Instructor's Guide to Accompany

A Problem Solving Approach to
Mathematics for Elementary School Teachers

Fourth Edition

Rick Billstein
Shlomo Libeskind
Johnny W. Lott

The Benjamin/Cummings Publishing Company, Inc.
Redwood City, California · Fort Collins, Colorado ·
Menlo Park, California · Reading, Massachusetts · New York ·
Don Mills, Ontario · Wokingham, U.K. · Amsterdam ·
Bonn · Sydney · Singapore · Tokyo · Madrid · San Juan

ISBN 0-8053-0391-X
ABCDEFGHIJ-AL-9543210

The Benjamin/Cummings Publishing Company, Inc.
390 Bridge Parkway
Suite 102
Redwood City, California 94065

TABLE OF CONTENTS

Sample Tests

PREFACE

The purpose of this Instructor's Resource Manual is to provide you with additional teaching materials that will supplement your use of our text, <u>A Problem Solving Approach to Mathematics for Elementary School Teachers</u>, fourth edition.

This supplement contains:

- Sample chapter tests that may be used as test questions or makeup tests.

- Answers to all sample test problems.

- Suggested answers to Questions From the Classroom.

- Answers to problems in the problem sets and chapter tests and solutions to the Brain Teasers.

- Bibliography.

Rick Billstein

Shlomo Libeskind

Johnny W. Lott

ACKNOWLEDGMENTS

With special thanks to John Lott and Nancy Stone.

J.W.L.

Sample Test

1. List the terms that complete a possible pattern in each of the following:

   (a) 6, 8, 10, 12, 14,___ ,___ ,___
   (b) 38, 33, 28, 23, 18,___ ,___ ,___
   (c) 640, 320, 160, 80,___ ,___ ,___
   (d) 7, 8, 15, 23, 38,___ ,___ ,___
   (e) 4, 8, 16, 32, 64,___ ,___ ,___
   (f) 0, 7, 26, 63, 124,___ ,___ ,___
   (g) 1,___ ,___ ,___ , 25, 36, 49

2. Classify each of the sequences in Problem 1 as arithmetic, geometric, or neither.

3. Find the nth term in each of the following:

   (a) 7, 11, 15, 19, ...
   (b) 2, 9, 28, 65, ...
   (c) 5, 25, 125, 625, ...

4. Find the first five terms of the sequences with n^{th} term given as follows:

   (a) $5n + 4$
   (b) $n^2 - n$
   (c) $3n + 7$
   (d) $n(n + 1)$

5. Find the following sums.

   (a) $6 + 8 + 10 + 12 + ... + 100$
   (b) $71 + 72 + 73 + 74 + ... + 89$

6. Complete the following magic square; that is, complete the square so that the sum in each row, column, and diagonal is the same.

46	33	32	43
	40		
39		37	42
34	45		

7. A person writing a book numbered the pages consecutively starting with 1 and had written 3200 digits. On what page was she at that point?

8.   Place the numbers 3, 4, 7, 9 in the squares below to obtain the greatest product.

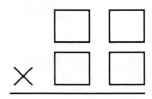

9.   How many different ways can you make change for a $100 bill using $5, $10, $20, and $50 bills?

10.   How many rectangles are in the following figure?

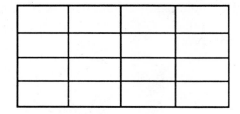

11.   A pencil and an eraser cost $1.45. The eraser costs 13¢ than the pencil. What is the cost of each?

12.   The third term in an arithmetic sequence is 11 and the 11th term is 35. Find the first term.

Sample Test

1. List the terms that complete a possible pattern in each of the following:

    (a) 2, 3, 5, 8, 12,___ ,___ ,___
    (b) 47, 87, 67, 107, 87,___ ,___ ,___
    (c) 100, 300, 900, 2700, 8100,___ ,___ ,___
    (d) 2, 10, 50, 250, 1250,___ ,___ ,___
    (e) 8, 15, 22, 29, 36,___ ,___ ,___
    (f) 4, 0, 8, 0, 16, 0,___ ,___,___
    (g) 5, 9, 13, 17, 21,___ ,___ ,___
    (h) 0, 15, 80, 255, 624,___ ,___ ,___

2. Classify each of the sequences in Problem 1 as arithmetic, geometric, or neither.

3. Find the nth term in each of the following:

    (a) 4, 9, 14, 19, 24, ...
    (b) 6, 12, 24, 48, 96, ...

4. Find the first five terms of the sequences with n^{th} term given as follows:

    (a) $4n + 7$
    (b) $n^2 + 2n$
    (c) $3n - 1$

5. Find the following sums:

    (a) $3 + 6 + 9 + 12 + 15 + ... + 84$
    (b) $183 + 182 + 181 + 180 + ... + 17$

6. Place the letters A, B, C, and D in the grid below so that no letter shows up twice in any row, column, or diagonal.

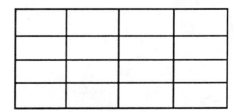

7. Igor won at cards three more times than he lost. If he played 11 times, how many times did he win?

8. Catarina had $2.00. This money was the value of the same number of nickels, dimes, and quarters only. How many of each did she have?

9. What is the 200th letter in the sequence A, B, C, D, E, F, A, B, C, D, E, F, ...?

10.   Gerald and Betty Joggette ran 5 blocks on their first day out. They increased their run by 3 blocks each day until they were running 35 blocks. How many days did it take to do this?

11.   Place the digits 2, 3, 4, 5, and 6 in the squares below to obtain the product shown.

12.   How many numbers are there between 100 and 1000 that contain the digits 7, 8, or 9?

13.   The second term in an arithmetic sequence is 18 and the 9th term is 46. Find the first term.

CHAPTER 2 FORM A

Sample Test

1. Write the set of vowels of the English language using set-builder notation.

2. List all the subset of {z, o, t}.

3. Let U = {x | x is a Tennessean};
   A = {x | x is a female};
   B = {x | x owns a pickup};
   C = {x | x owns a dog}

   Describe in words a member of each of the following:

   (a) $\overline{B}$

   (b) $B \cup C$

   (c) A - C

   (d) $\overline{A \cup C}$

   (e) B - A

   (f) $\overline{A}$

4. Let U = {u, n, i, t, e, d};
   A = {n, i, t};
   B = {n, e, d};
   C = {u, n, i, t, e};
   D = {d, u, e}

   Find each of the following:

   (a) $A \cap B$

   (b) $C \cup D$

   (c) $\overline{D}$

   (d) $\overline{A \cup D}$

   (e) $B \cap \overline{C}$

   (f) $(B \cap C) \cap D$

   (g) $(A \cup B) \cap (C \cup D)$

   (h) $(C - D) \cap \overline{A}$

   (i) n (C)

   (j) n (C ∪ D)

5. Indicate the following sets by shading.

   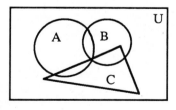

   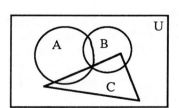

   (a) $(A - B) \cup C$

   (b) $A - (B \cup C)$

6. Let C = {m, i, n, u, s}. How many proper subsets does C have?

7. Show one possible one-to-one correspondence between sets D and E if D = {w, h, y} and E = {n, o, t} ?

8.   How many different one-to-one correspondences between sets D and E are possible in Problem 7?

9.   Use a Venn diagram to determine whether $A \cap (B - C) = (B \cap A) - C$ for all sets A, B, and C.

10.   Describe using symbols, the shaded portion in each of the following:

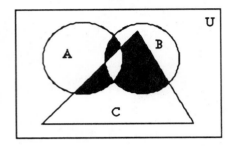   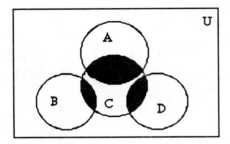

      (a)   (b)

11.   If $A = \{o, n, e\}$, $B = \{t, w, o\}$, and $C = \{z, e, r, o\}$, illustrate the equality $A \times (B \cup C) = (A \times B) \cup (A \times C)$.

12.   Classify each of the following as true or false. If false, tell why or give an example showing that it is not true.

      (a)   For all sets A and B, $A - B = B - A$.

      (b)   For all sets A, $\emptyset \subseteq \overline{A}$.
      (c)   For all sets A, $A \cap \emptyset \subseteq A \cup \emptyset$.
      (d)   The set $\{r, s, t, ..., z\}$ is a finite set.
      (e)   No set can be equivalent to all of its subsets.

13.   In an interview of 50 math majors,
      12 liked calculus and geometry
      18 liked calculus but not algebra
      4 like calculus, algebra, and geometry
      25 liked calculus
      15 liked geometry
      10 liked algebra but neither calculus nor geometry
      1 liked geometry and algebra but not calculus.
      Of those surveyed, how many like calculus and algebra?

14.   Which of the following relations are functions from the set of first components to the set of second components?

      (a)   { (b, a), (d, c), (a, e), (g, f) }
      (b)   { (a, b), (b, a), (c, c) }
      (c)   { (b, a), (c, a), (b, b), (c, b) }

15. Given the following function rules and domains, find the associated ranges.

   (a) $f(x) = 5x - 3$; Domain = {0, 1, 2, 3, 4}
   (b) $f(x) = x^2$; Domain = {1, 9, 4}
   (c) $f(x) = 2x - x^2$; Domain = {1, 0, 2}

16. If $f(x) = 3x - 7$, find the element of the domain associated with each of the following:

   (a) 2   (b) 8

17. What properties do each of the following relations defined on the set of all people have?

   (a) owns the same brand of bicycle
   (b) has more hair than
   (c) is a cousin of
   (d) is the maternal grandmother of

18. The following graphs show the cost and revenue functions in dollars for producing ten-speed bicycles. From the graphs estimate the following.

   (a) The break-even point—that is, the number of ten-speed bicycles that must be sold to meet expenses exactly.
   (b) The profit or loss on the first 25 ten-speed bicycles produced and sold.
   (c) The number of ten-speed bicycles that must be sold to gain a $2000 profit.

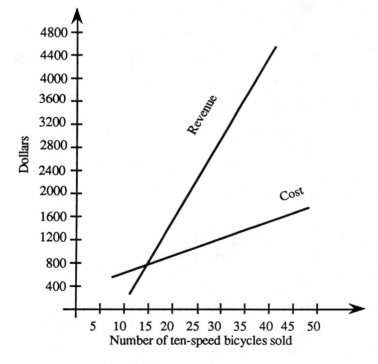

*19 Which of the following are statements?
   (a) Richard Feynman won a Nobel Prize in physics.
   (b) How many skinks does it take to create a stink?
   (c) It takes 3 college professors to screw in a light bulb.
   (d) $x - 3 = 15$

7

*20.   Negate each of the following:

    (a)   Butterflies are born free.
    (b)   Yogi Bear always says "How de do Boo Boo."
    (c)   Some umpire calls are incorrect.
    (d) $7 + 3 = 10$.

*21.   Write truth tables for each of the following:

    (a) $[p \wedge (\sim q)] \to p$ (b) $[p \vee (\sim q)] \to q$

    (c) $[p \to (\sim q)] \leftrightarrow [(\sim q) \to p]$ (d) $p \to p$

*22.   Decide whether or not the following are equivalent:

    (a) $\sim q; \ (p \to q)$ (b) $\sim q \to p; \ \sim (\sim p \to q)$

*23.   Write the converse, inverse, and contrapositive of the following. If the masked man was the Lone Ranger, the horse was Silver.

*24.   Find a valid conclusion for the following arguments.

    (a)   If I don't get an increase in salary, I will quit. I do not get an increase in salary.
    (b)   If the map is in the plane, it takes no more than four colors to color it. It takes more than four colors to color the map.
    (c)   All women mathematicians are well known. Emmy Noether is a woman mathematician.

*25.   Write the following argument symbolically and then determine its validity.

If a nail is lost, then a shoe is lost.
If a shoe is lost, then a horse is lost.
If a horse is lost, then a rider is lost.
If a rider is lost, then a battle is lost.
If a battle is lost, then a kingdom is lost.
Therefore, if a nail is lost, then a kingdom is lost.

*26.   Determine whether or not each of the following arguments is valid.

    (a)   All pine trees are conifers.
          All conifers keep their needles all year long.
          Therefore, all pine trees deep their needles all year long.
    (b)   No spiders are insects.
          All insects are not arachnids.
          Therefore, no spiders are arachnids.
    (c)   If a cat is spayed, then it cannot have kittens.
          My cat has kittens.
          Therefore, my cat is not spayed.
    (d)   If John works in stained glass, then he makes butterflies.
          If John does not make butterflies, then he is not a glazier.
          John works in stained glass.
          Therefore, John is not a glazier

Sample Test

1. Use set notation to write the days of the week having six letters in their name.

2. Write the set M = {2, 4, 6, 8, 10} using set-builder notation.

3. List all the nonempty proper subsets of {a, b, c}.

4. Let U = {x | x is an American}
 C = {x | x is a smoker}
 D = {x | x has a health problem}
 E = {x | x is a female}

 (i) Describe a person who is an element of each of the following sets:

 (a) $\overline{C}$ (b) $\overline{C} \cap \overline{D}$ (c) $C \cap D$
 (d) $D - C$ (e) $D \cup C$

 (ii) Use the sets above, along with the set operations to describe a set of which each of the following is a representative number.

 (a) A healthy American (b) An unhealthy male smoker
 (c) A nonsmoking healthy female
 (d) An American who is either a female or a nonsmoker

5. Classify the following as true or false, where A and B are any two sets. If false, give a counterexample.

 (a) If $A \cup B = A$, then $A \subseteq B$.

 (b) If $A \subseteq B$, then $A \cup B = A$.

 (c) $(A \cup B) \cup C = A \cup (B \cup C)$

 (d) $A \cap \overline{A} = \varnothing$

 (e) $A \cup \overline{A} = \varnothing$

 (f) $A - \overline{A} = \varnothing$

 (g) $A \times \overline{A} = \varnothing$
 (h) $\varnothing \subseteq \varnothing$

6. If $U = \{q, u, e, s, t, i, o, n\}$, $A = \{q, u, s, e, t\}$, $B = \{s, i, t\}$, and $C = \{n, o, t\}$, find each of the following:

 (a) $A \cup B$

 (b) $A \cap \overline{C}$

 (c) $A \cup \overline{(B \cap C)}$

6.   (cont.)

(d) $\overline{A} \cap \overline{B}$
(e)   A - B
(f) $(A \cup B) \cap (A \cup C)$

(g) $A \cup \overline{A}$
(h)   n (B - A)

7.   Let A = {1, 2} and B = {a}. Find the following:

(a)   A x B
(b)   B x A
(c)   B x B
(d)   A x A
(e)   A x Ø
(f)   Is A x A a function from A to A?
(g)   Is B x B a function from B to B?
(h)   n (A x Ø)

8.   (a)   Illustrate a one-to-one correspondence between the following sets:

$$N = \{1, 2, 3, 4, ..., n, ...\}$$
$$F = \{6, 11, 16, 21, ...\}$$

(b)   In your correspondence, what number corresponds to 57? Explain why.
(c)   In your correspondence, what element of F corresponds to n?
(d)   Does the correspondence that you have illustrated prove that N is an infinite set?
        Why or why not?

9.   Given the function rules and domains, find the associated ranges.

(a)   f(x) = 2x + 7, domain = {1, 2, 0}
(b)   f(x) = 0, domain = {0, 1, 2}

10.   Shade the Venn diagram to illustrate $\overline{A} \cap \overline{B}$.

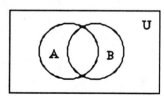

11.   Describe in symbols the shaded portion of the Venn diagram below.

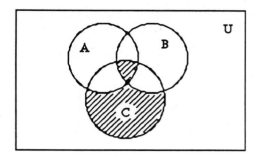

12.   A survey was made of 200 students to study their use of the public library system. The findings were as follows:

    59 used the Reader's Guide
    28 used both the card catalog and the information booth.
    68 used the information booth.
    83 did not use the library.
    44 used only the card catalog.

Explain how the above information can be used to conclude that some students must use both the information booth and the Reader's Guide.

13.   Does the given one-to-one correspondence illustrate that set A is infinite? Why or why not?

$$A = \{10, 20, 30, 40, 50, ..., 10n, ...\}$$
$$\updownarrow \quad \updownarrow \quad \updownarrow \quad \updownarrow \quad \updownarrow \qquad \updownarrow$$
$$B = \{5, 10, 15, 20, 25, ..., 5n, ...\}$$

14.   If $A = \{a, b, c, d\}$ and $B = \{1, 2, 3, 4\}$, how many different one-to-one correspondences can be made?

15.   Which of the following relations are functions from the set of first components to the set of second components?

    (a)   {(1, 2), (1, 1), (2, 1), (2, 2)}
    (b)   {(5, 10), (10, 10), (15, 10), (20, 10)}

16.   What properties do each of the following relations defined on the set of all people have?

    (a)   uses the same mouthwash as
    (b)   drinks more coffee than
    (c)   is an aunt of
    (d)   is the grandfather of

17.   The following graphs show the cost and revenue functions in dollars for producing washing machines. From the graphs estimate the following.

    (a)   The break-even point—that is, the number of washing machines that must be sold to meet expenses exactly.
    (b)   The profit or loss on the first 20 washing machines produced and sold.

11

17.   (cont.)

(c)   The number of units that must be sold to gain a $6000 profit

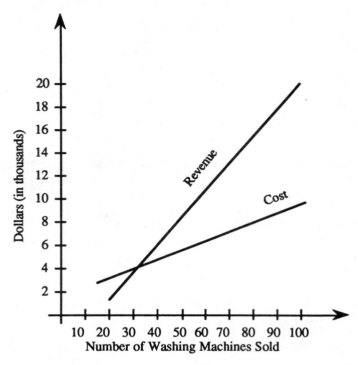

*18.   Which of the following are statements?

(a)   Bishop Desmond Tutu won a Nobel Peace Prize.
(b)   Is there a Nobel Prize for mathematics?
(c)   Every person who works for the government is a bureaucrat.
(d) $15 + x = x + 15$

*19.   Negate each of the following:

(a)   *The Clan of the Cave Bear* was written by Jean Auel.
(b)   All realtors get commissions on houses that they sell.
(c)   There exists an honest used car salesman.
(d) $5 - 2 = 3$

*20.   Write truth tables for each of the following:

(a) $(p \lor q) \to (p \to \sim q)$

(b) $(p \to q) \leftrightarrow \sim (p \land \sim q)$

(c) $(p \lor q) \land (p \lor r)$

*21.   Decide whether or not each of the following are equivalent.

(a) $[(\sim q \to \sim p) \land \sim q]; \ \sim p$

(b) $(p \to q) \land \sim q; \ \sim p$

*22.   Write the converse, inverse, and the contrapositive of the following: If Clark Kent is Superman, then he came from Krypton.

*23.   Find a valid conclusion for the following argument:

    (a)   If you understand a problem, then you can solve it.
          You cannot solve a problem.
    (b)   No students like 8:00 classes.
          You like 8:00 classes.
    (c)   It always snows in Montana.
          I will go skiing if it snows in Montana.
          If I go skiing, then I will get cold.

*24.   Write the following argument symbolically and then determine its validity.

If I pay attention to my job, I will get a salary increase.
If I shirk my job, then I will not get a raise.
I shirk my job.
Therefore, I did not pay attention to my job.

*25.   Determine whether or not each of the following arguments is valid.

    (a)   If you do not understand this test, then you enjoy logic.
          You do not enjoy this test.
          Therefore, you do not understand this test.
    (b)   No dogs are cats.
          All cats are finicky.
          Therefore, no dogs are finicky.
    (c)   If I eat a piece of fudge, I will gain weight.
          I will not gain weight.
          Therefore, I did not eat a piece of fudge.

CHAPTER 3 FORM A

Sample Test

1. Convert each of the following to base ten.

    (a)   CMXLVI   *(b) 233_{four} *(c) TEO_{twelve}

    *(d) 1101_{two} *(e) 2153_{six}

2. Convert each of the following base ten numerals to numerals in the indicated system.

    (a)   897 to Roman   *(b)   346 to base four

    *(c)   1440 to base twelve   *(d)   27 to base twelve

    *(e)   829 to base nine

3. Simplify each of the following, if possible. Write your answers in exponential form, that is, a^b.

    (a) $5^3 \cdot 5^5 \cdot 5^6$ (b) $3^{13} \cdot 3^{11}$ (c) $4^2 + 3 \cdot 4^2$

4. For each of the following, identify the whole-number properties which are illustrated.

    (a) $2 \cdot (3 + 4) = 2 \cdot 3 + 2 \cdot 4$ (b) $5 + 7 = 7 + 5$

    (c) $1 \cdot 14 = 14 = 14 \cdot 1$ (d) $5 \cdot (9 + 3) = 5 \cdot 9 + 5 \cdot 3$

    (e) $2 + (3 + 2) = 2 + (2 + 3)$ (f) $2 \cdot (3 \cdot 4) = (2 \cdot 3) \cdot 4$

5. Using the definition of less than or greater than, prove that each of the following inequalities is true.

    (a) $2 < 9$ (b) $13 > 4$

6. Explain why the product $38 \cdot 100$--namely, 3800--has zeroes in the tens and unit places.

7. Use both the scratch and traditional algorithms to perform each of the following.

    (a)   312
               889
            + 611

    (b) 312_{twelve}
               889_{twelve}
            $+ 611_{twelve}$

8. Use both the lattice and traditional multiplication algorithms to perform each of the following.

    (a)   514
            $\times \ 89$

    *(b) 216_{nine}
            $\times \ 54_{nine}$

9. Use both the repeated subtraction and the traditional algorithms to perform each of the following.

    (a) $81 \overline{)5607}$ (b) $101_{two} \overline{)11011_{two}}$

10. Use the division algorithm to check your answers in Problem 9.

11. For each of the following base ten numerals, tell the place value for each of the circled digits.

    (a)   ⑥72   (b)   ③910   (c)   29③28

12. For each of the following, find all possible whole-number replacements that make the following true statements.

    (a) $3 \cdot \square - 27 < 36$
    (b) $4986 = \square \cdot 48 + 42$
    (c) $\square \cdot (5 + 3) = \square \cdot 5 + \square \cdot 3$
    (d) $38 - \square \geq 4$

13. Use the number line to perform each of the following operations.

    (a)   16 - 9   (b)   11 + 3
    (c) $3 \cdot 4$ *(d) $2_{five} + 4_{five}$

14. Use the distributive property of multiplication over addition and addition and subtraction facts to rename each of the following, if possible.

    (a) $3x + 4x + 7x$ (b) $6x^3 + 7x^3 + 5x^3$
    (c) $q \cdot (r + s + v)$

15. Solve each of the following:

    (a)   Jean had 6 dresses, 7 blouses, and 3 skirts. How many garments did she have?
    (b)   Carolyn had 32 students and only 4 books. How many students were there for each book?
    (c)   Jim had 6 shirts, each with 5 buttons. How many buttons were there in all?
    (d)   Perry paid $36 for a pair of pants. He used a $50 bill. How much change did he receive?

16. What number comes after each of the following:

    (a) EOE_{twelve}
    (b)   XXXVIII

17. Hugo's checking account at the beginning of the month had a balance fo $360. During the month he wrote three checks for $12, two checks for $18, and one check for $187. He made one deposit of $42. What is his new balance?

18. Use numbers to illustrate each of the following properties of whole numbers.

    (a)   Commutative Property for Addition
    (b)   Associative Property for Multiplication
    (c)   Identity Property for Addition

19. Tom, Dick, and Mary decided to share expenses for a class party. Tom bought $18 worth of pizza, Dick bought $10 worth of ice cream, and Mary bought $14 worth of soft drinks. How much should each person pay in order that each of them spend the same amount and how might they accomplish this?

20. Kim's new bicycle cost $102. She paid $30 down and was to make six equal size payments on the balance. If no interest was charged, how much were her monthly payments?

21. Sandy began a two-week exercise program where she walked 3 blocks the first day and then 2 blocks more than the previous day for each day of the two-week period. At the end of 2 weeks, how many blocks had she walked using this scheme?

22. A certain model car comes in 5 different exterior colors and 4 different interior colors. How many different looking cars can be ordered?

23. Find the missing numbers in each of the following.

(a)
```
   _28_
 + 1_13
  ─────
   65__
```

(b)
```
   _5_8
 − 152_
  ─────
   6_12
```

24. Which is greater $2^{40} + 2^{40}$ or 2^{80}?

25. I am thinking of a number. If I multiply it by 3, then subtract 3 and add 9, I get 15. What is my number?

Sample Test

1. Convert each of the following to base ten.

   (a) $\overline{\text{MCDIX}}$ *(b) 413_{five} (c) $\text{T1E}_{\text{twelve}}$
   *(d) 10111_{two} *(e) 106_{seven}

2. Convert each of the following base ten numerals to numerals in the indicated system.

   (a) 454 to Roman   *(b) 233 to base five
   *(c) 1590 to base twelve   *(d) 29 to base nine
   *(e) 27 to base three

3. Simplify each of the following, if possible. Write your answers in exponential form, that is a^b.

   (a) $3^4 \cdot 3 \cdot 3^8$ (b) $4^{11} \cdot 4^{79}$ (c) $6^6 + 5 \cdot 6^6$

4. For each of the following, identify the whole-number properties which are illustrated.

   (a) $4 \cdot (6 + 7) = 4 \cdot (7 + 6)$ (b) $5 \cdot (7 \cdot 3) = (5 \cdot 7) \cdot 3$
   (c) $5 \cdot (7 + 3) = 5 \cdot 7 + 5 \cdot 3$ (d) $5 \cdot 1 = 5 = 1 \cdot 5$
   (e) $0 + 1$ is a whole number   (f) $5 \cdot (7 \cdot 3) = 5 \cdot (3 \cdot 7)$

5. Using the definition of less than or greater than, prove each of the following is true.

   (a) $8 < 12$ (b) $1 > 0$

6. Explain why the product $12 \cdot 100$, namely 12,000, has zeroes in the hundreds, tens, and units places.

7. Use both the scratch and traditional algorithms to perform each of the following.

   (a)   62   (b) 214_{five}
          78   232_{five}
          34             $+ \ 223_{\text{five}}$
      $+ \ \underline{79}$

8. Use both lattice and traditional multiplication to perform each of the following.

   (a)   518   *(b) 212_{five}
       $\times \ \underline{34}$ $\times \ \underline{23_{\text{five}}}$

9. Use both the repeated subtraction and the traditional algorithms to perform each of the following.

   (a) $9 \ \overline{)3287}$ *(b) $12_{\text{three}} \ \overline{)2021_{\text{three}}}$

10. Use the division algorithm to check your answers in Problem 9.

11. For each of the following base ten numerals, tell the place value for each of the circles digits.

   (a) 52⑧4   (b) 3②,583   (c) 528⓪

12. For each of the following, find all possible whole-number replacements that make the following statements true.

   (a) $5 \cdot \square = \square \cdot 5$ (b) $98 = 6 \cdot 16 + \square$

   (c) $2 \cdot \square - 15 < 17$ (d) $8 - \square \geq 3$

13. Use the number line to perform each of the following operations.

   (a) $5 + 4$ (b) $8 - 2$
   (c) $4 \cdot 2$ *(d) $3_{four} \cdot 2_{four}$

14. Use the distributive property of multiplication over addition and addition and subtraction facts to rename each of the following, if possible.

   (a) $5x^2 + 2x^2 + 7x^2$ (b) $8x + 9x + 11x$
   (c) $(a + b)(c + d)$

15. What number comes after each of the following?

   (a) DCLXVIII   *(b) E0E$_{twelve}$

16. If a plane can carry 195 people and made 52 fully loaded flights, how many total people did it carry?

17. Sam's operating expenses for driving a car are $40 per week. If his expenses for driving a motorcycle for 30 weeks are $720, how much did he save for the 30 week period?

18. Christen scored 6 more points in a basketball game than Molly. If Molly doubled the number of points she scored and added 1, the result would equal Christen's points. How many points did Molly score?

19. Tina had $83 in her checking account. She wrote 3 checks for $5 and 2 checks for $12. She then deposited $9. What was her balance?

20. Sandy took a seven day trip on which she drove 80 miles the first day. Each day after the first she drove 20 miles more than the day before. How many total miles did she drive?

21. Find the missing numbers in each of the following.

   (a)
   ```
     _ 3 _ 8
   +4 8 3 _
     6 _ 7 3
   ```
   (b)
   ```
    8 _ 6 _
   - _ 2 _ 4
    _ _ _ _
   ```

22. Which is greater $2^{20} + 2^{20}$ or 2^{21}?

23. I am thinking of a number. If I add 3, multiply the result by 5 and then subtract 5, I get 20. What is my number?

18

Sample Test

1.   Find the additive inverse of each of the following.

      (a) $^-7$ (b)   x   (c) $2 + x$ (d) $x - y$

2.   Perform the following operations:

      (a) $(^-12 - {}^-18) + 4$ (b) $^-3 \, (^-2) - 2$
      (c) $^-12 - 3 \, (^-4) + 2 \, (^-8)$ (d) $(3)^6 \div (^-3)^2$
      (e) $(^-4)^4 - 4^4$ (f) $(^-7 - 3) \, (7 - 3)$

3.   For each of the following find all integer values of x, if they exist, that make the equations true.

      (a) $x + (^-5) = {}^-3$ (b) $x^2 = 9$
      (c) $|x| = 7$ (d) $|^-x| = 5$
      (e) $4 - 3x < 2x + 84$ (f) $|x + 2| = 7$
      (g) $^-3 \, (^-2x + {}^-7) \leq {}^-x + 7$ (h) $(x - 3)^2 = 64$

4.   Factor each of the following expressions.

      (a) $5x - 3x^2$
      (b) $25 - x^2$
      (c) $(a + 1) \, (a - b) + (a + 1)$
      (d) $5 + 5x$

5.   Use any method to demonstrate that $(^-1) \, (^-1) = 1$.

6.   Use the concept of the additive inverse to prove that $^-(^-a) = a$.

7.   Evaluate the following when $x = {}^-3$, if possible.

      (a) ^-x (b) $|x|$
      (c) x^3 (d) $^-x^3$
      (e) $(^-x)^3$ (f) $0 \div x$

8.   Classify each of the following as true or false, where a and b are any integers. If false, tell why.

      (a)   If $ac > bc$, then $a > b$.
      (b)   If $^-x > {}^-7$, then $x > 7$.
      (c)   If $^-3x + 7 \geq x + 14$, then $^-3x + 7 + {}^-7 \geq x + 14 + {}^-7$.
      (d) $|x|$ is always equal to x.
      (e) $^-12 - {}^-7 = {}^-5$.
      (f) $a^2 + b^2 = (a + b) \, (a + b)$
      (g) $a^2 - b^2 = (a + b) \, (a - b)$

19

9. Classify each of the following as true or false. If false, tell why.

    (a) All whole numbers are integers.
    (b) Subtraction is commutative on the set of integers.
    (c) Multiplication is associative on the set of integers.
    (d) The set of integers is closed with respect to division.

10. What conditions must be satisfied so that the product of two integers is positive?

11. In the football game, O.J. Samson gained 5 yards on each of 2 plays, gained 16 yards on one play, made no gain on one play and lost 9 yards on one play. How many total yards did he end up with for the day?

12. The temperature dropped 15 degrees from the high temperature of $^-6°$ C. What was the high temperature?

13. After Freon was added to a freezer, the temperature dipped from $10°$ to $^-30°$. What was the change in temperature?

14. A pound of rose food costs $2. A pound of enriched compost costs $6. If Jernigan's Greenhouses wishes to sell 20 pounds of a mixture of the two as fertilizer at $3 per pound, how much of each should they use?

15. The sum of two integers is 14. Their difference is 8. What are the integers?

16. Demonstrate the addition $^-5 + {^-3} = {^-8}$ using each of the following models:

    (a) Number line
    (b) Charged field

Sample Test

1. Find the additive inverse of each of the following.

   (a) 13   (b) ^-x
   (c) $^-3 + x$
   (d) $^-x + y$

2. Perform each of the following operations:

   (a) $(5 - {}^-3) + 13$ (b) $6\,({}^-8) + ({}^-5)$
   (c) $^-8 + 3 \cdot ({}^-2) - ({}^-8) \cdot ({}^-2)$ (d) $({}^-5)^8 \div ({}^-5)^6$
   (e) $8^3 + ({}^-8)^3$ (f) $({}^-8 + 6)({}^-8 - 6)$

3. For each of the following find all integer values of x, if they exist, that makes the equations true.

   (a) $^-x - 3 = {}^-8$ (b) $x^3 = {}^-27$
   (c) $|x| = 16$ (d) $|{}^-x| = 9$
   (e) $8 - 5x < 2x - 20$ (f) $|{}^-x + 5| = 8$
   (g) $^-6\,(3x + {}^-2) \leq 2x - 48$ (h) $(x - 2)^4 = 16$

4. Factor each of the following expressions.

   (a) $9x^2 - 3x$
   (b) $4x^2 - 9$
   (c) $(a + 1)\,x + (a + 1)$
   (d) $11x - 11$

5. Use any method to demonstrate that $1 \cdot ({}^-1) = {}^-1$

6. Use the concept of the additive inverse to prove that $({}^-a)\,b = {}^-(ab)$.

7. Evaluate the following when $x = {}^-2$, if possible.

   (a) $^-x^2$ (b) $|{}^-x|$ (c) $^-|x|$
   (d) x^3 (e) $({}^-x)^3$ (f) $2x^3$

8. Classify each of the following as true or false. If false, tell why.

   (a) If $a > b$ then $a + c > b + c$.
   (b) If $^-x > 2$ then $x > {}^-2$.
   (c) If $3x = 6$ then $^-6x = 12$.
   (d) $|{}^-x|$ is always equal to ^-x.
   (e) $^-5 - 8 \cdot 3 = {}^-39$
   (f) $a^2 \cdot b^2 = (ab)^2$
   (g) $a^2 - b^2 = (a - b)(a - b)$

9. Classify each of the following as true or false. If false, tell why.

   (a) Every integer is a whole number.
   (b) Subtraction is associative on the set of integers.
   (c) Multiplication is closed on the set of integers.
   (d) Addition is commutative on the set of integers.

10. What conditions must be satisfied so that the product of two integers is negative?

11. Ann had a balance of $25 in her checking account. She wrote three checks for $5.00 each, one check for $28, and two checks for $22 each. What was her new balance?

12. The temperature was 18° C and it dropped 37° C. What was the new temperature?

13. The temperature dropped 37° C from the high temperature to reach a low of ⁻8° C. What was the high temperature?

14. Bill mixes 40 pounds of nuts worth 60¢/pound with 60 pounds of nuts worth 45¢/pound. How much should he sell them for in order to make the same amount of money as when he sold the nuts separately?

15. The difference between two integers is 22. The greater integer is equal to three times the smaller integer plus 8. What are the two integers?

16. Demonstrate ⁻8 + 2 = ⁻6 using the following models.

   (a) Number line
   (b) Charged field

CHAPTER 5 FORM A

Sample Test

1. Determine all possible digits to fill in the blanks to make each of the following true.

   (a) $5 \mid 728\_$ (b) $3 \mid 482\_$ (c) $11 \mid 5\_64$

   (d) $6 \mid 24\_36$ (e) $4 \mid 62\_$ (f) $8 \mid 632\_$

2. Let N be the three-digit number whose hundreds digit is a, tens digit is b, and units digit is c. If $9 \mid (a + b + c)$, prove that $9 \mid N$.

3. Classify each of the following as true or false. If false, give a counterexample or tell why.

   (a) If a and b are different and prime, then GCD(a, b) = 1.
   (b) If a and b are even, then GCD(a, b) = 2.
   (c) If $a \mid b$, then LCM(a, b) = a.
   (d) If $12 \mid a$, then $6 \mid a$.
   (e) $0 \mid a$ for all natural numbers a.
   (f) $a \mid 0$ for all natural numbers a.

4. Circle the given numbers that divide 444,444.

   2, 3, 4, 5, 6, 7, 8, 9, 10, 11, 12, 15, 22, 25

5. Find the least whole number with exactly seven positive divisors.

6. Determine whether each of the following numbers is prime or composite.

   (a) 217   (b) 517
   (c) 1001   (d) 87

7. Find each of the following

   (a) GCD(38, 95)   (b) LCM(38, 95)
   (c) GCD(12, 26, 42)   (d) LCM(12, 26, 42)

8. Use the Euclidean Algorithm to find the GCD of 74 and 19,192.

9. If $a = 2^3 \cdot 3^7 \cdot 5^8 \cdot 11^4$ and $b = 2^2 \cdot 3^5 \cdot 7^2 \cdot 11 \cdot 13$, find the following.

   (a) GCD(a, b)
   (b) LCM(a, b)

10. What is the greatest prime that must be checked in order to determine if each of the following is prime?

    (a) 1217
    (b) 811

11. Find all positive divisors of 288.

12. Describe a divisibility test for 45.

13. Jane cut her cake into 12 pieces of equal size. Lori cut her cake into 8 pieces of equal size. If the cakes must now be cut so that they are identical, into how many pieces should each cake be cut?

14. In their freshman years, Jacqueline took 43 credit hours and Jean took 47 credit hours. If Jacqueline took only 5-credit courses and Jean took only 3-credit courses after their freshman years, how many credits did they have when they had the same number?

*15. Christmas falls on Monday this year. On what day will it fall next year if next year is not a leap year?

*16. Find the remainder for each of the following.

    (a) 7^{100} is divided by 19
    (b) 19^{1990} is divided by 14
    (c) 19^{1991} is divided by 20

CHAPTER 5 FORM B

Sample Test

1. Determine all possible digits to fill in the blanks to make each of the following true.

   (a) 9 | _543   (b) 3 | 24_3   (c) 11 | 8_62

   (d) 4 | 7_4   (e) 6 | 28_20   (f) 5 | 37,28_

2. Prove the test for divisibility for 4 for a 4-digit number n such that
   $n = a \cdot 10^3 + b \cdot 10^2 + c \cdot 10 + d$.

3. Classify each of the following as true or false. If false, give a counterexample or tell why.

   (a) GCD(a, B) = a for all a ε N.
   (b) LCM(a, a) = a for all a ε N.
   (c) If LCM(a, b) = ab, then GCD(a, b) = 1.
   (d) If LCM(a, b) = 1, then a =1 and b = 1 if a, b ε W.
   (e) If 2 | a and 6 | a then 12 | a.

   (f) If 2 | a, and 3 | a and 5 | a then 30 | a.

4. Circle the given numbers that divide 353,430.

   2, 3, 4, 5, 6, 7, 8, 9, 10, 11, 12, 15, 22, 25

5. Find the least whole number with exactly 4 distinct prime divisors.

6. Determine whether each of the following numbers is prime or composite.

   (a) 241   (b) 391   (c) 1147
   (d) 199

7. Find each of the following.

   (a) GCD(67,79)   (b) LCM(67,69)
   (c) GCD(156, 84, 294)   (d) LCM(156, 84, 294)

8. Use the Euclidean Algorithm to find the GCD of 120 and 468,468.

9. If $a = 5^3 \cdot 7 \cdot 11 \cdot 13$ and $b = 2^3 \cdot 5^2 \cdot 7^3 \cdot 17$, find the following.

   (a) GCD(a, b)   (b) LCM(a,b)

10. What is the greatest prime that must be checked in order to determine if each of the following is prime?

   (a) 241   (b) 811

11. Find all positive divisors of 444.

12. Describe a divisibility test for 22.

13. Becky's class size will be either 16, 24, or 32 students. She would like to bring exactly enough treats to have available an equal number for each student. What is the minimum number she should bring?

14. Joel's dog barks every 9 minutes. Billy's dog barks every 15 minutes. They both barked at exactly 1:00 P.M.. When is the next time they will bark at the same time?

*15. Christmas is on Tuesday this year. In how many years will it be on Friday if no leap years are involved?

*16. Find the remainders for each of the following.

   (a) $13^{100} \cdot 12^{88}$ is divided by 11
   (b) 2^{64} is divided by 14
   (c)   100! is divided by 98!

CHAPTER 6 FORM A

Sample Test

1. For each of the following, draw a diagram illustrating the fraction.

   (a) $\dfrac{1}{5}$

   (b) $\dfrac{5}{6}$

2. Write three rational numbers equal to $\dfrac{-2}{3}$.

3. Reduce each of the following rational numbers to simplest form.

   (a) $\dfrac{28}{35}$ (b) $\dfrac{cy^3}{dy^2}$ (c) $\dfrac{0}{5}$

   (d) $\dfrac{108}{96}$ (e) $\dfrac{b + x}{b^2 + bx}$ (f) $\dfrac{16}{256}$

4. Place >, <, or = between each of the following pairs to make true sentences.

   (a) $\dfrac{4}{5}$ and $\dfrac{120}{200}$ (b) $\dfrac{3}{4}$ and $\dfrac{4}{5}$

   (c) $\dfrac{-6}{5}$ and $\dfrac{-7}{6}$ (d) $\dfrac{-4}{20}$ and $\dfrac{6}{-30}$

   (e) $\dfrac{0}{10}$ and $\dfrac{0}{-10}$ (f) $\left(\dfrac{6}{5}\right)^{30}$ and $\left(\dfrac{7}{6}\right)^{30}$

5. Perform each of the following computations. Leave your answers in simplest form.

   (a) $\dfrac{2}{3} + \dfrac{4}{5}$ (b) $\dfrac{4}{5} - \dfrac{2}{3}$

   (c) $\dfrac{8}{9} \cdot \dfrac{27}{40}$ (d) $\dfrac{4}{5} \div \dfrac{2}{3}$

   (e) $\left(3\dfrac{1}{4} + 7\dfrac{1}{8}\right) \div 3\dfrac{1}{2}$

6. Find the additive and multiplicative inverses for each of the following.

   (a) 4 (b) $2\dfrac{1}{5}$

   (c) 0.36 (d) $\dfrac{3}{8}$

   (e) $\dfrac{-2}{3}$

7. Simplify each of the following. Write your answer in the form $\frac{a}{b}$, where a and b are integers, b ≠ 0.

(a) $\dfrac{\frac{2}{3} - \frac{3}{4}}{\frac{1}{5} + \frac{1}{6}}$

(b) $\dfrac{\frac{2}{3} \cdot \frac{3}{5}}{\frac{1}{4}}$

8. Solve each of the following for x, where x is a real number.

(a) $3\left(\frac{1}{x} + \frac{1}{3}\right) = 5$

(b) $\frac{2}{3}x - \frac{3}{4} \le \frac{1}{3}(2 - 3x)$

9. If the ratio of cans of peas to cans of tomatoes in Ouida's pantry is 3 to 7 and the ratio of cans of peas to cans of tomatoes in Pam's is the same, and if you know that there are 14 cans of tomatoes in Pam's pantry, how many cans of peas are in her pantry?

10. Write each of the following in simplest form with nonnegative exponents in the final answer.

(a) $\left(\frac{1}{2}\right)^5 \cdot 2^{-10}$

(b) $3^4 \div 3^{-4}$

(c) $\left(\left(\frac{2}{3}\right)^4\right)^{-3}$

11. Sunflower seeds are packed in packages each weighing $3\frac{1}{4}$ ounces. If there is a supply of $10\frac{1}{2}$ pounds of sunflower seeds, how many packages of seeds can be packed? How many ounces of sunflower seeds will be left over?

12. A student says that he found a quick way to divide mixed numbers. He demonstrates his method as follows

$$9\frac{1}{4} \div 3\frac{3}{4} = 3\frac{1}{3} \quad \text{since } 9 \div 3 = 3 \text{ and } \frac{1}{4} \div \frac{3}{4} = \frac{1}{3},$$
$$20\frac{3}{5} \div 4\frac{3}{5} = 5\frac{1}{1}, \text{ or } 6 \text{ since } 20 \div 4 = 5 \text{ and } \frac{3}{5} \div \frac{3}{5} = 1$$

Is the student correct? Why or why not?

13. Estimate each of the following, indicating if the actual answer is greater than (+) or less than (-) the estimate.

(a) $\dfrac{31}{15} + \dfrac{199}{198}$

(b) $4\frac{10}{11} + 3\frac{8}{9} + \frac{13}{14}$

(c) $5\frac{19}{20} - 2\frac{9}{10} + 1\frac{1}{100}$

14.   Estimate by rounding the fractions.

(a) $7\frac{8}{9} \cdot 5\frac{1}{13}$

(b) $3\frac{19}{39} \cdot 4$

(c) $\dfrac{34\frac{9}{10}}{4\frac{9}{10}}$

(d) $\dfrac{14\frac{19}{39}}{\frac{19}{39}}$

CHAPTER 6 FORM B

Sample Test

1. Reduce each of the following rational numbers to simplest form.

   (a) $\dfrac{3^2}{4^2}$

   (b) $\dfrac{3^9 \cdot 5^1}{39 \cdot 3^8}$

   (c) $\dfrac{xy^3}{x^3y}$

   (d) $\dfrac{3 + 9x}{x + 3x^2}$

2. Perform each of the following computations.

   (a) $\dfrac{5}{8} + \dfrac{7}{12}$

   (b) $1 - \dfrac{1}{2} + \dfrac{1}{3} - \dfrac{1}{4} + \dfrac{1}{5}$

   (c) $(5\dfrac{2}{7} + 2\dfrac{3}{7}) \div 2\dfrac{1}{7}$

3. If possible, find the additive and multiplicative inverses for each of the following.

   (a) $-2\dfrac{1}{5}$

   (b) $\dfrac{3}{8}$

   (c) $\dfrac{0}{1}$

   (d) $\dfrac{1}{x}$

4. Simplify each of the following. Write your answer in the form $\dfrac{a}{b}$, where a and b are integers and $\dfrac{a}{b}$ is reduced to its simplest form.

   (a) $\dfrac{\dfrac{2}{3} - \dfrac{1}{6}}{\dfrac{2}{3} + \dfrac{1}{6}}$

   (b) $\dfrac{\dfrac{2}{9} \cdot \dfrac{3}{4}}{\dfrac{2}{3}}$

   (c) $\dfrac{\left(\dfrac{1}{2}\right)^2 + \left(\dfrac{2}{4}\right)^2}{\dfrac{1}{2} + \dfrac{3}{4}}$

5. Find the greatest rational number x such that $\dfrac{3}{4}x \geq \dfrac{1}{5} + x$.

6. Is the following statement true or false? (Justify your answer.) For all positive integers a, b such that $b \geq 2$, $\dfrac{a + 1}{b - 1} > \dfrac{a}{b}$.

7. Solve each of the following for x:

   (a) $\dfrac{x}{3} \geq x$

   (b) $\dfrac{3}{4}\left(\dfrac{2}{3}x - 1\right) \geq \dfrac{1}{2} - x$

   (c) $\dfrac{3}{4} = \dfrac{3 + x}{5}$

8. Write the following in simplest form with nonnegative exponents in the final answer.

    (a) $\left(\frac{1}{3}\right)^{14}\left(\frac{1}{9}\right)^{-7}$

    (b) $\left(\left(\frac{3}{4}\right)^{-5}\right)^{3}$

    (c) $\dfrac{\left(\frac{2}{3}\right)^{-4}}{\left(\frac{3}{2}\right)^{6}}$

9. A car travels 54 miles per hour and a plane travels 15 miles per minute. How far does the car travel when the plane travels 500 miles?

10. A $46\frac{5}{16}$ lb of nuts is packaged into $1\frac{3}{4}$ lb containers. The remaining nuts are given to the person packing the nuts. Does the person get more or less than $\frac{1}{2}$ lb of nuts? Approximately how much does the person get? Justify your answers.

11. Write in increasing order all the rational numbers satisfying the following conditions: (i) the rational numbers are greater than 0 and less than 1 (ii) the denominators are positive and less than or equal to 5.

12. If the ratio of boys to girls in a class is 3 to 8, will the ratios of boys to girls change, become greater, or become smaller if 2 boys and 2 girls leave the class? Justify your answer.

13. Estimate each of the following, indicating if the actual answer is greater than (+) or less than (-) the estimate.

    (a) $\dfrac{29}{15}+\dfrac{198}{199}$

    (b) $5\frac{12}{13}+2\frac{9}{10}+\frac{19}{20}$

    (c) $10\frac{4}{9}-5\frac{1}{2}+\frac{99}{100}$

14. Estimate each of the following.

    (a) $7\frac{33}{100}\cdot 3$

    (b) $2\frac{25}{99}\cdot 8$

    (c) $\dfrac{\frac{25}{13}}{2\frac{1}{100}}$

    (d) $\dfrac{4\frac{10}{99}}{\frac{1}{10}}$

Sample Test

1. Place >, <, or = between each of the following pairs to make true sentences.

   (a) $4.\overline{9}$ and 5

   (b) $0.\overline{44}$ and $\frac{1}{25}$

   (c) $0.\overline{46}$ and $0.4\overline{6}$

   (d) $\sqrt{3}$ and 1.7

2. Perform each of the following computations.

   (a)   3.0001 - 0.998
   (b)   0.14 + 2.157 + 36.001 - 0.04
   (c)   0.04 · 3.62
   (d)   2.178 ÷ 0.13 (to nearest tenth)

3. Find the additive and multiplicative inverses for each of the following.

   (a)   4.2

   (b)   0.36

4. Solve each of the following for x, where x is a real number.

   (a) $x\sqrt{3} - 2 = 5x\sqrt{3}$

   (b) $0.4x - 0.68 \geq \frac{1}{2}(x - 3.8)$

   (c)   16% of x is 3200

   (d)   11 is x percent of 55

   (e)   13 is 50% of x

   (f) $0.\overline{4} + x = 1$

   (g) $0.\overline{9} - x = 1$

   (h)   5.2x - 0.01 < 0.2x + 3.6

5. Use fractions to justify the algorithm for the subtraction in the following.

   $$\begin{array}{r} 23.6 \\ - \quad 8.34 \\ \hline \end{array}$$

6. Answer each of the following.

   (a)   7 is what percent of 3.5?
   (b)   What is 210% of 50?
   (c)   18 is 40% of what number?

7. Change each of the following to percents.

   (a) $\frac{1}{5}$

   (b) $\frac{3}{80}$

   (c)   5.36

   (d)   0.013

8. Change each of the following percents to decimals.

   (a)   40%

   (b) $\frac{1}{6}\%$

   (c)   200%

9. Round each of the following numbers as specified.

    (a) 508.576 to the nearest hundredth
    (b) 508.576 to the nearest tenth
    (c) 508.576 to the nearest hundred

10. Convert each of the following rational numbers to the form $\frac{a}{b}$, where a and b are integers and $b \neq 0$.

    (a) 0.27   (b) 3.104   (c) $0.2\overline{4}$ (d) $0.\overline{24}$

11. Convert each of the following fractions to decimals that either terminate or repeat.

    (a) $\frac{3}{40}$

    (b) $\frac{3}{24}$

    (c) $\frac{2}{13}$

12. Find an approximation for $\sqrt{15}$ rounded to the nearest thousandth.

13. Write each of the following in scientific notation.

    (a) 5,268,000
    (b) 0.000325

14. Classify each of the following as a rational or irrational number.

    (a) 6.76776777677776...   (b) $\frac{1}{\sqrt{15}}$

    (c) $\frac{8}{3}$ (d) 0.22332233...

15. Great Home Realty receives a 7% commission on each piece of property it sells. If it sold a house for $132,000, how much commission did the real estate office receive?

16. The teacher was hired at a salary of $18,200 and was to receive raises of 5.5 after the first year and 4% after the second year. What should be her salary after the two-year period?

17. Tony took an 80-item test and missed 18 questions. What percent did he get correct?

18. What is the number of significant digits in each of the following:

    (a) 3,287,000   (b) 3,028
    (c) 0.0328   (d) 2.380

*19. Find the simplest form for each of the following.

    (a) $\sqrt{363}$ (b) $\sqrt{576}$ (c) $\sqrt{480}$ (d) $\sqrt[3]{343}$

33

*20. Write each of the following in simplest form with non-negative exponents in the final answer.

(a) $\left(\frac{1}{3}\right)^3 \cdot \left(\frac{1}{3}\right)^8$

(b) $5^{-12} \div 5^{-3}$

(c) $\left(\left(\frac{1}{4}\right)^{-3}\right)^5$

(d) $5^{19} \cdot 5^7$

*21. A credit union offered a saving account that paid 8% annual interest compounded quarterly. What is the value, rounded to the nearest cent, of $500 if it is left in the account for exactly 2 years?

CHAPTER 7 FORM B

Sample Test

1. Place >, <, or = between each of the following pairs to make true sentences.

    (a) $2.\overline{23}$ and $\sqrt{5}$

    (b) $0.\overline{3}$ and $\frac{1}{3}$

    (c) $0.\overline{4} + 0.\overline{5}$ and 1

    (d) $3.\overline{78}$ and $3.7\overline{8}$

2. Perform each of the following computations.

    (a) 5.082 - 0.34
    (b) (3.2) · (3.4) + 0.001 - 15.3
    (c) $\dfrac{(2.4) \cdot (0.03)}{0.6}$
    (d) 2.782 ÷ 0.23 (to the nearest tenth)

3. Find the additive and multiplicative inverses for each of the following.

    (a) 0.4

    (b) $2.\overline{6}$

4. Solve each of the following for x, where x is a real number.

    (a) $5x\sqrt{2} - x\sqrt{2} = 7x\sqrt{2} + 5$

    (b) $\dfrac{x}{0.4} + 80 = 0.5x + 0.8$

    (c) 18% of x = 58.32

    (d) $0.\overline{3} + x = 0.\overline{7}$

    (e) 36 is x percent of 48

    (f) 6.6 is 30% of x

    (g) $1.\overline{9} - x = 2$

    (h) $x - \dfrac{0.5}{3} = \dfrac{1}{3}(3.7 + 2x)$

5. Use fractions to justify the algorithm for the subtraction in the following.

    8.07 - 2.3

6. Answer each of the following.

    (a) 8 is what percent of 2?
    (b) What is 25% of 8?
    (c) 12 is 60% of what number?

7. Change each of the following to percents.

    (a) $\dfrac{4}{6}$

    (b) $\dfrac{5}{80}$

    (c) 2.06

    (d) $2.\overline{4}$

8. Change each of the following percent to decimals.

    (a) 45%   (b) $\frac{4}{5}$%   (c) 320%

9. Round each of the following numbers as specified.

    (a) 483.765 to the nearest hundredth
    (b) 483.765 to the nearest unit
    (c) 483.765 to the nearest hundred

10. Convert each of the following rational numbers to the form $\frac{a}{b}$, where a and b are integers and b ≠ 0.

    (a) 0.38   (b) 2.607   (c) $0.4\overline{7}$ (d) $0.\overline{324}$

11. Convert each of the following fractions to decimals that either terminate or repeat.

    (a) $\frac{7}{30}$ (b) $\frac{11}{40}$ (c) $\frac{5}{11}$

12. Find an approximation for $\sqrt{11}$ rounded to the nearest thousandth.

13. Write each of the following in scientific notation.

    (a) 3,286
    (b) 0.0000032

14. How many significant digits are there in each part of Problem 13?

15. Classify each of the following as a rational or an irrational number.

    (a) $\sqrt{2} + 8$ (b) $\frac{7}{22}$
    (c) $0.\overline{23}$ (d) 3.14114111411114...

16. Marcy agreed to try to sell her brother's car if he would give her a 5% commission on the selling price. If she sells the car for $3250, how much commission will she receive?

17. Audrey's salary this year is $18,200. She received a 4% raise from last year to this year. What was her last year's salary rounded to the nearest dollar?

18. Tony got 80% of his test questions correct. If there were 80 questions on the test, how many questions did he miss?

*19. Find the simplest form for each of the following.

    (a) $\sqrt{117}$ (b) $\sqrt{700}$
    (c) $\sqrt{588}$ (d) $\sqrt[3]{192}$

*20. Write each of the following in simplest form with nonnegative exponents in the final answer.

(a) $\left(\frac{2}{5}\right)^3 \cdot \left(\frac{2}{5}\right)^8$

(b) $(3^2 \cdot 3^3)^2 \div 3^3$

(c) $(5^{-3} \div 5^{-5})^{-1}$

(d) $\left(\left(\frac{2}{3}\right)^3\right)^{-4}$

*21. A credit union offered a savings account that paid 6% annual interest compounded monthly. What is the value, rounded to the nearest cent, of $800 if it is left in the account for exactly 1 year?

Sample Test

1. Suppose the names of the months of the year are placed in a hat and a name is drawn at random.

    (a) List the sample space for this experiment.
    (b) List the event consisting of the outcomes that the month drawn starts with the letter J.
    (c) What is the probability of drawing the name of a month that starts with J?

2. A fair coin was flipped 5 times and landed heads five times. What is the probability of a head on the next toss?

3. A bag contains five red candies, six white candies, and seven blue candies. Suppose one piece of candy is drawn at random. Find the probability for each of the following.

    (a) A white candy is drawn.
    (b) A red or blue candy is drawn.
    (c) Neither a white nor a blue candy is drawn.
    (d) A red candy is not drawn.

4. One card is selected at random from an ordinary deck of 52 cards. Find the probability of each of the following events.

    (a) A spade is drawn.
    (b) A spade and a king are drawn.
    (c) A heart or a face card is drawn.
    (d) The two of clubs is not drawn.

5. A box contains three blue cards and four white cards. If two cards are drawn one at a time, find the probability that both cards are blue if the draws are made as follows:

    (a) With replacement   (b) Without replacement

6. In a NASA rocket firing, the probability of the success of stage 1 is 95%, at stage 2, 97%, and at stage 3, 98%. What is the probability for success for the three-stage rocket?

7. If a letter is drawn from container 1, shown below, and placed in container 2, and then a letter is drawn from container 2, what is the probability that the letter is a T?

WHAT   WATT

#1   #2

8. Use the containers in Problem 7. Select a container at random, and then select a letter from the chosen container. What is the probability that the letter is a T?

9. If a couple plans to have 3 children, what is the probability of having at least 2 boys?

10. If two die are rolled 360 times, approximately how many times should you expect the sums of 2, 3, or 12?

11. A teacher has prepared a 5-item test with the first three items being true or false and the last two items being multiple choice with 4 choices each. What is the probability that a student will score 100 percent if every answer is chosen at random?

12. Two cards are drawn from an ordinary deck of 52 playing cards. What is the probability that they are both aces given the following?

   (a)   The first card is replaced before the second card is drawn.
   (b)   The first card is not replaced before the second card is drawn.

13. A committee of 2 is selected at random from a set consisting of 5 Democrats, 8 Republicans, and 2 Independents.

   (a)   What is the probability that the committee consists of all Democrats?
   (b)   What is the probability that the committee consists of no Republicans?

14. There were 7 nominees for president and 16 nominees for vice president. In how many ways can the slate be chosen?

15. Compute $\dfrac{101!}{99!}$.

16. How many different 3-person committees can be formed from a group of 6 people?

17. If automobile license plates consist of 2 letters followed by 4 digits, how many different possible license plates are possible if letters and numbers can be repeated?

18. Given the spinner below, find each of the following.

   (a)   P(A)   (b)   P(B)

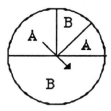

19. Find the number of ways to rearrange the letters in the following words.

   (a)   ENGLISH
   (b)   MATHEMATICS

*20. A hat contains the letters in PROBABILITY. If 6 letters are drawn from the hat one at a time with replacement, what are the odds against obtaining the outcome RABBIT?

*21. If the odds in favor of the Cardinals winning the game are 8 to 5, what is the probability that they will win?

*22. Two standard die are rolled. What are the odds in favor of rolling a sum of 3?

*23.　What are the odds against drawing a jack of spades when one card is drawn from an ordinary deck of playing cards?

*24.　A sorority sold 132 tickets in a raffle for a $299 television set. What is the expected value of a single ticket if only one ticket wins?

*25.　A game consists of rolling two die. Rolling doubles, for example (3, 3), pays $60. Rolling anything but doubles pays $6.00. What is the expected value for the game?

*26.　How could each of the following be simulated using a random digit table?

　　(a)　Tossing a fair coin.
　　(b)　Picking a day of the week at random.
　　(c)　Picking three dates at random in the month of April.

CHAPTER 8 FORM B

Sample Test

1.   Suppose the letters of the alphabet are placed in a hat and a letter is drawn at random.

        (a)   List the sample space for this experiment.
        (b)   List the event consisting of the outcomes that the letter drawn is a vowel.
        (c)   What is the probability of drawing a letter that is a vowel?

2.   What is the probability of a fair coin landing heads five times in a row?

3.   A box contains 4 red marbles, 8 white marbles, and 5 blue marbles. If one marble is drawn at random, find the probability for each of the following.

        (a)   A blue marble is drawn.
        (b)   A red or a blue marble is drawn.
        (c)   Neither a red nor a blue marble is drawn.
        (d)   A blue marble is not drawn.

4.   One card is drawn from an ordinary deck of 52 playing cards. Find the probability of each of the following events.

        (a)   A spade or a club is drawn.
        (b)   A face card and a heart is drawn.
        (c)   A face card or a heart is drawn.
        (d)   An ace is not drawn.

5.   A box contains 4 red marbles, 8 white marbles, and 5 blue marbles. If 2 marbles are drawn one at a time, find the probability that both marbles are white if draws are made as follows.

        (a)   With replacement   (b)   Without replacement

6.   The probability of Ann passing her math test is 90%. The probability she passes her English test is 80%. The probability she passes her Chemistry test is 70%. What is the probability she passes all 3 tests?

7.   If a letter is drawn from container number 1, shown below, and placed in container number 2, then a letter is drawn from container 2, what is the probability that the letter is an H?

                        MATH   HISTORY
                         #1   #2

8.   Use the containers in Problem 7. If a letter is drawn from container number 1 and then a letter is drawn from container number 2, what is the probability of the outcome MY?

9.   If a couple plans to have 3 children, what is the probability of having at least 1 girl?

10.   If two die are rolled 360 times, approximately how many times should you expect a sum which is a prime number?

11.   A teacher has prepared a 5-item test with the first two items being true or false and the last three items being multiple choice with four choices each. What is the probability that a student will score 0 if every answer is chosen at random?

12.   Two cards are drawn from an ordinary deck of 52 playing cards. What is the probability that they are both face cards given the following?

   (a)   The first card is replaced before the second card is drawn.
   (b)   The first card is not replaced before the second card is drawn.

13.   A committee of 2 is selected at random from a set of people consisting of 2 Democrats, 4 Republicans, and 1 Independent.

   (a)   What is the probability that the committee has no Republicans?
   (b)   What is the probability that the committee has all Republicans?

14.   There were 8 nominees for president and 11 nominees for vice president. In how many ways can the slate be chosen?

15.   Compute $\dfrac{26!}{24!\ 2!}$.

16.   How many different 4-person committees can be formed from a group of 7 people?

17.   If automobile license plates consist of 3 letters followed by 3 digits, how many different license plates are possible if letters and numbers can be repeated?

18.   Given the spinner below, find each of the following.

   (a)   P(A)   (b)   P(B)

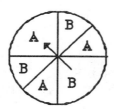

19.   Find the number of ways to rearrange the letters in the following words.

   (a)   FACTOR   (b)   PROBABILITY

*20.   A hat contains the letters in the word MATHEMATICS. If 4 letters are drawn from the hat one at a time without replacement, what are the odds against spelling the word MATH?

*21.   If the odds against the Tigers winning their next game are 9 to 4, what is the probability that they will win?

*22.   Two standard die are rolled. What are the odds in favor of rolling a sum of 6?

*23.   What are the odds against drawing a face card that is a heart when one card is drawn from an ordinary deck of playing cards?

*24.   Joe's baseball team sold 500 chances to win a $250 set of golf clubs. What is the expected value of a single chance if only one chance wins?

*25.   A game consists of rolling a die. If a number greater than 4 is rolled, you receive the number of dollars showing on the die. If any other number shows, you receive $1.00. What is the expected value of this game?

*26.   How could each of the following be simulated using random digit table?

(a)   Picking a letter of the alphabet at random.
(b)   Picking one of the five oceans at random.
(c)   Spinning the spinner shown below.

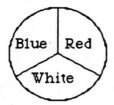

Sample Test

1. Claude paid $38.80 for dinner for himself and two friends. If one friend's meal cost twice as much as Claude's and Claude's meal cost the same as his other friend, answer the following:

    (a) What is the mean cost of the meals?
    (b) What is the median cost of the meals?
    (c) What is the mode cost of the meals?

2. Find the mean, median, mode, and range, of the following scores.

98	98	98	98	45
84	84	52	45	37

3. Use the scores in Problem 2 to make a frequency table for the data.

4. The budget for the Women's Center is $1,000,000. If $500,000 is spent on advertising, $150,000 is spent on conferences, and the remainder is spent on long-term securities, draw a circle graph to indicate how the money is spent.

5. If the median is higher than the mean on a set of test scores, describe the distribution.

6. The following are the weights in kilograms to the nearest tenth of Miss Brown's class. Construct a stem and leaf plot for the data with the stem defined to be all digits to the left of the decimal point.

28.3	27.3	25.6	29.0	27.4
22.7	21.9	22.4	23.7	20.9
21.5	20.1	24.1	21.2	21.9
26.4	23.5	22.5	26.4	23.6
30.1	28.7	27.5	24.6	28.2

7. Twenty test scores are shown below.

31	30	23	27	19
26	28	38	17	29
26	34	21	32	32
22	12	26	39	25

    (a) Make a grouped frequency table for these scores, using 12 to start the first class and making six classes.
    (b) Draw a histogram for the grouped data.
    (c) Draw a frequency polygon for the data.

8. The mean age of members of a class reunion was 71.9. The next year the mean age was 71.5 years. How can the mean age decrease when all the class members are a year older?

9. The mean age of 5 persons in a room is 30 years. A 36-year-old person walks in. What is the mean age of the persons in the room now?

10. The quiz scores for Mr. Brown and Miss Burke's classes are given below.

    (a) Draw a line plat for each set.
    (b) Draw a back-to-back stem and leaf plot for the two classes.
    (c) Give the interquartile range for each set of scores.
    (d) Are there any outliers for either set of data? If yes, what are they?
    (e) Draw box plots to compare the two sets of data.
    (f) What can you say about the two sets of data.

Mr. Brown	Miss Burke
75	78
82	76
91	79
85	78
90	92
92	86
94	74
90	78
94	80
92	90
90	82
90	80

*11. An advertisement claims "Four out of five doctors surveyed recommend Tielitnot for their patients with arthritis." State why you would or would not accept this as a valid claim to product superiority.

*12. A standardized test has a mean of 500 with a standard deviation of 70. If 2000 students took the test and their scores approximated a normal curve, how many scores are between 360 and 640?

*13. Use the information in Problem 12 to find:

    (a) P_{16} (b) D_5 (c) P_{84}

*14. On a final exam the mean was 72 with a standard deviation of 15. Find the grade corresponding to a z score of -1.

CHAPTER 9 FORM B

Sample Test

1. The grades of a coed on her examinations were as follows: 84, 91, 72, 68, 87, and 78. Find the coed's mean.

2. If (a) 77 and (b) 130 scores are arranged in an array, how would you find the median of the scores?

3. The reaction times in seconds of an organism to certain stimuli were recorded as follows: 0.53, 0.46, 0.55, 0.44, 0.52, 0.49, and 0.53. What is the mode of this set of data?

4. The mean annual salary paid to the employees at Pay-Less Food Store was $5000. The mean annual salaries paid to female and male employees at the store were $5200 and $4200 respectively. Determine the percentages of females and males employed by the store.

5. Given the set of numbers below:

5, 18, 12, 6, 7, 3, 15, 10

Find the following:

(a) range
(b) mean
(c) median
(d) standard deviation

6. The table below shows the number of bushels of soybeans produced in Tennessee's driest county in the 1950's. Draw a bar graph to depict the information.

Year	Number of Bushels of Soybeans
1950	200
1951	185
1952	225
1953	250
1954	240
1955	195
1956	210
1957	225
1958	250
1959	230
1960	235

7. Construct a stem and leaf plot using the numbers of bushels of soybeans in Problem 6.

8. In the table on the following page are the weights in pounds of 40 students at the Huntsville Space Camp Summer Program.

(a) Construct a frequency table for the data above with 12 classes starting the least class with 118.
(b) Draw a histogram depicting the data.

8.   (cont.)

146	163	142	147	135	153	140	135
146	158	140	147	136	148	152	144
168	126	138	176	163	119	154	165
138	164	150	132	144	125	149	157
161	145	135	142	150	156	145	128

9.   In a teachers' meeting, a principal was overheard to remark that no student should have a mathematics score on a standardized test below the national mean. Comment on this.

10.   On an English 101 exam two instructors gave the same test and both classes had the same mean. However, the standard deviation of one class was twice the standard deviation of the other class. Which class would appear to be the easiest to teach? Why?

11.   The quiz scores for Mr. Read and Miss Sol's classes are given below.

   (a)   Draw a line plot for each set.
   (b)   Draw a back-to-back stem and leaf plot for the two classes.
   (c)   Give the interquartile range for each set of scores.
   (d)   Are there any outliers for either set of data? If yes, what are they?
   (e)   Draw box plots to compare the two sets of data.
   (f)   What can you say about the two sets of data.

Mr. Read	Miss Sol
72	90
78	88
85	78
92	83
75	96
76	92
89	90
96	84
78	75
92	98
90	93
80	92

*12.   Use the information in Problem 8 to find the following:

   (a) P_{50} (b) D_5

*13.   Two students received z-scores of 0.8 and -0.4 respectively on a test. If their scores on the test were 88 and 64 respectively, what are the mean and standard deviation on the test?

*14.   A standardized test has a mean of 300 with a standard deviation of 45. If 1000 students took the test and their scores approximated a normal curve, how many scores are between 255 and 390?

CHAPTER 10 FORM A

Sample Test

1. Construct two rays $\overrightarrow{AB}$ and $\overrightarrow{CD}$, for which $\overline{AB} \cap \overline{CD}$ is a set containing one point and the intersection of $\overrightarrow{AB}$ and $\overrightarrow{CD}$ is a ray.

2. Sketch and name two adjacent angles that are complementary.

3. What is the least number of faces that a polyhedron may have?

4. (a) Sketch a square pyramid.
    (b) Count the number of vertices, edges, and faces for the pyramid in part (a) and determine if Euler's Formula holds for this pyramid.

5. Classify the following as true or false.

    (a) Two distinct lines can have no more that one point in common.
    (b) Two skew lines determine one and only one plane.
    (c) If a plane contains one point of a line, then it must contain the entire line.
    (d) A plane separates space into three distinct sets of points.

    (e) For any two distinct points A and B, $\overleftrightarrow{AB} = \overleftrightarrow{BA}$.
    (f) A ray contains its endpoint.

6. Describe each of the following sets of points with reference to the given figure.

    (a) $å \cap ʃ$
    (b) (plane XYZ) $ʃ$
    (c) $\overleftrightarrow{AF} \cap \overline{BE}$
    (d) $\overline{CE} \cap \triangle ADF$
    (e) $\overrightarrow{AE} \cup \overrightarrow{AF}$
    (f) $\alpha \cap \overrightarrow{BD}$
    (g) interior ($\triangle ADF$) $\cap \overleftrightarrow{AF}$

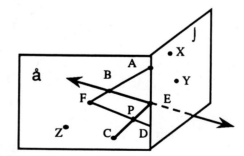

7. If the measure of an angle is 13°26'49", what is the measure of its supplement?

8. If the non-base angle of an isosceles triangle has a measure of 68°, what is the measure of each base angle?

9. Sketch a heptagonal prism and show that Euler's formula holds for it.

10. If 5x° and (7x - 12)° are the measures for supplementary angles, what is the measure of each angle?

11. Is a rectangle a trapezoid? Explain your answer.

12. Given the figure shown with $\overleftrightarrow{AX} \parallel \overleftrightarrow{DY}$, find the following:

   (a) m(∠1)
   (b) m(∠2)
   (c) m(∠3)
   (d) m(∠4)
   (e) m(∠5)

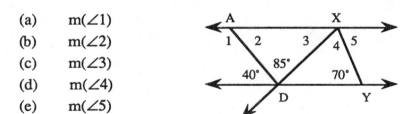

13. Determine if points A, B, and C are inside or outside the given curves.

   (a)

   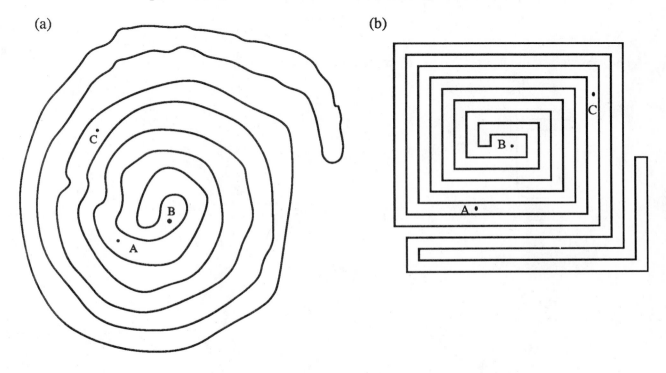

   (b)

*14. Given △ABC with ∠BCA and ∠CDA as right angles. Show that ∠A is congruent to ∠DCB.

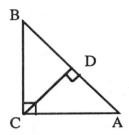

*15.   Which of the figures are traversable? Show a path for those that are.

(a)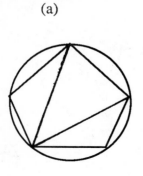

(b)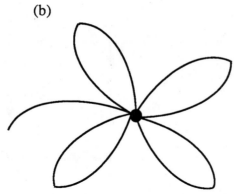

(c)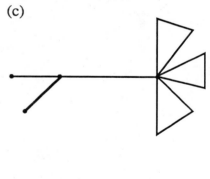

*16.   Which of the figures below, if any, are topologically equivalent?

(a)

Glass

(b)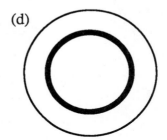

Cup

(c)

Spool

(d)

Plate

(e)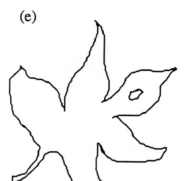

Leaf

(f)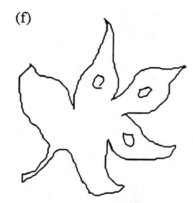

Leaf with three holes

*17. Write a Logo procedure to construct a pair of complementary angles given the measure of one angle, :A.

Sample Test

1. Construct two segments $\overline{AB}$ and $\overline{CD}$, for which $\overrightarrow{AB} \cap \overrightarrow{CD}$ is a set containing one point and $\overline{AB} \cap \overline{CD} = \emptyset$.

2. Sketch and name two angles that have a common vertex and a common side, but are not adjacent angles.

3. What is the least number of sides a polygon can have?

4. If planes α and β are distinct planes having points X, Y, and Z in common, what conclusion can you make about points X, Y, and Z? Why?

5. Classify the following as true or false.

    (a) For any line $\overleftrightarrow{AB}$ and point C such that $C \,\varepsilon\, \overleftrightarrow{AB}$, there is one and only one plane containing both C and $\overleftrightarrow{AB}$.

    (b) Two intersecting lines determine one and only one plane.

    (c) If a plane contains a segment, it contains the line of which the segment is a subset.

    (d) A line separates space into three disjoint sets.

    (e) For any two distinct points A and B, $\overrightarrow{AB} = \overrightarrow{BA}$.

    (f) If $\overrightarrow{AB} = \overrightarrow{CB}$, then A must be a different name for C.

    (g) A line has three endpoints.

6. Describe each of the following sets of points with reference to the given figure.

    (a) $\alpha \cap \beta$
    (b) (Plane XYZ) $\cap \beta$
    (c) $\overleftrightarrow{AF} \cap \overline{BE}$
    (d) $\overline{CE} \cap \Delta ADF$
    (e) $\overline{AE} \cup \overleftrightarrow{FE}$
    (f) $\alpha \cap \overrightarrow{BD}$
    (g) interior $(\Delta ADF) \cap \overleftrightarrow{AF}$
    (h) $\overline{AE} \cup \overline{EF}$

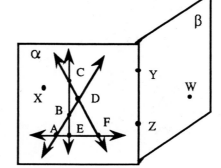

7. (a) What is the measure of each angle in a regular decagon?
    (b) How many diagonals does a decagon have?

8.   Show that Euler's formula holds for an octagonal pyramid.

9.   (a)   Can a rhombus have four acute angles? Justify your answer.
        (b)   A rectangle has been defined as a parallelogram in which one of the angles is a right
                angle. Explain why a rectangle must have four right angles.

10.   If 5x° and (7x - 12)° are the measures for vertical angles formed by two intersecting lines,
        what is the measure of each angle?

11.   (a)   Find 18°19'46" - 6°48'59".
        (b)   Express 6.82° in terms of degrees, minutes, and seconds.

12.   Given the figure shown with $\overleftrightarrow{AX}$ || $\overleftrightarrow{DY}$, find the following.

        (a)   m(∠1)
        (b)   m(∠3)
        (c)   m(∠4)
        (d)   m(∠2)
        (e)   m(∠5)

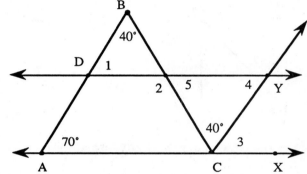

13.   Determine if points A, B, and C are inside or outside the given curves.

        (a)   (b)

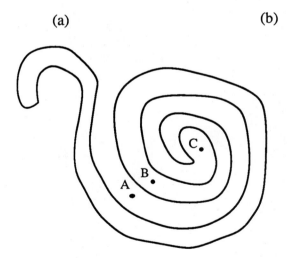
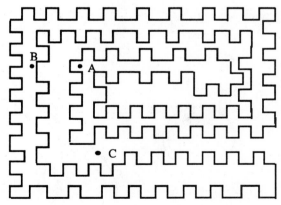

*14. Given ΔABC with $\overrightarrow{CA}$, as pictured. If $\overrightarrow{AX}$ bisects ∠DAB and $\overrightarrow{AY}$ bisects ∠BAC, show $\overrightarrow{AX} \perp \overrightarrow{AY}$.

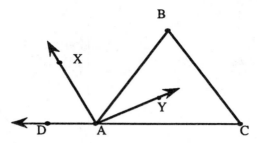

*15. Which of the figures are traversable? Show a path for those that are.

(a)   (b)   (c)

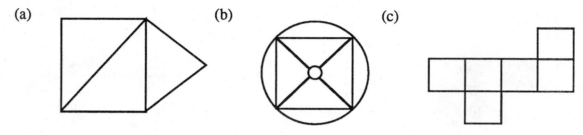

*16. Which of the figures below, if any, are topologically equivalent?

(a)   (b)   (c)

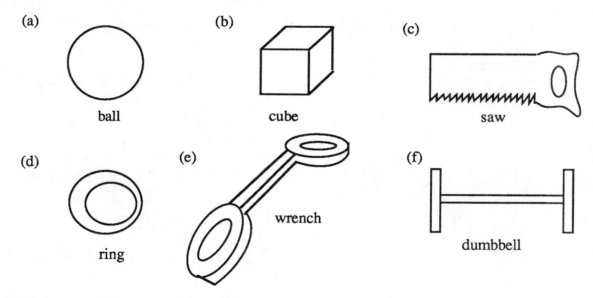

ball   cube   saw

(d)   (e)   (f)

ring   wrench   dumbbell

*17. Write a Logo procedure to construct a pair of supplementary angles given the measure of one angle, :A.

Sample Test

1. Given the figures, state whether the triangles are congruent based upon the given conditions. If your answer is yes, name the theorem or postulate abbreviation to justify your answer.

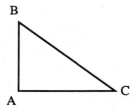 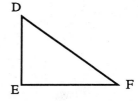

(a) $\angle A \cong \angle E$, $\angle B \cong \angle D$, $\overline{AB} \cong \overline{ED}$

(b) $\angle A$ and $\angle E$ are right angles. $\overline{BC} \cong \overline{DF}$; $\angle C \cong \angle F$.

(c) $\triangle ABC$ and $\triangle EDF$ are right triangles and $\overline{AC} \cong \overline{EF}$. $\angle B \cong \angle D$, and they are not right angles.

(d) $\overline{AC} \cong \overline{EF}$; $\angle C \cong \angle F$; $\overline{BC} \cong \overline{DF}$

(e) $\overline{AC} \cong \overline{EF}$; $\overline{BC} \cong \overline{DF}$; $\overline{AB} \cong \overline{ED}$

2. In each of the parts, there is at least one pair of congruent triangles. Identify them and tell why they are congruent.

(a)

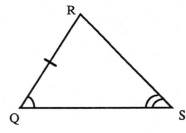 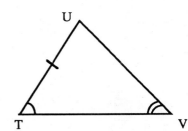

(b)

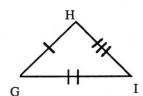 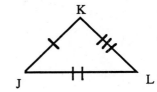

2.   (cont.)

(c)

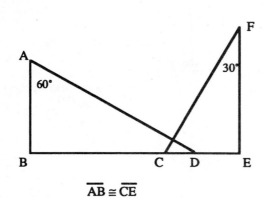

(d)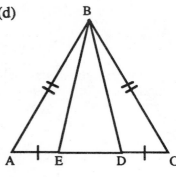

$$\overline{AB} \cong \overline{CE}$$

3.   Construct each of the following using (i) compass and straightedge, (ii) paper folding.

(a)   Angle bisector of ∠A

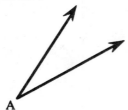

(b)   Perpendicular bisector of $\overline{AB}$

(c)   Altitude of △ABC from A

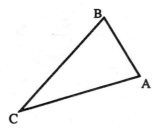

(d)   Parallel to ... through M

. M

4. For each of the following pairs of similar triangles, find the missing measure.

(a)

(b)

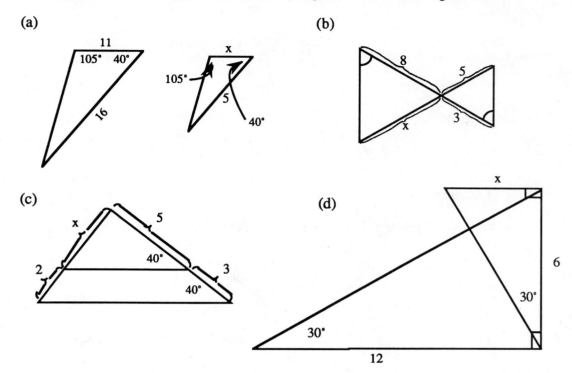

(c)

(d)

5. Divide the given segment into three congruent parts.

A   B

6. Construct the center of the circle containing AB.

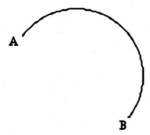

7. Determine whether each of the following is true or false. If false, explain why.

(a) A diameter of a circle is a chord of the circle.
(b) A chord may be a tangent of the circle.
(c) If a radius is perpendicular to a chord, the radius bisects the chord.
(d) A sphere may intersect a plane in a circle.

8.   A person 122 cm tall casts a 37-cm shadow at the same time a tree casts a 148-cm shadow. How tall is the tree?

9.   Given any circle, explain how to inscribe a regular octagon in it using only a compass and a straightedge.

10.   In each of the following, answer true or false. Justify your answer.

(a)   The center of the circle circumscribing a triangle is always in the interior of the triangle.

(b)   In every triangle the center of the inscribed circle is different from the center of the circumscribing circle.

(c)   If the three circles with centers at O_1, O_2, and O_3 (shown below) are tangent to $\overleftrightarrow{AB}$ and $\overleftrightarrow{AC}$ then A, O_1, O_2, and O_3 are collinear.

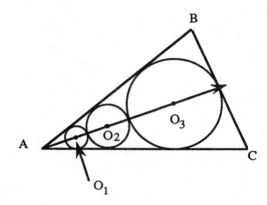

CHAPTER 11 FORM B

Sample Test

1.   Assume that each of the pairs of triangles is congruent and write an appropriate symbolic congruence in each case.

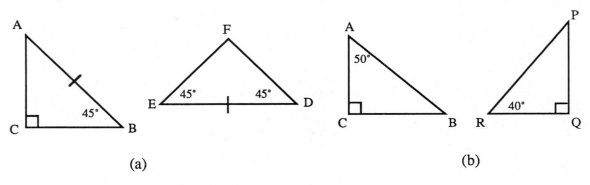

                             (a)   (b)

2.   Using a compass and straightedge construct each of the following:

    (a)   An equilateral triangle.
    (b)   A 30° angle.
    (c)   A 75° angle.

3.   Given $\overline{AM} \cong \overline{MC}$ and $\overline{BM} \cong \overline{MD}$ why are the following true?
Justify your answer.

    (a) $\overline{AB} \cong \overline{CD}$

    (b) $\overline{AB} \, || \, \overline{CD}$

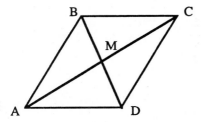

4.   Use a straightedge and compass to construct the circle which circumscribes the given triangle and the circle that is inscribed in the triangle.

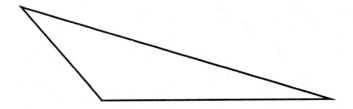

5.   In each of the following find x and y if possible.

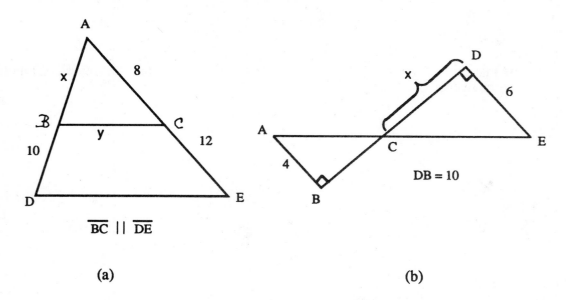

(a)   (b)

6.   Use a compass and a straightedge to divide the segment $\overline{AB}$ into 3 congruent parts.

A ————————————— B

7.   In each of the following answer true or false. Justify your answers.

    (a)   Congruent triangles are also similar.
    (b)   Two similar triangles are also congruent triangles.
    (c)   Any two equilateral triangles are similar.
    (d)   Two isosceles triangles are similar.
    (e)   The diagonals of a trapezoid divide it into four triangles, two of which are similar.
    (f)   If three sides of one triangle are parallel, respectively, to three sides of a second triangle, then the triangles are similar.

8.   Use a compass and a straightedge to divide the square below into 25 congruent squares.

9. Given ∆ABC below, construct a similar triangle whose sides are twice as great.

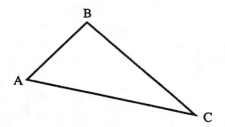

10. Construct a circle that contains points A, B, and C.

• B

A •

• C

Sample Test

1.　Complete each of the following motions.

(a)

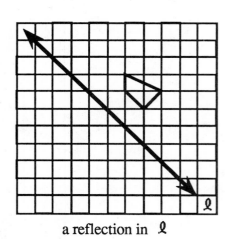

a reflection in　ℓ

(b)

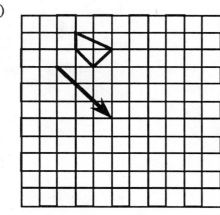

a translation as pictured

(c)

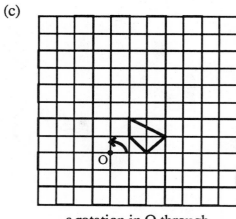

a rotation in O through
the given arc

*(d)

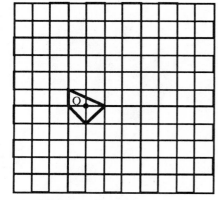

a size transformation with
center O and scale factor 2

2.   How many lines of symmetry, if any, does each of the following figures have?

(a)

(b)

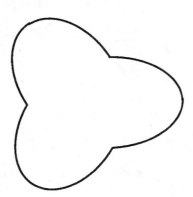

3.   The following pairs of figures are congruent. Tell which transformations will take (1) to (2).

(a)

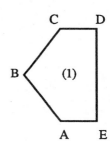

(b)

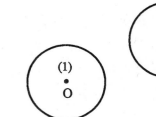

4.   For each of the following transformations, construct the image of $\overline{AB}$.

(a)   A reflection in ℓ

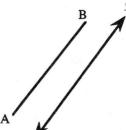

(b)   A translation which takes M to N

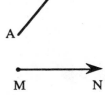

4. (cont.)

(c) A rotation in O as indic

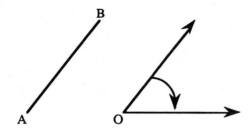

5. Describe objects which have each of the following types of symmetry.

(a) line
(b) point
(c) plane
(d) 45° rotational

6. For each of the following pairs of figures, determine which transformation might take one figure to the other.

(a)

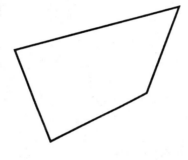

(b)

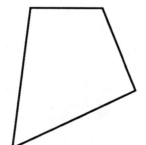
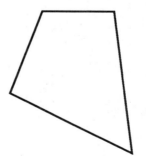

6. (cont.)

   (c)

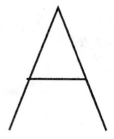 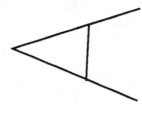

7. Find the minimum number of lines that can be used to accomplish each of the isometries in Problem 6.

8. If possible, describe a geometric figure that can be transformed into itself by each of the following:

   (a)   reflection
   (b)   rotation
   (c)   translation
   (d)   glide reflection

9. Use a reflection to argue that the base angles of an isosceles triangle are congruent.

10. Given points A and B and △DEF below, find point C on △DEF such that △ABC is isosceles.

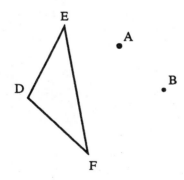

11. Let l' be the image of l under a half-turn about point O. If A' is the image of A and B' the image of B and $\overline{OB} \perp l$ answer each of the following true of false. Justify your answers.

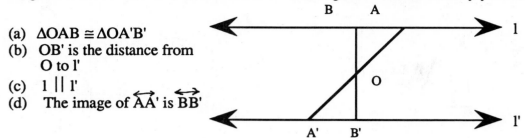

(a) $\triangle OAB \cong \triangle OA'B'$
(b) OB' is the distance from O to l'
(c) $1 \parallel 1'$
(d) The image of $\overleftrightarrow{AA'}$ is $\overleftrightarrow{BB'}$

12. Explain why a regular pentagon cannot tessellate the plane.

*13. Write a Logo procedure called H that will draw a strip of H's similar to the one below.

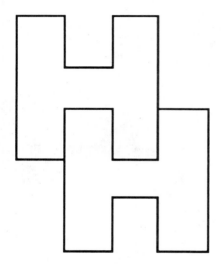

Sample Test

1.   Complete each of the following motions.

(a)

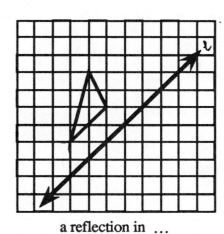

a reflection in ...

(b)

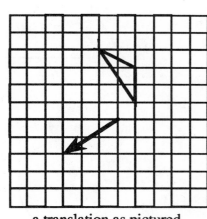

a translation as pictured

(c)

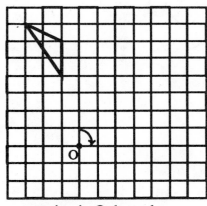

a rotation in O through
the given arc

(d)

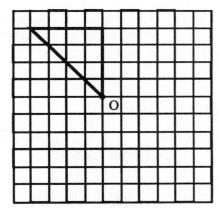

a size transformation with
center O and scale factor 1/2

2.   For each of the following transformations construct the image of the indicated figure.

   (a)   A reflection of ∆ABC in ℓ

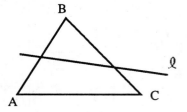

   (b)   A translation of the circle along the arrow from M to N.

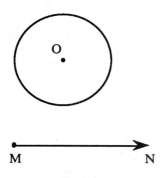

   (c)   A half-turn of the line ℓ in O.

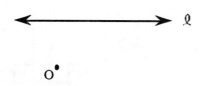

   (d)   A 60° rotation counterclockwise of ∆ABC in A.

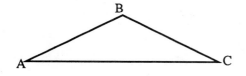

3.   Tessellate the plane with the quadrilateral given below.

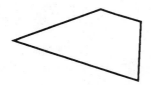

4.   How many lines of symmetry, if any, does each, of the following figures have?

(a)

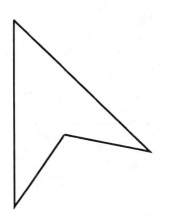

(b)

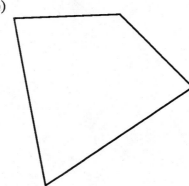

(c)

(d)

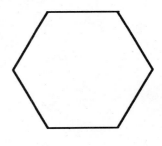

5.   Describe point symmetry and rotational symmetries, if any, of the parts of Problem 4.

6. For each of the following pairs of figures, determine which transformation might take one figure to the other.

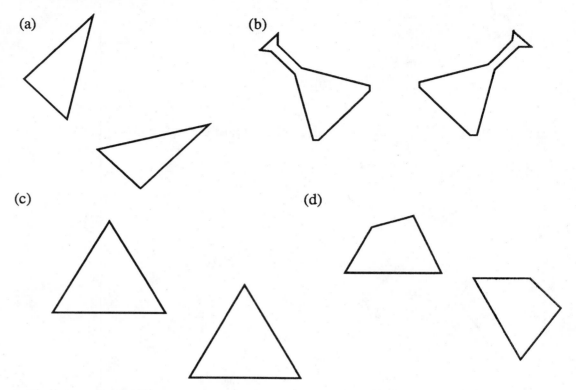

(a)

(b)

(c)

(d)

7. Find the minimum number of reflecting lines needed to accomplish the isometries in Problem 6.

8. Use a reflection to argue that the base angles of an isosceles trapezoid are congruent.

9. Given points A and B and circle O below, find a chord $\overline{CD}$ of a circle O such that $\overline{AB} \cong \overline{CD}$
.

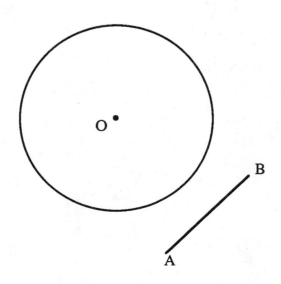

10.   What regular figure can be used with a regular octagon to tessellate the plane? Why?

*11.   Write a Logo procedure called HOUSE to draw a strip of houses similar to the ones below.

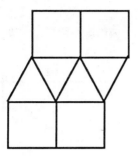

Sample Test

1. Complete the following table converting metric measures.

	mm	cm	m	km
(a)		6200		
(b)			360	
(c)				0.3
(d)	2,300,000			

2. For each of the following choose an appropriate metric unit: Millimeter, centimeter, meter or kilometer.

   (a) The thickness of a dime
   (b) The length of a straw
   (c) The diameter of a penny
   (d) The distance the winner travels at the Talledega 500
   (e) The height of a desk
   (f) The length of a football field

3. Find the area of each of the following.

   (a) 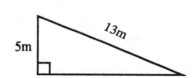   (b)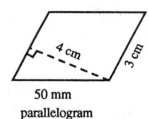

4. Find the surface area of the square prism whose base has a side of length 4 cm and a height of 6 cm.

5. Find the area of the shaded region on the following geoboard if the unit of measurement is 1 cm^2.

6.   Is it possible to have a square with area 11 cm^2? Explain why or why not.

7.   Explain how the formula for the area of a triangle can be determined by using the formula for the area of a parallelogram.

8.   Answer the following.

(a)   If the volume of a sphere is $\frac{500\pi}{3}$ m^3, what is the radius?

(b)   Find the volume of a cylinder whose height is 2 m and whose base has an area of $\frac{9\pi}{4}$ m^2.

9.   What is the area of the figure below?

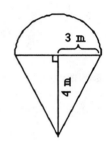

10.   For each of the following, can the measures represent sides of a right triangle? Explain your answers.

(a)   6 m, 8 m, 10 m   (b) $\sqrt{2}$ cm, $\sqrt{3}$ cm, $\sqrt{5}$ cm

11.   Complete each of the following.

(a)   500 cm^2 = ____ m^2 (b)   81 km = _____ m
(c)   4738 g = _____ kg   (d)   300 mL = _____ L
(e)   17 ha = _____ m^2 (f)   0.10222 kL = _____ mL
(g)   0.027 L = _____ cm^3
(h)   4738 kL of water at 4°C has a mass of _____ kg.

12.   Complete the following. (Use a calculator whenever convenient.)

(a)   1.7 mi = _____ yd
(b)   40 ft = _____ yd
(c)   1400 ft^2 = _____ yd^2
(d)   4.3 mi^2 = _____ acres
(e) $\frac{1}{4}$ yd^3 = _____ ft^3
(f)   0.4 ft^3 = _____ in^3
(g)   4.5 lb = _____ oz
(h)   68 oz = _____ lb
*(i)   32°C = _____ °F
*(j)   105° = _____ °C

13. (a) Suppose one edge of a cubic tank is 7 m and the tank is filled with water at 4°C; find the volume of the tank in cubic meters.
    (b) Find the capacity of the tank of (a) in liters.
    (c) Find the mass of the water of (a) in kilograms.

14. Complete each of the following.

    (a) 3 dm³ of water has a mass of _____ g.
    (b) 2 L of water has a mass of _____ g.
    (c) 13 cm³ of water has a mass of _____ g.
    (d) 4.2 L of water has a mass of _____ g.
    (e) 3.01 L of water has a volume of _____ m³.

15. Find the volume of a cone whose slant height is 50 cm and whose height is 0.4 m.

16. If the diameter of a circle is 14 cm, find each of the following.

    (a) The circumference of the circle
    (b) The area of the circle
    (c) The area of a sector of the circle that corresponds to a central angle of 18°.

17. Find the perimeters of each of the following if all arcs shown are semicircles.

    (a)

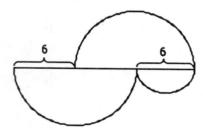

    (b)

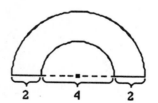

74

Sample Test

1.   Find the area of ΔABC in each of the following.

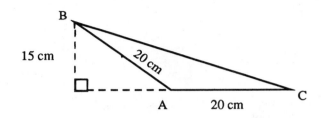 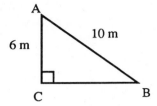

2.   Assume that the only area formula you know is the formula for the area of a triangle and derive the formula for the area of a trapezoid.

3.   A toy manufacturer wants to design a wooden square pyramid whose volume is 8000 cm^3.

   (a)   Design such a pyramid. Make a sketch and show the dimensions of the base and the altitude.
   (b)   How many such pyramids are possible? Why?

4.   Suppose the surface area of a box is S cm^2 and the volume is V cm^3. If each dimension of the box is quadrupled, what is the new surface area and the new volume?

5.   Complete each of the following:

   (a)   10 km = _____ m
   (b)   25 m = _____ dm
   (c)   52813 g = _____ kg
   (d)   26,000,000 mm = _____ m

6.   A rectangular box has dimensions 60 cm, 40 cm, 2 m.

   (a)   Find the surface area of the box in square meters.
   (b)   Find the volume of the box in cubic meters.
   (c)   Find the volume of the box in liters.

7.   A cone whose base is a circle with radius 50 cm and whose slant height is 90 cm is cut along a slant height (after the base in removed) and flattened into a sector of a circle. Find the opening angle.

8.　A box shaped container has a 2 m by 3 m rectangular base. It is filled with water and the height of the water is 50 cm.

    (a)　How many liters of water are in the container?
    (b)　Find the weight of the water in kg.
    (c)　If 60 liters of water are added into the container, how much will the water rise?

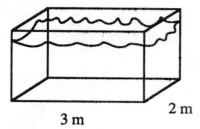

2 m

3 m

9.　The base of a right pyramid is a regular hexagon with the sides of length 12 m. The altitude of the pyramid is 9 m. Find the following:

    (a)　The area of the base of the pyramid.
    (b)　The lateral surface area of pyramid.

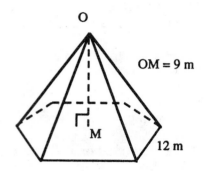

O

OM = 9 m

M

12 m

10.　Find x in each of the following:

(a)

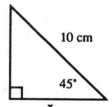

10 cm

45°

x

(b)

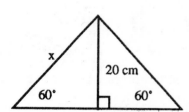

x

20 cm

60°　60°

(c)

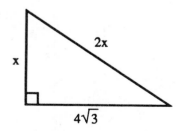

2x

x

$4\sqrt{3}$

11.　Complete the following. (Use a calculator whenever convenient.)

    (a)　0.4 mi = _____ yd
    (b)　4.8 yd = _____ ft

11. (cont.)

    (c) $2.8 \text{ yd}^2 = $ _____ ft^2

    (d) $4.8 \text{ acres} = $ _____ mi^2

    (e) $0.7 \text{ yd}^3 = $ _____ ft^3

    (f) 48034 ft^3 _____ yd^3

    (g)   8.64 lb = _____ oz

    (h)   48.5 oz = _____ lb

  *(i)   -40°C = _____ °F

  *(j)   85°F = _____ °C

CHAPTER 14 FORM A

Sample Test

1. Sketch a picture of a line for each of the following conditions.

   (a) A positive slope
   (b) A negative slope
   (c) Slope of 0
   (d) A negative slope with y-intercept $^-2$
   (e) No slope

2. For each of the following conditions, write the equation of the line determined.

   (a) The line through $(4, ^-7)$ and $(^-8, ^-3)$
   (b) The line through $(4, ^-7)$ with y-intercept 8
   (c) The line through $(4, ^-7)$ parallel to $y = 3x + 15$
   (d) The line through $(4, ^-7)$ perpendicular to the x-axis

3. Sketch the graph of each of the following.

   (a) $x^2 + y^2 = 16$
   (b) $(x + 3)^2 + (y + 4)^2 = 16$
   (c) $x^2 + y^2 \leq 9$
   (d) $3x - 2y = 6$
   (e) $4y = 3x - 12$
   (f) $\frac{x}{2} + \frac{y}{3} = 1$
   (g) $x \geq y + 4$
   (h) $y \leq 4x + 1$

4. Find the equation of the circle whose center is at $(^-2, ^-6)$ and which passes through the point $(7, 8)$.

5. Find the perimeter of the triangle with vertices at A $(0, 0)$, B $(4, 3)$, and C $(^-6, 0)$.

6. Solve each of the following systems, if possible. Indicate whether the system has a unique solution, infinitely many solutions, or no solutions.

   (a) $4x - 3y = 8$
       $4x + 3y = 8$
   (b) $3x - 5y = 7$
       $^-6x + 10y = ^-14$

   (c) $2x + 3y = 8$
       $7x + 4y = 13$

7. Graphically show the solution to the following system of inequalities.

   $3x - 7y \leq 14$
   $y \geq x + 3$

8. In each part, determine if the three points are collinear.

   (a) $(0, 7)$, $(0, 3)$, and $(0, 9)$
   (b) $(2, 3)$, $(4, 6)$, and $(6, 9)$
   (c) $(0.1, ^-3)$, $(0.2, ^-4)$, and $(0.3, ^-5)$

9. Find the equation of the line passing through the y-intercept of the line $x = 3y + 1$ and perpendicular to that line.

Sample Test

1. Without relying on an accurate drawing show that the following points are the vertices of a parallelogram.

    A (3, 4), B (5, 8), C (8, 3), D (6, ⁻1)

2. Find the coordinates of 3 different points (not on the x or y axis) which are on the circle $x^2 + y^2 = 1$.

3. The lines $\overleftrightarrow{AB}$ and $\overleftrightarrow{BC}$ are the graphs of $y = 2 - 2x$ and $y = x - 4$. The line $\overleftrightarrow{CD}$ contains the point D whose coordinates are (0,5) and is parallel to the x axis. Find the coordinates of A, B and C.

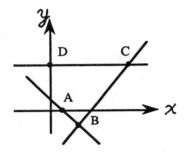

4. The vertices of ABC are A(⁻1, 5), B(3, 5) and C (5, ⁻7).
    Find the following.

    (a)   The equation of the median to side $\overline{BC}$.
    (b)   The length of the median in (a).
    (c)   The equation of the line through C and parallel to the x axis.

5. Solve each of the following systems if possible. Indicate whether the system has a unique solution, infinitely many solutions, or no solution.

    (a)   x + 2y = 3   (b)   x = 3y + 5
          4x + 5y = 6   6y = 2x - 10

    (c)   2x - 3y = 1
          $\frac{3}{4}y - \frac{1}{2}x = 13$

6. Find the equation of the circle whose diameter has endpoints at A(3, ⁻5) and B (7, 1).

7. Graph each of the following.

    (a)   x ≤ ⁻1   (b)   x - y ≤ 1
          y ≥ 2   y - x ≤ 3
          x ≥ ⁻3

8.   Find a system whose graph is shaded below.

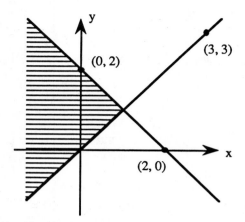

9.   David has $50.05 in quarters and dimes. How many coins of each kind does he have if he has a total of 301 coins?

10.   Company A produces $\frac{3}{4}$ of the cars that company B produces annually. If it is known that company A produces 23,000,000 fewer cars than B, how many cars does each company produce?

11.   The vertices of $\triangle ABC$ are at A (0, 0), B (3, 0) and C (1, 4). Find the coordinates of the point where the altitude to $\overline{AB}$ intersects the altitude to $\overline{AC}$.

CHAPTER 1 FORM A

Answers to Sample Test

1.   (a)   16, 18, 20   (b)   13, 8, 3
     (c)   40, 20, 10   (d)   61, 99, 160
     (e)   128, 256, 512   (f)   215, 342, 511
     (g)   4, 9, 16

2.   (a)   arithmetic   (b)   arithmetic
     (c)   geometric   (d)   neither
     (e)   geometric   (f)   neither
     (g)   neither

3.   (a) $4n + 3$ (b) $n^3 + 1$ (c) 5^n

4.   (a)   9, 14, 19, 24, 29   (b)   0, 2, 6, 12, 20
     (c)   10, 13, 16, 19, 22   (d)   2, 6, 12, 20, 30

5.   (a)   2544   (b)   1520

6.

46	33	32	43
35	40	41	38
39	36	37	42
34	45	44	31

7.   1077

8.   93
     $\times\,74$

9.   49 ways if not all must be used in any given time.

10. 100

11. The pencil costs 79¢ and the eraser costs 66¢.

12. 5

Answers to Sample Test

1.   (a)   17, 23, 30   (b)   127, 107, 147
     (c)   24300, 72900, 218700   (d)   6250, 31250, 156250
     (e)   43, 50, 57   (f)   0, 64, 0
     (g)   25, 29, 33   (h)   1295, 2400, 4095

2.   (a)   neither   (b)   neither
     (c)   geometric   (d)   geometric
     (e)   arithmetic   (f)   neither
     (g)   arithmetic   (h)   neither

3.   (a) $5n - 1$ (b) $6 \cdot 2^{n-1}$

4.   (a)   11, 15, 19, 23, 27   (b)   3, 8, 15, 24, 35
     (c)   2, 5, 8, 11, 14

5.   (a)   1218   (b)   16700

6.   Answers may vary.

A	B	C	D
D	C	B	A
B	A	D	C
C	D	A	B

7.   Igor won 7 times and lost 4 times.

8.   Caterina had 5 of each coin.

9.   B   10. 11

11.   465
    × 23   12. 606

13.   14

Answers to Sample Test

1. V = {x | x is a vowel of the English language}

2. Ø, {z}, {o}, {z, o}, {t}, {z, t}, {t, o}, {z, o, t}

3. (a) x is a Tennessean who does not own a pickup.
    (b) x is a Tennessean who either owns a pickup or a dog or both.
    (c) x is a Tennessee female who does not own a dog.
    (d) x is a Tennessee male who does not own a dog.
    (e) x is a Tennessean who owns a pickup but is not a female.
    (f) x is a Tennessee male.

4. (a) {n}   (b) {u, n, i, t, e, d} or C
    (c) {n, i, t} or A   (d) Ø
    (e) {d}   (f) {e}
    (g) {n, i, t, e, d}   (h) Ø
    (i) 5   (j) 6

5.

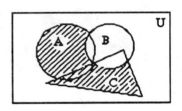

(a)

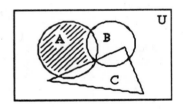

(b)

6. 31

7. w h y
    ↕ ↕ ↕
    n o t

8. 6

9.

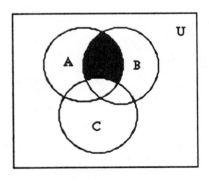

A ∩ (B - C)

=

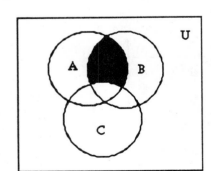

(B ∩ A) - C

10. Answers may vary.
    (a) [(A ∩ B) ∪ (A ∩ C) ∪ (B ∩ C)] - (A ∩ B ∩ C)
    (b) (A ∩ C) ∪ (B ∩ C) ∪ (D ∩ C)

11. $A \times (B \cup C) = \{(o, t), (o, w), (o, o), (o, z), (o, e), (o, r), (n, t), (n, w), (n, o), (n, z),$
$(n, e), (n, r), (e, t), (e, w), (e, o), (e, z), (e, e), (e, r)\}$

$(A \times B) \cup (A \times C) = \{(o, t), (o, w), (o, o), (n, t), (n, w), (n, o), (e, t), (e, w), (e, o),$
$(o, z), (o, e), (o, r), (n, z), (n, e), (n, r), (e, z), (e, e), (e, r)\}$

12.   (a)   False; Let $A = \{1, 2\}$ and $B = \{1\}$
      (b)   True
      (c)   True
      (d)   True
      (e)   False; The empty set is equivalent to itself.

13.   7

14.   (a)   Yes   (b)   Yes   (c)   No

15.   (a) $\{-3, 2, 7, 12, 17\}$
      (b) $\{1, 81, 16\}$
      (c) $\{1, 0, 0\}$

16.   (a)   3   (b)   5

17.   (a)   Reflexive, symmetric, and transitive
      (b)   Transitive
      (c)   Symmetric
      (d)   None

18.   (a)   15   (b) $1400   (c)   32

19.   (a)   Yes   (b)   No   (c)   Yes   (d)   No

20.   (a)   There exists a butterfly that was not born free.
      (b)   Sometimes Yogi Bear does not say "How de do Boo Boo."
      (c)   All umpire calls are correct.
      (d) $7 + 3 \neq 10$

21.   (a)

p	q	$\sim q$	$p \wedge (\sim q)$	$[p \wedge (\sim q)] \to p$
T	T	F	F	T
T	F	T	T	T
F	T	F	F	T
F	F	T	F	T

      (b)

p	q	$\sim q$	$p \vee (\sim q)$	$[p \vee (\sim q)] \to p$
T	T	F	T	T
T	F	T	T	F
F	T	F	F	T
F	F	T	T	F

21. (cont.)

(c)

p	q	~q	p→(~q)	(~q)→p	[p→(~q)] ↔ [(~q)→p]
T	T	F	F	T	F
T	F	T	T	T	T
F	T	F	T	T	T
F	F	T	T	F	F

(d)

p	p→p
T	T
F	T

22. (a)   No   (b)   No

23. Converse: If the horse was Silver, the masked man was the Lone Ranger.
    Inverse: If the masked man was not the Lone Ranger, the horse was not Silver.
    Contrapositive: If the horse was not Silver, the masked man was not the Lone Ranger.

24. (a)   I quit.
    (b)   The map is not in the plane.
    (c)   Emmy Noether is well known.

25. Let   p be the statement: A nail is lost;
          q be the statement: A shoe is lost;
          r be the statement: A horse is lost;
          s be the statement: A rider is lost;
          t be the statement: A battle is lost;
          u be the statement: A kingdom is lost.

$$[(p \to q) \land (q \to r) \land (r \to s) \land (s \to t) \land (t \to u)] \to (p \to u)$$

The argument is valid using the Chain Rule several times.

26. (a) Valid   (b)   Invalid
    (c) Valid   (d)   Invalid

CHAPTER 2 FORM B

Answers to Sample Test

1. D = {Sunday, Monday, Friday}

2. M = {x | x is an even natural number less than 12}

3. Ø, {a}, {b}, {c}, {a, b}, {a, c}, {b, c}

4. (i) (a) A nonsmoking American
        (b) A healthy nonsmoking American
        (c) An American smoker with a health problem
        (d) An American nonsmoker with a health problem
        (e) An American who is either a smoker or unhealthy or both

    (ii) (a) $\overline{D}$

        (b) $D \cap \overline{E} \cap C$

        (c) $\overline{C} \cap \overline{D} \cap E$

        (d) $E \cup \overline{C}$

5. (a) F. Let A = {1, 2, 3} and B = {1}.
    (b) F. Let A = {1} and B = {1, 2}.
    (c) T
    (d) T

    (e) F. $A \cup \overline{A} = U$

    (f) F. $A - \overline{A} = A$

    (g) F. Let A = {1}, and U = {1, 2}. Then $\overline{A}$ = {2} and A x $\overline{A}$ = {(1, 2)}.
    (h) T

6. (a) {q, u, e, s, t, i}
    (b) {q, u, e, s}
    (c) {q, u, e, s, t, i, o, n}, or U
    (d) {o, n}
    (e) {q, u, e}
    (f) {q, u, e, s, t}
    (g) U
    (h) 1

7. (a) A x B = {(1, a), (2, a)}
    (b) B x A = {(a, 1), (a, 2)}
    (c) B x B = {(a, a)}
    (d) A x A = {(1, 1), (1, 2), (2, 1), (2, 2)}
    (e) Ø
    (f) No
    (g) Yes
    (h) 0

8.   (a)

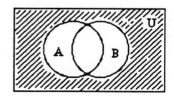

$\{1, \quad 2, \quad 3, \quad 4, \quad ..., \quad n, \quad ...\}$

$\{6, \quad 11, \quad 16, \quad 21, \quad ..., 5n + 1, ...\}$

    (b)   286, because 5 (57) + 1 = 286
    (c)   5n + 1
    (d)   Yes. F is a proper subset of N and it is in a one-to-one correspondence with N.

9.   (a)   {9, 11, 7}   (b)   {0}

10.

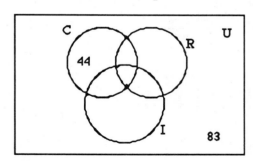

$\overline{A} \cap \overline{B}$

11. $(A \cap B \cap C) \cup [C - (A \cup B)]$

12.   Use a Venn Diagram as shown below, where C represents card catalog users, R represents Reader's Guide users and I represents the users of the information booth.

If there was no overlap between the users of the information booth and the Reader's Guide, we would have the following: n (R) + n (I) + 44 + 83 = 200. Thus, n (R) + n (I) = 73, but n (R) = 59 and n (I) = 68. Since 59 + 68 ≠ 73, there must be an overlap.

13.   Yes, A is in a one-to-one correspondence with B, an infinite set.

14. $4 \cdot 3 \cdot 2 \cdot 1 = 24$

15.   (a)   No. 1 corresponds with both 2 and 1.
    (b)   It is a function.

16.   (a)   Reflexive, symmetric, and transitive
    (b)   Transitive
    (c)   None
    (d)   None

17.   (a)   30   (b) $2000 loss
    (c)   70 units

18. (a) Yes   (b) No
    (c) Yes   (d) Yes

19. (a) The Clan of the Cave Bear was not written by Jean Auel.
    (b) There exists a realtor who does not get a commission on a house the realtor sold.
    (c) All used car salesmen are dishonest.
    (d) $5 - 2 \neq 3$

20. (a)

p	q	~q	p ∨ q	p → (~q)	(p ∨ q) → (p → ~q)
T	T	F	T	F	F
T	F	T	T	T	T
F	T	F	T	T	T
F	F	T	F	T	T

(b)

p	q	~q	p → q	(p ∧ ~q)	~(p ∧ ~q)	(p → q) ↔ ~(p ∧ ~q)
T	T	F	T	F	T	T
T	F	T	F	T	F	T
F	T	F	T	F	T	T
F	F	T	T	F	T	T

(c)

p	q	r	p ∨ q	p ∨ r	(p ∨ q) ∧ (p ∨ r)
T	T	T	T	T	T
T	T	F	T	T	T
T	F	T	T	T	T
T	F	F	T	T	T
F	T	T	T	T	T
F	T	F	T	F	F
F	F	T	F	T	F
F	F	F	F	F	F

21. (a) Yes   (b) Yes

22. Converse: If he came from Krypton, then Clark Kent is Superman.
Inverse: If Clark Kent is not Superman, then he did not come from Krypton.
Contrapositive: If he did not come from Krypton, then he is not Clark Kent.

23. (a) You did not understand the problem.
    (b) You are not a student.
    (c) I will get cold.

24. Let   p be the statement: I pay attention to my job;
            q be the statement: I will get a salary increase;
            r be the statement: I shirk my job.

Symbolically, we have $[(p \rightarrow q) \wedge (r \rightarrow \sim q) \wedge q] \rightarrow \sim p$

25. (a) Not valid   (b) Not valid   (c) Valid

Answers to Sample Test

1. (a) 946 (b) 47 (c) 1572
   (d) 13 (e) 501

2. (a) DCCCXCVII (b) 11122_{four} (c) $T00_{twelve}$
   (d) 23_{twelve} (e) 1121_{nine}

3. (a) 5^{14} (b) 3^{24} (c) 4^3

4. (a) Distributive Property of Multiplication over Addition
   (b) Commutative Property for Addition
   (c) Multiplicative Identity
   (d) Distributive Property of Multiplication over Addition
   (e) Commutative Property for Addition
   (f) Associative Property for Multiplication

5. (a) Let $k = 7$. Since $2 + 7 = 9$, then $2 < 9$.
   (b) Let $k = 9$. Since $13 = 9 + 4$, then $13 > 4$.

6. Because $38 \cdot 100 = (3 \cdot 10 + 8) \cdot 10^2 = 3 \cdot 10^3 + 8 \cdot 10^2 = 3 \cdot 10^3 + 8 \cdot 10^2 + 0 \cdot 10 + 0$, the tens digit and units digit are 0.

7. (a)
$$\begin{array}{r} {}^{13}{}^1 2 \\ 889 \\ + 611 \\ \hline 1812 \end{array} \qquad \begin{array}{r} {}^{13}{}^1 2 \\ 889 \\ + 611 \\ \hline 1812 \end{array}$$

   (b)
$$\begin{array}{r} 3^1 1 2_{twelve} \\ 889_{twelve} \\ + 611_{twelve} \\ \hline 15E0_{twelve} \end{array} \qquad \begin{array}{r} 3^1 1 2_{twelve} \\ 889_{twelve} \\ + 611_{twelve} \\ \hline 15E0_{twelve} \end{array}$$

8. (a)

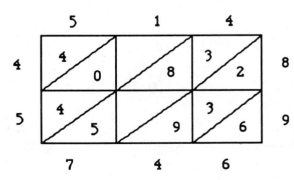

$$\begin{array}{r} 514 \\ \times\ 89 \\ \hline 4626 \\ 4112 \\ \hline 45746 \end{array}$$

   Answer: 45,746

8.   (cont.)

(b)

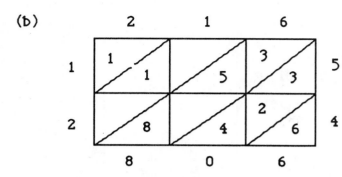

$$216_{nine}$$
$$\times\ 54_{nine}$$
$$\overline{866}$$
$$\underline{1183}$$
$$12806_{nine}$$

Answer: 12806_{nine}

9.   (a)

```
81  | 5607                         69
        810    10 81s        81 | 5607
       4797                        486
       3240    40 81s              747
       1557                        729
        810    10 81s               18
        747
        729     9 81s
         18 R   69 Quotient
```

(b)

```
101_two | 11011_two                    101
          10100   100 101s     101_two | 11011_two
            111                          101
            101     1 101                111
             10 R  101 Quotient          101
                                          10 R
```

10.   (a) $81 \cdot 69 + 18 = 5607$ (b) $(101 \cdot 101 + 10 = 11011)_{two}$

11.   (a)   Hundreds   (b)   Thousands   (c)   Hundreds

12.   (a) $\{9, 10, 11, ..., 20\}$ (b) $\{103\}$
       (c)   W   (d) $\{0, 1, 2, ..., 34\}$

13.   (a)

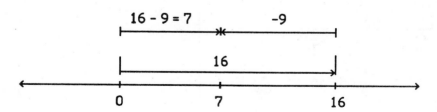

13. (cont.)

(b)

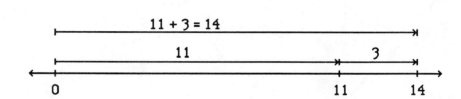

(c)

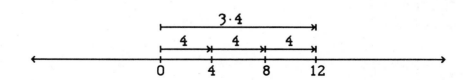

(d)

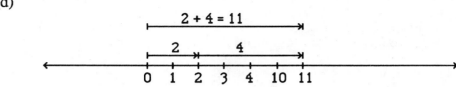

14. (a) $14x$ (b) $18x^3$ (c) $qr + qs + qv$

15. (a) 16   (b) 8   (c) 30   (d) $14

16. (a) $E10_{twelve}$ (b) XXXIX

17. $143

18. Answers may vary. For example:

(a) $2 + 3 = 3 + 2$
(b) $2 \cdot (3 \cdot 4) = (2 \cdot 3) \cdot 4$
(c) $3 + 0 = 3 = 0 + 3$

19. Each pay $14. Dick should pay Tom $4.00.

20. $12/month

21. 224 blocks

22. 20 cars

23. (a)
$$\begin{array}{r} 5286 \\ +\ 1313 \\ \hline 6599 \end{array}$$
     (b)
$$\begin{array}{r} 7538 \\ -\ 1526 \\ \hline 6012 \end{array}$$

24. 2^{80}

25. 3

CHAPTER 3 FORM B

Answers to Sample Test

1.   (a)   1,000,409   (b)   108   (c)   1463
     (d)   23   (e)   55

2.   (a)   CDLIV   (b) 1413_{five} (c) $E06_{\text{twelve}}$
     (d) 32_{nine} (e) 1000_{three}

3.   (a) 3^{13} (b) 4^{90} (c) 6^{7}

4.   (a)   Commutative Property for Addition
     (b)   Associative Property for Multiplication
     (c)   Distributive Property for Multiplication over Addition
     (d)   Identity Property for Multiplication
     (e)   Closure Property for Addition
     (f)   Commutative Property for Multiplication

5.   (a)   Let $k = 4$. Since $8 + 4 = 12$, then $8 < 12$.
     (b)   Let $k = 1$. Since $0 + 1 = 1$, then $1 > 0$.

6.   Because $12 \cdot 1000 = (1 \cdot 10 + 2) \, 10^3 = 1 \cdot 10^4 + 2 \cdot 10^3 = 1 \cdot 10^4 + 2 \cdot 10^3 + 0 \cdot 10^2 + 0 \cdot 10 + 0 \cdot 1$, the hundreds, tens and units digit are 0.

7.   (a)

$$
\begin{array}{r}
^2 6\ 2 \\
7\,_5 8\,0 \\
3\ 4 \\
+\ 7\,5\,_9 3 \\
\hline
2\ 5\ 3
\end{array}
\qquad
\begin{array}{r}
^2 6\ 2 \\
7\ 8 \\
3\ 4 \\
+\ 7\ 9 \\
\hline
2\ 5\ 3
\end{array}
$$

  (b)

$$
\begin{array}{r}
^{1}2^{1}1\ 4_{\text{five}} \\
2\,_0 3\,_0 2\,1_{\text{five}} \\
+\ 2\ 2\ 3_{\text{five}} \\
\hline
1\ 2\ 2\ 4_{\text{five}}
\end{array}
\qquad
\begin{array}{r}
^{1}2^{1}1\ 4_{\text{five}} \\
2\ 3\ 2_{\text{five}} \\
+\ 2\ 2\ 3_{\text{five}} \\
\hline
1\ 2\ 2\ 4_{\text{five}}
\end{array}
$$

8.   (a)

$$
\begin{array}{r}
518 \\
\times\ 34 \\
\hline
2072 \\
1554 \\
\hline
17612
\end{array}
$$

8.   (cont.)

(b)

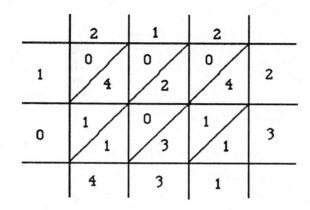

$$\begin{array}{r} 212_{\text{five}} \\ \times\ 23_{\text{five}} \\ \hline 1141 \\ 424 \\ \hline 10431_{\text{five}} \end{array}$$

9.   (a)

$$\begin{array}{r} 9\ \overline{|3287} \\ 2700 \\ \hline 587 \\ 540 \\ \hline 47 \\ 45 \\ \hline 2\ R \end{array} \begin{array}{l} 300\ 9\text{'s} \\[2mm] 60\ 9\text{'s} \\[2mm] \underline{5}\ 9\text{'s} \\ 365 \end{array}$$

$$\begin{array}{r} 365 \\ 9\ \overline{|3287} \\ 27 \\ \hline 58 \\ 54 \\ \hline 47 \\ 45 \\ \hline 2 \end{array}$$

(b)

$$12_{\text{three}}\ \overline{|2021_{\text{three}}} \quad \begin{array}{l} 100\ 12\text{'s} \end{array}$$
$$\begin{array}{r} 1200 \\ \hline 121 \\ 120 \\ \hline 1\ R \end{array} \begin{array}{l} \\ \underline{10}\ 12\text{'s} \\ 110_{\text{three}} \end{array}$$

$$\begin{array}{r} 110_{\text{three}} \\ 12_{\text{three}}\ \overline{|2021_{\text{three}}} \\ 12 \\ \hline 12 \\ 12 \\ \hline 01 \\ 0 \\ \hline 1\ R \end{array}$$

10.   (a) $9 \cdot 365 + 2 = 3287$
(b) $(12 \cdot 110 + 1 = 2021)_{\text{three}}$

11.   (a)   Tens
(b)   Thousands
(c)   Units

12.   (a)   W
(b)   2
(c)   {8, 9, 10, 11, 12, 13, 14, 15}
(d)   {0, 1, 2, 3, 4, 5}

13.

(a)

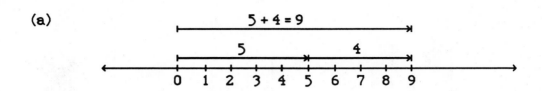

(b)

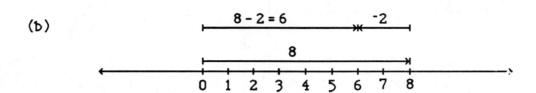

(c)

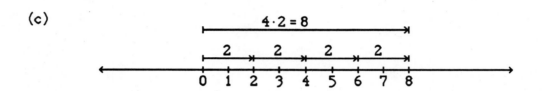

(d)

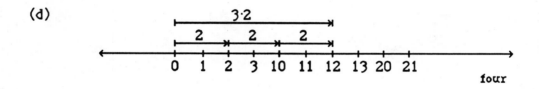

four

14.　(a)　$14x^2$　　　　(b)　$28x$　　　(c)　$ac + ad + bc + bd$

15.　(a)　DCLXIX　　　　　(b)　$E10_{twelve}$

16.　10,140 passengers

17.　$480

18.　5 points

19.　$53

20.　980 miles

21　(a)　$\begin{array}{r} 1338 \\ +\ 4835 \\ \hline 6173 \end{array}$　　　　　(b)　$\begin{array}{r} 8669 \\ -\ 6234 \\ \hline 2435 \end{array}$

22.　They are the same.

23.　2

Answers to Sample Test

1.   (a)   7   (b) ^-x (c) $^-2 - x$ (d) $^-x + y$

2.   (a)   10   (b)   4   (c) $^-16$ (d)   81
       (e)   0   (f) $^-40$

3.   (a)   2   (b)   3, $^-3$
       (c)   7, $^-7$ (d)   5, $^-5$
       (e) $x > {}^-16, x \, \varepsilon \, I$ (f)   5, $^-9$
       (g) $x \leq {}^-2, x \, \varepsilon \, I$ (h)   11, $^-5$

4.   (a) $x (5 - 3x)$ (b) $(5 - x) (5 + x)$
       (c) $(a + 1) (a - b + 1)$ (d) $5 (1 + x)$

5.   Answers may vary.

6.   The additive inverse of a is $^-$a. Also, the additive inverse of $^-$a is $^-(^-$a). Since additive inverses are unique and both a and $^-(^-$a) are additive inverses of $^-$a, then a = $^-(^-$a).

7.   (a)   3   (b)   3   (c) $^-27$ (d)   27
       (e)   27   (f)   0

8.   (a)   F (unless c > 0)
       (b)   F. If $^-$x > $^-$7, then $(^-1) (^-$x) < $(^-1) (^-$7), or x < 7.
       (c)   T
       (d)   F (unless x $\geq$ 0)
       (e)   T
       (f)   F. $(a + b) (a + b) = a^2 + 2ab + b^2$
       (g)   T

9.   (a)   T
       (b)   F. For example, 5 - 3 $\neq$ 3 - 5.
       (c)   T
       (d)   F. For example, 5 $\div$ 3 $\notin$ I

10.   They must be nonzero integers with like signs, that is, they must both be positive or both be negative.

11.   17 yards

12.   9° C

13.   a drop of 40°

14.   15 pounds of rosefood and 5 pounds of enriched compost

15.   11 and 3

16. (a)

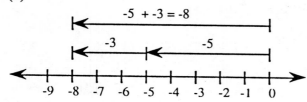

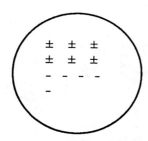   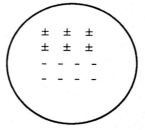

-5 charge on field   Add 3 negative charges; net result is -8 charge on field.

(b)

CHAPTER 4 FORM B

Answers to Sample Test

1.   (a)   ⁻13   (b)   x   (c)   3 - x   (d)   x - y

2.   (a)   21   (b)   ⁻53   (c)   ⁻30   (d)   25
      (e)   0   (f)   28

3.   (a)   5   (b)   ⁻3
      (c)   16, ⁻16   (d)   9, ⁻9
      (e) $x > 4, x \in I$ (f)   ⁻3, 13
      (g) $x \geq 3, x \in I$ (h)   0, 4

4.   (a)   3x (3x - 1)   (b)   (2x - 3) (2x + 3)
      (c)   (a + 1) (x + 1)   (d)   11 (x - 1)

5.   Answers may vary.

6.   From the definition of the additive inverse, we know that ab + ⁻(ab) = 0. Also
      ab + (⁻a) (b)   = (a + (⁻a)) · b = 0 · b = 0. Because ⁻(ab) and (⁻a) (b) are both additive
      inverses of ab and because the additive inverse must be unique, then ⁻(ab) = (⁻a) (b).

7.   (a)   ⁻4   (b)   2
      (c)   ⁻2   (d)   ⁻8
      (e)   8   (f)   ⁻16

8.   (a)   T
      (b)   F. For example, let x = ⁻5.
      (c)   F. ⁻6x = ⁻12
      (d)   F. For example, let x = 2, then 2 ≠ ⁻2.
      (e)   F. ⁻5 - 8 · 3 = ⁻5 - 24 = ⁻29 ≠ ⁻39
      (f)   T
      (g)   F. $a^2 - b^2 = (a - b) (a + b)$

9.   (a)   F. ⁻5 ∉ W
      (b)   F. For example, 5 - (3 - 2) ≠ (5 - 3) - 2
      (c)   T
      (d)   T

10.   They must be nonzero integers with unlike signs.

11.   -$62   12.   ⁻19° C

13.   29° C

14.   51¢/pound

15.   7 and 29

16. (a)

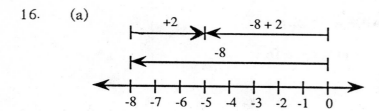

(b)

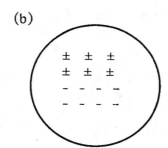

-8 charge on field

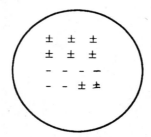

Add 2 positive charges; net result is -6 charge on field.

CHAPTER 5 FORM A

Answers to Sample Test

1.   (a)   0 or 5   (b)   1, 4, or 7   (c)   7
       (d)   0, 3, 6, or 9   (e)   0, 4, or 8   (f)   0 or 8

2. $9 \mid (a + b + c)$; $9 \mid 9$ implies the following: $9 \mid 9b$ and $9 \mid 9 \cdot 11a$, or $9 \mid 99a$. Thus

$$9 \mid [(a + b + c) + 9b + 99a]$$

$$9 \mid (100a + 10b + c)$$

$$9 \mid N$$

3.   (a)   T
       (b)   F. Let $a = 4$ and $b = 8$.
       (c)   F. Let $a = 4$ and $b = 8$.
       (d)   T
       (e)   F. 0 does not divide any number.
       (f)   T

4.   2, 3, 4, 6, 7, 11, 12, 22

5. 2^6, or 64

6.   (a)   Composite   (b)   Composite
       (c)   Composite   (d)   Composite

7.   (a)   19   (b)   190
       (c)   2   (d) $2^2 \cdot 3 \cdot 7 \cdot 13$, or 1092

8.   2

9.   (a) $2^2 \cdot 3^5 \cdot 11$ (b) $2^3 \cdot 3^7 \cdot 5^8 \cdot 7^2 \cdot 11 \cdot 13$

10.   (a)   31   (b)   23

11.   1, 2, 4, 8, 16, 32, 3, 6, 12, 24, 48, 96, 9, 18, 36, 72, 144, 288

12.   For a number to be divisible by 45, it must be divisible by both 5 and 9.

13.   24 pieces

14.   53

15.   Tuesday

16.   (a)   7   (b)   1   (c)   19

1. (a)   6   (b)   0, 3, 6, 9   (c)   1
    (d)   0, 2, 4, 6, 8   (e)   0, 3, 6, 9   (f)   0, 5

2. $n = a \cdot 10^3 + b \cdot 10^2 + c \cdot 10 + d$. Because $4 \mid 10^2$, then $4 \mid b \cdot 10^2$, $4 \mid a \cdot 10^3$ and $4 \mid (a \cdot 10^3 + b \cdot 10^2)$. Therefore if $4 \mid (c \cdot 10 + d)$ then $4 \mid (a \cdot 10^3 + b \cdot 10^2) + (c \cdot 10 + d)$ or $4 \mid n$.

3. (a)   T
    (b)   T
    (c)   F. Let a = b.
    (d)   T
    (e)   F. Let a = 6.
    (f)   T

4. 2, 3, 5, 6, 7, 9, 10, 11, 15, 22

5. 210

6. (a)   Prime   (b)   Composite
    (c)   Composite   (d)   Prime

7. (a)   1   (b)   5293
    (c)   6   (d) $2^3 \cdot 3 \cdot 7^2 \cdot 13$ or 7644

8. 12

9. (a) $5^2 \cdot 7$ (b) $2^3 \cdot 5^3 \cdot 7^3 \cdot 11 \cdot 13 \cdot 17$

10. (a)   13   (b)   37

11. 1, 2, 3, 4, 6, 12, 37, 74, 111, 148, 222, 444

12. For a number to be divisible by 22, it must be divisible by both 2 and 11.

13. 96

14. 1:45 P.M.

15. 3 years

16. (a)   1
    (b)   2
    (c)   0

1. (a)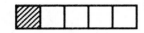

    (b)

2. $\dfrac{^-4}{6}, \dfrac{2}{^-3}, \dfrac{4}{^-6}$, and so on

3. (a) $\dfrac{4}{5}$ (b) $\dfrac{cy}{d}$ (c) $\dfrac{0}{1}$

    (d) $\dfrac{9}{8}$ (e) $\dfrac{1}{b}$ (f) $\dfrac{1}{16}$

4. (a) $>$ (b) $<$ (c) $<$ (d) $=$
    (e) $=$ (f) $>$

5. (a) $\dfrac{22}{15}$ (b) $\dfrac{2}{15}$ (c) $\dfrac{3}{5}$

    (d) $\dfrac{6}{5}$ (e) $\dfrac{83}{28}$

6. (a) $^-4$ and $\dfrac{1}{4}$ (b) $^-2\dfrac{1}{5}$ and $\dfrac{5}{11}$

    (c) $^-0.36$ and $\dfrac{100}{36}$, or $\dfrac{25}{9}$ (d) $\dfrac{^-3}{8}$ and $\dfrac{8}{3}$

    (e) $\dfrac{2}{3}$ and $\dfrac{^-3}{2}$

7. (a) $\dfrac{^-5}{22}$

    (b) $\dfrac{8}{5}$

8. (a) $x = \dfrac{3}{4}$

    (b) $x \le \dfrac{17}{20}$

9. 6

10. (a) $\dfrac{1}{2^{15}}$ (b) 3^8 (c) $\left(\dfrac{3}{2}\right)^{12}$

11. 51 boxes, and $\dfrac{1}{13}$ ounces will be left over.

12. The student is wrong. He considers $\dfrac{9 + \frac{1}{4}}{3 + \frac{3}{4}}$ and $\dfrac{9}{3} + \dfrac{\frac{1}{4}}{\frac{3}{4}}$ to be equal, and they are not. In general, $\dfrac{a + b}{c + d} \neq \dfrac{a}{c} + \dfrac{b}{d}$.

13. (a) 3$^+$
    (b) 10$^-$
    (c) 4$^+$

14. (a) 40
    (c) 7
    (b) 14
    (d) 29

Answers to Sample Test

1.   (a) $\dfrac{9}{16}$ (b) $\dfrac{51}{13}$ (c) $\dfrac{y^2}{x^2}$ (d) $\dfrac{3}{x}$

2.   (a) $\dfrac{29}{24}$ (b) $\dfrac{3}{5}$ (c) 5

3.   (a) $2\dfrac{1}{5}$ and $\dfrac{-5}{11}$ (b) $\dfrac{-3}{8}$ and $\dfrac{8}{3}$

       (c)   0 and no multiplicative inverse   (d) $\dfrac{-1}{x}$ and x

4.   (a) $\dfrac{3}{5}$ (b) $\dfrac{1}{4}$ (c) $\dfrac{13}{20}$

5. $\dfrac{-4}{5}$

6.   True. When the denominator of a fraction (whose numerator and denominator are positive) decreases, the fraction increases. When the numerator increases the fraction increases as well. A more formal approach follows: $\dfrac{a+1}{b-1} > \dfrac{a}{b}$ if and only if $ab + b > ab - a$ or $b > -a$. The last inequality is true because $a > 0$ and $b \geq 2$.

7.   (a) $x \leq 0$ (b) $x \geq \dfrac{5}{6}$ (c) $x = \dfrac{3}{4}$

8.   (a) 1 (b) $\left(\dfrac{4}{3}\right)^{15}$ (c) $\dfrac{4}{9}$

9.   30 miles

10.   Less than $\dfrac{1}{2}$. The person gets approximately $\dfrac{1}{2}$ lb of nuts. $45\dfrac{5}{16} \div 1\dfrac{3}{4} = 26 + \dfrac{13}{28}$. However $\dfrac{13}{28} < \dfrac{1}{2}$.

11. $\dfrac{1}{5}, \dfrac{1}{4}, \dfrac{1}{3}, \dfrac{2}{5}, \dfrac{1}{2}, \dfrac{3}{5}, \dfrac{2}{3}, \dfrac{3}{4}, \dfrac{4}{5}$

12.   It will become smaller because $\dfrac{3x}{8x} > \dfrac{3x-2}{8x-2}$.

13.   (a) 3^- (b) 10^- (c) 6^-

14.   (a)   22   (b)   18
       (c)   1   (d)   41

CHAPTER 7 FORM A

Answers to Sample Test

1.   (a) $4.\overline{9} = 5$ (b) $0.\overline{44} > \frac{1}{25}$

        (c) $0.\overline{46} < 0.4\overline{6}$ (d) $\sqrt{3} > 1.7$

2.   (a)   2.0021   (b)   38.258   (c)   0.1448

        (d)   16.8

3.   (a) $^{-}4.2$ and $\frac{1}{4.2}$, or $\frac{10}{42}$ or $\frac{5}{21}$

        (b) $^{-}0.36$ and $\frac{100}{36}$, or $\frac{25}{9}$

4.   (a) $\frac{-1}{2\sqrt{3}}$ or $\frac{-\sqrt{3}}{6}$ (b) $x \leq 12.2$

        (c)   20,000   (d)   20%

        (e)   26   (f) $\frac{5}{9}$ or $0.\overline{5}$

        (g) $x = 0$ (h)   0.722

5. $23.6 - 8.34 = 23.60 - 8.34$

$$= \frac{2360}{100} - \frac{834}{100}$$

$$= \frac{1526}{100}$$

$$= 15.26$$

6.   (a)   200%   (b)   105   (c)   45

7.   (a)   20%   (b) $3\frac{3}{4}$% or 3.75%

        (c)   536%   (d)   1.3%

8.   (a)   0.40   (b) $0.001\overline{6}$ (c)   2

9.   (a)   508.58   (b)   508.6   (c)   500

10.   (a) $\frac{27}{100}$ (b) $\frac{3104}{1000}$ (c) $\frac{22}{90}$ (d) $\frac{24}{99}$

11.   (a)   0.075

        (b)   0.125

        (c) $0.\overline{153846}$

12.   3.873

13.   (a) 5.268×10^6 (b) 3.25×10^{-4}

14.   (a)   Irrational if pattern continues
       (b)   Irrational
       (c)   Rational
       (d)   Rational if pattern continues repeating

15. $9240

16. $19,874.40

17.   77.5%

18.   (a)   4   (b)   4   (c)   3   (d)   3

19.   (a) $11\sqrt{3}$ (b)   24   (c) $4\sqrt{30}$ (d)   7

20.   (a) $\left(\dfrac{1}{3}\right)^{11}$, or $\dfrac{1}{3^{11}}$ (b) $\dfrac{1}{5^9}$

       (c) 4^{15} (d) 5^{26}

21. $585.83

Answers to Sample Test

1.   (a)   <   (b)   =   (c)   =   (d)   <

2.   (a)   4.742   (b)   ⁻4.419   (c)   0.12   (d)   12.1

3.   (a)   ⁻0.4 and $\frac{10}{4}$ or $\frac{5}{2}$ or 2.5

       (b)   ⁻2.$\overline{6}$ and $\frac{3}{8}$ or 0.375

4.   (a) $\frac{-5}{3\sqrt{2}}$ or $\frac{-5\sqrt{2}}{6}$ (b)   ⁻39.6

       (c)   324   (d)   0.$\overline{4}$ or $\frac{4}{9}$

       (e)   75   (f)   22

       (g)   0   (h)   4.2

5. $8.07 - 2.3 = \frac{807}{100} - \frac{23}{10}$

$$= \frac{807}{100} - \frac{230}{100}$$

$$= \frac{807 - 230}{100}$$

$$= \frac{577}{100}$$

$$= 5.77$$

6.   (a)   400%   (b)   2   (c)   20

7.   (a)   66.$\overline{6}$% or $66\frac{2}{3}$%   (b)   6.25%

       (c)   206%   (d)   244.$\overline{4}$% or $244\frac{4}{9}$%

8.   (a)   0.45   (b)   0.008   (c)   3.2

9.   (a)   483.77   (b)   484   (c)   500

10.   (a) $\frac{38}{100}$ or $\frac{19}{50}$ (b) $\frac{2607}{1000}$

       (c) $\frac{43}{90}$ (d) $\frac{324}{999}$ or $\frac{108}{333}$

11.   (a)   0.2$\overline{3}$ (b)   0.275

       (c)   0.$\overline{45}$

12.   3.317

13.   (a) $3.286 \cdot 10^3$ (b) $3.2 \cdot 10^{-6}$

14.   (a)   4   (b)   2

15.   (a)   Irrational
      (b)   Rational
      (c)   Rational
      (d)   Irrational (if pattern continues)

16. $162.50

17. $17,500

18.   16

19.   (a) $3\sqrt{13}$ (b) $10\sqrt{7}$ (c) $14\sqrt{3}$ (d) $4\sqrt[3]{3}$

20.   (a) $\left(\dfrac{2}{5}\right)^{11}$ or $\dfrac{2^{11}}{5^{11}}$ (b) 3^7

      (c) $\dfrac{1}{5^2}$ (d) $\left(\dfrac{2}{3}\right)^{12}$ or $\dfrac{2^{12}}{3^{12}}$

21. $849.34

CHAPTER 8 FORM A

Answers to Sample Test

1.   (a)   {January, February, March, April, May, June, July, August, September, October, November, December}

       (b)   {January, June, July}

       (c) $\frac{3}{12}$ or $\frac{1}{4}$

2. $\frac{1}{2}$

3.   (a) $\frac{6}{18}$ or $\frac{1}{3}$ (b) $\frac{12}{18}$ or $\frac{2}{3}$

       (c) $\frac{5}{18}$ (d) $\frac{13}{18}$

4.   (a) $\frac{13}{52}$ or $\frac{1}{4}$ (b) $\frac{1}{52}$

       (c) $\frac{22}{52}$ or $\frac{11}{26}$ (d) $\frac{51}{52}$

5.   (a) $\frac{9}{49}$ (b) $\frac{6}{42}$ or $\frac{1}{7}$

6.   0.90307   7. $\frac{9}{20}$

8. $\frac{3}{8}$ 9. $\frac{1}{2}$

10. $\frac{4}{36}$ or $\frac{1}{9}$ 11. $\frac{1}{128}$

12.   (a) $\frac{16}{2704}$ or $\frac{1}{169}$ (b) $\frac{12}{2652}$ or $\frac{1}{221}$

13.   (a) $\frac{20}{210}$ or $\frac{2}{21}$ (b) $\frac{42}{210}$ or $\frac{1}{5}$

14.   112 ways   15.   10,100

16.   20   17.   6,760,000

18.   (a) $P(A) = \frac{3}{8}$ (b) $P(B) = \frac{5}{8}$

19.   (a)   7! or 5040   (b) $\frac{11!}{2! \; 2! \; 2!}$ or 4,989,600

20. $\dfrac{1,771,533}{8}$

21. $\dfrac{8}{13}$

22. $\dfrac{2}{34}$ or $\dfrac{1}{17}$

23. 51 to 1

24. Approximately $2.27

25. $15

26. Answers vary, for example,

    (a) Let an even number represent a head and an odd number represent a tail.

    (b) Let the days of the week be represented by the digits 0 through 6 and choose one digit at random. If the digit is not in this range, continue until a number in this range is found.

    (c) Let the numbers 01, 02, 03, 04, 05, ..., 29, 30 represent the dates of the month. Pick a starting place and mark off blocks of 2 until three of the digits are obtained.

CHAPTER 8 FORM B

Answers to Sample Test

1. (a) {a, b, c, d, e, f, ..., x, y, z}

   (b) {a, e, i, o, u}

   (c) $\dfrac{5}{26}$

2. $\dfrac{1}{32}$

3. (a) $\dfrac{5}{17}$ (b) $\dfrac{9}{17}$ (c) $\dfrac{8}{17}$ (d) $\dfrac{12}{17}$

4. (a) $\dfrac{26}{52}$ or $\dfrac{1}{2}$ (b) $\dfrac{3}{52}$

   (c) $\dfrac{22}{52}$ or $\dfrac{11}{26}$ (d) $\dfrac{48}{52}$ or $\dfrac{12}{13}$

5. (a) $\dfrac{64}{289}$ (b) $\dfrac{56}{272}$

6. 0.504   7. $\dfrac{5}{32}$

8. $\dfrac{1}{28}$ 9. $\dfrac{7}{8}$

10. 150   11. $\dfrac{27}{256}$

12. (a) $\dfrac{144}{2704}$ or $\dfrac{9}{169}$ (b) $\dfrac{132}{2652}$ or $\dfrac{33}{676}$

13. (a) $\dfrac{1}{7}$ (b) $\dfrac{2}{7}$

14. 88 ways   15. 325

16. 35   17. $26^3 \cdot 10^3$ or 17,576,000

18. (a) $P(A) = \dfrac{1}{2}$ (b) $P(B) = \dfrac{1}{2}$

19. (a) 6! or 720   (b) $\dfrac{11!}{2!\,3!}$ or 9,979,200

20. 7912 to 8 or 989 to 1   21. $\dfrac{4}{13}$

22. **5 to 31**

23. 49 to 3

24. **$.50**

25. $2.50

26. **Answers** may vary, for example,

(a) Mark off the digits in blocks of two. Let the numbers 01, 02, 03, 04, 05, ..., 25, 26 represent the consecutive letters of the alphabet. Disregard blocks of two not in this range.

(b) Let each of the oceans be represented by one of the numerals 1, 2, 3, 4, or 5. Disregard the rest of the digits.

(c) Let Red be represented by the digits 1, 2, and 3; let Blue be represented by the digits 4, 5, and 6; and let White be represented by the digits 7, 8, and 9. Disregard the digit 0.

111

Answers to Sample Test

1. (a) Approximately $12.93
    (b) $9.70
    (c) $9.70

2. Mean, 73.9;
    median, 84;
    mode, 98;
    range, 61

3.

Scores	Frequency
98	4
84	2
52	1
45	2
37	1

4.

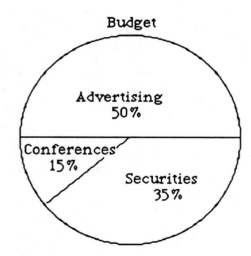

5. There are more high scores than low ones, but the low ones lower the mean.

6.

Weights of Miss Brown's Students

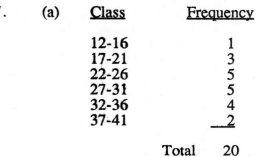

20	19
21	2599
22	457
23	567
24	16
25	6
26	44
27	345
28	237
29	0
30	1

25 │ 6 represents 25.6 kg

7. (a)

Class	Frequency
12-16	1
17-21	3
22-26	5
27-31	5
32-36	4
37-41	2
Total	20

Histogram of Scores

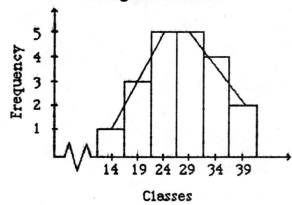

(b) and (c) on the same graph

8. All that it could mean is that more of the older members have died or did not attend.

9. 31

10.   (a)

Mr. Brown's Class Scores

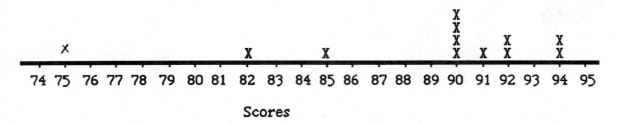

Scores

Miss Burke's Class Scores

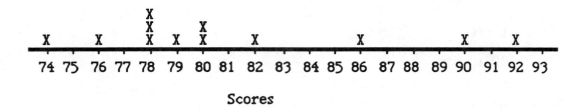

Scores

(b)

TEST SCORES

Miss Burke's Class		Mr. Brown's Class	
988864	7	5	
6200	8	25	9|4 = 94
20	9	000012244	

(c)   Brown's IQR = 4.5
        Burke's IQR = 6

(d)   Yes, the score of 75 in Mr. Brown's class is an outlier.

(e)

TEST SCORES

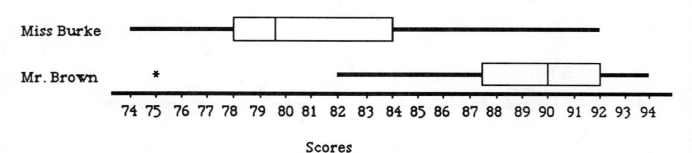

Scores

(f)   Mr. Brown's class scored considerably higher than Miss Burke's class. All of Mr.
        Brown's class, except the outlier of 75, scored above the median for Miss Burke's
        class.

11. **You do not know who was surveyed, how many were** surveyed, or what type of questions **were asked. The claim should not be taken at face value** without more information.

12. **1900 students**

13. (a)   430   (b)   500   (c)   570

14. 57

CHAPTER 9 FORM B

Answers to Sample Test

1. 80

2. (a) Arrange the scores in order from least to greatest and counting from the least score, take the 39th score. This is the median.
    (b) Arrange the scores in order from least to greatest; count from the least score and find the arithmetic mean of the 65th and 66th scores.

3. 0.53

4. 80% males and 20% females

5. (a) 15   (b) 9.5
    (c) 8.5   (d) Approximately 4.8

6.

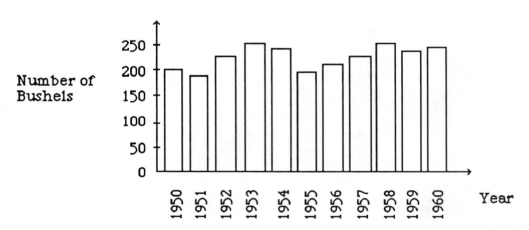

Tennessee Soybean Crop for 1950-1960

7.

Tennessee Soybean Crop (1950 – 60)

18	5
19	5
20	0
21	0
22	5 5
23	0 5
24	0
25	0 0

18|5 represents 185 bushels

8.   (a)

Class of Weights	Frequency
118-122	1
123-127	2
128-132	2
133-137	4
138-142	6
143-147	8
148-152	5
153-157	4
158-162	2
163-167	4
168-172	1
173-177	1

Total 40

(b)

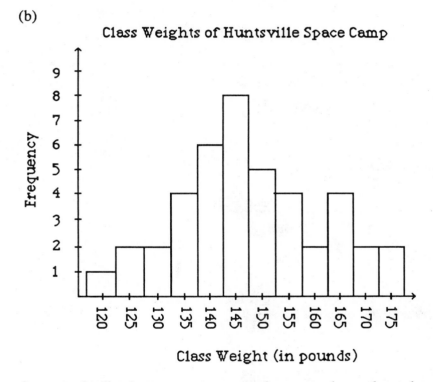

9.   On a standardized test, or on any test, there must be students that score below the mean. Without more information, there is no reason to believe that every student in any given school should score above the national mean on a test.

10.   It would appear that it would be easier to teach the class in which the standard deviation was not twice the standard deviation of the other for the reason that the group appears to be more homogeneous.

11. (a)

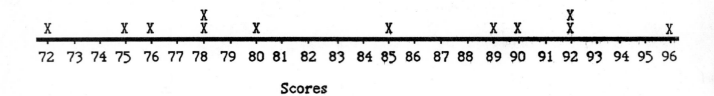

Mr. Read's Class Scores

Scores

Miss Sol's Test Scores

Scores

(b)

TEST SCORES

Miss Sol's Class		Mr. Read's Class
85	7	25688
843	8	059
8632200	9	0226

9|8 = 98

(c)   The IQR for Mr. Read is 14. The IQR for Miss Sol is 9.
(d)   There are no outliers for either set of data.

(e)

TEST SCORES

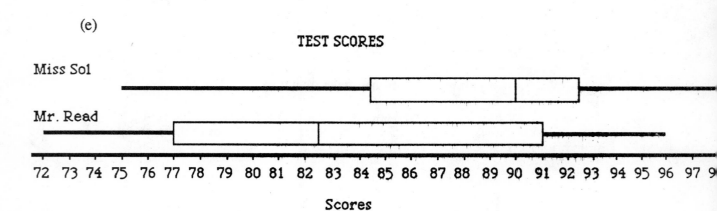

Miss Sol

Mr. Read

Scores

11.   (cont.)

    (f)   Miss Sol's class did better on the quiz than Mr. Read's class. 75% of Miss Sol's class scored above the median in Mr. Read's class.

*12.   (a)   146   (b)   146

*13.   Mean, 72; Standard deviation, 20

*14.   815

Answers to Sample Test

1. Answers may vary. For example,

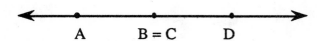

2. Answers may vary. For example,

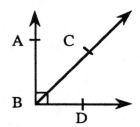

∠ABC and ∠CBD are such angles

3. 4

4. (a)

    (b) There are 5 vertices, 5 faces and 8 edges. Euler's Formula holds because
         $5 + 5 - 8 = 2$.

5. (a) True
    (b) False
    (c) False
    (d) True
    (e) True
    (f) True

6. (a) $\overleftrightarrow{AD}$

    (b) $\overleftrightarrow{XY}$
    (c) Point B
    (d) Points P and E
    (e) Point A

    (f) $\overrightarrow{BD}$
    (g) ∅

7. 166°33'11"

8. 56°

9. Answers may vary. For example,

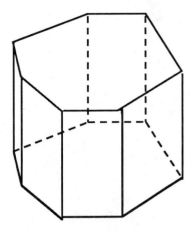

The number of faces is 9; the number of edges is 21; and the number of vertices is 14. Euler's Formula holds because 9 + 14 - 21 = 2.

10. 80° and 100°

11. Yes. A rectangle is a parallelogram and a parallelogram is a special type of trapezoid.

12. (a) 140°   (b) 40°   (c) 55°   (d) 55°
     (e) 70°

13. (a) Points A and C are inside and point B is outside.
     (b) Points B and C are inside and point A is outside.

14. ∠A and ∠DCA are complementary because they are the acute angles in a right triangle.

     ∠DCB and ∠DCA are complementary angles because together they are adjacent angles whose measures sum to a right angle. Therefore, angles DCB and A are congruent because they are complements of the same angle.

15. (a) The figure is traversable. One possibility is shown.

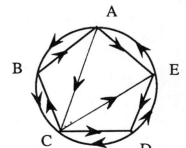

Path ABACBCDCEDEAE

15.   (cont.)

(b)   The figure is traversable. **One possibility is shown.**

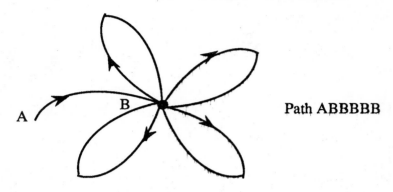

Path ABBBBB

(c)   The figure is not traversable.

16.   The figures in (a), (d), and (e) are topologically equivalent; the figures in (b) and (c) are topologically equivalent.

17.   One possibility follows:

```
TO COMP.ANGLES :A
  FD 100
  BK 100
  RT :A
  FD 100
  BK 100
  RT 90-:A
  FD 100
  BK 100
  LT 90
END
```

Answers to Sample Test

1.

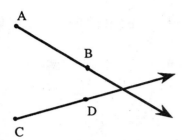

2.

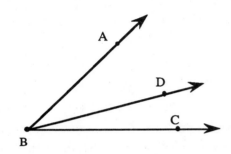

∠ABC and ∠DBC

3. Three; the polygon with the smallest number of sides is a triangle.

4. X,Y, and Z are collinear because if two distinct planes intersect, they intersect in a line.

5. (a) F (b) T (c) T (d) F
   (e) F (f) T (g) F

6. (a) $\overleftrightarrow{YZ}$

   (b) $\overleftrightarrow{YZ}$

   (c) point E

   (d) points B and E

   (e) $\overline{AE}$

   (f) $\overrightarrow{BD}$

   (g) $\emptyset$

   (h) $\overline{AF}$

7.   (a)   144°

      (b)   35

8. $V + F - E = 9 + 9 - 16 = 2$

9.   (a)   No. The sum of the measures of the angles must be equal to 360°. This could not be the case if they were all acute angles.

      (b)   Let ABCD be an rectangle as shown, with ∠A as a right angle.

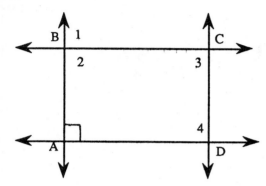

Because rectangle ABCD is a parallelogram, $\overset{\leftrightarrow}{BC}$ ‖ $\overset{\leftrightarrow}{AD}$ and $\overset{\leftrightarrow}{AB}$ ‖ $\overset{\leftrightarrow}{DC}$.
Corresponding angles, ∠BAD and ∠1 are congruent, and thus ∠1 is a right angle.
Because ∠1 and ∠2 are supplementary, ∠2 is a right angle. Similarly, it can be proved that ∠3 and ∠4 are right angles.

10.   30°

11.   (a)   11°30'47"

       (b)   6°49'12"

12.   (a)   70°

       (b)   70°

       (c)   70°

       (d)   110°

       (e)   70°

13.   (a)   Points A and C are outside, but point B is inside.

       (b)   Points A and B are inside and point C is outside.

14. $\overrightarrow{AX}$ bisects ∠DAB, so ∠DAX ≅ ∠XAB. $\overrightarrow{AY}$ bisects ∠BAC, so ∠BAY ≅ ∠YAC.
m(∠DAX) + m(∠XAB) + m(∠BAY) + m(∠YAC) = 180°
Hence, 2m(∠XAB) + 2m(∠BAY) = 180° and m(∠XAB) + m(∠BAY) = 90°.

Therefore, ∠XAY is a right angle. Hence, $\overrightarrow{AX} \perp \overrightarrow{AY}$.

15.

(a)

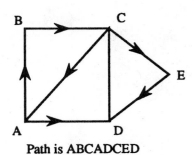

Path is ABCADCED

(b)   Not traversable
(c)   Not traversable

16.   (a), (b), and (f) are topologically equivalent; (c) and (d) are topologically equivalent.

17.   TO SUPP. ANGLES :A
      FD 100
      BK 50
      RT :A
      FD 50
      BK 50
      RT 180-:A
      LT 180
      BK 50
    END

Answers to Sample Test

1.   (a)   Yes. ASA   (b)   Yes. AAS   (c)   Yes. AAS
       (b)   Yes. SAS   (e)   Yes. SSS

2.   (a) $\Delta QRS \cong \Delta TUV$ by AAS

       (b) $\Delta GHI \cong \Delta JKL$ by SSS.

       (c) $\Delta ABD \cong \Delta CEF$ by ASA. (It must first be determined that m($\angle FCE$) is 60°.)

       (d) $\Delta ABE \cong \Delta CBD$ by SAS. (It must first be determined that $\angle A \cong \angle C$, because they are base angles of an isosceles triangle.)

4.   (a) $\dfrac{55}{16}$ (b) $\dfrac{40}{3}$ (c) $\dfrac{10}{3}$ (d)   3

7.   (a)   T
       (b)   F. A chord intersects a circle in two points.
       (c)   T
       (d)   T

8.   488 cm

9.   Draw any diameter. Construct a diameter perpendicular to it. Bisect the right angles formed. The points of intersection of the diameters with the circle, and the angle bisectors with the circle are the vertices of the octagon.

10.   (a)   False. In case of an obtuse triangle the center is in the exterior.
       (b)   False. In an equilateral triangle the two centers are the same. (This is because in an equilateral triangle the angle bisectors and the perpendicular bisectors of the sides are the same.)

       (c)   True. Each center is the same distance from $\overleftrightarrow{AB}$ as from $\overleftrightarrow{AC}$ and hence each center is on the angle bisector of $\angle A$.

Answers to Sample Test

1. (a) $\triangle ABC \cong \triangle EDF$ (b) $\triangle ABC \cong \triangle PRQ$

3. (a)   Follows from $\triangle AMB \cong \triangle CMD$ which are congruent by SAS.

    (b)   From $\triangle AMB \cong \triangle CMB$ it follows that $\angle BAM \cong \angle DCM$ and hence that $\overline{AB} \parallel \overline{CD}$.

5. (a)   y cannot be determined from the given data.
    (b) $x = 6$

7. (a)   True by AA.
    (b)   False. In similar triangles the ratio between corresponding sides does not have to be 1.
    (c)   True by AA since all the angles are 60° angles.
    (d)   False. Two isosceles triangles may have non-congruent base angles.

    (e)   True. $\triangle BCE \sim \triangle DAE$ by AA; $\angle CBE \cong \angle EDA$ as they are alternate interior angles

    between the parallels $\overleftrightarrow{BC}$ and $\overleftrightarrow{AD}$ and the transversal $\overleftrightarrow{BD}$, and the angles at E are congruent as vertical angles.

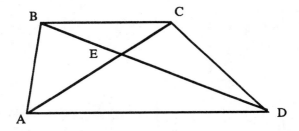

    (f)   True. If two sides of one angle are parallel respectively to two sides of a second angle, the angles must be congruent. (If a proof is desired extend two non-parallel sides of the angles and use corresponding angles to show that the angles are congruent.) Consequently the statement follows by AA.

10.   Divide each of two adjacent sides of the square into five congruent segments and then construct lines parallel to the sides of the square.

CHAPTER 12 FORM A

Answers to Sample Test

1.

(a)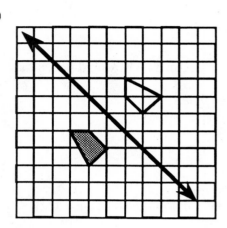

(b)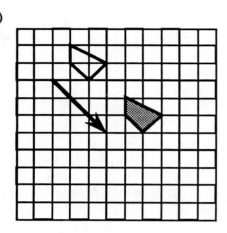

(c)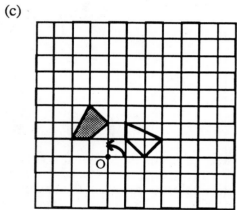

(d)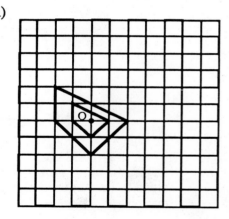

2. (a) 6   (b) 3

3. (a) Reflection
    (b) Slide, reflection, or rotation

5. Answers may vary.

6. (a) Rotation   (b) Reflection   (c) Rotation

7. (a) 2   (b) 1   (c) 2

8. Answers may vary.

9. Hint: Use the angle bisector of the non-base angle as a reflecting line.

10. Hint: Use the perpendicular bisector of $\overline{AB}$.

11. (a) True. $\triangle OAB \cong \triangle OA'B'$ by SAS since $\overline{OA} \cong \overline{OA'}$, $\overline{OB} \cong \overline{OB'}$ and the angles at O are vertical angles.

    (b) True. From (a) by CPCTC $\angle B' \cong \angle B$ and hence $\angle B'$ is a right angle. Because $\overline{OB} \cong \overline{OB'}$ and $\overline{OB'} \perp \ell'$, OB' is the distance from O to ℓ'.

    (c) True. The angles at B are alternate interior angles between ℓ and ℓ' and the transversal $\overleftrightarrow{BB'}$.

    (d) False. The image of $\overleftrightarrow{AA'}$ is $\overleftrightarrow{AA'}$.

12. The measure of each interior angle in a regular pentagon is $\dfrac{3 \cdot 180}{5}$ or 108°. Because 360 is not divisible by 108 a regular pentagon cannot tessellate the plane.

13.
```
TO H :S
  IF YCOR > 80 TOPLEVEL
  HE :S
  FORWARD 2*:S
  LEFT 90
  FORWARD :S
  RIGHT 90
  H :S
END

TO HE :S
  FORWARD 3*:S
  RIGHT 90
  FORWARD :S
  RIGHT 90
  FORWARD :S
  LEFT 90 FORWARD :S
  LEFT 90 FORWARD :S
  RIGHT 90 FORWARD :S RIGHT 90
  FORWARD 3*:S
  RIGHT 90 FORWARD :S
  RIGHT 90 FORWARD :S
  LEFT 90 FORWARD :S
  LEFT 90 FORWARD :S
  RIGHT 90 FORWARD :S RIGHT 90
END
```

1.

(a)

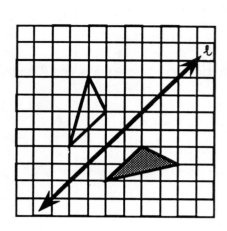

(b)

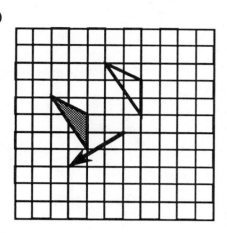

(c)

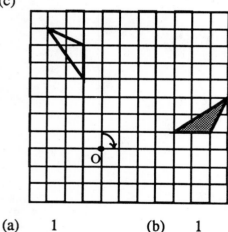

(d)

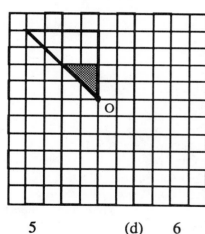

4. (a) 1   (b) 1   (c) 5   (d) 6

5. (a) Neither
    (b) Neither
    (c) Rotational symmetries of 72°, 144°, 216°, 288°
    (d) Rotational symmetries of 60°, 120°, 180°, 240°, 300°; Also has point symmetry

6. (a) Reflection   (b) Reflection   (c) Translation   (d) Rotation

7. (a) 1   (b) 1   (c) 2   (d) 2

8. Hint: Use the line through the midpoints of parallel sides.

9. Hint: Find a reflecting line which will reflect $\overline{AB}$ onto circle O.

10.   A square with side the same length as a side of the octagon.

11.    ```
TO HOUSE :S
  IF XCOR > 80 TOPLEVEL
  HOUS :S
  SETUP1 :S
  HOUS :S
  SETUP1 :S
  HOUSE :S
END
```
(In AppleLogo II, replace TOPLEVEL with [THROW "TOPLEVEL].)
```
TO HOUS :S
  SQUARE :S
  FORWARD :S
  TRIANGLE :S
END

TO SQUARE :S
  REPEAT 4[FORWARD :S RIGHT 90]
END

TO TRIANGLE :S
  REPEAT 3[FORWARD :S RIGHT 120]
END

TO SETUP1 :S
  FORWARD :S RIGHT 30
  FORWARD :S LEFT 30
  REPEAT 2[FORWARD :S RIGHT 90]
END
```
```

1.

	mm	cm	m	km
(a)	62,000	6200	62	0.062
(b)	360,000	36,000	360	0.360
(c)	300,000	30,000	300	0.3
(d)	2,300,000	230,000	2300	2.3

2. (a) Millimeter   (b) Centimeter
    (c) Centimeter or Millimeter   (d) Kilometer
    (e) Meter or centimeter   (f) Meter

3. (a) $30 \, m^2$ (b) $12 \, cm^2$

4. $128 \, cm^2$ 5. $5 \, cm^2$

6. Yes. The sides must be of length $\sqrt{11}$ cm.

7. Given any triangle ABC as shown, another triangle A'B'C' can be constructed and placed to form parallelogram ABA'C. The area of parallelogram ABA'C is bh. Thus, the area of $\triangle ABC$ is $\frac{1}{2}bh$.

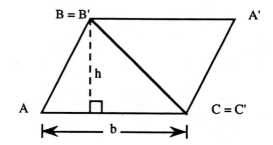

8. (a) 5m
    (b) $\frac{9}{2}\pi \, m^2$

9. $(12 + \frac{9}{2}\pi) \, m^2$

10. (a) Yes. $6^2 + 8^2 = 10^2$
    (b) No. $(\sqrt{2})^2 + (\sqrt{3})^2 \neq 5^2$

11.   (a)   0.05   (b)   81,000   (c)   4.738
       (d)   0.3   (e)   170,000   (f)   27
       (g)   27   (h)   4,738,000

12.   (a)   8976   (b)   13.3   (c)   155.6
       (d)   2752   (e)   6.75   (f)   691.2
       (g)   72   (h)   4.25   (i)   89.6
       (j)   40.6

13.   (a)   343 m^3 (b)   343,000 L   (c)   343,000 kg

14.   (a)   3000   (b)   2000   (c)   13
       (d)   4200   (e)   0.00301

15.   12,000π cm^3

16.   (a)   14π cm   (b)   49π cm^2 (c) $\frac{49}{20}\pi$ cm^2

17.   (a)   15π (b)   6π

Answers to Sample Test

1. (a)   150 cm^2 (b)   24 m^2

2. See text

3. (a)

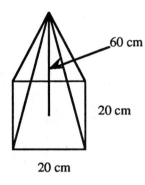

    60 cm

    20 cm

    20 cm

  (b)   There are infinitely any possible pyramids. If a is the length of the side of the base and h the height of the pyramid, then the volume of the pyramid is $\frac{1}{3}$ a^{2}h.

      We have $\frac{1}{3}$ a^{2}h = 8000 or h = $\frac{24000}{a^2}$. Thus we may assign an arbitrary value for a and obtain a value for h which will correspond to a pyramid whose volume is 8000 cm^3.

4. 16 S cm^2 and 64 V cm^3.

5. (a)   10,000 m   (b)   250 dm
    (c)   52.813 kg   (d)   2600 m

6. (a)   4.48 m^2 (b)   0.48 m^3 (c)   480 liters

7. 200°

8. (a)   3,000 liters   (b)   3,000 kg   (c)   1 cm

9. (a)   216$\sqrt{3}$ (b)   108$\sqrt{21}$

10. (a)   5$\sqrt{2}$ (b) $\frac{40\sqrt{3}}{3}$ (c)   4

11. (a)   691.2   (b)   14.4
    (c)   25.2   (d)   0.0075
    (e)   18.9   (f)   1779.0
    (g)   138.24   (h)   3.03
    (i)   -40   (j)   29.4

1.   Answers may vary.

2.   (a) $y = \dfrac{-1}{3}x - \dfrac{17}{3}$

      (b) $y = \dfrac{-15}{4}x + 8$

      (c) $y = 3x - 19$
      (d) $x = 4$

3.   (a)

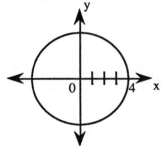

(b)

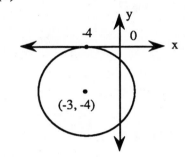

(c)

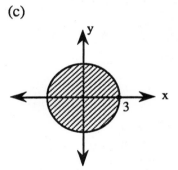

(d)

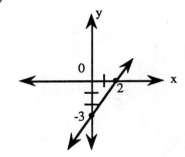

(e)

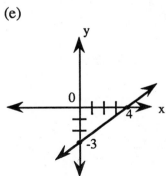

(f)

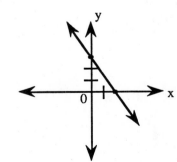

3.   (cont.)

(g)   (h)

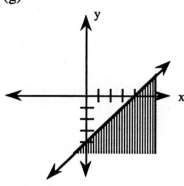

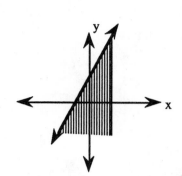

4. $(x + 2)^2 + (y + 6)^2 = 277$

5. $11 + \sqrt{13}$

6.   (a)   One solution, $(2, 0)$
        (b)   Infinitely many solutions
        (c)   One solution, $(\frac{15}{13}, \frac{74}{39})$

7.

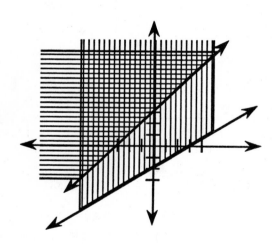

8.   (a)   Yes   (b)   Yes   (c)   Yes

9. $y = {}^-3x - \frac{1}{3}$

CHAPTER 14 FORM B

Answers to Sample Test

1. The slope of $\overleftrightarrow{AB}$ is $\frac{8-5}{5-3}$ or 2. The slope of $\overleftrightarrow{CD}$ is $\frac{3-(-1)}{8-6}$ or 2. Because the lines have the same slope they are parallel. Similarly the slopes of $\overleftrightarrow{BC}$ and $\overleftrightarrow{AD}$ are equal (each equals $\frac{-5}{3}$.) Thus $\overleftrightarrow{BC} \parallel \overleftrightarrow{AD}$ and therefore ABCD is a parallelogram.

2. Answers vary.

3. A (0, 1), B(2, -2), C (5, 9)

4. (a) $6x + 5y = 19$ or $y = \frac{-6}{5}x + \frac{19}{5}$

   (b) $\sqrt{61}$
   (c) $y = -7$

5. (a) $x = -1, y = 2$
   (b) The system has infinitely many solutions; all x and y satisfying $x = 3y + 5$
   (c) No solutions.

6. $(x - 5)^2 + (y + 2)^2 = 52$

7. (a)   (b)

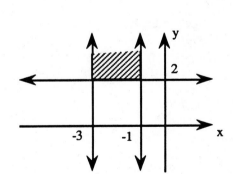   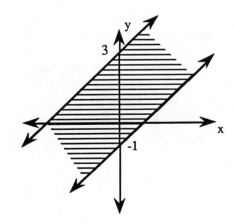

8. $y \le 2 - x$ 9.   133 quarters and 168 dimes
   $y \ge x$

10. A produces 69,000,000 cars while B produces 92,000,000 cars.

11. $(1, \frac{1}{2})$

137

Questions from the Classroom

1.   One way to designate the empty set is { }. Anything we enclose the the braces is an element of the set. Thus, {∅} is a set having one element, so it is not empty. The difficulty usually arises from the reluctance to consider the empty set as a set from lack of experience with sets whose elements are sets themselves. Examples of sets whose elements are sets themselves should be provided for the student.

2.   In fact it is true that $A \cup B = \{a, b, c, d, c, d\}$; however, because the agreement is not to list any element in a set more than once, $\{a, b, c, b, c, d\} = \{a, b, c, d\}$. For further discussion of this question, read the article by Geddes and Lipsey listed in the Chapter 2 bibliography.

3.   A set is finite if the set can be put into one-to-one correspondence with the set $\{1, 2, 3, ..., n\}$, for some whole number n. Otherwise, the set is infinite. Another criterion is that a set is infinite if and only if it can be put into one-to-one correspondence with a proper subset of itself.

4.   The student is right. To show that the hypothesis implies $B = C$ we show that $B \subseteq C$ and $C \subseteq B$. To show that $B \subseteq C$ let $x \in B$, then $x \in A \cup B$ and because $A \cup B = A \cup C$, $x \in A \cup C$. Consequently $x \in A$ or $x \in C$. If $x \in C$ then $B \subseteq C$. If $x \in A$ then since we started with $x \in B$ it follows that $x \in A \cap B$. Because $A \cap B = A \cap C$ we conclude that $x \in A \cap C$ and therefore $x \in C$. Thus $B \subseteq C$. Similarly starting with $x \in C$ it can be shown that $x \in B$ and hence that $C \subseteq B$.

5.   No. For example, the set of all rational numbers greater than or equal to 0 and less than or equal to 1 is an infinite set whose greatest element is 1.

6.   The student is incorrect. The student is distributing the complement bar over A and B. It might be helpful to point out that many other operations, like taking the square root or squaring, cannot be distributed over addition. For example, $\sqrt{9 + 16} \neq \sqrt{9} + \sqrt{16}$ and $(2 + 3)^2 \neq 2^2 + 3^2$. The student should be encouraged to check the assertion $\overline{A \cap B} = \overline{A} \cap \overline{B}$ with an example and with a Venn diagram.

7.   What the student said is true if $\overline{A} = B$. However, in general, $\overline{A} \cap B \neq \overline{A}$. Consider $U = \{1, 2, 3, 4\}$, $A = \{1, 2\}$ and $B = \{2\}$. Here $\overline{A} = \{3, 4\}$ and $\overline{A} \cap B = \emptyset$.

8.   Since "formula" is not defined, it is really impossible to answer the question. Most likely, students view a formula as a single equation. If this is the case, the concepts are not the same. Students are usually misled by the fact that many functions which appear in mathematical applications are given by equations. However, not every equation represents a function; for example, let $x = y^2$, when x takes values from the domain which is the set of natural numbers. For every $x \neq 0$, there are two corresponding values of y, and hence the equation does not define a function.

9.   The student is wrong. If, for example, A = {1, 2, 3} and B = {2, 3, 4}, then neither A ⊆ B nor B ⊆ A.

10.   Even though the Cartesian product of sets includes all pairings in which each element of the first set is the first component in a pair with each element of the second set, this is not necessarily a one-to-one correspondence. A one-to-one correspondence implies that there must be the same number of elements in each set. This is not the case in Cartesian product. For example, consider sets A = {1} and B = {a, b}.

11.   There is no definitive answer to this question. Many mathematics educators feel that teachers should know the mathematics behind the sorting, classifying, and counting taught in elementary school. While it is possible to teach these concepts and never have a knowledge of the language of sets, the development of set concepts helped to build a foundation for mathematics and the language involved may help teachers to converse with mathematics educators and mathematicians.

CHAPTER 3

Questions from the Classroom

1. The expressions are not equal because $2 \cdot (3 \cdot 4) = 2 \cdot 12 = 24$ and $(2 \cdot 3) \cdot (2 \cdot 4) = 6 \cdot 8 = 48$. There is no distributive property of multiplication over multiplication.

2. No. The first equation is true because $39 + 41 = 39 + (1 + 40) = (39 + 1) + 40 = 40 + 40$. Now, $39 \cdot 41 = (40 - 1)(40 + 1) = (40 - 1) \cdot 40 + (40 - 1) \cdot 1 = 40^2 - 40 + 40 - 1 = 40^2 - 1$, and $40^2 - 1 \neq 40^2$.

3. Yes. If $a < b$, we can write $a = bq + r$, where $q = 0$ and $r = a$. Notice that in this case, we still have $0 \leq r < b$. For example, if $a = 3$ and $b = 5$, then $3 = 0 \cdot 5 + 3$.

4. They are equal in value because multiplication is commutative; 5 times 4 means $5 \cdot 4$; 5 multiplied by 4 is $4 \cdot 5$; and $5 \cdot 4 = 4 \cdot 5$.

5. $0 \div 0 = x$ if and only if $0 = 0 \cdot x$. Any number x solves the last equation, and consequently $0 \div 0$ does not have a unique value. Suppose $0 \div 0 = 1$. Because $0 = 0 \cdot 2$, if we divide both sides of the equation by 0, then $1 = 1 \cdot 2$ or $1 = 2$. Thus, $0 \div 0 = 1$ leads to a contradiction, and consequently it cannot be defined as 1.

6. Evidently the student does not understand the process of long division. The subtraction method should help in understanding the above mistake.

```
6 | 36
    6 | 1 six
    30
    30 | 5 sixes
       | 6 sixes
```

Instead of adding 1 and 5, the student wrote 15.

7. It is correct. Since M is a special symbol for 1000, it is preferable to write MI for 1001 rather than $\bar{\text{II}}$. Romans usually reserved the bar for numbers greater than 4000.

8. The student probably incorrectly generalized the associative property as follows: $(x + 7) \div 7 = x + (7 \div 7) = x + 1$. The teacher should emphasize that the associative property holds only when all the operations performed are additions or all are multiplications. When other operations are performed, the associative property does not generally hold.

9. No, $x \div x = 1$ if and only if $x \neq 0$. If $x = 0$, then $x \div x = 0 \div 0$, which is not defined. (See Question 5.)

10. The following should be discussed. $(2^3)^2 = 2^3 \cdot 2^3 = 2^6$. On the other hand $2^{(3^2)} = 2^9$.

11. In general, $a \div (b - c) \neq (a \div b) - (a \div c)$. For example, $100 \div (25 - 5) \neq (100 \div 25) - (100 \div 5)$. In fact the right-hand side is $4 - 20$, which is not defined in the set of whole numbers. However, the right distributive property of division over subtraction does hold

provided each expression is defined in the set of whole numbers; that is $(b - c) \div a = (b \div a) - (c \div a)$.

12. The student has probably in mind the fact that if $a \varepsilon W$, $a - 0 = a$. If should be pointed out that 0 would be the identity for subtraction if $0 - a = a$ was also true. Since $0 - a$ is not defined in the set of whole numbers, $0 - a \neq a$ and therefore 0 is not the identity for subtraction.

13. Zero is different from nothing. For example, if you are holding two pencils in your hand, you can say that you have zero pieces of chalk in your hand, but you cannot say you have nothing in your hand. Zero is the whole number that tells how many elements are in the empty set.

14. Any number can be represented by a directed arrow of a given length. In this case the directed arrow represents 3 units. Any arrow 3 units in length can be used to represent 3, regardless of its starting point.

CHAPTER 4

Questions from the Classroom

1. The algorithm is correct, and the student should be congratulated for finding it. One way to encourage such creative behavior is to name and refer to the procedure after the student who invented it--for example, "David's subtraction method." In fourth grade the technique can be explained by using a money mode. Suppose you have $4 in one checking account and $80 in another, for a total of $84. You spent $27 by withdrawing $7 from the first account and $20 from the second. The first checking account is overdrawn by $3; that is, the balance is $^-$$3. The balance in the second account is $60. After transferring $3 from the second account to the first, the balance in the first account is $0 and in the second $57; that is, the total balance is $57.

2. The student is correct that a debt of $5 is greater than a debt of $2. However, what this means is that on a number line $^-$5 is farther to the left than is $^-$2. The fact that $^-$5 is farther to the left than $^-$2 on a number line implies that $^-5 < {^-}2$.

3. The student does not complete the argument in details. Indeed $a - b = a + {^-}b$. However, $b - a = b + {^-}a$. In general, $a + {^-}b \neq b + a$. For example, $5 + {^-}2 \neq 2 + {^-}5$.

4. The student is using an analogy in thinking that multiplication and addition behave in the same way. If such arguments were always correct, it would follow that since $a \cdot 1 = a$, then $a + 1 = a$. An example such as $(2 + 3)^2 \neq 2^2 + 3^2$ shows that the general case cannot be true. The proofs for the general case can be given to show the difference in the two expressions. By the associative and commutative properties of multiplication, $(ab)^2 = (ab)(ab) = (aa)(bb) = a^2b^2$. A complete expansion of $(a + b)^2$ using the distributive property gives the following: $(a + b)^2 = (a + b)(a + b) = (a + b)a + (a + b)b = a^2 + ba + ab + b^2 = a^2 + 2ab + b^2$.

5. The solution set of the given inequality has infinitely many elements, and it would be impossible to substitute all the solutions into the original inequality. However, it is possible to check and see if a particular element of the solution set satisfies the original inequality. For example, $x = 1$ is indeed a solution since $1 < 2$. To see if $x = 1$ is a solution, we substitute $x = 1$ in the original inequality and obtain $1 - 2 \cdot 1 > 1 - 5$, or $^-1 > {^-}4$. Since the inequality is true, $x = 1$ is a solution.

    There is a method of showing that all x such that $x < 2$ satisfies the original inequality. By reversing the process by which the original inequality was solved, we have: $x < 2$ implies $3x < 6$ and hence $3x - 5 < 6 - 5$, or $3x - 5 < 1$. Adding $^-$2x to both sides of the last inequality, the original inequality $1 - 2x > x - 5$ is obtained.

6. This student does not fully understand the order of operations. The teacher should emphasize that in order to avoid ambiguity, mathematicians agree that multiplication is performed before addition or subtraction. A few simpler examples like $10 - 2 \cdot 3$ should be helpful.

7. This is not a correct procedure in all cases. Since for all integers c, $^-c = (^-1)c$, the effect of performing the opposite of an algebraic expression is the same as multiplying the

expression by ⁻1. However, in the expression x - (2x - 3), the - is used to denote subtraction not simply finding the opposite. If the expression is first rewritten as x + ⁻(2x + ⁻3), then it is the case that ⁻(2x + ⁻3) = ⁻1(2x + ⁻3) or ⁻2x + 3. Now the expression can be rewritten as x + ⁻2x + 3 which a student might obtain from the father's rule, but a person using such a rule shows no real understanding of the subtraction operation.

8. No. The check only shows that the equations are correctly solved. It is possible that the equations were not set up correctly; that is, that they do not represent the information given in the word problem. In such a case, without following the written information, it would be impossible to detect the error.

9. It is quite possible that the student has used a circular argument in this proof. The teacher would need to know how the cancellation property of multiplication involving integers was proved. Most likely, the proof used the fact that (⁻1)(⁻1) =1. If so, then there is an error in the reasoning.

CHAPTER 5

Questions from the Classroom

1. Yes. Notice that $a \mid a$ implies that $a \neq 0$, and hence the student's conclusion is that $a \mid 0$, for $a \neq 0$.

2. The student is right. By definition, $0 \mid 0$ if there is an integer k such that $0 = k \cdot 0$. Because the last equation is true for any k, the definition is satisfied..

3. The student is generalizing the statement "if $d \mid a$ and $d \mid b$, then $d \mid (a + b)$" to the corresponding statement for "does not divide." (Generalizations have to be checked carefully.) The statement the student wrote is false, since—for example—$3 \nmid 7$ and $3 \nmid 2$ but $3 \mid (7 + 2)$. The student's statement should not be immediately rejected, but instead called a conjecture; the student should be encouraged to try to prove or disprove it.

4. It has been shown that any four-digit number n can be written in the form $n = a \cdot 10^3 + b \cdot 10^2 + c \cdot 10 + d = (a \cdot 999 + b \cdot 99 + c \cdot 9) + (a + b + c + d)$. The test for divisibility by some number g will depend on the sum of the digits $a + b + c + d$ if and only if $g \mid (a \cdot 999 + b \cdot 99 + c \cdot 9)$ regardless of the values of a, b, and c. Since the only numbers greater than 1 that divide 9, 99, 999 are 3 and 9, the test for divisibility by dividing the sum of the digits by the number works only for 3 and 9. A similar argument works for any n-digit number.

5. The student is wrong. For example, 1029 is divisible by 7, but neither 29 or 10 is divisible by 7. However, it is true that a number with an even number of digits is divisible by 7 if each of the numbers formed by pairing the digits into groups of two is divisible by 7. The proof for any six-digit number follows. (The proof for any number with an even number of digits is similar.) Let $n = a \cdot 10^5 + b \cdot 10^4 + c \cdot 10^3 + d \cdot 10^2 + e \cdot 10 + f$ be any six digit number such that 7 divides each of the two-digit numbers $a \cdot 10 + b$, $c \cdot 10 + d$ and $e \cdot 10 + f$. The number, n, can be written as follows: $n = a \cdot 10^5 + b \cdot 10^4 + c \cdot 10^3 + d \cdot 10^2 + e \cdot 10 + f = (a \cdot 10 + b) \, 10^4 + (c \cdot 10 + d) \, 10^2 + (e \cdot 10 + f)$. Since 7 divides $(e \cdot 10 + f)$, $(c \cdot 10 + d)$, and $(a \cdot 10 + b)$ it follows from the basic properties of divisibility that $7 \mid [(a \cdot 10 + b) \, 10^4 + (c \cdot 10 + d) \, 10^2 + (e \cdot 10 + f)]$.

6. It is very hard to refute the student's claim, since there are infinitely many primes. We can say that unlike finding successive counting numbers, where it is possible to produce the next number by adding one, there is no known way to produce the next prime from a given prime number.

7. It is true that a number is divisible by 21 if and only if it is divisible by 3 and by 7. However, the general statement is false. For example, 12 is divisible by 4 and by 6 but not by $4 \cdot 6$, or 24. One part of the statement is true—that is, "if a number is divisible by $a \cdot b$, then it is divisible by a and by b." The statement "if a number is divisible by a and by b, it is divisible by ab" is true if a and b are relatively prime. To see why this is true, suppose that $GCD(a, b) = 1$ and m is an integer such that $a \mid m$ and $b \mid m$. Since $a \mid m$, $m = ka$ for some integer k. Now $b \mid m$ implies that $b \mid ka$. Since a and b are relatively prime, it

follows from the Fundamental Theorem of Arithmetic and the fact that b | ka that b | k (Why?), and therefore k = jb, for some integer j. Substituting k = jb in m = ka, we obtain m = jba, and consequently ab | m.

8. The student is partially correct. If a and b are distinct natural numbers, then the student is correct. By definition, a ≤ LCM(a, b); b ≤ LCM(a, b). Also GCD(a, b) ≤ a and GCD(a, b) ≤ b. Hence, GCD(a, b) ≤ LCM(a, b). However, the equality holds if a = b.

9. x = 3k, y = 4k, z = 5k satisfies the equation for any integer k. Hence the student is right.

CHAPTER 6

Questions from the Classroom

1. Since nothing has been said about the domain of x, the student's answer is correct if the student assumes and states the assumption that x is an integer. If the domain is the set of rational numbers or the set of real numbers, then the answer is not correct.

2. The student is wrong unless n = 0 or p = m. For example, $\frac{5}{6} = \frac{3+2}{4+2} \neq \frac{3}{4}$. Notice that $\frac{m+n}{p+n} = \frac{m}{p}$ is equivalent to each of the following: $(m+n)p = (p+n)m$, $mp + np = pn + nm$, $np = nm$. The last equation is equivalent if n = 0 or p = m. That is, $\frac{m+n}{p+n} = \frac{m}{p}$ if and only if n = 0 or m = p.

3. It is true that the rule "invert and multiply" follows from the fact that division is the inverse of multiplication. This by itself, however, is not a justification of the rule. Because division is defined in terms of multiplication, it follows that $\frac{a}{b} \div \frac{c}{d} = x$ if and only if $\frac{a}{b} = x \cdot \frac{c}{d}$. This solution of the last equation is $\frac{a}{b} \cdot \frac{d}{c}$, which justifies the rule "invert and multiply."

4. The student is generalizing the distributive property of multiplication over addition into the distributive property of multiplication over multiplication, which does not hold. For example, $\frac{1}{2}(\frac{1}{3} \cdot \frac{1}{4}) = \frac{1}{2} \cdot \frac{1}{12} = \frac{1}{24}$, but $(\frac{1}{2} \cdot \frac{1}{3})(\frac{1}{2} \cdot \frac{1}{4}) = \frac{1}{6} \cdot \frac{1}{8} = \frac{1}{48}$.

5. It is true that the new ratio in the class is $\frac{2+4}{3+6}$, or $\frac{6}{9}$; however, this ratio does not equal $\frac{2}{3} + \frac{4}{6}$. Also, $\frac{2}{3} + \frac{4}{6} = \frac{4}{3}$; however, $\frac{2+4}{3+6} = \frac{6}{9} = \frac{2}{3}$. Hence $\frac{2}{3} + \frac{4}{6} \neq \frac{2}{3}$. The student's definition of addition of fractions contradicts many properties of addition. For example, $\frac{1}{2} + \frac{1}{2}$ is greater than 1; however, using the student's definition of addition, we obtain $\frac{1}{2} + \frac{2}{2} = \frac{1+2}{2+2} = \frac{3}{4}$, which is less than 1.

6. The teacher was right; Nat obtained the correct answer by using an incorrect method because in general $a + b(x + c) \neq (a + b)(x + c)$. Some advanced student could be encouraged to find other equations for which a similar mistake will produce a correct answer. This will happen if the equations $a + b(x + c) = x + d$ and $(a + b)(x + c) = x + d$ have the same solution. This can be shown to happen if and only if $d = a + b + c - 1$. Consequently a, b and c can be chosen at will but d is determined by the above equation.

7. $\frac{0}{6}$ is not in simplest form. A fraction $\frac{a}{b}$ is in simplest form if and only if GCD(a, b) = 1; however GCD(0, 6) = 6. The simplest form of $\frac{0}{6}$ is $\frac{0}{1}$.

8. Let the number be a. One half of a is $\frac{1}{2} \cdot a = \frac{a}{2}$. Dividing a by $\frac{1}{2}$ is $a \div \frac{1}{2} = a \cdot \frac{2}{1} = 2a$. Consequently, the student is wrong.

9. The first student's approach is correct. What the second student has done is to treat the problem as if had been $\frac{1}{5} \cdot \frac{5}{3} = \frac{1}{3}$, when in reality, the problem is $\frac{15}{53}$. Writing the problem as $\frac{10 + 5}{50 + 3}$ may help him or her understand the problem.

10. The student has incorrectly applied the property which says that multiplying both sides of an inequality by a negative number reverses the inequality. When both sides of the inequality $\frac{x}{7} < {}^-1$ are multiplied by 7, a positive number, we obtain, $x < {}^-7$, and not $x > {}^-7$.

    Probably the student seeing $^-1$ in $\frac{x}{7} < {}^-1$ thinks that the inequality is multiplied by $^-1$ and consequently reverses the inequality.

11. (a) No. Because $\frac{2}{3} - \frac{1}{2} = \frac{1}{6}$ and $\frac{3}{4} - \frac{2}{3} = \frac{1}{12}$, there is no fixed number that can be added to each term in order to obtain the next term.

    (b) No. The difference between each term and the preceding one is not fixed. In fact, this is a geometric sequence because each term can be multiplied by $(\frac{1}{2})^{-3}$ to obtain the next term.

12. Yes, the student is correct. Suppose that the fractions are positive and $\frac{a}{b} < \frac{c}{d}$. This inequality is equivalent to $ad < bc$. The student claims that $\frac{a}{b} < \frac{a+c}{b+d} < \frac{c}{d}$. This is equivalent to $a(b + d) < b(a + c)$ and $(a + c)d < c(b + d)$. However, each of the last inequalities is equivalent to $ad < bc$.

13. Yes, the student is correct. Let $\frac{a}{b} = \frac{c}{d} = r$. Then $a = br$, $c = dr$, and therefore $\frac{a + c}{b + d} = \frac{br + dr}{b + d} = \frac{r(b + d)}{b + d} = r$.

14. No. For example, $\frac{1}{-3} < \frac{1}{2}$, but $^-3$ is not greater than 2. However, if x and y are both positive or both negative, the conclusion is true. (To prove this, multiply both sides of $\frac{1}{x} < \frac{1}{y}$ by xy.)

CHAPTER 7

Questions from the Classroom

1. $3\,1/4\% = 3\% + 1/4\% = 3/100 + (1/4)/100 = 0.03 + 0.0025 = 0.0325$. Knowing the $1/4 = 0.25$, the student incorrectly wrote $1/4\% = 0.25$.

2. The principal square root of 25, written, $\sqrt{25}$ is defined to be the nonnegative number whose square is 25. Consequently, $\sqrt{25} = 5$.

3. The principal square root of a^2 is always nonnegative. Hence $\sqrt{a^2} = a$ if $a > 0$. If $a < 0$, then -a is positive, and hence $\sqrt{a^2} = {}^-a$. For example, if $a = {}^-5$, then $\sqrt{({}^-5)^2} = {}^-({}^-5) = 5$. Consequently the student is wrong.

4. All properties of integral exponents do not automatically extend to rational exponents. The corresponding properties for rational exponents have to be justified. The property $(a^m)^n = a^{mn}$ is true when a in nonnegative and m and n are rational numbers. For $a < 0$, m is an even integer and $n = 1/m$, the property is false. For example, $(({}^-5)^2)^{1/2} \neq {}^-5$.

5. Most likely, the student thinks that ^-x is a negative number. This is wrong. Depending upon the value of x, ^-x can be positive, negative, or 0. If $x < 0$, then $^-x > 0$. In fact, $x = {}^-9$ is the solution of the given equation.

6. In the second method, the student did not use the distributive property correctly. Notice that $(8 + 1/2)(6 + 1/2) = (8 + 1/2)6 + (8 + 1/2)(1/2)$. Because $(8 + 1/2)6 = 8 \cdot 6 + (1/2)6 = 48 + 3$, the 3 is missing in the student's example. Adding 3 to the student's answer results in the correct answer of $55\,1/4$.

7. The student assumed that $\sqrt{{}^-7}$ could not be done. That is correct, but does not answer the question. Every real number squared is greater than or equal to $^-7$.

8. It is possible to mark up a product 150%. For example, if a product sells for $10, then a 150% markup is $1.5(\$10) = \$15$. Thus, the product would sell for $25.

9. Scientific notation is typically used for very great numbers or very small numbers (numbers close to 0). In scientific notation, a number N is written in the form $N = A \cdot 10^n$ where $1 \leq A < 10$. Thus, negative numbers are not considered in this definition. If this notation is to be used with negative numbers, we can work with the number as if it was a positive number and then annex a negative sign at the end, for example, $^-2,390,000$ could be written as $^-2.39 \cdot 10^6$.

CHAPTER 8

Questions from the Classroom

1. Each toss of a fair coin is independent of the previous one. Hence the probability of a tail on each toss is $\frac{1}{2}$ regardless of how many tails appeared in previous tosses.

2. If the four areas corresponding to the colors were equal in size, the events of the spinner landing on each of the colors would be equally likely, and the student would be correct. However, since the four areas are different in size, the events are not equally likely, and the student is wrong. Since the area corresponding to the color green is the largest, the probability of green appearing is greater than the probability of either red or blue appearing.

3. Tossing 3 heads on the first 3 tosses of a coin does not imply the coin is unfair. Only when a fair coin is tossed a much greater number of times can we expect to get approximately equal numbers of tails and heads. The probability of 3 heads in 3 tosses is $\frac{1}{8}$.

4. The student is wrong. The sample space for this event is not {HH, HT, TT}, but rather {HH, HT, TH, TT}. Consequently the probability of HH is $\frac{1}{4}$.

5. The student is correct if by the student's statement he or she means that an understanding of the concept of permutations and combinations based on the Fundamental Counting Principle is sufficient rather than recalling the formula. For example, if we are given n objects, the first object can be chosen in n ways, the second in (n - 1) ways, the third in (n - 2) ways, and the fourth in (n - 3) ways. Notice that the fourth object is not chosen in (n - 4) ways but in (n - 3) or (n - 4 + 1) ways. If this pattern continues, the rth object can be chosen (n - r + 1) ways. The pattern does continue and by the Fundamental Counting Principle, the number of permutations is $n \cdot (n - 1) \cdot (n - 2) \cdot ... \cdot (n - r + 1)$. This expression is equivalent to the permutation formula as shown below.

$$n \cdot (n - 1) \cdot (n - 2) \cdot ... \cdot (n - r + 1) =$$

$$\frac{[n \cdot (n - 1) \cdot (n - 2) \cdot ... \cdot (n - r + 1)] \cdot [(n - r) \cdot (n - r - 1) \cdot ... \cdot 2 \cdot 1]}{(n - r) \cdot (n - r - 1) \cdot ... \cdot 2 \cdot 1}$$

$$= \frac{n!}{(n - r)!}$$

To find the number of combinations possible, the number of permutations can be divided by the number of ways in which r objects can be arranged. Since any r objects can be rearranged in r! ways (Why?), we divide the number of permutations by r!.

Tree diagrams are also useful in permutation and combination problems.

6. The Multiplication Rule for Probabilities states that for events A and B in a sample space and $P(B) \neq 0$, then $P(A \cap B) = P(B) \cdot P(A \mid B)$. The Multiplication Rule for Probabilities

justifies multiplying probabilities the way we do on tree diagrams. For example, suppose we have a box containing the letters H, A, T and we draw two letters from the box without replacement. If we wish to compute the probability of obtaining the outcome HA we could use a tree diagram as follows.

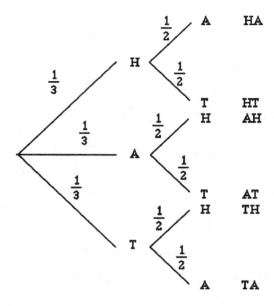

Thus, the probability of obtaining the outcome HA is $\left(\frac{1}{3}\right) \cdot \left(\frac{1}{2}\right)$ or $\frac{1}{6}$. The reason we can multiply in this way along the branches follows from the Multiplication Rule of Probabilities. What we are really doing is multiplying $P(H)$ and $P(A \mid H)$ which is exactly an application of the Multiplication Rule for Probabilities.

7. The student is not correct. The confusion probably lies in the fact that the student thinks that probabilities are additive. The student does not understand the Multiplication Rule for Probabilities. A tree diagram for the experiment could possibly help. A partial tree diagram is given below

$$\xrightarrow{\frac{1}{6}} 5 \xrightarrow{\frac{1}{6}} 5$$

Thus $P(5, 5) = \frac{1}{6} \cdot \frac{1}{6} = \frac{1}{36}$.

8. For an experiment with sample space S with equally likely outcomes, the probability of an event A is given by $P(A) = \frac{n(A)}{n(S)}$. Because an event A must be a subset of S, the smallest that $n(A)$ could be is 0. This occurs when $A = \varnothing$. Because $n(S)$ is never negative and $n(A)$ is never negative, then the $P(A)$ can never be negative.

9.   The probability of an event is a ratio and does not necessarily reflect the number of elements in the event or in the sample space. For example, if $n(S) = 20$ and $n(A) = 12$, then $P(A) = \dfrac{12}{20}$ which could also be reported as $P(A) = \dfrac{3}{5}$.

CHAPTER 9

Questions from the Classroom

1. The median and the mode are unchanged. The new mean is
    $$\frac{9 \cdot (10000) + 20000}{10} = 11,000.$$ Consequently the new mean has increased by $1000.

2. The mode is used if it is desirable to know which value occurs most often in a distribution. For example, if a store wants to know which size pants is most frequently sold, the mode is the most appropriate average to use.

3. The student is not correct. The stem and leaf plot is very useful when trying to organize information that will later be used to make a bar graph or a frequency polygon. It is not the most useful when trying to depict information that will be organized into a circle graph for example.

4. Since the median is 90, at least half of the class had grades of 90 or more. Since Tom scored 80, he did not do better than half of the class.

5. A graph displays the data in a way that is possible to see at a glance how parts of the data compare to each other. One of the disadvantages of graphical representation is that it is not always possible to obtain accurate readings from graphs.

6. In a grouped frequency table, the precise value of the raw data is not displayed, and hence it is impossible to conclude from the table which value occurs most often. Consequently it is impossible to find the exact mode from the information given in a grouped frequency table. In this situation the mode is usually given as a class interval.

7. If the mean is less than the median, then one can be certain that there were more scores above the mean than below it. The low scores tend to be further from the mean than the high scores.

8. No, it is not possible to have a standard deviation of -5. By definition, the standard deviation is the positive square root of the variance.

9. Mel did not really miss the cut-off by a single point. He would have had to increase his score on each of the 10 tests by a single point to reach an average of 90 or increase his total score for the 10 tests by 10 points to reach an average of 90.

CHAPTER 10

Questions from the Classroom

1. The distinct lines are parallel if they do not intersect and are contained in a single plane. Lines which do not intersect and are not contained in any single plane are called skew lines. Many of the properties of parallel lines depend upon the fact that they are contained in a single plane and therefore do not share these properties with skew lines.

2. The measure of an angle has nothing to do with the fact that rays cannot be measured. The measure of an angle in degrees is based on constructing a circle with center at the vertex of the angle and dividing the circle into 360 congruent parts. The number of parts in the arc that the angle intercepts is the measure of the given angle in degrees. The number of parts in the intercepted arc is the same regardless of the size of the circle (or protractor).

3. A regular polygon is a polygon in which all the angles are congruent and all the sides are congruent. In general, neither condition implies the other, and hence neither is sufficient to describe a regular polygon. For example, a rhombus that is not a square has all sides congruent, but all its angles are not congruent. A rectangle, not a square, has all its angles congruent, but not all its sides are congruent.

4. Let n be the number of sides of a regular polygon, all of whose angles measure 90 degrees. The sum of the measures of all the interior angles in $n \cdot 90$ and also $(n - 2)180$. Consequently, $n \cdot 90 = (n - 2)180$. This equation has the solution $n = 4$. Thus, the polygon must have 4 sides, and therefore it is necessarily a square.

5. If two parallel lines are defined as lines which are in the same plane and do not intersect, then two identical lines cannot be parallel, because their intersection is nonempty. It is possible to define two identical lines as parallel or nonparallel. Some books define it one way; other books the other way.

6. The student is wrong. Some pairs of such lines are indeed skew lines; others, however, are parallel. For example, consider the line determined by the intersection of the same wall and the floor. These two lines are in the planes of the classroom ceiling and classroom floor and are parallel. They are contained in the plane of the wall.

7. The answer is no. If lines were great circles, then all lines would intersect in two points.

8. Since an angle is a set of points determined by two rays with the same endpoint, to say that two angles are equal implies that the two sets of points determining the angles are equal. The only way this can happen is if the two angles are actually the same angle. To say that two angles are congruent is to say that the angles have the same size or measure.

9. The student is incorrect. While the degree is the basic unit of angle measure, it can be further subdivided. This in itself would prove that the student is incorrect. However, many geometry books also consider a Protractor Postulate which puts all the rays in a half-plane emanating from a point in a one-to-one correspondence with the real numbers greater than or equal to 0 and less than 180. This would allow infinitely many rays emanating from one point.

CHAPTER 11

Questions from the Classroom

1. The symbol $\cong$ is used only for congruent parts. Because AB and CD designate length of segments and not the segments themselves, it is not true that $AB \cong CD$. Notice that if segments are congruent, then they are of the same length; hence it is correct to write $AB = CD$.

2. Some of the constructions that cannot be done using a compass and straightedge are angle trisection, duplication of a cube, and squaring the circle. Given any angle, it is impossible with only a compass and straightedge to find two rays which divide the angle into three congruent angles. Some angles, but not all, can be trisected with straightedge and compass. For example, a right angle can be trisected. The duplication of a cube involves constructing the edge of a cube whose volume is twice as great as the volume of a given cube. Squaring a circle involves constructing a square which has the same area as a given circle. For over 2000 years mathematicians tried to perform these three constructions. In the nineteenth century it was finally proved that these constructions cannot be done with straightedge and compass alone. A clear exposition of these proofs can be found in the book by Courant and Robbins, <u>What Is Mathematics?</u> (London: Oxford University Press, 1941 and 1969, pp. 117-140).

3. Perhaps the "best" definition relies on transformational geometry. Two figures can be defined to be congruent if and only if one figure can be mapped onto the other by a translation, reflection, rotation, or glide reflection.

4. For a detailed discussion of the trisection problem, see <u>The Trisection Problem</u>, by Robert Yates (Washington, D. C.: NCTM Publications, 1971).

5. The student is wrong. $\angle 1 \cong \angle 2$ implies that $\overline{AD}$ and $\overline{BC}$ are parallel, but does not imply that the other two sides are parallel.

6. This is false. Consider, for example, a rectangle which is not a square. The polygon resulting from connecting the midpoints of the sides of the rectangle is a rhombus with no right angles. Such a rhombus is not similar to the rectangle.

7. The symbol $=$ is used for identical objects. Two triangles are equal if they represent the same set of points. Congruent triangles are not necessarily identical because their positions may be different.

8. The student is wrong. The student is forgetting that when we say $\triangle ABC$ is congruent to $\triangle BCA$, this means that there is a one-to-one correspondence set up among the vertices so that corresponding sides are congruent. If $\triangle ABC$ is congruent to $\triangle BCA$, then $\overline{AB} \cong \overline{BC}$, $\overline{AC} \cong \overline{BA}$, and $\overline{BC} \cong \overline{CA}$. This is not true in a general triangle.

9. This is incorrect. For example, a circle cannot be inscribed in a general rectangle.

CHAPTER 12

Questions from the Classroom

1. The answer is no. If you are given only a single point and its image, then either of a translation, rotation, reflection, or glide reflection could be used. It takes three noncollinear points to determine the isometry.

2. Again, having only a segment and its image is not enough to determine the transformation. It requires three noncollinear points. For a further examination of this problem, see <u>Transformational Geometry</u>, by Richard Brown (Palo Alto, CA: Dale Seymour Publications, 1989).

3. A kite always has one line of symmetry. This line of symmetry contains one of the diagonals. It is the diagonal through the vertices of the angles of the kite which are not necessarily congruent.

4. The student is correct. The two dimensional analogue of the plane is a line.

5. What the student says is true if only single points are being considered. However, the student is incorrect when one considers the entire plane or even a triangle. A reflection reverses orientation while a rotation does not. The orientation must be considered any time three noncollinear points are used.

6. We do have a function that is sometimes called a point transformation. Since it is not a one-to-one mapping of the plane to the plane, it is not a true transformation. The student is correct.

CHAPTER 13

Questions from the Classroom

1. The units have to be the same because volume is measured in cubic units. A cubic unit is the volume of a cube having all its dimensions measured in the same units.

2. Yes, the same type of relationship does hold. For a proof and discussion, see G. Polya, <u>Mathematics and Plausible Reasoning</u>, vol. 1 (Princeton, N.J.: Princeton University Press, 1954, pp. 15-17).

3. No. An angle is a union of two rays. The student probably means the area of the interior of an angle. However, since the interior of an angle occupies an infinite part of a plane, it does not have a measurable area.

4. The area of the interior of any simple closed curve can be described as the sum of the areas of the finitely many nonoverlapping parts into which it can be divided. In the student's case, the square is divided into <u>infinitely</u> many parts, and hence the above property does not apply.

5. Consider a box whose base is a square with sides of 5 cm each and height 30 cm long. Its volume is 750 cm^3 and its surface area is $20 \cdot 30 + 2 \cdot 25 = 650$ cm^2. Since $750 > 650$, the volume is a greater number than the surface area.

6. The metric system is much simpler than the English system of measurement. For example, converting from one unit to another within the metric system requires only multiplication or division by a power of 10. Almost all the countries in the world are using the metric system. In order for the United States to be able to trade effectively with other countries, it is essential that it uses the same system as everybody else. For more information read the article by Arthur E. Hallerberg "The Metric System: Past, Present, Future" <u>Arithmetic Teacher</u> 20 (April 1973): 247-255.

7. Using the student's reasoning, in a right isosceles triangle the side opposite to the 90° angle should be twice as long as the side opposite the 45° angle.

    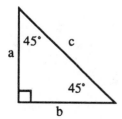

    Thus, $c = 2a$. However, the sum of the length of two sides in any triangle is always greater than the length of the third side. In particular $a + a > c$; That is, $2a > c$. This contradicts $c = 2a$, and hence the student's reasoning is wrong for an isosceles right triangle. A similar contradiction can be established for a 30°, 60°, 90° triangle. (Complete the details!)

8. The given box has a volume of 125 cm^3 and not 5 cm^3. The student most likely thinks of 5 cm^3 as (5 cm)^3. The teacher can remind the student that $ab^3 \neq (ab)^3$; for example, $2 \cdot 4^3 = (2 \cdot 4)^3$.

9.	The ratio will not change; it is a number without any dimensions. Suppose the circumference is a cm long and the diameter is b cm long. Then the ratio is $\dfrac{a \text{ cm}}{b \text{ cm}} = \dfrac{a}{b}$.

Now suppose that 1 cm = x in., then $\dfrac{a \text{ cm}}{b \text{ cm}} = \dfrac{ax \text{ in.}}{bx \text{ in.}} = \dfrac{a}{b}$.

10.	We use square centimeters or square inches to indicate the area of a square 1 cm or 1 in. on a side. However we cannot have a square with 1 are or 1 hectare on a side because are and hectare are not linear measures. 1 a is defined as the area of a square 10 m on a side and 1 ha is the area of a square 100 m on a side.

1. If the vertical line intersects the x-axis at $x = a$, any two points on the line can be written as (a, y_1) and (a, y_2), where $y_1 \neq y_2$. Using the formula for slope, we obtain $\frac{y_2 - y_1}{0}$.

    Since division by zero is not defined, $\frac{y_2 - y_1}{0}$ is meaningless, and hence the slope cannot be defined. The teacher may also want to give the following explanations. If a vertical line has a slope m, the equation of the y-axis would have to be $y = mx$ for some m, $m \neq 0$. (Why?) However, none of the points on the y-axis, except $(0, 0)$, satisfy the equation. For example, the point $(0, 1)$ cannot satisfy the equation $y = mx$ because $y = m \cdot 0 = 0$ no matter what the value of m is. Consequently, it is impossible to assign a slope to a vertical line.

2. It is difficult to refute this argument since it is based on a faulty assumption. "Zero is nothing" is a false statement. The student has a problem in his or her understanding of zero. Until this is cleared up, any further discussion is futile.

3. The following figure illustrates the values of $x_2 - x_1$ and $\frac{x_2 - x_1}{2}$.

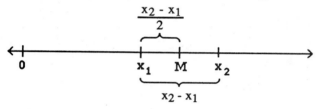

    Notice that the x-coordinate of M is $x_1 + \frac{x_2 - x_1}{2}$ rather than $\frac{x_2 - x_1}{2}$. Also, $x_1 + \frac{x_2 - x_1}{2} = \frac{2x_1 + x_2 - x_1}{2} = \frac{x_1 + x_2}{2}$. Since the midpoint of a segment is half the way between the endpoints of a segment, the student has confused the concept of half the distance between the points with that of the midpoint.

4. If a mistake was made in the steps of obtaining the simpler equivalent equations from the original equations and no mistakes were made thereafter, the mistake will not be detected if the answer is checked in the simpler equivalent equations. For example, consider the system $3x - 5 = y - 3$ and $y = x$. Substituting x for y in the first equation, we obtain $3x - 5 = x - 3$. Suppose the following mistake was made solving the last equation: $3x + x = 5 - 3$. The solution of this equation is $x = \frac{1}{2}$. Since $y = x$, then $y = \frac{1}{2}$. Now substituting $\frac{1}{2}$ for x in $3x + x = 5 - 3$ yields a true statement, but $x = \frac{1}{2}$ and $y = \frac{1}{2}$ do not satisfy the original system.

5. The student's claim is false whenever $b < 0$. For example, $x - y + 3 > 0$ represents the half-plane below the line $x - y + 3 = 0$. On the other hand, $x - y + 3 < 0$ represents the half-plane above the line. Notice that $ax + by + c > 0$ is equivalent to $by > -ax - c$. If

$b > 0$, this inequality is equivalent to $y > -\frac{a}{b}x - \frac{c}{a}$, representing a half-plane below the line. Consequently, the student's claim is true if and only if $b > 0$.

6. The student is making a mistake because in general $\sqrt{a + b} \neq \sqrt{a} + \sqrt{b}$. The student should be encouraged to exhibit counterexamples, such as $\sqrt{4 + 9} \neq \sqrt{4} + \sqrt{9}$.

7. If line k has slope m_1, then the line k', it's reflection in the x axis, has slope $^-m_1$. Consequently, the product of the slopes of lines k' and l is $(^-m_1)m_2$. Because $m_1m_2 = 1$, it follows that $(^-m_1)m_2 = {}^-(m_1m_2) = {}^-1$. Consequently, the lines k' and l are perpendicular.

Answers to Problems

CHAPTER 1

Problem Set 1-1

1. **(a)** $5 \times 6, 6 \times 7, 7 \times 8$ **(b)** $000000, \square\square\square\square\square\square$, 00000000 **(c)** 45, 41, 37 **(d)** 15, 20, 26 **(e)** 26, 37, 50 **(f)** X, Y, X (answers may vary) **(g)** 1, 18, 1 **(h)** 34, 55, 89 **(i)** 111111, 1111111, 11111111 **(j)** 123456, 1234567, 12345678 **(k)** $6 \cdot 2^6, 7 \cdot 2^7, 8 \cdot 2^8$ **(l)** $2^{32}, 2^{64}, 2^{128}$ **(m)**

, ,

(n) 15, 25, 40 **(o)** 21, 35, 49 **(p)** $\frac{3}{2}, \frac{5}{2}, \frac{7}{2}$ **(q)** 44, 88, 110

2. **(a)** Arithmetic; 11, 13, 15 **(b)** Arithmetic; 250, 300, 350 **(c)** Geometric; 96, 192, 384 **(d)** Geometric; 10^6, 10^7, 10^8 **(e)** Geometric; 5^7, 5^8, 5^9 **(f)** Arithmetic; 66, 77, 88 **(g)** Geometric; 2^{11}, 2^{13}, 2^{15} **(h)** Arithmetic; 33, 37, 41 **(i)** Neither, $6^3, 7^3, 8^3$ **(j)** Geometric; 486, 1458, 4374

3. **(a)** 12, 14 **(b)** 18, 21

4. **(a)** 30, 42, 56 **(b)** $100 \cdot 101 = 10,100$ **(c)** $n(n + 1) = n^2 + n$

5. **(a)** $6 + 9 \cdot 5 = 51$ **(b)** $6 + (n - 1) \cdot 5$ or $5n + 1$

6. **(a)** $1 + 10 \cdot 4 = 41$ **(b)** $1 + n \cdot 4$ or $4n + 1$

7. 1200 students

8. 15 liters

9. $1225

10. **(a)** $1660 **(b)** $7500 **(c)** 103 months

11. 19

12. **(a)** Yes. The difference between terms in the new sequence is the same as in the old sequence. **(b)** Yes. If the fixed number is k, the difference between terms of the second sequence is k times the difference between terms of the first sequence.

13. **(a)** No **(b)** Yes, the resulting sequence will be a geometric sequence. The ratio between each term (starting from the second term) and the preceding term of the resulting sequence is the same as the ratio of the corresponding terms in the original sequence.

14. **(a)** 1, 5, 12, 22, 35, 51 **(b)** 14,950

15. **(a)** 3, 5, 9, 15, 23, 33 **(b)** 4, 6, 10, 16, 24, 34 **(c)** 15, 17, 21, 27, 35, 45

16. **(a)** 299, 447, 644 **(b)** 56, 72, 90 **(c)** 108, 190, 304

17. **(a)** 100 **(b)** 101 **(c)** 100 **(d)** 61 **(e)** 200

18. The resulting sequence is always an arithmetic sequence.

19. **(a)** 3, 6, 11, 18, 27 **(b)** 4, 9, 14, 19, 24 **(c)** 9, 99, 999, 9999, 99999 **(d)** 5, 8, 11, 14, 17

20. **(a)** 1, 1, 2, 3, 5, 8, 13, 21, 34, 55, 89, 144 **(b)** Yes **(c)** 143 **(d)** The sum of the first n terms equals the $(n + 2)$th term minus 1.

21. **(a)** 199; $2n - 1$ **(b)** $50 \cdot 99$, or 4950; $50(n - 1)$ **(c)** $3 \cdot 2^{99}$; $3 - 2^{n-1}$ **(d)** 10^{100}; 10^n **(e)** 5^{101}; 5^{n+1} **(f)** 1100; $11n$ **(g)** 2^{199}; 2^{2n-1} **(h)** 405; $9 + 4(n - 1)$, or $4n + 5$ **(i)** 100^3, or 1,000,000; n^3 **(j)** $2 \cdot 3^{99}$; $2 \cdot 3^{n-1}$

22. **(a)** 11, 15, 19 **(b)** 1

23. Yes; the common ratio is the same as the ratio of the original sequence.

24. The sequence in (b) becomes greater than the sequence in (a) on the 12th term.

Brain Teaser (p. 16)

(a) N, T, E (Rule: <u>O</u>ne, <u>T</u>wo, <u>T</u>hree, <u>F</u>our, <u>F</u>ive, <u>S</u>ix, <u>S</u>even, <u>E</u>ight, <u>N</u>ine, <u>T</u>en, <u>E</u>leven) **(b)** Letters composed of only line segments go above the line. Letters with curves go below the line.

Section 1-2 Time Out

1. None, no dirt in a hole.

2. Fifty-cent piece and a nickel. (One coin is not a fifty-cent piece but the other one is.)

3. 4

4. 3

5. 6 hours (1 cigarette can be made with the butts from the first 5)

6.

7.

3	5	
0	5	(fill $\boxed{5}$)
3	2	(empty $\boxed{5}$ into $\boxed{3}$)
0	2	(empty $\boxed{3}$)
2	0	(pour $\boxed{2}$ into $\boxed{3}$)
2	5	(fill $\boxed{5}$)
3	④	(empty $\boxed{5}$ into $\boxed{3}$)

8. 1 hr 20 min. = 80 min.

9. 25

10. No extra dollar. There is no reason the 2nd column should sum to $50.

11. $63

12. They didn't play each other.

13. None, Noah took animals on the ark, not Adam

14. 68 ft.

15. 5 in.

16. Pour the contents of the 2nd glass into the 5th glass.

Problem Set 1-2

1. Yes; it works with an even or an odd number of numbers.

2. 18

3. $1.19

4. Answers may vary.

6	7	2
1	5	9
8	3	4

5. 325

6. Start both the 7-minute and 11-minute timers. When the 7-minute timer stops, put the egg on. When the 11-minute timer stops, restart it. When it stops this time, the egg is done.

7. 12

8. 24

9. 10

10. 12 dogs, 10 boys

11. $2.45

12. 16 days

13. 17 rungs

14. (1) Applejack (2) Null Set (3) Fast Jack (4) Lookout (5) Bent Leg

15. (a) Weigh 4 against 4, pick the heavier side, weigh 2 against 2, and finally, weigh 1 against 1. (b) Divide them into groups of 3, 3, and 2 and weigh 3 against 3. If they balance, only one more weighing is necessary. If they do not balance, select any 2 from the heavier side and weigh 1 against 1. Either they balance or they do not. Thus only one more weighing is necessary.

16. (a) 11 (b) 63

17. 310 feet and 230 feet

18. No. To do so, each domino must cover a black and a white square. Because there are only 30 white squares, while there are 32 black squares, this is impossible.

19. (a) 1001 (b) 300 (c) 150

20. (a) 260,610 (b) 100,701 (c) 20,503

21. 170

22. Yes; she can use the $8\frac{1}{2}$-inch side twice to get 17 inches and then use the 11-inch side to get back to 6 inches.

23. $13,500

24. 35 moves

25. (a) 21, 24, 27 (b) 243, 2, 729

26. $22 + (n - 1) \cdot 10$ or $10n + 12$

27. 21

28. 903

Brain Teaser (p. 36)

Thursday

Problem Set 1-3

1. (a) (i) $\begin{array}{r} 541 \\ \times 72 \\ \hline \end{array}$ (ii) $12\overline{)754}$

(b) (i) $\begin{array}{r} 257 \\ \times 14 \\ \hline \end{array}$ (ii) $75\overline{)124}$

2. (b)

3. $3.99, $5.87, $6.47

4. Hint: $259 \times 429 = 111,111$

5. 17

6. 275,000,000

7. Depends upon calculator.

8. Answers may vary.

9. Answers may vary.

10. $5,256,000

11. Answers may vary.

12. 625

13. 3,628,800

14. (a) If the product were abcd, then $a + c = 9$ and $b + d = 9$ (b) If the product were *abcde*, then $c = 9$, $a + d = 9$ and $b + e = 9$

15. $1 \div 30$

16. Answers may vary.

17. Play second and make sure that the sum showing when you hand the calculator to your opponent is a multiple of 3.
18. Play first and press 4. After that, make sure that each time that you hand your opponent the calculator, it displays 4 more than a multiple of 5.
19. Play first and press 3. After that, make sure that each time you hand your opponent the calculator, it displays 3 more than a multiple of 10.
20. Play second. Make sure that the calculator displays a multiple of 3 each time you hand your opponent the calculator.
21. Play second; use a strategy similar to that of problem 20 but use a multiple of 4.
22. Play first and subtract 3; after that, make sure that the calculator displays a multiple of 10 each time you hand your opponent the calculator.
23. (a) 35, 42, 49 (b) 1, 16, 1
24. $20n - 8$
25. 21
26. 9

Brain Teaser (p. 43)
Christmas (Notice that there is no L (NOEL) in the display.)

Chapter Test
1. (a) 15, 21, 28 (b) 32, 27, 22 (c) 400, 200, 100
(d) 21, 34, 55 (e) 17, 20, 23 (f) 256, 1024, 4096
(g) 5, 25 (h) 16, 20, 24 (i) 125, 216, 343
2. (a) Neither (b) Arithmetic (c) Geometric
(d) Neither (e) Arithmetic (f) Geometric
(g) Geometric (h) Arithmetic (i) Neither
3. (a) $3n + 2$ (b) n^3 (c) 3^n
4. (a) 5, 8, 11, 14, 17 (b) 2, 6, 12, 20, 30 (c) 3, 7, 11, 15, 19
5. (a) 10,100 (b) 10,201
6.

16	3	2	13
5	10	11	8
9	6	7	12
4	15	14	1

7. 89 years since there is no year 0.
8. 10 days
9. 26
10. $2.00
11. 21
12. 128
13. $3 \cdot 5 \cdot 9 \cdot 11 \cdot 13$
14. 44,000,000
15. 20
16. 39
17. 48

CHAPTER 2

Brain Teaser (p. 57)
If Joe belongs to A then he shaves himself. Because Joe shaves only those who do not shave themselves, he cannot shave himself. Consequently Joe does not belong to A. If Joe belongs to B then he does not shave himself. But then the order he got implies that he shaves himself and hence does not belong to B. Consequently Joe does not belong to either set. This is a popularized version of the famous Russel Paradox, discovered by Bertrand Russel in 1901.

Problem Set 2-1
1. (c) is well defined; (a) and (b) are not.
2. (a) $\{m, a, t, h, e, i, c, s\}$ (b) empty set
(c) $\{January, June, July\}$, or $\{x | x$ is a month which begins with J$\}$ (d) $\{21, 22, 23, 24, 25, \ldots\}$, or $\{x | x \in N$ and x is greater than 20$\}$ (e) $\{x | x$ is a state in the United States$\}$ (f) $\{M, I, S, P\}$ (g) $\varnothing$
(h) $\{California, Oregon, Washington, Alaska, Hawaii\}$
3. (a) $B = \{x, y, z, w\}$ (b) $3 \notin B$ (c) $\{1, 2\} \subset \{1, 2, 3, 4\}$ (d) $D \not\subseteq E$ (e) $A \not\subset B$ (f) $A = \{x | x \in N$ and $x < 5\}$ (g) $0 \in \varnothing$ (h) $A = \{0\} \neq \varnothing$
4. Answers may vary.
5. Answers may vary.
6. (a) Yes (b) No (c) Yes (d) No (e) No
7. $1 \leftrightarrow a$ and $1 \leftrightarrow b$
 $2 \leftrightarrow b$ and $2 \leftrightarrow a$
8. (a) $4 \cdot 3 \cdot 2 \cdot 1 = 24$ (b) $5 \cdot 4 \cdot 3 \cdot 2 \cdot 1 = 120$
(c) $n \cdot (n - 1) \cdot (n - 2) \cdot \ldots \cdot 3 \cdot 2 \cdot 1$
9. (a) cardinal (b) ordinal (c) ordinal (d) cardinal
10. $\{\varnothing, \{x\}, \{y\}, \{z\}, \{x, y\}, \{x, z\}, \{y, z\}, \{x, y, z\}\}$
11. $A = C = D; E = H$
12. $\overline{A} = \{x | x$ is a college student that does not have a straight-A average$\}$
13. One, if $B = \varnothing$
14. Sets C and D are equal.
15. No; $\varnothing \not\subset \varnothing$.
16. (a) $\in$ (b) $\in$ (c) $\notin$ (d) $\notin$ (e) $\notin$ (f) $\notin$ (g) $\notin$ (h) $\notin$ (i) $\in$ (j) $\notin$
17. (a) $\not\subseteq$ (b) $\not\subseteq$ (c) $\not\subseteq$ (d) $\not\subseteq$ (e) $\subseteq$ (f) $\not\subseteq$ (g) $\subseteq$ (h) $\subseteq$ (i) $\not\subseteq$ (j) $\not\subseteq$
18. No; suppose $A = \{1, 2\}$ and $B = \{3\}$. Then $A \not\subseteq B$ and $B \not\subseteq A$.
19. (a) True (b) False; for example, let $A = \{1, 2\}$ and $B = \{1, 2\}$. Then $A \subseteq B$, but $A \not\subset B$.
20. (a) $\{a, b\}$ is equivalent to $\{x, y\}$ a proper subset of $\{x, y, z, w\}$ (b) $\{a, b, c\}$ is equivalent to $\{1, 2, 3\}$ a proper subset of $\{1, 2, 3, \ldots, 100\}$ (c) is equivalent to itself, a proper subset of $\{1, 2, 3\}$
21. In the definition of "less than" replace "proper subset" by "subset".
22. (a) $2^6 = 64$ subsets; $2^6 - 1 = 63$ proper subsets
(b) $2^n - 1$ proper subsets
23. 35

24. (a) $\{1, 3, 5, 7, 9, \ldots, 2n - 1, \ldots\}$
$\{3, 5, 7, 9, 11, \ldots, 2n + 1, \ldots\}$
(b) $\{100, 101, 102, 103, \ldots, n + 99, \ldots\}$
$\{101, 102, 103, 104, \ldots, n + 100, \ldots\}$

Problem Set 2-2
1. (a) yes **(b)** yes **(c)** yes **(d)** yes **(e)** no **(f)** yes
2. (a) True **(b)** False. Let $A = \{1, 2, 4\}$ and $B = \{2, 3\}$. Then $A - B = \{1, 4\}$ and $B - A = \{3\}$.
(c) True **(d)** False. Let $A = \{1\}$, $B = \{1, 2\}$, and $U = \{1, 2, 3\}$. $\overline{A \cap B} = \{2, 3\}$ and $\overline{A} \cap \overline{B} = \{3\}$.
(e) True **(f)** True **(g)** True
3. (a) B **(b)** A
4. (a)   **(b)**   **(c)**

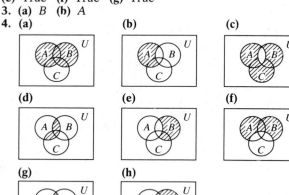

(d)   **(e)**   **(f)**

(g)   **(h)**

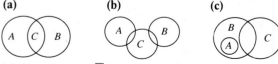

5. (a) U **(b)** U **(c)** S **(d)** $\varnothing$ **(e)** S **(f)** U **(g)** $\varnothing$
(h) S **(i)** $\overline{S}$ **(j)** S **(k)** $\varnothing$ **(l)** $\overline{S}$
6. (a) Yes. If $a \in A \cap B$, then a must belong to both A and B. Thus, it belongs to at least one of them. Hence, $a \in A \cup B$. **(b)** No, not necessarily. Let $A = \{a, b, c\}$ and $B = \{b, c\}$. Then $a \in A \cup B$, but $a \notin A \cap B$.
7. (a) A **(b)** $\varnothing$ **(c)** $\varnothing$ **(d)** $\varnothing$
8. (a)   **(b)**   **(c)**

  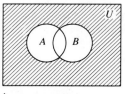

9. (a) $B - A$, or $B \cap \overline{A}$ **(b)** $A \cap B \cap C$ **(c)** $(A \cap C) - B$, or $(A \cap C) \cap \overline{B}$ **(d)** $\overline{A \cup B}$, or $\overline{A} \cap \overline{B}$ **(e)** $A \cap B$
(f) $[(A \cup C) - B] \cup (A \cap C \cap B)$
10. (a)   **(b)**   **(c)**

(d)

11. (a) False **(b)** False
12. (a) (i) 5 (ii) 2 **(b)** (i) $n + m$ (ii) the lesser number of m and n
13.

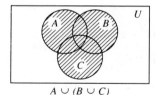

$A \cup (B \cup C)$ $(A \cup B) \cup C$

14. (a) No **(b)** No **(c)** No
15. (a) $\overline{A \cup B} = \overline{A} \cap \overline{B}$ **(b)** $\overline{A \cap B} = \overline{A} \cup \overline{B}$

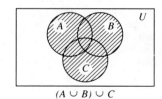 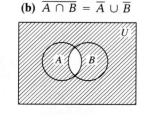

(c) Answers may vary.
16. $A = B$
17. (a) The set of college basketball players more than 200 cm tall. **(b)** The set of humans who are not college students or who are more than 200 cm tall. **(c)** The set of college students who are either basketball players or who are more than 200 cm tall. **(d)** The set of humans who are not college basketball players and who are not college students more than 200 cm tall. **(e)** The set of college students who are more than 200 cm tall but do not play basketball. **(f)** The set of college basketball players whose height is less than or equal to 200 cm.
18. (a) is the set of all students at Paxson School taking band but not choir. **(b)** is the set of all students at Paxson taking both choir and band. **(c)** is the set of all students at Paxson taking choir but not band. **(d)** is the set of all students at Paxson taking neither choir nor band.
19. 18
20. 4
21. (a) region $\overline{A}$ **(b)** 3
22. (a) 20 **(b)** 10 **(c)** 10
23. (a) False; let $A = \{a\}$ and $B = \{b\}$ **(b)** False; let $A = B$ **(c)** False; let $A \subseteq B$ **(d)** True **(e)** False; let $A = \{2, 4, 6, 8, \ldots\}$ and $B = \{1, 2, 3, 4, \ldots\}$
(f) False; let $A = \{1, 2\}$ and $B = \{4, 5, 6\}$
24. Cowboys vs. Giants   Steelers vs. Jets   Vikings vs. Packers   Redskins vs. Bills
25. (a) $\{(x, a), (x, b), (x, c), (y, a), (y, b), (y, c)\}$
(b) $\{(0, a), (0, b), (0, c)\}$ **(c)** $\{(a, x), (a, y), (b, x), (b, y), (c, x), (c, y)\}$ **(d)** $\varnothing$ **(e)** $\{(0, 0)\}$ **(f)** $\varnothing$ **(g)** $\{(x, 0), (y, 0), (a, 0), (b, 0), (c, 0)\}$ **(h)** $\{(x, 0), (y, 0), (a, 0), (b, 0), (c, 0)\}$ **(i)** $\varnothing$ **(j)** $\varnothing$
26. (a) $C = \{a\}, D = \{b, c, d, e\}$ **(b)** $C = \{1, 2\}, D = \{1, 2, 3\}$ **(c)** $C = \{0, 1\}, D = \{0, 1\}$

164

27. (a) 3 **(b)** 6 **(c)** 9 **(d)** 20 **(e)** $m \cdot n$
(f) $m \cdot n \cdot p$
28. (a) 3 **(b)** 0 **(c)** 0
29. 5
30. Yes
31. 30
32. 60
33. (a) No **(b)** No
34. 93
35. Answers may vary.
36. $\varnothing$, {a}, {b}, {c}, {a, b}, {a, c}, {b, c}, {a, b, c}
37. Yes
38. {p}, {q}, {r}, {s}, {p, q}, {p, r}, {p, s}, {q, r}, {q, s}, {r, s}, {p, q, r}, {q, r, s}, {p, r, s}, {p, q, s}
39. (a) {Massachusetts, Maryland, Mississippi, Minnesota, Missouri, Michigan, Maine, Montana}
(b) {x|x is a state in the United States starting with the letter M}

Brain Teaser (p. 68)
There are 5 doohickeys that are neither doodads nor thingamajigs.

Problem Set 2-3
1. Answers may vary. **(a)** The second component is the square of the first component. **(b)** The second component is the husband of the first component. **(c)** The second component is the capital of the first component. **(d)** The second component is the cost of the first component.
2. (a) We can tell directly that a is taller than m, a is taller than n, c is taller than m. We can tell indirectly that a is taller than c, b is the shortest, b is shorter than or the same height as m and n. **(b)** We can tell directly a is taller than m, b is taller than m, c is taller than m and n. We can tell indirectly that n is taller than m, c is the tallest person in either group, and m is the shortest in either group. Also, n is the same height or taller than a or b.
3. Answers may vary.
4.

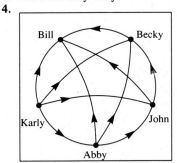

5. (a) no properties, not an equivalence relation
(b) reflexive, symmetric, transitive; an equivalence relation **(c)** reflexive, symmetric, transitive; an equivalence relation **(d)** symmetric; not an equivalence

relation **(e)** reflexive, symmetric, transitive; an equivalence relation **(f)** symmetric; not an equivalence relation **(g)** reflexive, symmetric, transitive; an equivalence relation **(h)** transitive; not an equivalence relation
6. (a) reflexive, symmetric, transitive; and equivalence relation **(b)** transitive, not an equivalence relation **(c)** symmetric, not an equivalence relation
7. (a) {Abe, Anna}, {George}, {Laura}, {Ben, Betty}, {Sue}, {Dax, Doug}, {Zachary}, {Mike, Mary}, {Carolyn} **(b)** {Abe, George, Sue, Mike}, {Laura, Anna}, {Ben, Carolyn}, {Betty, Zachary, Mary}, {Dax}, {Doug} **(c)** {Abe, Ben, Sue, Dax, Anna}, {George}, {Laura, Betty}, {Zachary, Carolyn}, {Doug, Mike, Mary}
8. Answers may vary **(a)** $3n - 1$ **(b)** $n^2 + 1$ **(c)** $n(n + 1)$ or $n^2 + n$
9. (a) $f(x) = 2x$ **(b)** $f(x) = x - 2$ **(c)** $f(x) = x + 6$ **(d)** $f(x) = x^2 + 1$
10. (a) No. 1 is paired with 2 elements, a and d. **(b)** No. Not every element from {1, 2, 3} is paired, namely 2. **(c)** Yes **(d)** No. Not every element from {1, 2, 3} is paired, namely 2 and 3.
11. Yes. Each element in the first set is used and each is associated with only one element in the second set.
12. (a) 5 **(b)** 11 **(c)** 35 **(d)** $3a + 5$
13. Answers may vary.
14. (a) No. a and b are paired with 2 different elements **(b)** Yes. It satisfies the definition.
15. (a)

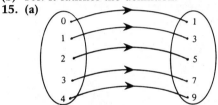

(b) {(0, 1), (1, 3), (2, 5), (3, 7), (4, 9)}
(c)

x	f(x)
0	1
1	3
2	5
3	7
4	9

(d)

16. (a) ⁻5 **(b)** 16 **(c)** 65
17. (a) $f(x) = (1/7)x$ **(b)** $f(x) = x + 5$ **(c)** $f(x) = (x - 5)/3$
18. (a) \$1.70 **(b)** $C = 20 + 15(W - 1)$ or $C = 15W + 5$; $W \leq 13$

19. (a) 30 chirps in 15 seconds, or 2 chirps/second
(b) 50 degrees F
20. $3.35
21. (a) 4 million **(b)** $4 million **(c)** 9 million
22. (a) $5n - 2$ **(b)** 3^n **(c)** $2n$
23. (a) Yes **(b)** No
24. (a)

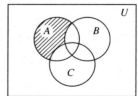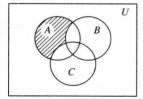

$$A - (B \cup C) = (A - B) \cap (A - C)$$

(b)

$$A \cup B = B$$

25. No; rich is not well-defined
26. (a) $\{x \in N: x > 12\}$ **(b)** $\{x \in N: 1 \le x < 14\}$
27. (a) $\{a, b, c, d\}$ or U **(b)** $\{a, d\}$ **(c)** $\varnothing$ **(d)** $\varnothing$
(e) $\varnothing$
28. Answers may vary.
29. Answers may vary.
30. (a) 6 **(b)** 9
31. $(A \cup B) \cup C = \{h, e, l, p, m\} \cup \{n, o, w\} = \{h, e, l, p, m, n, o, w\}$; $A \cup (B \cup C) = \{h, e, l, p\} \cup \{m, e, n, o, w\} = \{h, e, l, p, m, n, o, w\}$

Brain Teaser (p. 85)
The plan fails because we have not accounted for the eleventh man. The first and second men are in room 1, the third through tenth men are in rooms 2 through 9. Where is the eleventh man? He has not been mentioned. If the extra man in room 1 is put in room 10, then the eleventh man still has no room. Confusion results from the fact that by the time we read that the tenth man has been put into room 9, we think that the extra man in the first room is the eleventh man, when actually he is either the first or second.

Problem Set 2-4
1. (a) False statement **(b)** Not a statement **(c)** False statement **(d)** Not a statement **(e)** Not a statement **(f)** Not a statement **(g)** True statement **(h)** Not a statement **(i)** Not a statement, ambiguous
2. (a) There exists a natural number x such that $x + 8 = 11$ **(b)** For all natural numbers x, $x + 0 = x$, or there exists a natural number x such that $x + 0 = x$.
(c) There exists a natural number x such that $x = 4$.
(d) For no natural numbers x, $x + 1 = x + 2$.

3. (a) For all natural numbers x, $x + 8 = 11$. **(b)** For no natural numbers x, $x + 0 = x$. **(c)** For no natural numbers x, $x^2 = 4$. **(d)** For all natural numbers x, $x + 1 = x + 2$, or there exists a natural number x such that $x + 1 = x + 2$.
4. (a) The book does not have 500 pages. **(b)** Six is not less than 8, or 6 is greater than or equal to 8. **(c)** Johnny is thin. **(d)** $3 \cdot 5 \ne 15$ **(e)** No person has blond hair. **(f)** Some dogs do not have four legs. **(g)** All cats have nine lives. **(h)** Some dogs can fly. **(i)** Some squares are not rectangles. **(j)** All rectangles are squares. **(k)** There exists a natural number x such that $x + 3 \ne 3 + x$. **(l)** There does not exist a natural number x such that $3 \cdot (x + 2) = 12$. **(m)** There exists a counting number which is not divisible by itself and one. **(n)** All natural numbers are divisible by 2. **(o)** There exists a natural number x such that $5x + 4x \ne 9x$.
5. (a)

p	$\sim p$	$\sim(\sim p)$
T	F	T
F	T	F

(b)

p	$\sim p$	$p \vee \sim p$	$p \wedge \sim p$
T	F	T	F
F	T	T	F

(c) Yes **(d)** No
6. (a) $q \wedge r$ **(b)** $r \cup (-q)$ **(c)** $\sim(q \cap r)$
(d) $\sim q$
7. (a) F **(b)** T **(c)** T **(d)** F **(e)** F **(f)** T **(g)** F **(h)** F **(i)** F **(j)** F
8. (a) F **(b)** F **(c)** T **(d)** T **(e)** F **(f)** T **(g)** F **(h)** T **(i)** T **(j)** T
9. (a) No **(b)** Yes **(c)** No **(d)** Yes
10.

p	q	$\sim p$	$\sim q$	$\sim p \vee q$
T	T	F	F	T
T	F	F	T	F
F	T	T	F	T
F	F	T	T	T

11. (a) Today is not Wednesday or the month is not June. **(b)** Yesterday I did not eat breakfast or I did not watch television. **(c)** It is not true that both it is raining and it is July.

Brain Teaser (p. 92)
The second native is an Abe and the third native is a Babe. This is true since no matter to which tribe the first native belonged, he would have responded that he was an Abe. The second native reported this truthfully; thus, he is an Abe. The third native lied about the first native's response, thus, he is a Babe. (Note that the first native could be either an Abe or a Babe.)

Problem Set 2-5
1. (a) $p \to q$ **(b)** $\sim p \to q$ **(c)** $p \to \sim q$ **(d)** $p \to q$ **(e)** $\sim q \to \sim p$ **(f)** $q \leftrightarrow p$

166

2. (a) Converse: If you are good in sports, then you eat Meaties. Inverse: If you do not eat Meaties, then you are not good in sports. Contrapositive: If you are not good in sports, then you do not eat Meaties.
(b) Converse: If you do not like math, then you do not like this book. Inverse: If you like this book, then you like math. Contrapositive: If you like math, then you like this book. **(c)** Converse: If you have cavities, then you do not use Ultra Brush toothpaste. Inverse: If you use Ultra Brush toothpaste, then you do not have cavities. Contrapositive: If you do not have cavities, then you use Ultra Brush toothpaste. **(d)** Converse: If your grades are high, then you are good at logic. Inverse: If you are not good at logic, then your grades are not high. Contrapositive: If your grades are not high, then you are not good at logic.

3. (a)

p	q	$p \vee q$	$p \rightarrow (p \vee q)$
T	T	T	T
T	F	T	T
F	T	T	T
F	F	F	T

(b)

p	q	$p \wedge q$	$(p \wedge q) \rightarrow q$
T	T	T	T
T	F	F	T
F	T	F	T
F	F	F	T

(c)

p	$\sim p$	$\sim(\sim p)$	$p \rightarrow \sim(\sim p)$	$\sim(\sim p) \rightarrow p$	$p \leftrightarrow \sim(\sim p)$
T	F	T	T	T	T
F	T	F	T	T	T

(d)

p	q	$p \rightarrow q$	$\sim(p \rightarrow q)$
T	T	T	F
T	F	F	T
F	T	T	F
F	F	T	F

4. (a) T **(b)** T **(c)** F **(d)** F **(e)** T **(f)** F
5. (a) T **(b)** F **(c)** T **(d)** T **(f)** F **(g)** T
6. No. When an implication is false, its converse is always true.
7. No. Tom can go to the movies or not and the implication is still true.
8. (b)
9. Answers may vary. For example, "If a number is not a multiple of 4, then it is not a multiple of 8.

10.

p	q	r	$p \rightarrow q$	$p \wedge r$	$(p \wedge r) \rightarrow q$	$(p \rightarrow q) \rightarrow [(p \wedge r) \rightarrow q]$
T	T	T	T	T	T	T
T	T	F	T	F	T	T
T	F	T	F	T	F	T
T	F	F	F	F	T	T
F	T	T	T	F	T	T
F	T	F	T	F	T	T
F	F	T	T	F	T	T
F	F	F	T	F	T	T

(b)

p	q	$p \rightarrow q$	$(p \rightarrow q) \wedge p$	$[(p \rightarrow q) \wedge p] \rightarrow q$
T	T	T	T	T
T	F	F	F	T
F	T	T	F	T
F	F	T	F	T

(c)

p	q	$p \rightarrow q$	$\sim q$	$\sim p$	$(p \rightarrow q) \wedge (\sim q)$	$[(p \rightarrow q) \wedge (\sim q)] \rightarrow \sim p$
T	T	T	F	F	F	T
T	F	F	T	F	F	T
F	T	T	F	T	F	T
F	F	T	T	T	T	T

(d)

p	q	r	$p \rightarrow q$	$q \rightarrow r$	$p \rightarrow r$	$(p \rightarrow q) \wedge (q \rightarrow r)$	$[(p \rightarrow q) \wedge (q \rightarrow r)] \rightarrow (p \rightarrow r)$
T	T	T	T	T	T	T	T
T	T	F	T	F	F	F	T
T	F	T	F	T	T	F	T
T	F	F	F	T	F	F	T
F	T	T	T	T	T	T	T
F	T	F	T	F	T	F	T
F	F	T	T	T	T	T	T
F	F	F	T	T	T	T	T

11. (a) $P \subset Q$ **(b)** $P = Q$ **(c)** $p \rightarrow q \wedge \sim p \rightarrow \sim q$ or equivalently $p \leftrightarrow q$. $A = B$.
12. (a) p is false. **(b)** False **(c)** Yes, see line 3 of Table 2-12
13. (a) p: Mary's little lamb follows her to school. q: The lamb breaks the rules. r: Mary is sent home. $p \rightarrow (q \cap r)$ **(b)** p: Jack is nimble. q: Jack is quick. r: Jack makes it over the candlestick. $\sim(p \wedge q) \rightarrow \sim r$
(c) p: The apple hit Isaac Newton on the head. q: The laws of gravity were discovered. $\sim p \rightarrow \sim q$
14. (a) valid **(b)** valid **(c)** valid **(d)** not valid **(e)** not valid **(f)** valid
15. (a) Helen is poor. **(b)** Some freshmen are intelligent. **(c)** If I study for the final, then I will look for a teaching job. **(d)** Some pigs are not eagles. **(e)** There may exist triangles that are not equilateral.
16. (a) If a figure is a square, then it is a rectangle. **(b)** If a number is an integer, then it is a rational number. **(c)** If a figure has exactly three sides, then it may be a triangle. **(d)** If it rains, then it must be cloudy.
17. Not valid. Consider the following table.

Rain	Wet	$r \rightarrow w$
T	T	T
T	F	F
F	T	T
F	F	T

Not raining in the park corresponds to F in the first column. However both T and F in the second column make the original statement true.

Chapter Test
1. $\{x \mid x$ is a letter of the English alphabet$\}$

167

2. $\{m\}, \{a\}, \{t\}, \{h\}, \{m, a\}, \{m, t\}, \{m, h\}, \{a, t\}, \{a, h\},$ $\{t, h\}, \{m, a, t\}, \{m, a, h\}, \{a, t, h\}, \{m, t, h\}, \{m, a, t, h\},$ empty set

3. (a) $\overline{A}$ is the set of people living in Montana who are less than 30 years old. **(b)** $A \cap C$ is the set of people living in Montana who are 30 years or older and own a gun. **(c)** $A \cup B$ is the set of people living in Montana. **(d)** $\overline{C}$ is the set of people living in Montana who do not own a gun. **(e)** $\overline{A} \cap \overline{C}$ is the set of people living in Montana who do not own a gun. **(f)** $A - C$ is the set of people living in Montana who are 30 years or older and do not own a gun.

4. (a) $\{r, a, v, e\}$ **(b)** $\{e, l\}$ **(c)** $\{u, n, i, v, r\}$ **(d)** $\{r, v\}$ **(e)** $\{u, v, s\}$ **(f)** $\{a, l, e\}$ **(g)** $\{i, n\}$ **(h)** $\{e\}$ **(i)** 5 **(j)** 16

5. (a)

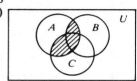

$A \cap (B \cup C)$

(b)

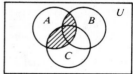

$\overline{A \cup B} \cap C$

6. (a) $\{(i, s), (i, e), (i, t), (d, s), (d, e), (d, t), (e, s), (e, e),$ $(e, t), (a, s), (a, e), (a, t)\}$ **(b)** $\{(s, s), (s, e), (s, t), (e, s),$ $(e, e), (e, t), (t, s), (t, e), (t, t)\}$ **(c)** 0 **(d)** 3

7. $2^6 - 1 = 63$

8. $t \leftrightarrow e$ There are $3 \cdot 2 \cdot 1 = 6$ different one-to-one $h \leftrightarrow n$ correspondences. $e \leftrightarrow d$

9.

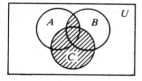

$A \cap (B \cup C) \neq (A \cap B) \cup C$

10. (a) $(A \cap C) \cup B$ **(b)** $B - C$, or $B \cap \overline{C}$

11. $(A \cap B) \cap C = \{3\} = A \cap (B \cap C); A \cup B =$ $\{1, 2, 3, 4, 5\} = B \cup A$

12. (a) F. Suppose $A = \{1\}$ and $b = \{a\}$; then $A \not\subseteq B$ and $B \not\subseteq A$. **(b)** F. It is not a proper subset of itself. **(c)** F. Suppose $A = \{1, 2\}$ and $B = \{a, b\}$; then $A \sim B$ but $A \neq B$. **(d)** F. It is an infinite set. **(e)** F. Infinite sets are equivalent to proper subsets of themselves. **(f)** F. Consider $A = \{1, 2, 3, 4, \ldots\}$ and $B = \{1, 2\}.$ $B \subseteq A$ and B is finite. **(g)** T **(h)** F. Consider $A = \{1, 2\}, B = \{a\}. A \cap B = \varnothing.$ **(i)** F. The empty set has no elements.

13.

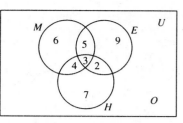

(a) 36 **(b)** 6 **(c)** 5

14. (a) This is a function from $\{a, c, e, f\}$ to $\{b, d, a, g\}$. **(b)** This is not a function, since the elements a and b are paired with more than one element. **(c)** This is a function from $\{a, b\}$ to $\{a, b\}$.

15. (a) 7 **(b)** 31 **(c)** 37

16. (a) 10 missiles **(b)** Profit = \$270 million **(c)** 35 million missiles

17. (a) $\{3, 4, 5, 6\}$ **(b)** $\{14, 29, 44, 59\}$ **(c)** $\{0, 1, 4, 9, 16\}$ **(d)** $\{5, 9, 15\}$

18. (a) $f(x) = x - 1$ **(b)** $f(x) = (-1/2)x$ **(c)** $f(x) = (-1/2)(x - 1)$ **(d)** $f(x) = (-1/2)x - 1$

19. (a) reflexive, symmetric, transitive **(b)** transitive **(c)** symmetric **(d)** none

20. (a) yes **(b)** yes **(c)** no **(d)** yes **(e)** no

21. (a) No women smoke. **(b)** $3 + 5 \neq 8$ **(c)** Some heavy metal rock is not loud. **(d)** Beethoven wrote some non-classical music.

22. (a)

p	q	$\sim q$	$p \vee (\sim q)$	$[p \vee (\sim q)] \vee p$
T	T	F	T	T
T	F	T	T	T
F	T	F	F	F
F	F	T	T	F

(b)

p	q	$\sim q$	$p \to (\sim q)$	$[p \to (\sim q)] \vee q$
T	T	F	F	T
T	F	T	T	T
F	T	F	T	T
F	F	T	T	T

(c)

p	q	$\sim q$	$p \to (\sim q)$	$[(\sim q) \to p]$	$[p \to (\sim q)] \wedge [(\sim q) \to p]$
T	T	F	F	T	F
T	F	T	T	T	T
F	T	F	T	T	T
F	F	T	T	F	F

(d)

p	q	$\sim p$	$\sim q$	$(\sim p) \vee (\sim q)$	$q \wedge p$	$[(\sim p \vee (\sim q)] \to (q \wedge p)$
T	T	F	F	F	T	T
T	F	F	T	T	F	F
F	T	T	F	T	F	F
F	F	T	T	T	F	F

23. (a) equivalent **(b)** not equivalent

24. Converse: If someone faints, we have a rock concert. Inverse: If we do not have a rock concert, no one will faint. Contrapositive: If someone does not faint, then we do not have a rock concert.

25. (a) Joe Czernyu loves Mom and apple pie.
(b) The Statue of Liberty will eventually rust.
(c) Albertina will pass Math 100.
26. p: You are fair skinned. q: You sunburn. r: You go to the dance. s: Your parents want to know why you didn't go to the dance.
$[(p \rightarrow q) \wedge (q \rightarrow \sim r) \wedge (\sim r \rightarrow s) \wedge \sim s] \rightarrow \sim p$
The argument is valid.
27. (a) valid **(b)** not valid **(c)** valid **(d)** valid

CHAPTER 3

Problem Set 3-1
1. (a) $\overline{\text{MCDXXIV}}$ **(b)** 46,032 **(c)** ▾▾ **(d)** ▲ ∩ | **(e)** ◁▷
2. (a) MCML; MCMXLVIII **(b)** $\overline{\text{MII}}$; $\overline{\text{M}}$ **(c)** M; CMXCVIII **(d)** << <▾▾; << <
(e) ▲99|; ▲9; ∩∩∩∩∩ ||||| / ∩∩∩ |||| **(f)** •• ; ••
3. (a) Use place value in columns as done in the Hindu-Arabic system. Group the numerals in each column; trade symbols and shift columns if possible. **(b)** Group all the same symbols for each number; trade if possible to make the sum using as few symbols as possible.
4. 9∩∩||| → ∩∩∩∩∩∩∩∩∩ΛΛΛΛ∩||||||||||| = ∩∩∩∩∩∩∩|||||||||
  −∩∩∩∩|||||
5. (a) CXXI **(b)** XLII **(c)** LXXXIX **(d)** $\overline{\text{V}}$CCLXXXII
6. (a) ∩∩∩∩∩ || **(b)** 9||| **(c)** ◁ ||| **(d)** ∩∩∩ ||||||
7. (a) ▾ <▾▾; ∩∩∩∩∩∩∩||; LXXII; ••
(b) 602; 999/999 ||; DCII; ••
(c) 1223; << << ▾▾▾; MCCXXIII; ••
(d) 667; <▾ ▾▾▾▾▾▾▾; 999999∩∩∩∩∩|||||||; ≡
(e) 106; ▾ <<<<▾▾▾▾▾; 9||||||; CVI
8. Answers may vary.
9. (a) Hundreds **(b)** Tens **(c)** Thousands **(d)** Hundred thousands
10. (a) 3,004,005 **(b)** 20,001 **(c)** 3,560 **(d)** 9,000,099
11. (a) 86 **(b)** 11
12. 811
13. 4,782,969
14. Assume an eight-digit display without scientific notation. **(a)** 98,765,432 **(b)** 12,345,678 **(c)** 99,999,999 **(d)** 11,111,111
15. (a) Answers vary, e.g. subtract 2020 **(b)** Answers vary, e.g. subtract 50

Brain Teaser (p. 115)
One box contains 2 nickels, one box contains 2 dimes, and one box contains a nickel and a dime. You would reach in the box labeled 15¢. If a nickel is drawn, the correct label for this box is 10¢. The 20¢ label would then be shifted to the box which was labeled 10¢ and then the 15¢ label would be placed on the remaining box. If a dime were drawn from the box labeled 15¢, then the 20¢ label would be placed on this box. Then the 10¢ label would be shifted to the box which was labeled 20¢ and the 15¢ label would be placed on the remaining box.

Problem Set 3-2
1. (a) $k = 2$ **(b)** $k = 3$
2. No. If $k = 0$, we would have $k = 0 + k$, implying $k > k$.
3. For example, let $A = \{1, 2\}$, $B = \{2, 3\}$, then $A \cup B = \{1, 2, 3\}$. Thus $n(A) = 2$, $n(B) = 2$, $n(A \cup B) = 3$, but $n(A) + n(B) = 2 + 2 = 4 \neq n(A \cup B)$.
4. (a)

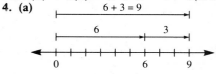

(b)

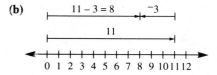

5. (a) 5 **(b)** 2 **(c)** 0, 1, 2 **(d)** 3, 4, 5, 6, . . .
6. (a) 3 **(b)** 13 **(c)** a **(d)** 0 **(e)** 3, 4, 5, 6, 7, 8, 9 **(f)** 10, 11, 12, . . .
7. (a) Yes **(b)** Yes **(c)** Yes **(d)** No, $3 + 5 \notin V$ **(e)** Yes
8. (a) $x = 119 + 213$ **(b)** $213 = x + 119$ **(c)** $213 = 119 + x$
9. (a) Commutative Property for Addition **(b)** Associative Property for Addition **(c)** Commutative Property for Addition
10. 9 pages
11. (a) 33, 38, 43 **(b)** 56, 49, 42
12. (a)

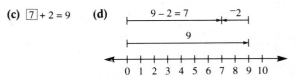

(c) $\boxed{7} + 2 = 9$ **(d)**

169

13. Answers may vary; for example, let $A = \{a, b\}$, $B = \{a, b, c, d\}$. Then $4 - 2 = n(B - A) = n(\{c, d\}) = 2$.

14. (a) For example, $5 - 3 \neq 3 - 5$ **(b)** $(7 - 5) - 1 \neq 7 - (5 - 1)$ **(c)** $4 - 0 \neq 0 - 4$ and $0 - 4 \neq 4$

15. (a) $a = b$ **(b)** If $c = 0$, then it is true for all whole number values for which $(a - b)$ is defined. **(c)** $a = 0$ **(d)** All whole number values of a, b, and c for which $(b - c)$ is meaningful.

16. 0

17. (a)

8	1	6
3	5	7
4	9	2

(b)

17	10	15
12	14	16
13	18	11

18.

8	3
4	12

19.

1	5	9
6	7	2
8	3	4

20.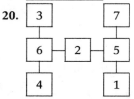

21. (a) Answers may vary **(b)** Yes, for example,

1	2
3	5
4	6

,

1	3
2	5
4	6

, or

1	4
2	5
3	6

22. 21
23. 24¢
24. 5 months
25. 45 points
26. 400
27. (a) 70 **(b)** 9000 **(c)** 1100 **(d)** 560 **(e)** 3470
28. Depends on the individual calculator.
29. Depends on the individual calculator.
30. 26
31. (a) CMLIX **(b)** XXXVIII
32. There are fewer symbols to remember and place value is used.
33. $5 \cdot 10^3 + 2 \cdot 10^2 + 8 \cdot 10^1 + 6 \cdot 1$

Brain Teaser (p. 125)
Answers may vary, for example,

1	2	3
8	9	4
7	6	5

or

9	8	7
2	1	6
3	4	5

Brain Teaser (p. 135)
Rosalie made $20 on the transaction. The best way for students to understand this problem is to use play money and act the problem out.

Problem Set 3-3
1.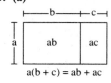

2. $35.00
3. (a) Yes **(b)** Yes **(c)** Yes **(d)** Yes **(e)** Yes **(f)** No, $2 \cdot 2 = 4$, which does not belong to the set.
4. $8 \cdot 3 = (6 + 2) \cdot 3 = 6 \cdot 3 + 2 \cdot 3 = 18 + 6 = 24$
5. (a) Commutative Property for Multiplication **(b)** Associative Property for Multiplication **(c)** Commutative Property for Addition **(d)** Zero Multiplication Property **(e)** Identity Property for Multiplication **(f)** Commutative Property for Multiplication **(g)** Distributive Property for Multiplication over Addition **(h)** Distributive Property for Multiplication over Addition
6. (a) 5 **(b)** 4 **(c)** 5 **(d)** Any whole number
7. (a) $ac + ad + bc + bd$ **(b)** $3x + 3y + 15$ **(c)** $\square \cdot \triangle + \square \cdot \bigcirc$ **(d)** $x^2 + xy + xz + yx + y^2 + yz$, or $x^2 + 2xy + xz + y^2 + yz$
8. (a) 11 **(b)** 16 **(c)** 16 **(d)** 13
9. $a(b + c + d) = a[(b + c) + d] = a(b + c) + ad = (ab + ac) + ad = ab + ac + ad$
10. Only (a).
11. (a) (i) $a^2 + ab + ba + b^2 = a^2 + 2ab + b^2$ **(ii)** 1508 **(b)** $(m + n)(x + y) = (m + n)x + (m + n)y = (mx + nx) + (my + ny) = mx + (nx + my) + ny = mx + (my + nx) + ny = mx + my + nx + ny$
12. (a) 6 **(b)** 0 **(c)** 4
13. (a)　　　　　　　　　　　　　**(b)**

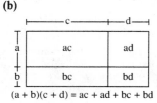

14. (a) $40 = 8 \cdot 5$ **(b)** $326 = 2 \cdot x$ **(c)** $48 = x \cdot 16$
(d) $x = 5 \cdot 17$ **(e)** $a = b \cdot c$ **(f)** $(48 - 36) = 6x$
15. (a) $2 \div 1 \neq 1 \div 2$ **(b)** $(8 \div 4) \div 2 \neq 8 \div$
$(4 \div 2)$ **(c)** $8 \div (2 + 2) \neq (8 \div 2) + (8 \div 2)$
(d) $3 \div 4 \notin W$
16. \$32
17. $(a \cdot b) \div b = a$ if and only if $a \cdot b = b \cdot a$. By the
Commutative Property for Multiplication, $a \cdot b = b \cdot a$,
for all whole numbers.
18. 2; 3 left
19. 9 minutes
20. (a)

□	△
0	34
1	26
2	18
3	10
4	2

(b) $\triangle = 66$ **(c)**

□	△
25	1
1	25

Also, $\square = 5$ and
$\triangle = 5$ if $\square = \triangle$.

21. 1 and 36   2 and 18   3 and 12   4 and 9   6 and 6
22. 12
23. 30
24. 12
25. (a) Yes **(b)** Yes **(c)** Yes, a **(d)** Yes
26. (a) 3 **(b)** 2 **(c)** 2 **(d)** 6 **(e)** 4
27. The answers depend upon the keys available on
your calculator.
(a)

$3 = 1 + 9 - 7$ $11 = 7 + 1 + \sqrt{9}$
$4 = 1^7 + \sqrt{9}$ $12 = 19 - 7$
$5 = 7 - \sqrt{9} + 1$ $13 = 91 \div 7$
$6 = 7 - 1^9$ $14 = 7(\sqrt{9} - 1)$
$7 = 7 \cdot 1^9$ $15 = 7 + 9 - 1$
$8 = 7 + 1^9$ $16 = (7 + 9) \cdot 1$
$9 = 1^7 \cdot 9$ $17 = 7 + 9 + 1$
$10 = 1^7 + 9$ $18 = \sqrt{9}(7 - 1)$
   $19 = ?$
   $20 = 7\sqrt{9} - 1$

(b) For example, $4 \cdot 4 - (4 \div 4) -$
$(4 \div 4) - (4 \div 4)$. **(c)** For example, $22 + 2$. **(d)** For
example, $111 - 11$.
28. (i) ∩∩∩∩∩∩∩IIIII **(ii)** LXXV

(iii) ▼<▼▼▼▼▼ **(iv)** ●●●

29. $3 \cdot 10^4 + 5 \cdot 10^3 + 2 \cdot 10^2 + 0 \cdot 10^1 + 6$
30. For example, $\{0, 1\}$.
31. No. For example, $5 - 2 \neq 2 - 5$.
32.

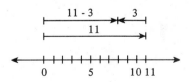

Problem Set 3-4
1. (a) $^1 3^2 7^1 8\ 9$
    $9\ 2\ 9\ 6$
    $+\ 6^3 8^1 4^8 3^5$
           $_2$
   $\overline{1\ 9\ 9\ 2\ 8}$

(b) $3\ 0^1 0\ 4$
   $+\ 9\ 8\ 7$
   $\overline{3\ 9\ 9\ 1}$

(c) $^1 5^2 2\ 4$
   $3\ 2\ 8$
   $5\ 6\ 7^2$
   $+\ 1^4 3^2 5_4$
   $\overline{1\ 5\ 5\ 4}$

2. The "scratch marks" represent the normal "carries."
3. The columns separate place value and show that
$7 + 8 = 15$ and $20 + 60 = 80$. Finally, $15 + 80 = 95$.
4. (a)
   981
  $+\ 421$
  $\overline{1402}$

(b)
   2025
   1196
  $+3148$
  $\overline{6369}$

(c)
   $1,069$
   $2,094$
   $9,546$
   $9,003$
  $+7,064$
  $\overline{28,776}$

(d)
   291
   451
  $+584$
  $\overline{1326}$

5. (a) 46,414 **(b)** 3453
(c)
   383
  -159
  $\overline{224}$

(d)
  13296
  $-\ 8309$
  $\overline{4987}$

6. (a) One possibility:
   863
  $+752$
  $\overline{1615}$

(b) One possibility:
   368
  $+257$
  $\overline{625}$

7. If only positive numbers are used: **(a)**
   876
  -235
  $\overline{641}$

(b)
   623
  -587
  $\overline{36}$

8. 15,782
9. (a) 34, 39, 44 **(b)** 82, 79, 76
10. 30¢
11. No, not all at dinner. He can have either the steak
or the salad.
12. Molly, 55 lbs; Karly, 50 lbs; Samantha, 65 lbs.
13. \$124

14. 340 cm

15. (a) (i) No, not clustered (ii) Yes, clustered around 500 **(b)** Answers vary

16. Too high

17. (a) They all sum to 265. **(b)** They all sum to 265.

(c)

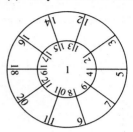

18. Answers vary

19. Answers may vary, for example,

$$
\begin{array}{r}
000 \\
770 \\
000 \\
330 \\
+011 \\
\hline
1111
\end{array}
$$

20. 8 + 8 + 8 + 88 + 888

21. (a)

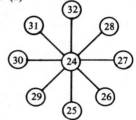

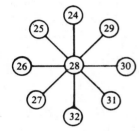

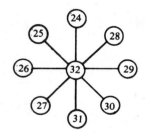

(b) 3

22. It is doubling the second number in the operation

23. (a) 34; 34; 34 **(b)** 34 **(c)** 34 **(d)** Yes **(e)** Yes

24. $5280 = 5 \cdot 10^3 + 2 \cdot 10^2 + 8 \cdot 10 + 0 \cdot 1$

25. For example, 2 + (3 + 4) = (2 + 3) + 4
$$
2 + 7 = 5 + 4 \\
9 = 9
$$

26.

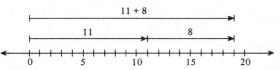

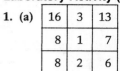

27. 1,000,410

28. (a) $a \cdot (x + 1)$ **(b)** $(3 + a) \cdot (x + y)$

29. 15

Brain Teaser (p. 154)
The license plate number is 10968.

Laboratory Activity (p. 154)

1. (a)

16	3	13
8	1	7
8	2	6

(b)

28	7	21
15	12	3
13	−5	18

Problem Set 3-5

1. (a)

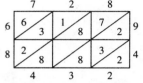

(b)

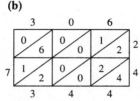

2. Diagonals separate place value as placement does in the traditional algorithm.

3. (a)

$$
\begin{array}{r}
426 \\
\times\ 783 \\
\hline
1278 \\
3408 \\
2982 \\
\hline
333558
\end{array}
$$

(b)

$$
\begin{array}{r}
327 \\
\times\ 941 \\
\hline
327 \\
1308 \\
2943 \\
\hline
307707
\end{array}
$$

4. Answers may vary.

5. (a) 5^{19} **(b)** 6^{15} **(c)** 10^{313} **(d)** 10^{12}

6. (a) 2^{100} **(b)** 2^{102}

7. 86,400; 604,800; 31,536,000 (365 Days)

8. (a)

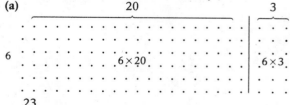

$$
\begin{array}{r}
23 \\
\times\ \ 6 \\
\hline
18\ (6 \times 3) \\
120\ (6 \times 20) \\
\hline
138
\end{array}
$$

172

(b)

20   3

10×20 10×5

8×20 8×5

```
    25
  × 18
    40   (8 × 5)
   160   (8 × 20)
    50   (10 × 5)
   200   (10 × 20)
   450
```

9. (a) $293 \cdot 476 = 139{,}468$ **(b)** Placement still indicates place value.

(c)
```
      363
   ×   84
     2904
     1452
    30492
```

10.
```
→17 ×    63        63
    8    126     +1008
    4    252      1071
    2    504
→   1   1008
```

11. (a) Let xy be the number. Then we want $(10x + y) + (10y + x)$ or $11 \cdot (x + y)$ to be close to 50. Therefore the sum we want must be a multiple of 11. 55 is the multiple of 11 closest to 50. Therefore the number could be 14, 23, 32, or 41. **(b)** By similar reasoning, the number could be 18, 27, 36, 45, 54, 63, 72, or 81.

12. (a) 21 **(b)** 355 **(c)** 304 **(d)** 164

13. (a) 22 **(b)** 190 **(c)** 7 **(d)** 39

14. (a) $15 \cdot (10 + 2) = 150 + 30 = 180$
(b) $14 \cdot (100 + 2) = 1400 + 28 = 1428$ **(c)** $30 \cdot 99 = 30(100 - 1) = 3000 - 30 = 2970$

15.
$$6 \cdot 411 = 6 \cdot (4 \cdot 10^2 + 1 \cdot 10 + 1)$$
$$= 6 \cdot (4 \cdot 10^2) + 6 \cdot (1 \cdot 10) + 6 \cdot 1$$
$$= (6 \cdot 4) \cdot 10^2 + (6 \cdot 1) \cdot 10 + 6 \cdot 1$$
$$= 24 \cdot 10^2 + 6 \cdot 10 + 6$$
$$= (2 \cdot 10 + 4) \cdot 10^2 + 6 \cdot 10 + 6$$
$$= (2 \cdot 10) \cdot 10^2 + 4 \cdot 10^2 + 6 \cdot 10 + 6$$
$$= 2 \cdot (10 \cdot 10^2) + 4 \cdot 10^2 + 6 \cdot 10 + 6$$
$$= 2 \cdot 10^3 + 4 \cdot 10^2 + 6 \cdot 10 + 6$$
$$= 2466$$

16.

a	b	$a \cdot b$	$a + b$
67	56	3752	123
32	78	2496	110
15	18	270	33

17. (a) 1332 **(b)** Jane, 330 more calories
(c) Maurice, 96 more calories
18. No, only 2352 calories
19. $60
20. 5
21. 157
22. (a) 77 remainder 7 **(b)** 8 remainder 10 **(c)** 10 remainder 91
23. (a) $3\overline{)876}$ **(b)** $8\overline{)367}$
24. (a) Monthly payments are more expensive.
(b) $3,700
25. She will finish on the eleventh day.
26. 65,536 bits
27. 3
28. 16 cars
29.

2	11
4	15
0	7
6	19
12	31

30. (f) Yes, suppose the 3 numbers are a, b, and c. The 6 different numbers are

```
 ab
 ac
 bc
 bd
 cb
+cd
```
The sum is $2(a + b + c) \cdot 10 + 2(a + b + c) = (a + b + c) \cdot 22$. Now if we divide by $(a + b + c)$, we always obtain 22.

31. (b) If $ab \cdot cd = ba \cdot dc$ then $ac = bd$
32. 1022
33. (a)
```
   763
 ×   8
  6104
```
(b)
```
   678
 ×   3
  2034
```

173

34. (a)
```
    762
  ×  83
 63,246
```
(b)
```
    378
  ×  26
  9,828
```

35. 7,500,000 cows

36. (a)
```
     37
   × 43
    111
   1480
   1591
```
(b)
```
     93
   × 36
    558
   2790
   3348
```
(c)
```
      13
  9)123
    − 9
     33
    −27
      6
```

37. (a) 1; 121; 12,321; 1,234,321; your calculator may not produce the pattern after this term, but it continues through 111,111,111 × 111,111,111. **(b)** 9801, 998001, 99980001, 9999800001, 999998000001

38. $60; $3600; $86,400; $604,800; $2,592,000 (30 days); $31,536,000 (365 days); $630,720,000 (aproximately)

39. 19

40. 999999∩∩∩∩∩∩∩IIIII

41. 300,260

42. For example, $3 + 0 = 3 = 0 + 3$.

43. (a) $x \cdot (a + b + 2)$ **(b)** $(3 + x)(a + b)$

44. 6979

45. 724

Brain Teaser (p. 165)
```
   570,140
  ×      6
 3,420,840
```

Problem Set 3-6

1. (a) $(1, 10, 11, 100, 101, 110, 111, 1000, 1001, 1010, 1011, 1100, 1101, 1110, 1111)_{two}$
(b) $(1, 2, 10, 11, 12, 20, 21, 22, 100, 101, 102, 110, 111, 112, 120)_{three}$
(c) $(1, 2, 3, 10, 11, 12, 13, 20, 21, 22, 23, 30, 31, 32, 33)_{four}$
(d) $(1, 2, 3, 4, 5, 6, 7, 10, 11, 12, 13, 14, 15, 16, 17)_{eight}$

2. 20

3. $2032_{four} = (2 \cdot 10^3 + 0 \cdot 10^2 + 3 \cdot 10 + 2)_{four} = 2 \cdot 4^3 + 0 \cdot 4^2 + 3 \cdot 4 + 2$

4. (a) 111_{two} **(b)** 555_{six} **(c)** 999_{ten} **(d)** EEE_{twelve}

5. (a) ETE_{twelve}; $EE1_{twelve}$ **(b)** 11111_{two}; 100001_{two}
(c) 554_{six}; 1000_{six} **(d)** 66_{seven}; 101_{seven} **(e)** 444_{five}; 1001_{five} **(f)** 101_{two}; 111_{two}

6. (a) There is no numeral 4 in base four. **(b)** There are no numerals 6 or 7 in base 5. **(c)** There is no numeral T in base three.

7. (a) 3212_{five} **(b)** 1177_{twelve} **(c)** 12110_{four}
(d) 100101_{two} **(e)** 1431304_{five} **(f)** $1E3T4_{twelve}$
(g) $9000E0_{twelve}$

8. 100010_{two}

9. (a) 117 **(b)** 45 **(c)** 1331 **(d)** 1451 **(e)** 157
(f) 181 **(g)** 211 **(h)** 194

10. 72¢; 242_{five}

11. 1 prize of $625, 2 prizes of $125, and 1 of $25.

12. 3 quarters, 4 nickels, and 2 pennies.

13. (a) 8 weeks, 2 days **(b)** 4 years, 6 months **(c)** 1 day, 5 hours **(d)** 5 feet, 8 inches

14. $E66_{twelve}$; 1662

15. (a) 6 **(b)** 1 **(c)** 9

16. 1 hour 34 minutes 15 seconds

17. 4; 1, 2, 4, 8; 1, 2, 4, 8, 16

18. 9 (4 quarters 3 nickels 2 pennies); 73 pennies

19. (a) 121_{five} **(b)** 20_{five} **(c)** 1010_{five} **(d)** 14_{five}
(e) 1001_{two} **(f)** 1010_{two}

20.

+	0	1	2	3	4	5	6	7
0	0	1	2	3	4	5	6	7
1	1	2	3	4	5	6	7	10
2	2	3	4	5	6	7	10	11
3	3	4	5	6	7	10	11	12
4	4	5	6	7	10	11	12	13
5	5	6	7	10	11	12	13	14
6	6	7	10	11	12	13	14	15
7	7	10	11	12	13	14	15	16

Base eight

·	0	1	2	3	4	5	6	7
0	0	0	0	0	0	0	0	0
1	0	1	2	3	4	5	6	7
2	0	2	4	6	10	12	14	16
3	0	3	6	11	14	17	22	25
4	0	4	10	14	20	24	30	34
5	0	5	12	17	24	31	36	43
6	0	6	14	22	30	36	44	52
7	0	7	16	25	34	43	52	61

Base eight

21. (a) 9 hours 33 minutes 25 seconds **(b)** 1 hour 39 minutes 40 seconds

22. (a) 2 quarts, 1 pint, 0 cups, or 1 half-gallon, 0 quarts, 1 pint, 0 cups **(b)** 1 pint, 0 cups
(c) 2 quarts, 1 pint, 1 cup

23.
```
   ³3̸ 2
   1¹3̸
   2 2⁰
   4 3̸
   2³3⁰
   1⁰2̸
        ⁰
  ─────────
   3 1 0_five
```

24. (a) 3 gross 10 dozen 9 ones **(b)** 6 gross 3 dozen 4 ones

25. (a) 22 students on Tuesday; **(b)** 1 gal., 1 half-gallon, 1 qt., 1 pint, and 1 cup

26. (a) 70 **(b)** 87

27. There is no numeral 5 in base five; $2_{five} + 3_{five} = 10_{five}$.

28. (a)
```
    231_five
  +  22_five
    303_five
```
(b)
```
   20010_three
  − 2022_three
   10211_three
```

29. (a) 233_{five} **(b)** 4_{five} remainder 1_{five} **(c)** 2144_{five}
(d) 31_{five} **(e)** 67_{eight} **(f)** 15_{eight} remainder 3_{eight}
(g) 110_{two} **(h)** 1101110_{two}

30. (a) Nine **(b)** Four **(c)** Six **(d)** Any base greater than or equal to 2.

31. 30221_{five}

32. (a) $10040T0_{twelve}$ **(b)** 8400000_{twelve}

Laboratory Activity (p. 175)

1. (a) A computer
2. When a person tells his or her age by listing cards, the person is giving the base two representation for his or her age. The number can then be determined by adding the numbers in the upper left-hand corners of the named cards.

Chapter Test

1. (a) 400,044 (b) 117 (c) 1704 (d) 11 (e) 1448
2. (a) CMXCIX (b) ∩∩∩∩∩∩∩∩||||| (c)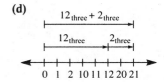

(d) 2341_{five} (e) 1000_{twelve} (f) 11011_{two} (g) 1241_{nine}
(h) 1011_{two}
3. (a) 3^{17} (b) 2^{21} (c) 3^5 (d) 2^{82}
4. (a) Distributive Property for Multiplication over Addition (b) Commutative Property for Addition (c) Identity Property for Multiplication (d) Distributive Property for Multiplication over Addition (e) Commutative Property for Multiplication (f) Associative Property for Multiplication
5. (a) $3 < 13$, since $3 + 10 = 13$ (b) $12 > 9$, since $12 = 9 + 3$
6. $1000 \cdot 438 = 10^3(4 \cdot 10^2 + 8 \cdot 10 + 3)$
$= 4 \cdot 10^5 + 8 \cdot 10^4 + 3 \cdot 10^3$
$= 4 \cdot 10^5 + 8 \cdot 10^4 + 3 \cdot 10^3 + 0 \cdot 10^2$
$+ 0 \cdot 10^1 + 0 \cdot 1$
$= 483,000$
7. (a) 1119 (b) $173E_{twelve}$
8. (a) 60,074 (b) 14150_{eight}
9. (a) 5 remainder 243 (b) 91 remainder 10
(c) 120_{five} remainder 2_{five} (d) 11_{two} remainder 10_{two}
10. (a) $5 \cdot 912 + 243 = 4803$ (b) $91 \cdot 11 + 10 =$ 1011 (c) $23_{five} \cdot 120_{five} + 2_{five} = 3312_{five}$
(d) $11_{two} \cdot 11_{two} + 10_{two} = 1011_{two}$
11. (a) tens (b) thousands (c) hundreds
12. (a) 9, 10, 11, 12, 13, 14, 15 (b) 10 (c) All whole numbers (d) 0, 1, 2, . . . , 26
13. (a)

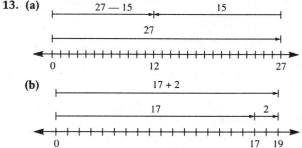

(b)

(c)

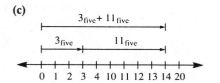

(d)

14. (a) $15a$ (b) $5x^2$ (c) $xa + xb + xy$
(d) $(x + 5)(3 + y)$
15. (a) Addition, 25 (b) Division, 8
(c) Multiplication, 72 (d) Subtraction, $26
16. $395
17. $4380
18. 2600
19. $3842
20. Several answers are possible. For example,

296	569
+541	+214
837	783

21. 69 miles
22. 40 cans
23. 12 outfits
24.

+	5	7	9
8	13	15	17
11	16	18	20
21	26	28	30

25. 26
26. $2.16
27. $6000 vs. $6400
28. There are 36 bikes and 18 trikes
29. $900E000T_{twelve}$

CHAPTER 4

Problem Set 4-1

1. (a) $^-2$ (b) 5 (c) ^-m (d) 0 (e) m (f) $^-(a + b)$ or $^-a + ^-b$
2. (a) 2 (b) m (c) 0
3. (a) 5 (5) 10 (c) $^-5$ (d) $^-5$

4. (a)

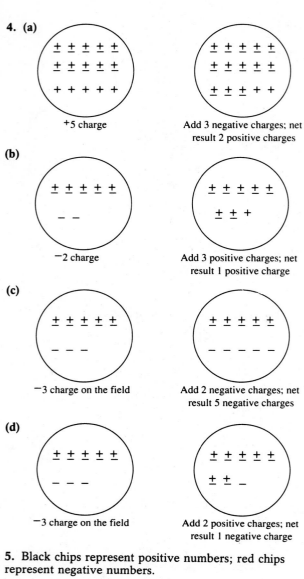

+5 charge

Add 3 negative charges; net result 2 positive charges

(b)

−2 charge

Add 3 positive charges; net result 1 positive charge

(c)

−3 charge on the field

Add 2 negative charges; net result 5 negative charges

(d)

−3 charge on the field

Add 2 positive charges; net result 1 negative charge

5. Black chips represent positive numbers; red chips represent negative numbers.

(a)

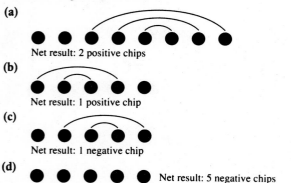

Net result: 2 positive chips

(b)

Net result: 1 positive chip

(c)

Net result: 1 negative chip

(d)

Net result: 5 negative chips

6. (a)

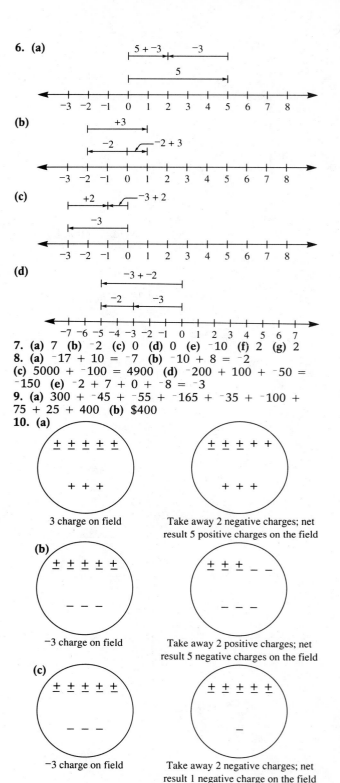

7. (a) 7 **(b)** ⁻2 **(c)** 0 **(d)** 0 **(e)** ⁻10 **(f)** 2 **(g)** 2

8. (a) ⁻17 + 10 = ⁻7 **(b)** ⁻10 + 8 = ⁻2
(c) 5000 + ⁻100 = 4900 **(d)** ⁻200 + 100 + ⁻50 = ⁻150 **(e)** ⁻2 + 7 + 0 + ⁻8 = ⁻3

9. (a) 300 + ⁻45 + ⁻55 + ⁻165 + ⁻35 + ⁻100 + 75 + 25 + 400 **(b)** \$400

10. (a)

3 charge on field

Take away 2 negative charges; net result 5 positive charges on the field

(b)

−3 charge on field

Take away 2 positive charges; net result 5 negative charges on the field

(c)

−3 charge on field

Take away 2 negative charges; net result 1 negative charge on the field

176

11. (a)

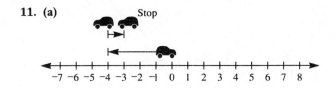

(b)

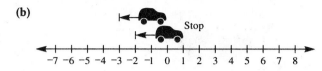

12. (a) $^-4 - 2 = ^-6$; $^-4 - 1 = ^-5$; $^-4 - 0 = ^-4$; $^-4 - ^-1 = ^-3$ **(b)** $3 - 1 = 2$; $2 - 1 = 1$; $1 - 1 = 0$; $0 - 1 = ^-1$; $^-1 - 1 = ^-2$; $^-2 - 1 = ^-3$

13. (a) $^-9$ **(b)** $^-10$ **(c)** 13 **(d)** $^-4$

14. (a) $^-9$ **(b)** 3 **(c)** 1 **(d)** $^-19$ **(e)** $^-13$ **(f)** $^-6$

15. (a) Yes **(b)** Yes

16. (a) $1 + 4x$ **(b)** $2x + y$ **(c)** $x - 2$

17. (a) All negative integers **(b)** All positive integers **(c)** All integers less than $^-1$ **(d)** 2 or $^-2$ **(e)** There are none. **(f)** All integers except 0 **(g)** There are none.

18. 783 B.C.

19. (a) I **(b)** W **(c)** $I - \{0\}$ **(d)** $\varnothing$ **(e)** $\varnothing$ **(f)** I^- **(g)** $\{0\}$ **(h)** W **(i)** I

20.

2	-13	8
5	-1	-7
-10	11	-4

21.

	6	4	
2	8	1	7
	5	3	

22. 33

23. (a) 59 **(b)** $^-269$ **(c)** 192 **(d)** Mileposts 56 or 80

24. (a) 0 **(b)** $^-101$ **(c)** 1 **(d)** $^-4$

25. (a) 9 **(b)** 2 **(c)** 0 or 2 **(d)** The set of all integers greater than or equal to 0

26. (a) All nonnegative integers **(b)** (i) 5 (ii) 5 (iii) 0 (iv) $^-7$

27. (a) $^-14$ **(b)** $^-24$ **(c)** 2 **(d)** 5

28. (a) $^-18$ **(b)** $^-106$ **(c)** $^-6$ **(d)** 22 **(e)** $^-11$ **(f)** 2 **(g)** $^-18$ **(h)** 23

29. (a) True **(b)** True **(c)** True **(d)** True **(e)** False; let $x = ^-1$ **(f)** False; let $x = ^-1$

Brain Teaser (p. 197)

$123 - 45 - 67 + 89 = 100$

Brain Teaser (p. 204)

Answers may vary.

$1 = 4^4/4^4$
$2 = (4 \cdot 4)/(4 \cdot 4)$
$3 = 4 - (4/4)^4$
$4 = [(4 - 4)/4] + 4$
$5 = 4 + 4^{(4 - 4)}$
$6 = 4 + [4 + 4)/4]$
$7 = (44/4) - 4$
$8 = 4 \cdot 4/4 \cdot 4$
$9 = 4 + 4 + 4/4$
$10 = (44 - 4)/4$

Problem Set 4-2

1. $3(^-1) = ^-1 + ^-1 + ^-1 = ^-3$; $2(^-1) = ^-1 + ^-1 = ^-2$; $1(^-1) = ^-1$; $0(^-1) = 0$; $^-1(^-1) = 1$ by continuing the pattern

2.

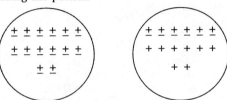

0 charge   Take away four groups of two negative charges; net result is eight positive charges.

3.

If you are now at 0 moving west at 4 km/h, you will be at 8 km west of 0 two hours from now.

4. (a) 12 **(b)** $^-15$ **(c)** $^-15$ **(d)** 0 **(e)** 30 **(f)** $^-30$ **(g)** 0 **(h)** 16

5. (a) 5 **(b)** $^-13$ **(c)** $^-11$ **(d)** 0 **(e)** Impossible; division by 0 is not defined **(f)** Impossible; division by 0 is not defined

6. (a) $^-10$ **(b)** $^-40$ **(c)** a; $b \neq 0$ or the division is not defined **(d)** $^-10$ **(e)** a; $b \neq 0$ or the division is not defined **(f)** $^-32$ **(g)** $^-5$ **(h)** 0 **(i)** Impossible **(j)** $^-4$ **(k)** Impossible **(l)** 13 **(m)** $^-1$ **(n)** $^-2$

7. (a) $4(^-11) = ^-44$ **(b)** 6 yd

8. $^-15°C$

9. 132,000 acres

10. (a) $^-1(^-5 + ^-2) = ^-1 \cdot ^-5 + ^-1 \cdot ^-2$ **(b)** $^-3(^-3 + 2) = ^-3 \cdot ^-3 + ^-3 \cdot 2$ **(c)** $^-5(2 + ^-6) = ^-5 \cdot 2 + ^-5 \cdot ^-6$

11. (a) $12/(^-2 + 4) \neq 12/^-2 + 12/4$ since $6 \neq ^-3$ **(b)** $^-20/(4 + ^-5) \neq ^-20/4 + ^-20/^-5$ since $20 \neq ^-1$ **(c)** $^-10/(1 + 1) \neq ^-10/1 + ^-10/1$ since $^-5 \neq ^-20$

12. (a) Yes **(b)** Yes **(c)** Yes **(d)** Yes

13. (a) $^-8$ **(b)** 16 **(c)** $^-1000$ **(d)** 81 **(e)** 1 **(f)** $^-1$ **(g)** 1 **(h)** $^-1$

14. (a) 12 **(b)** 0 **(c)** $^-5$ **(d)** 19 **(e)** 9 **(f)** $^-9$ **(g)** $^-13$ **(h)** $^-8$ **(i)** $^-32$ **(j)** $^-16$

15. (a) and (f) are always negative; (b), (c), (g), and (h) are always positive.

16. (b) and (c); (d) and (e); (g) and (h)

17. (a) xy (b) $2xy$ (c) 0 (d) ^-x (e) $x + 2y$ (f) b (g) x (h) y

18. (a) $^-13, ^-17, ^-21$ (b) $^-12, ^-14, ^-16$ (c) $^-9, 3, ^-1$ (d) $^-5, ^-2, 1$

19. (a) $^-2$ (b) 2 (c) 0 (d) $^-6$ (e) $^-36$ (f) 6 (g) All integers except 0 (h) All integers except 0 (i) No solution is possible with integers. (j) 3 or $^-3$ (k) No solution is possible with integers. (l) All integers except 0 (m) All integers except 0 (n) All integers (o) All integers

20. (a) $^-2x + 2$ (b) $^-2x + 2y$ (c) $x^2 - xy$ (d) $^-x^2 + xy$ (e) $^-2x - 2y + 2z$ (f) $^-x^2 + xy + 3x$ (g) $^-25 - 10x - x^2$ (h) $x^2 - y^2 - 1 - 2y$ (i) $^-x^4 + 3x^2 - 2$

21. (a) $(50 + 2)(50 - 2) = 2496$ (b) $5^2 - 100^2 = ^-9975$ (c) $x^2 - y^2$ (d) $4 - 9x^2$ (e) $x^2 - 1$ (f) $(213 - 13)(213 + 13) = 200 \cdot 226 = 45,200$

22. No; it is not of the form $(a - b)(a + b)$.

23. (a) $(3 + 5)x = 8x$ (b) $(a + 2)x$ (c) $x(y + 1)$ (d) $(a - 2)x$ (e) $x(x + y)$ (f) $(3 - 4 + 7)x = 6x$ (g) $(3y + 2 - z)x$ (h) $(3x + y - 1)x$ (i) $a(bc + b - 1)$ (j) $(a + b)(c + 1 - 1) = (a + b)c = ac + bc$ (k) $(4 - a)(4 + a)$ (l) $(x - 3y)(x + 3y)$ (m) $(2x - 5y)(2x + 5y)$ (n) $(x + y)(x - y + 1)$

24. (a) Commutative Property of Multiplication (b) Closure Property of Addition (c) Associative Property of Multiplication (d) Distributive Property of Multiplication over Addition

25. (a) False (b) True (c) True (d) True

26. (a) The sums are 9 times the middle number.
(b) Let x be the first number. Then we have the following 9 numbers:

$$
\begin{array}{ccc}
x & x + 1 & x + 2 \\
x + 7 & x + 8 & x + 9 \\
x + 14 & x + 15 & x + 16
\end{array}
$$

The sum of these numbers is $9x + 72$ or $9(x + 8)$ which is 9 times the middle number.

27. (a) The additive inverse of $^-(ab)$ is ab. Also, $(^-a)b + ab = [(^-a) + a]b = 0 \cdot b = 0$. Thus, the additive inverse of $(^-a)b$ is also ab. Hence, by the uniqueness of additive inverses, $(^-ab) = ^-(ab)$. (b) The additive inverse of ab is $^-(ab)$, or $(^-a)b$ by part (a). Also, $(^-a)b + (^-a)(^-b) = (^-a) \cdot 0 = 0$. Thus, the additive inverse of $(^-a)(^-b)$ is also $(^-a)b$. Hence, by the uniqueness of additive inverses, $ab = (^-a)(^-b)$. (c) The additive inverse of $^-(a + b)$ is $a + b$. Also,

$$
\begin{aligned}
(^-a + {}^-b) + (a + b) &= {}^-a + (^-b + a) + b \\
&= {}^-a + (a + {}^-b) + b \\
&= (^-a + a) + (^-b + b) \\
&= 0 + 0 \\
&= 0
\end{aligned}
$$

Thus, the additive inverse of $(^-a + {}^-b)$ is also $a + b$. Hence, by the uniqueness of additive inverses, $^-(a + b) = {}^-a + {}^-b$.

28. (a) $^-81$ (b) 184 (c) $^-2$ (d) 2

29. (a) $^-3$ (b) 1 (c) 13 (d) 3 (e) $^-3$ (f) $^-13$

30.

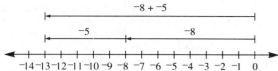

31. (a) 5 (b) $^-7$ (c) 0

32. (a) 14 (b) 21 (c) $^-4$ (d) 22

33. 400 lb

Brain Teaser (p. 206)
0 because $(x - x) = 0$.

Brain Teaser (p. 220)
The part of the explanation that is incorrect is the division by $e - a - d$ which is equal to 0. Division by 0 is impossible.

Problem Set 4-3

1. (a) $^-20, ^-13, ^-5, ^-3, 0, 4$ (b) $^-6, ^-5, 0, 5, 6$ (c) $^-100, ^-20, ^-15, ^-13, 0$ (d) $^-3, ^-2, 5$ 13

2. (a) $^-5 + 2 = ^-3$ (b) $^-6 + 6 = 0$ (c) $^-10 + 2 = ^-8$ (d) $^-5 + 9 = 4$

3. (a) $^-18$ (b) $x > ^-18$ and x is an integer (c) 18 (d) $x < 18$ and x is and integer (e) $^-18$ (f) $x \le ^-18$, and x is an integer (g) $^-7$ (h) $x < ^-7$ and x is an integer (i) $^-2$ (j) $x \ge ^-2$ and x is an integer (k) $^-1$ (l) $x < ^-1$ and x is an integer (m) $^-2$ (n) $x < ^-3$ and x is an integer

4. (a) True (b) False (c) True (d) True (e) True (f) False

5. (a) $1, ^-2, 0$ (b) 9 (c) $^-6, ^-7$ (d) $^-3, ^-2, ^-1, 0, 1, 2, 3$

6. (a) $^-3$ (b) 0 (c) 1 (d) 0

7. (a) $n - 6$ or $6 - n$ (b) $n + 14$ (c) $4n - 7$ (d) $8 + 3n$ (e) $n + 10$ (f) $4n$ (g) $13 - n$ (h) $n - 4$

8. The area of North America is 6,942,000 mi^2; the area of South America is 5,756,000 mi^2; the area of Europe is 2,559,000 mi^2, the area of Asia is 14,866,000 mi^2.

9. Tom is older than 11.

10. $^-5$

11. Rick has $100; David has $300.

12. Nureet is 10; Ran is 14.

13. Let x be the distance from B to A. Point A is twice as far from point C as point B is from point A can be translated as "point A is $2x$ from point C and point B is x from point A." From this information, we can infer that the distance from B to C is also x. The distance from B to C in 5 in. Hence, the distance from A to C is 10 in.

14. Factory A produces 2800; B produces 1400; C produces 3100.

15. 40 lb of $.60-per-pound tea and 60 lb of $.45-per-pound tea

16. 524

17. 78, 79, and 80

18. 78, 80, and 82

19. 14, 7

20. Eldest, $30,000; middle, $24,000; youngest, $10,000

21. (a) Yes. $x^2 + y^2 \geq 2xy$ if and only if $x^2 - 2xy + y^2 \geq 0$ and $x^2 - 2xy + y^2 = (x - y)^2 \geq 0$. **(b)** $x = y$

22. Proof: $0 < a < b$ implies that $0 < a$ and $0 < b$. Now $a < b$ and $0 < a$ imply $a^2 < ab$. Also $a < b$ and $0 < b$ imply $ab < b^2$. Hence $a^2 < b^2$.

23. No; $^-5 < 2$, but $(^-5)^2 > 2^2$.

24. Proof: $a < b$ implies $^-a > ^-b$. Hence $c + ^-a > c + ^-b$, or $c - a > c - b$.

25. (a) $^-3, ^-2, ^-1, 0, 1$ **(b)** $^-2, ^-3, ^-4, \ldots$

26. (a) 7 **(b)** $^-5$ **(c)** $^-3$ **(d)** $^-10$

27. (a) $^-10$ **(b)** 4 **(c)** $^-4$ **(d)** 10 **(e)** $^-21$ **(f)** 21 **(g)** $^-4$ **(h)** $^-3$ **(i)** 3 **(j)** $^-4$ **(k)** 7 **(l)** $^-21$ **(m)** 21 **(n)** 56 **(o)** 15 **(p)** $^-1$

28.

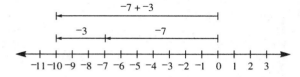

Chapter 4 Test

1. (a) $^-3$ **(b)** a **(c)** 0 **(d)** $^-x + ^-y$ **(e)** $x + ^-y$ **(f)** 32 **(g)** 32 **(h)** $^-16$

2. (a) $^-7$ **(b)** 8 **(c)** 8 **(d)** 0 **(e)** 8 **(f)** 15

3. (a) 3 **(b)** $^-5$ **(c)** Any integer except 0 **(d)** No integer will work **(e)** $^-41$ **(f)** Any integer

4. $2(^-3) = ^-3 + ^-3 = ^-6; 1(^-3) = ^-3; 0(^-3) = 0; ^-1(^-3) = 3; ^-2(^-3) = 6$

5. (a)
$$\begin{aligned}(x - y)(x + y) &= (x - y)x + (x - y)y \\ &= x^2 - yx + xy - y^2 \\ &= x^2 - xy + xy - y^2 \\ &= x^2 - y^2\end{aligned}$$
(b) $4 - x^2$

6. (a) ^-x **(b)** $^-x + y$ **(c)** $3x - 1$ **(d)** $2x^2$ **(e)** 0 **(f)** $^-9 - 6x - x^2$

7. (a) $x(1 - 3) = ^-2x$ **(b)** $x(x + 1)$ **(c)** $(x - 6)(x + 6)$ **(d)** $(9y^3 - 4x^2)(9y^3 + 4x^2)$ **(e)** $5(1 + x)$ **(f)** $(x - y)(x + 1 - 1) = (x - y)x$

8. (a) $^-2$ **(b)** 5 or $^-5$ **(c)** x is any non-negative integer **(d)** $^-3, ^-4, ^-5, ^-6, \ldots$

9. (a) False **(b)** False **(c)** False **(d)** True **(e)** False

10. (a) $2/1 \neq 1/2$ **(b)** $3 - (4 - 5) \neq (3 - 4) - 5$ **(c)** $1/2 \notin I$ **(d)** $8/(4 - 2) \neq 8/4 - 8/2$

---

11. (a)

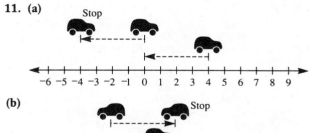

(b)

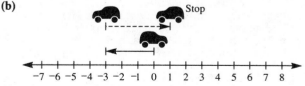

(c) If you are at 0, moving west at 3 km/h, you were 12 km east of 0 four hours ago.

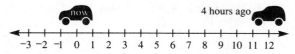

12. $^-7°C$

13. 14 lb

14. 35 1-kg packages and 115 2-kg packages

15. 7 nickels and 17 dimes

16. 1010 seniors, 895 juniors, 2020 sophomores, and 1790 freshmen

17. 42 gallons

CHAPTER 5

Problem Set 5-1

1. (a) T **(b)** T **(c)** T **(d)** T **(e)** T **(f)** F

2. (a) $7|(14 + 21)$ or $7|35$ **(b)** $d|(213 - 57 + 57)$, or $d|213$ **(c)** $d|(a - b + b)$, or $a|a$

3. (a) $7|217$ **(b)** $d|213$ **(c)** $d|a$

4. Yes. $9 \nmid 1379$

5. No

6. (a) Theorem 5-3 **(b)** Theorem 5-1(b) **(c)** None **(d)** Theorem 5-1(b) **(e)** Theorem 5-3

7. (a) No, since $17|34000$ and $17 \nmid 15$ **(b)** Yes, since $17|34000$ and $17|51$ **(c)** No, since $19|19000$ and $19 \nmid 31$ **(d)** No, since $31 \nmid 19000$ and $31|31$. **(e)** No, since $2^{14}|2^{64}$ and $2^{14} \nmid 1$ **(f)** No, since 2, 3, 5, 7, 13, and 17 divide $2 \cdot 3 \cdot 5 \cdot 7 \cdot 13 \cdot 17$ but none of these numbers divides 1

8. (a) F. $5|(2 + 3)$, but $5 \nmid 2$ and $5 \nmid 3$. **(b)** F. $5|(2 + 3)$, but $5 \nmid 2$ and $5 \nmid 3$. **(c)** T. Use Theorem 5-3. **(d)** F. $6|2 \cdot 3$, but $6 \nmid 2$ and $6 \nmid 3$. **(e)** T. $ab|c$ means $abx = c$ for some integer x or $a \cdot (bx) = c$, which in turn means $a|c$. Similarly, $b|c$. **(f)** T. $1 \cdot a = a$ for all integers a. **(g)** T. Since it is given that $d \neq 0$. $0 = d \cdot 0$. **(h)** F. $-1|1$ and $1|-1$, yet $1 \neq -1$. **(i)** T. **(j)** F. $3 \nmid 7$ and $3 \nmid 5$, yet $3|(7 + 5) = 12$ **(k)** F. $9|6^2$ yet $9 \nmid 6$ **(l)** F. $9 \nmid 6$, yet $9|6^2$ **(m)** T

9. (a) 5 (b) 0
10. (a) T (b) F (c) F (d) T (e) T (f) F (g) T
11. (a) Always (b) Sometimes (c) Sometimes
(d) Always (e) Sometimes (f) Sometimes
(g) Always
12. (a) A number N is divisible by 16 if and only if the number formed by the last 4 digits is divisible by 16. (b) A number N is divisible by 25 if and only if the number formed by the last two digits is divisible by 25.
13. A number is divisible by 12 if and only if the number is divisible by 3 and 4. A number is divisible by 15 if and only if the number is divisible by both 3 and 5.
14. Yes.
15. $0.19
16. 85,041
17. (a) Divisible by 2, 3, 4, 6, 11, 12 (b) Divisible by 2, 3, 6, 9 (c) Divisible by 2, 3, 5, 6, 10, 15 (d) Divisible by 2, 3, 4, 6, 12 (e) Divisible by 3, 5, 15 (f) Divisible by 2, 4 (g) Divisible by 7, 11 (h) None (i) Divisible by 2, 4, 5, 10
18. (a) No. Suppose that the number is divisible by 10; then it must be divisible by 5, a contradiction. (b) Yes. For example, $10 \nmid 5$, but $5 \mid 5$
19. (a) 747 (b) 83,745 (c) 6655
20. Because each digit, except 0, appears three times, 3 divides the sums of all like digits. Also $3 \mid 0$, so that 3 divides the sum of all digits.
21. $a \mid b$ implies $a \cdot m = b$ for some integer m. $b \mid c$ implies $b \cdot n = c$ for some integer n. Substituting am for b, we have $(am)n = c$, or $a(mn) = c$. Therefore, $a \mid c$.
22. (a) Yes (b) No (c) Yes (d) Yes
23. (a) Every 4-digit palindrome is in the form $xyyx$. The divisibility text for 11 always yields 0 which is divisible by 11. Thus, the palindrome is divisible by 11. (c) No, for example, $11 \nmid 12321$. (d) Every 6-digit palindrome is in the form $xyzzyx$. The divisibility text for 11 always yields 0 which is divisible by 11. Thus, the palindrome is divisible by 11.
24. (a) The difference is always equal to 9. (b) The difference is always equal to 2×9 or 18. (c) Let ab be a 2-digit number. Then $ab - ba = (10a + b) - (10b - a) = 9a - 9b = 9(a - b)$. Since $a, b \in I$, then $9 \mid (ab - ba)$. (d) The difference is always a multiple of 9.
25. $3 \mid 6$ and $3 \mid 15$, yet $3 \nmid 286$, so there is no solution.
26. Only (a), (b), (c) and (e) can be shown not to have solutions. Justification: (a) Since $9 \mid 18$ and $9 \mid 27$, yet $9 \nmid 3111$ (b) Since $2 \mid 2$ and $2 \mid 6$, yet $2 \nmid 113$ (c) Since $5 \mid 10$ and $5 \mid 25$, yet $5 \nmid 1007$ (e) Since $4 \mid 8$ and $4 \mid 108$, yet $4 \nmid 4001$
27. (a) Any integer can be written as $3q$, $3q + 1$, or $3q + 2$ where $q \in I$. If $n = 3q$ then $3 \mid n$. If $n = 3q + 1$ then $n + 1 = 3p + 2$, $n + 2 = 3p + 3$ and hence $3 \mid n + 2$. If $n = 3p + 2$ then $n + 1 = 3q + 3$ and hence $3 \mid n + 1$. (b) Among any n consecutive integers there is always one that is divisible by n.

28. (a) $d \mid a$ means $dx = a$, where $x \in I$. Suppose $d \mid (a + b)$. Then $dy = a + b$, where $y \in I$. Hence, $dy - dx = a + b - a$ and $dy - dx = b$, or $d \cdot (y - x) = b$. Thus $d \mid b$, which is a contradiction. Therefore, $d \nmid (a + b)$. (b) $d \nmid b$ implies $d \nmid (-b)$; then use Theorem 5-1, part b.
29. Let $N = a_4 \cdot 10^4 + a_3 \cdot 10^3 + a_2 \cdot 10^2 + a_1 \cdot 10^1 + a_0$.
$9 \mid 9$ implies $9 \mid 9a_1$
$9 \mid 99$ implies $9 \mid 99a_2$
$9 \mid 999$ implies $9 \mid 999a_3$
$9 \mid 9999$ implies $9 \mid 9999a_4$
Thus $9 \mid (9999a_4 + 999a_3 + 99a_2 + 9a_1)$. Because $N = (9999a_4 + a_4) + (999a_3 + a_3) + (99a_2) + (9a_1 + a_1) + a_0$, then $9 \mid [[9999a_4 + 999a_3 + 99a_2 + 9a_1) + (a_4 + a_3 + a_2 + a_1 + a_0)]$ if and only if $9 \mid (a_4 + a_3 + a_2 + a_1 + a_0)$
30. 243; Yes; $7 \cdot 11 \cdot 13 = 1001$ and any number of the form $abcabc$ is divisible by 1001.
31. 11-$50 checks and 3-$20 checks

Brain Teaser (p. 238)
The number is 381-65-4729.

Problem Set 5-2
1. (a) $504 = 2^3 \cdot 3^2 \cdot 7$ (b) $2475 = 3^2 \cdot 5^2 \cdot 11$ (c) $11,250 = 2 \cdot 3^2 \cdot 5^4$
2. (a) Yes (b) No (c) Yes (d) Yes (e) Yes (f) No
3. 73
4. The greatest prime whose square is less than 50 is 7. That is the greatest one which must be checked.
5. 53, 59, 61, 67, 71, 73, 79, 83, 89, 97, 101, 103, 107, 109, 113, 127, 131, 137, 139, 149, 151, 157, 163, 167, 173, 179, 181, 191, 193, 197, 199
6. 90
7. (a) $1 \cdot 48$; $2 \cdot 24$; $3 \cdot 16$; $4 \cdot 12$ (b) Only one; $1 \cdot 47$
8. Yes; 59 groups of 3 or 3 groups of 59.
9. (a) 3, 5, 15, or 29 members (b) 145 committees of 3; 87 committees of 5; 29 committees of 15; or 15 committees of 29.
10. (a) $1 \cdot 36$; $2 \cdot 18$; $3 \cdot 12$; $4 \cdot 9$; $6 \cdot 6$ (b) $1 \cdot 28$; $2 \cdot 14$; $4 \cdot 7$ (c) $1 \cdot 17$ (d) $1 \cdot 144$; $2 \cdot 72$; $3 \cdot 48$; $4 \cdot 36$; $6 \cdot 24$; $8 \cdot 18$; $9 \cdot 16$; $12 \cdot 12$
11. 2^6, or 64
12. (a) $82^2 - 82 + 41 = 6683 = 41 \cdot 163$ (b) Let $n = 41a$ where $a \in N$. Then $n^2 - n + 41 = (41a)^2 - 41a + 41 = 41(41a^2 - a + 1)$.
13. 27,720
14. No. For any two consecutive integers, a and b, one of a or b is even and greater than 2, so it must be prime.
15. 3 and 5; 11 and 13; 17 and 19; 29 and 31; 41 and 43; 59 and 61; 71 and 73; 101 and 103; 107 and 109; 137 and 139; 149 and 151; 179 and 181; 191 and 193; 197 and 199

16. (a) If $2 \mid n$, then 2 appears in the prime fractorization of n. If $3 \mid n$, then 3 appears in the prime factorization of n. Hence, $n = (2 \cdot 3)x = 6x$, where x is some integer. Therefore, $6 \mid n$. **(b)** Yes. $a \mid n$ implies $ax = n$, where $x \in I$. $b \mid n$ implies $by = n$, where $y \in I$. Therefore, $(ax) \cdot (by) = n^2$, or $(ab) \cdot (xy) = n^2$. Hence $ab \mid n^2$.

17. No. The student who checked for divisibility by 12 using 2 and 6 is incorrect because $2 \mid n$ and $6 \mid n$ do not imply that $12 \mid n$. They imply only that $6 \mid n$.

18. (a) Yes **(b)** No. $4 \mid 2 \cdot 2$, but $4 \nmid 2$.

19. For example, $6 = 2 \cdot 3$ or $6 = 1 \cdot 2 \cdot 3$. Therefore, 6 would have at least two prime factorizations.

20. 1, 2, 3, 6, 7, 14, 21

21. No. 2^x is always even and 3^y is always odd, so $2^x 3^y$ is always even. Yet 5^z is always odd, so they can never be equal.

22. If we designate a solution as (x, y), then the required solutions are: (1, 60), (2, 30), (3, 20), (4, 15), (5, 12), (6, 10), (10, 6), (12, 5), (15, 4), (20, 3), (30, 2), (60, 1)

23. (a) 1, 2, 4, 8, 16, 32, 64, 128, 256 **(b)** 1, 3, 9, 27, 81, 243 **(c)** 54 **(d)** $(k + 1) \cdot (m + 1)$

24. (a) 49, 121, 169. These numbers are the squares of prime numbers. **(b)** 81, 625, 2401. These numbers are the primes raised to the 4th power. **(c)** 38, 39, 46. These numbers are the product of 2 primes or the cube of primes.

25. 9409

26. If any prime q in the set $\{2, 3, 5, \ldots, p\}$ divides N, then $q \mid 2 \cdot 3 \cdot 5 \cdot \ldots \cdot p$. Because $q \nmid 1$ by Theorem 5-1(b), $q \nmid (2 \cdot 3 \cdot 5 \cdot \ldots \cdot p + 1)$; that is, $q \nmid N$.

27. (a) $5 \cdot 3 \cdot 2^3$ **(b)** 11^2 **(c)** $7 \cdot 5^2 \cdot 3^4 \cdot 2^8$ **(d)** $7^3 \cdot 5^6 \cdot 3^{12} \cdot 2^{24}$ **(e)** $7 \cdot 5 \cdot 3^6 \cdot 2^7$

28. (a) If $2 \le n \le 100$ then n appears in the product of $100!$. Hence $n \mid 100!$. Because $n \nmid 1$, by Theorem 5.1(b), $n \nmid 100! + 1$. **(b)** If $2 \le q \le p$, then q appears in the product of $p!$. Hence $q \mid p!$. Because $q \nmid 1$, by Theorem 5.1(b), $q \nmid p! + 1$. **(c)** 0 **(d)** 24

29. 111 is composite since $3 \mid 111$. Also, 111111 is composite since $3 \mid 111111$. Thus whenever n has d digits where $3 \mid d$, n will be composite. We can find infinitely many such n.

30. Whenever n is odd, $3n + 1$ will be even and thus divisible by 2.

31. Primes result when $n = 1, 2, 3, 4, 5, 6, 7, 8, 9, 10, 11, 12, 13, 14, 15$.

32. (a) F **(b)** T **(c)** T **(d)** T

33. (a) 438,162 is divisible by 2, 3, and 6. **(b)** 2,345,678,910 is divisible by 2, 3, 5, 6, 9, and 10

34. Let N be a number such that $12 \mid N$. $12 \mid N$ implies $12m = N$, $3 \cdot 4 \cdot m = N$, $3 \cdot (4 \cdot m) = N$, where $m \in I$. Therefore, $3 \mid N$.

35. No, it is not divisible by 7.

Problem Set 5-3

1. (a) 2; 90 **(b)** 12; 72 **(c)** 4; 312

2. (a) 12; 5544 **(b)** 65; 1690 **(c)** 6; 50,400 **(d)** 36; 1080 **(e)** 21; 441 **(f)** 125; 15000

3. (a) 4 **(b)** 1 **(c)** 16

4. (a) 72 **(b)** 1440 **(c)** 630

5. (a) 160,280 **(b)** 158,433,320 **(c)** 941,866,496

6. (a) 8 **(b)** 4 **(c)** 164 **(d)** 504 **(e)** 984 **(f)** 70,299

7. 24

8. 24

9. 15

10. 2:30 A.M.

11. 36 minutes

12. (a) ab **(b)** a; a **(c)** a; a^2 **(d)** a; b **(e)** 1; ab **(f)** $a \mid b$ **(g)** $b \mid a$

13. (a) T. If a and b are both even, then $GCD(a, b)$ is at least 2. **(b)** T. If $GCD(a, b) = 2$, then $2 \mid a$ and $2 \mid b$. **(c)** F. For example, $a = 12$, $b = 20$. **(d)** F. If $a = 8$ and $b = 4$, then $LCM(a, b) = 8$ and $GCD(a, b) = 4$, and $8 \nmid 4$. **(e)** T. $LCM(a, b) \cdot GCD(a, b) = ab$ **(f)** T. A divisor is always less than or equal to the number into which it divides. **(g)** T. A multiple is always greater than or equal to one of its divisors.

14. 15

15. No. $GCD(2, 4, 6) = 2$; $LCM(2, 4, 6) = 12$; $2 \cdot 12 = 24 \ne 2 \cdot 4 \cdot 6$.

16. (a) The only divisors of 4 are 1, 2, and 4. The only one of these numbers that divides 97,219,988,751 is 1. **(b)** $11 \nmid 181,345,913$ because $11 \nmid [(3 + 9 + 4 + 1 + 1) - (1 + 5 + 3 + 8)]$. Also, 11 and 1 are the only divisors of 11. Thus, 1 is the only common divisors of 11 and 181,345,913. **(c)** The divisors of 33 are 1, 3, 11 and 33. Because 3 and 11 do not divide 181,345,913, then 33 does not divide 181,345,913. Thus, 1 is the only common divisor.

17. 1, 2, 3, 4, 6, 7, 8, 9, 11, 12, 13, 14, 16, 17, 18, 19, 21, 22, 23, 24.

18. (a) 7/12 **(b)** 7/11 **(c)** 13/32 **(d)** 1/4

19. (a) 28 **(b)** $1 + 2 + 4 + 5 + 10 + 11 + 20 + 22 + 44 + 55 + 110 = 284$; $1 + 2 + 4 + 71 + 142 = 220$.

20. Yes. $d \mid GCD(a, b)$ and $GCD(a, b) \mid a$ so $d \mid a$. Similarly, $d \mid b$.

21. $10^6 = 2^6 \cdot 5^6 = 15625 \cdot 64$

22. (a) 83151, 83451, 83751 **(b)** 83691, 86691, **(c)** 10396

23. No. $3 \mid 3111$

24. 2^5, or 32

25. $2^3 \cdot 3^2 \cdot 5 \cdot 7 \cdot 11 = 27, 270$

26. 43

Brain Teaser (p. 257)

If w is the width of the rectangle and ℓ is the length of the rectangle, then the number of squares the diagonal crosses is $(\ell + w) - GCD(\ell, w)$ or $(\ell + w) - 1$.

Problem Set 5-4

1. (a) 3 **(b)** 2 **(c)** 6 **(d)** 8 **(e)** 3 **(f)** 4 **(g)** Impossible **(h)** 10

2. (a) 2 **(b)** 1 **(c)** 2 **(d)** 4 **(e)** 2 **(f)** 1 **(g)** 2 **(h)** 4

3. (a)

$\oplus$	1	2	3	4	5	6	7
1	2	3	4	5	6	7	1
2	3	4	5	6	7	1	2
3	4	5	6	7	1	2	3
4	5	6	7	1	2	3	4
5	6	7	1	2	3	4	5
6	7	1	2	3	4	5	6
7	1	2	3	4	5	6	7

(b) 6; 4 **(c)** Each subtraction problem $a - b = x$ can be rewritten as $a = b + x$. If every number x shows up exactly once in every row and column, then no matter what a and b are, x can be found.

4. (a)

$\otimes$	1	2	3	4	5	6	7
1	1	2	3	4	5	6	7
2	2	4	6	1	3	5	7
3	3	6	2	5	1	4	7
4	4	1	5	2	6	3	7
5	5	3	1	6	4	2	7
6	6	5	4	3	2	1	7
7	7	7	7	7	7	7	7

(b) 2; 3

(c) Yes, with the exception of the rows and columns containing 7, every row and every column contains all the numbers 1 through 6.

5. (a)

$\otimes$	1	2	3
1	1	2	3
2	2	1	3
3	3	3	3

$\otimes$	1	2	3	4
1	1	2	3	4
2	2	4	2	4
3	3	2	1	4
4	4	4	4	4

$\otimes$	1	2	3	4	5	6
1	1	2	3	4	5	6
2	2	4	6	2	4	6
3	3	6	3	6	3	6
4	4	2	6	4	2	6
5	5	4	3	2	1	6
6	6	6	6	6	6	6

$\otimes$	1	2	3	4	5	6	7	8	9	10	11
1	1	2	3	4	5	6	7	8	9	10	11
2	2	4	6	8	10	1	3	5	7	9	11
3	3	6	9	1	4	7	10	2	5	8	11
4	4	8	1	5	9	3	6	10	3	7	11
5	5	10	4	9	3	8	2	7	1	6	11
6	6	1	7	2	8	3	9	4	10	5	11
7	7	3	10	6	2	9	5	1	8	4	11
8	8	5	2	10	7	4	1	9	6	3	11
9	9	7	5	3	1	10	8	6	4	2	11
10	10	9	8	7	6	5	4	3	2	1	11
11	11	11	11	11	11	11	11	11	11	11	11

(b) 3 and 11 **(c)** On the n-hour clocks on which divisions can be performed, n is prime.

6. (a) 10 **(b)** 9 **(c)** 7 **(d)** 7 **(e)** 1 **(f)** 6

7. Wednesday

8. (a) 4 **(b)** 0 **(c)** 0 **(d)** 7

9. (a) $8|(81 - 1)$ **(b)** $10|(81 - 1)$ **(c)** $13|(1000 - {}^-1)$ **(d)** $10 \equiv 1 \pmod 9$ implies $10^{84} \equiv 1 \pmod 9$ **(e)** $10 \equiv {}^-1 \pmod{11}$ implies $10^{100} \equiv ({}^-1)^{100} \equiv 1 \pmod{11}$ **(f)** $100|(937 - 37)$

10. If $m|a$, then $m|(a - 0)$, which implies $a \equiv 0 \pmod m$. If $a \equiv 0 \pmod m$, then $m|(a - 0)$, or $m|a$.

11. (a) $24 \equiv 0 \pmod 8$ **(b)** ${}^-90 \equiv 0 \pmod 3$ **(c)** $n \equiv 0 \pmod n$

12. (a) $x = 2k$, where $k \in I$ **(b)** $x = 2k + 1$, where $k \in I$ **(c)** $x = 5k + 3$, where $k \in I$

13. (a) 1 **(b)** 5 **(c)** 10 **(d)** 1

14. (a) ${}^-1$ **(b)** 12

15. Let $N = a_k \cdot 10^k + a_{k-1} \cdot 10^{k-1} + \cdots + a_2 \cdot 10^2 + a_1 \cdot 10^1 + a_0$. $4|N$ if and only if $4|(a_1 \cdot 10 + a_0)$. Proof: $100 \equiv 0 \pmod 4$. Hence, $N = 100(a_k 10^{k-2} + a_{k-1} 10^{k-3} + \cdots + a_2) + a_1 10 + a_0 \equiv a_1 10 + a_0 \pmod 4$. Consequently, $4|N$ if and only if $4|(a_1 \cdot 10 + a_0)$.

16. (a) For example, $2 \cdot 3 \equiv 2 \cdot 1 \pmod 4$, but $3 \not\equiv 1 \pmod 4$. **(b)** For example, $2^2 \equiv 4^2 \pmod 6$, but $2 \not\equiv 4 \pmod 6$.

17. (1) $a \equiv a \pmod m$, since $m|(a - a)$. (2) If $a \equiv b \pmod m$, then $b \equiv a \pmod m$. Proof: $a \equiv b \pmod m$ means $m|(a - b)$, which implies $m|({}^-1)(a - b)$, or $m(b - a)$. Hence $b \equiv a \pmod m$. (3) If $a \equiv b \pmod m$, and $b \equiv c \pmod m$, then $a \equiv c \pmod m$. Proof: Since $a - b = k_1 m$ and $b - c = k_2 m$ for some integers k_1 and k_2, it follows that $(a - b) + (b - c) = k_1 m + k_2 m$, or $a - c = (k_1 + k_2)m$. Hence, $a \equiv c \pmod m$. (4) If $a \equiv b \pmod m$, then $a + c \equiv b + c \pmod m$. Proof: Because $a - b = km$ for some integer k, it follows that $a + c - (b + c) = a - b = km$, and hence that $a + c \equiv b + c \pmod m$. (5) If $a \equiv b \pmod m$, then $ac \equiv bc \pmod m$. Proof: Because $a - b = km$ for some integer k, $ac - bc = (a - b)c = (km)c = (kc)m$. Since kc is an integer, it follows that $ac \equiv bc \pmod m$. (6) If $a \equiv b \pmod m$ and $c \equiv d \pmod m$, then $ac \equiv bd \pmod m$. Proof: By (5), $a \equiv b \pmod m$ implies $ac \equiv bc \pmod m$ and $c \equiv d \pmod m$ implies $bc \equiv bd \pmod m$. Now applying (3) to $ac \equiv bc \pmod m$ and $bc \equiv bd \pmod m$, we obtain $ac \equiv bd \pmod m$.

Brain Teaser (p. 263)
There are no primes in this list.

Chapter Test

1. (a) F **(b)** F **(c)** T **(d)** F **(e)** F

2. (a) F. $7|7$ and $7 \nmid 2$, but $7|7 \cdot 2$ **(b)** F $7 \nmid (7 + 2)$, but $7|7$ **(c)** T **(d)** T **(e)** T **(f)** F. $4 \nmid 2$ and $4 \nmid 6$, but $4|2 \cdot 6$

3. (a) 83,160 is divisible by 2, 3, 4, 5, 6, 7, 8, 9, 11. **(b)** 83,193 is divisible by 3 and 11.

4. $17 | 10,007$ and $17|17$, so that $17 | (10,007 + 17)$ or $17 \nmid 10,024$.

5. (a) 2, 5, 8 **(b)** 1, 4, 7 **(c)** 17, 46, 75

6. (a) 143 is not prime **(b)** 223 is prime

7. The number must be divisible by both 8 and 3. Since $3|4152$ and $8|4152$, then $24|4152$.

8. (a) 4 **(b)** 73

9. (a) $2^4 \cdot 5^3 \cdot 7^4 \cdot 13 \cdot 29$ **(b)** $278 \cdot 279$, or $77,562$

10. $2^4 = 16$, for example.

11. 1, 2, 3, 4, 6, 8, 9, 12, 16, 18, 24, 36, 48, 72, 144

12. (a) $2^2 \cdot 43$ **(b)** $2^5 \cdot 3^2$ **(c)** $2^2 \cdot 5 \cdot 13$ **(d)** $3 \cdot 2 \cdot 37$

13. 15 minutes

14. $0.31

15. 9:30 A.M.

16. $N = a \cdot 10^2 + b \cdot 10 + c = (99a + 9b) + (a + b + c)$. Since $9|9(11a + b)$, then using Theorem 5-1, $9|N$ if and only if $9|(a + b + c)$

17. (a) 1 **(b)** 4 **(c)** 3

CHAPTER 6

Problem Set 6-1

1. (a) The solution to $8x = 7$ is $(7/8)$. **(b)** Jane ate seven eighths of Jill's candy. **(c)** The ratio of boys to girls is seven to eight.

2. (a) 1/6 **(b)** 1/4 **(c)** 2/6 **(d)** 1/2 **(e)** 7/12 **(f)** 2/16

3. (a) 2/3 **(b)** 4/6 **(c)** 6/9 **(d)** 8/12. The diagram illustrates the Fundamental Law of Fractions

4. (a)

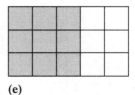

(b)

(c)

(d)

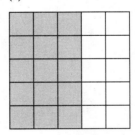

(e)

(f)

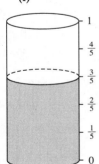

5. (a) 3/8 **(b)** 1/2 **(c)** 1/6 **(d)** 1/3

6. (a) 4/18, 6/27, 8/36 **(b)** $-4/10$, $2/-5$, $-10/25$ **(c)** 0/1, 0/2, 0/4 **(d)** $2a/4$, $3a/6$, $4a/8$

7. (a) 52/31 **(b)** 3/5 **(c)** $-5/7$ **(d)** 0/1 **(e)** 144/169 **(f)** Reduced

8. Impossible to determine. Because $20/25 = 24/30 = 4/5$, so the same fraction of students passed in each class, but the actual scores in one class could have been higher than in the other.

9. (a) undefined **(b)** undefined **(c)** 0 **(d)** cannot be simplified **(e)** cannot be simplified **(f)** 2/3 **(g)** 5/3

10. (a) 1 **(b)** $2x/9y$ **(c)** a **(d)** $(a^3 + 1)/(a^3b)$ **(e)** $1/(3 + b)$ **(f)** $a/(3a + b)$

11. Only the fractions in (d) are not equal.

12. Only the fractions in (c), (e), and (f) are equal.

13. (a) 32/3 **(b)** -36 **(c)** x is any rational number except 0.

14. (a) $a = b$, $c \neq 0$ **(b)** $b = c \neq 0$ or $a = 0$, but $b \neq 0$ and $c \neq 0$.

15. (a) T **(b)** T **(c)** F **(d)** F **(e)** T

16. Only the fractions in (c) are equal.

Problem Set 6-2

1.

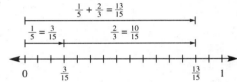

2. (a) $\dfrac{-11}{16}$ **(b)** $\dfrac{-4}{12}$, or $\dfrac{-1}{3}$ **(c)** $\dfrac{19}{18}$ **(d)** $\dfrac{-5}{42}$

3. (a) $\dfrac{-31}{20}$ **(b)** $\dfrac{58}{35}$ **(c)** $\dfrac{-19}{40}$ **(d)** $\dfrac{5y - 3x}{xy}$

4. (a) $\dfrac{15}{14}$ **(b)** $\dfrac{-23}{21}$ **(c)** $\dfrac{-6y + 6x - 1}{4xy}$

(d) $\dfrac{-9y + 5x + 42y^2}{6x^2y^2}$

5. (a) $18\dfrac{2}{3}$ **(b)** $2\dfrac{4}{5}$ **(c)** $-\left(2\dfrac{93}{100}\right)$ **(d)** $-\left(5\dfrac{7}{8}\right)$

6. (a) $\dfrac{27}{4}$ **(b)** $\dfrac{15}{2}$ **(c)** $\dfrac{-29}{8}$ **(d)** $\dfrac{-14}{3}$

7. (a) $\dfrac{7}{12}$ **(b)** $\dfrac{49}{12}$ **(c)** $\dfrac{71}{24}$ **(d)** $\dfrac{-23}{3}$ **(e)** $\dfrac{43}{2^4 \cdot 3^4}$

(f) $\dfrac{472}{45}$

8. (a) $\dfrac{41}{24}$ **(b)** $\dfrac{-23}{12}$ **(c)** $\dfrac{36,037}{168,070,000}$ **(d)** $\dfrac{-1}{2}$

(e) $3\dfrac{9}{16}$

9. (a) $1/3^-$ **(b)** $1/6^+$ **(c)** $3/4^+$ **(d)** $1/2^-$

10. (a) Beavers **(b)** Ducks **(c)** Bears **(d)** Tigers **(e)** Lions **(f)** Wildcats

11. (a) $1/2^-$ **(b)** $1/2^+$ **(c)** 0^+ **(d)** $3/4^-$ **(e)** 1^- **(f)** 1^+ **(g)** 1^+ **(h)** 0^- **(i)** $3/4^+$ **(j)** $1/2^+$ **(k)** $1/2^-$ **(l)** 1^+ **(m)** 1^-

12. (a) 2 (b) 3/4 (c) 1/3 (d) 0
13. (a) 10^- (b) 0^+ (c) 13^- (d) 151^-
14. (a) No (b) No
15. (a) 1/4 (b) 5-1/8 (c) 0 (d) 10
16. (a) $\dfrac{d-a}{bc}$ (b) $\dfrac{12a+2b}{a^2-b^2}$ (c) $\dfrac{a^3bd-bc^2}{adc}$
17. (a) $\dfrac{dc+a}{bc}$ (b) $\dfrac{a^2+2ab-b^2}{a^2-b^2}$ (c) $\dfrac{a-ab-b^2}{a^2-b^2}$
18. (a) $\dfrac{3+3}{3} \neq \dfrac{3}{3}+3$ (b) $\dfrac{4}{2+2} \neq \dfrac{4}{2}+\dfrac{4}{2}$
(c) $\dfrac{ab+c}{a} \neq \dfrac{\not{a}b+c}{\not{a}}$ (d) $\dfrac{a \cdot a - b \cdot b}{a-b} \neq \dfrac{\not{a} \cdot a - \not{b} \cdot b}{\not{a}-\not{b}}$
(e) $\dfrac{a+c}{b+c} \neq \dfrac{a+\not{c}}{b+\not{c}}$
19. 1/4
20. She saves 1/20
21. $\dfrac{7}{30}$ miles
22. $6\dfrac{7}{12}$ yards
23. $\dfrac{1}{16}$
24. $1\dfrac{7}{8}$ cups
25. $1\dfrac{3}{4}$ cups
26. $2\dfrac{1}{6}$ hours
27. $2\dfrac{5}{6}$ yards
28. $22\dfrac{1}{8}$ inches
29. Answers vary.
30. (a) $\dfrac{1}{2}+\dfrac{3}{4}=\dfrac{5}{4} \in Q$ (b) $\dfrac{1}{2}+\dfrac{3}{4}=\dfrac{3}{4}+\dfrac{1}{2}=\dfrac{5}{4}$
(c) $\dfrac{1}{2}=\dfrac{2}{4}, \dfrac{1}{2}+\dfrac{1}{4}=\dfrac{3}{4}$, and $\dfrac{2}{4}+\dfrac{1}{4}=\dfrac{3}{4}$
(d) $\left(\dfrac{1}{2}+\dfrac{1}{3}\right)+\dfrac{1}{4}=\dfrac{13}{12}$ and $\dfrac{1}{2}+\left(\dfrac{1}{3}+\dfrac{1}{4}\right)=\dfrac{13}{12}$

31. (a) Yes. If a, b, c, and d are integers, then $\dfrac{a}{b}-\dfrac{c}{d}=$ $\dfrac{ad-bc}{bd}$ is a rational number. (b) No. For example, $\dfrac{1}{2}-\dfrac{1}{4} \neq \dfrac{1}{4}-\dfrac{1}{2}$. (c) No. For example, $\dfrac{1}{2}-\left(\dfrac{1}{4}-\dfrac{1}{8}\right) \neq \left(\dfrac{1}{2}-\dfrac{1}{4}\right)-\dfrac{1}{8}$. (d) No. If there is an identity for subtraction it must be 0, since only for 0 does $\dfrac{a}{b}-0=$ $\dfrac{a}{b}$. However, in general $0-\dfrac{a}{b} \neq \dfrac{a}{b}-0$, and hence

there is no identity. (e) No. Since there is no identity, an inverse cannot be defined. (f) Yes. If $\dfrac{a}{b}=\dfrac{c}{d}$, then by the addition property of equality $\dfrac{a}{b}+\left(\dfrac{-e}{f}\right)=\dfrac{c}{d}+\left(\dfrac{-e}{f}\right)$. Hence, $\dfrac{a}{b}-\dfrac{e}{f}=\dfrac{c}{d}-\dfrac{e}{f}$.

32. (a) $1\dfrac{1}{2}, 1\dfrac{3}{4}, 2$; arithmetic, $\dfrac{1}{2}-\dfrac{1}{4}=\dfrac{3}{4}-\dfrac{1}{2}=$ $1-\dfrac{3}{4}=\dfrac{5}{4}-1$ (b) $\dfrac{6}{7}, \dfrac{7}{8}, \dfrac{8}{9}$; not arithmetic; $\dfrac{2}{3}-\dfrac{1}{2} \neq \dfrac{3}{4}-\dfrac{2}{3}$ (c) $\dfrac{17}{3}, \dfrac{20}{3}, \dfrac{23}{3}$; arithmetic; $\dfrac{5}{3}-\dfrac{2}{3}=\dfrac{8}{3}-\dfrac{5}{3}=\dfrac{11}{3}-\dfrac{8}{3}=\dfrac{14}{3}-\dfrac{11}{3}$ (d) $\dfrac{1}{7}, \dfrac{1}{8}, \dfrac{1}{9}$; not arithmetic; $\dfrac{1}{3}-\dfrac{1}{2} \neq \dfrac{1}{4}-\dfrac{1}{3}$ (e) $\dfrac{-5}{4}, \dfrac{-7}{4}, \dfrac{-9}{4}$; arithmetic; $\dfrac{3}{4}-\dfrac{5}{4}=\dfrac{1}{4}-\dfrac{3}{4}=$ $\dfrac{-1}{4}-\dfrac{1}{4}=\dfrac{-3}{4}-\left(\dfrac{-1}{4}\right)$

33. (a) $\dfrac{1}{4}n$ (b) $\dfrac{n}{n+1}$ (c) $\dfrac{3n-1}{3}$ (d) $\dfrac{1}{n+1}$
(e) $\dfrac{-2n+7}{4}$

34. $1, \dfrac{7}{6}, \dfrac{8}{6}, \dfrac{9}{6}, \dfrac{10}{6}, \dfrac{11}{6}, 2$

35. (a) (i) $\dfrac{3}{4}$ (ii) $\dfrac{25}{12}$ (iii) 0 (b) (i) $\dfrac{1}{4}$ (ii) $\dfrac{-7}{4}$ (iii) $\dfrac{-1}{4}$

36. (a) $f(0)=-2$ (b) $f(-2)=0$ (c) $f(-5)=\dfrac{1}{2}$
(d) $f(5)=\dfrac{7}{4}$

37. (b) $\dfrac{1}{n}=\dfrac{1}{n+1}+\dfrac{1}{n(n+1)}$ (c) $\dfrac{1}{n+1}+\dfrac{1}{n(n+1)}$ $=\dfrac{n}{n(n+1)}+\dfrac{1}{n(n+1)}=\dfrac{n+1}{n(n+1)}=\dfrac{1}{n}$

38. (a) $\dfrac{2}{3}$ (b) $\dfrac{13}{17}$ (c) $\dfrac{25}{49}$ (d) $\dfrac{a}{1}$, or a (e) Reduced
39. (a), (b), (c), and (e) are equal.

Brain Teaser (p. 287)
Let x = number of students, $\dfrac{1}{2}x+\dfrac{1}{7}x+20=x$
$$20=\dfrac{5}{14}x$$
$$56=x$$

Brain Teaser (p. 298)
Observe that after crossing each bridge, the prince was left with half the number of bags he had previously minus one additional bag of gold. To determine the

184

number he had prior to crossing the bridge, we can use the inverse operations; that is, add 1 and multiply by 2. The prince had one bag left after crossing the fourth bridge. He must have had two before he gave the guard the extra bag. Finally he must have had four bags before he gave the guard at the fourth bridge any bags. The entire procedure is summarized in the following table.

Bridge	Bags After Crossing	Bags Before Guard Given Extra	Bags Prior to Crossing
Fourth	1	2	4
Third	4	5	10
Second	10	11	22
First	22	23	46

Problem Set 6-3

1. (a) $\frac{1}{4} \cdot \frac{1}{3} = \frac{1}{12}$ (b) $\frac{2}{5} \cdot \frac{3}{5} = \frac{6}{25}$

2. (a) (b)

(c)

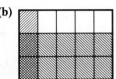

3. (a) $\frac{3}{4}$ (b) $\frac{3}{8}$ (c) $\frac{-5a}{3b}$

4. (a) $\frac{1}{5}$ (b) $\frac{b}{a}$ (c) $\frac{za}{x^2 y}$ (d) $\frac{35}{4}$ (e) $\frac{44}{3}$ (f) $\frac{-25}{4}$

5. (a) $10\frac{1}{2}$ (b) $8\frac{1}{3}$ (c) $24{,}871\frac{1}{20}$

6. (a) -3 (b) $\frac{5}{3}$ (c) $\frac{1}{2}$ (d) $\frac{3}{10}$ (e) $\frac{y}{x}$ (f) $\frac{-1}{7}$

7. (a) 27 (b) $\frac{8}{7}$ (c) $\frac{-6}{7}$ (d) $\frac{y}{x}$ (e) $\frac{27}{64}$ (f) $\frac{1}{12}$

(g) $\frac{32}{21}$ (h) $\frac{7}{10}$ (i) $\frac{-14}{5}$

8. (a) $\frac{11}{5}$ (b) $\frac{77}{12}$ (c) $\frac{22}{3}$ (d) $\frac{5}{2}$ (e) 5 (f) -42

(g) 2 (h) $\frac{z}{y}$ (i) z (j) $\frac{5}{x}$ (k) $\frac{xy}{z}$

9. (a) 20 (b) 16 (c) 2 (d) 1

10. (a) 18 (b) 25 (c) 7 (d) 6

11. (a) Less than 1 (b) Less than 1 (c) Greater than 2 (d) Less than 4 (e) Greater than 4 (f) Less than 4 (g) Greater than 4

12. (a) 48^- (b) 12^+ (c) 45^- (d) 12^+

13. (a) 26 (b) 30 (c) 92 (d) 18

14. (a) 6 (b) 7 (c) 9 (d) $2\frac{1}{4}$

15. (a) $\frac{21}{8}$ (b) $\frac{3}{35}$ (c) -28 (d) $\frac{-56}{5}$ (e) $\frac{1}{5}$ (f) $\frac{15}{32}$

(g) $\frac{-45}{28}$ (h) $\frac{-7}{15}$ (i) $\frac{-15}{2}$

16. 51 and 52

17. 400

18. $\frac{1}{6}$

19. (a) 39 uniforms (b) $\frac{1}{4}$ yards left

20. Answers vary. (a) $\frac{3}{4}$ (b) $\frac{5}{12}$ (c) $\frac{9}{16}$ (d) $2\frac{1}{2}$

(e) $\frac{7}{10}$ (f) 24 feet (g) \$300,000

21. (a) $2 \div 1 \neq 1 \div 2$ (b) $(1 \div 2) \div 3 \neq 1 \div (2 \div 3)$ (c) There is no rational number a such that $2 \div a = a \div 2 = 2$. (d) Because there is no identity, there can be no inverse.

22. 29/36

23. 9600

24. $\$266\frac{2}{3}$

25. (a) \$121,000 (b) \$90,000 (c) \$300,000

26. 1/4

27. $x = 50$

28. \$225

29. 18

30. 7 ounces

31. (a) $\frac{1}{32}, \frac{1}{64}$; geometric, ratio = $\frac{1}{2}$ (b) $\frac{-1}{32}, \frac{1}{64}$; geometric, ratio = $-\frac{1}{2}$ (c) $\frac{81}{256}, \frac{243}{1024}$; geometric, ratio = $\frac{3}{4}$ (d) $\frac{5}{3^4}, \frac{6}{3^5}$; not geometric, $\frac{2}{3^2} \div \frac{1}{3} \neq \frac{3}{3^3} \div \frac{2}{3^2}$

32. (a) $n(n + 1) + \left(\frac{1}{2}\right)^2$ (b) $\left(n + \frac{1}{2}\right)^2 = n^2 + 2n \cdot \frac{1}{2} + \left(\frac{1}{2}\right)^2 = n^2 + n + \left(\frac{1}{2}\right)^2 = n(n + 1) + \left(\frac{1}{2}\right)^2$

33. (a) (i) $\frac{1}{2}$ (ii) $\frac{4}{5}$ (iii) $\frac{1}{5}$ (b) (i) $\frac{-2}{3}$ (ii) $\frac{-2}{3}$ (iii) $\frac{-4}{3}$

34. (a) (i) $\frac{-4}{5}$ (ii) $\frac{-26}{17}$ (iii) $\frac{-14}{33}$ (b) (i) $\frac{-4}{3}$ (ii) $\frac{-30}{7}$ (iii) $\frac{-3}{10}$ (c) $\frac{5}{4}$

35. (a) First 3, second 4, third 5. Guess 6. The guess is correct since

$$\left(1 + \frac{1}{1}\right)\left(1 + \frac{1}{2}\right)\left(1 + \frac{1}{3}\right)\left(1 + \frac{1}{4}\right)\left(1 + \frac{1}{5}\right) =$$

$$5 \cdot \left(1 + \frac{1}{5}\right) = 6. \quad \textbf{(b)} \ 102 \quad \textbf{(c)} \ n + 2$$

36. $c = 0$ or $a = b$, where $b \neq 0$.

37. (a) $2S = 2\left(\dfrac{1}{2} + \dfrac{1}{2^2} + \cdots + \dfrac{1}{2^{64}}\right) = 1 + \dfrac{1}{2} + \dfrac{1}{2^2} +$

$\cdots + \dfrac{1}{2^{63}}$ **(b)** Note that $2S = 1 + S - \dfrac{1}{2^{64}}$. Hence,

$2S - S = 1 + S - \dfrac{1}{2^{64}} - S = 1 - \dfrac{1}{2^{64}}$. **(c)** $1 - \dfrac{1}{2^n}$

38. $3737\dfrac{1}{2}$

39. (a) $1\dfrac{49}{99}$ **(b)** $25 \cdot \left(2\dfrac{49}{99}\right)$

40. (a) $\dfrac{25}{16}$ **(b)** $\dfrac{25}{18}$ **(c)** $\dfrac{5}{216}$ **(d)** $\dfrac{259}{30}$ **(e)** $\dfrac{37}{24}$

(f) $\dfrac{-117}{12}$

41. 120 students

42. (a) $\dfrac{16}{15x}$ **(b)** $\dfrac{-x + 3y - xy}{x^2y^2}$

Brain Teaser (p. 302)

No. The legacy is impossible because the fractions of cats to be shared do not add up to the whole unit of cats. Let x equal the number of cats.

$\dfrac{1}{2}x + \dfrac{1}{3}x + \dfrac{1}{9}x = \dfrac{17}{18}x$, but the sum should be $1x$,

or $\dfrac{18}{18}x$.

Brain Teaser (p. 310)

Both cyclists covered the same distance, so it follows that the one who rode longer is the slower one. If we denote David's riding time in hours (or any other unit of time) by d and Sara's riding time, also in hours, by s, it would be sufficient to determine if $d < s$. Because David rode three times as long as Sara rested, we can deduce that Sara rested one third as long as David rode, that is, $\dfrac{d}{3}$ hours. Similarly, because Sara rode four times as long as David rested, we can deduce that David rested one fourth as long as Sara rode, that is, $\dfrac{s}{4}$. Using the expressions $\dfrac{d}{3}$ and $\dfrac{s}{4}$, we can write expressions for the total time of the trip, as shown in the following table.

	Riding Time	Resting Time	Total Time of Trip
David	d	$\dfrac{s}{4}$	$d + \dfrac{s}{4}$
Sara	s	$\dfrac{d}{3}$	$s + \dfrac{d}{3}$

Both cyclists started and returned at the same time, so their total trip times are the same. As shown in the table, David's total trip time is $d + \dfrac{s}{4}$ and Sara's total trip time is $s + \dfrac{d}{3}$. Consequently, we have the following equation and solution in terms of s.

$$d + \frac{s}{4} = s + \frac{d}{3}$$
$$d + \frac{d}{3} = s - \frac{s}{4}$$
$$\frac{2}{3}d = \frac{3}{4}s$$
$$d = \frac{3}{2} \cdot \frac{3}{4}s$$
$$d = \frac{9}{8}s$$

Because $\frac{9}{8} > 1$, it follows that $\frac{9}{8}s > s$, or that $d > s$. Thus, it took David longer to travel the same distance that Sara traveled, so Sara rode faster than David.

Problem Set 6-4

1. (a) > **(b)** > **(c)** < **(d)** < **(e)** = **(f)** =

2.

3. (a) $\dfrac{11}{13}, \dfrac{11}{16}, \dfrac{11}{22}$ **(b)** $3, \dfrac{33}{16}, \dfrac{23}{12}$ **(c)** $\dfrac{-1}{5}, \dfrac{-19}{36}, \dfrac{-17}{30}$

4. (a) $x \leq \dfrac{27}{16}$ **(b)** $x < \dfrac{17}{5}$ **(c)** $x \geq \dfrac{115}{3}$ **(d)** $x \geq \dfrac{141}{22}$

5. (a) No. Multiplication by bd, which is negative, reverses the order. **(b)** Yes. Multiplication by bd, which is positive, retains same order.

6. (a) $399\dfrac{80}{81}$ **(b)** $180\dfrac{89}{100}$ **(c)** $3\dfrac{699}{820}$

7. (a) over 7 **(b)** under 13 **(c)** under 1 **(d)** over 6 **(e)** over 6

8. (a) 20 and 201/2 **(b)** 51/2 and 6 **(c)** 5 and 51/2 **(d)** 10 and 101/2

9. (a) about 180 **(b)** about 729 **(c)** about 468 **(d)** about 6 **(e)** about 3

10. Every 3 pounds of birdseed yields about 4 packages. Thus, there are about 28 packages.

11. (a) A proper fraction is greater than its square.

(b) Let $\dfrac{a}{b}$ be a positive proper fraction, that is

$0 < \dfrac{a}{b} < 1$. Therefore, $\dfrac{a}{b} > 0$, $\dfrac{a}{b} < 1$ implies $\dfrac{a}{b} \cdot \dfrac{a}{b} <$

$1 \cdot \dfrac{a}{b}$ or $\left(\dfrac{a}{b}\right)^2 < \dfrac{a}{b}$. **(c)** If a fraction is greater than 1, it

is less than its square. **(d)** Let $\dfrac{a}{b}$ be a fraction greater

than 1. Then $\dfrac{a}{b} \cdot \dfrac{a}{b} > 1 \cdot \dfrac{a}{b}$ or $\left(\dfrac{a}{b}\right)^2 > \dfrac{a}{b}$.

12. $\dfrac{a}{b} < 1$ and $\dfrac{c}{d} > 0$ imply $\dfrac{a}{b} \cdot \dfrac{c}{d} < 1 \cdot \dfrac{c}{d}$ or $\dfrac{a}{b} \cdot \dfrac{c}{d} < \dfrac{c}{d}$

13. $xy > y$ because $x > 1$ and $y > 0$ implies $x \cdot y > 1 \cdot y$ or $xy > y$.

14. We need to show that $\dfrac{n}{n+1} < \dfrac{n+1}{n+2}$. This
inequality is equivalent to $n^2 + 2n < n^2 + 2n + 1$,
or $0 < 1$.

15. Answers vary.

16. (a) There is no whole number between two consecutive whole numbers—for example, between 0 and 1. **(b)** Same as (a).

17. Answers may vary. The following are possible answers. **(a)** $\dfrac{10}{21}, \dfrac{11}{21}$ **(b)** $\dfrac{-22}{27}, \dfrac{-23}{27}$ **(c)** $\dfrac{997}{1200}, \dfrac{998}{1200}$

(d) $0, \dfrac{1}{2}$

18. (a) 33 **(b)** 132 **(c)** $x < 4/7$ so $x = 0$ **(d)** no such x exists

19. (a) 28 **(b)** -301 **(c)** 10 **(d)** no such x exists

20. $0 < \dfrac{a}{b} < \dfrac{c}{d}$ so that $0 < \dfrac{1}{2} \cdot \dfrac{a}{b} < \dfrac{1}{2} \cdot \dfrac{c}{d}$. Also, $0 < \dfrac{a}{b} =$

$\dfrac{1}{2} \cdot \dfrac{a}{b} + \dfrac{1}{2} \cdot \dfrac{a}{b} < \dfrac{1}{2} \cdot \dfrac{a}{b} + \dfrac{1}{2} \cdot \dfrac{c}{d} = \dfrac{1}{2}\left(\dfrac{a}{b} + \dfrac{c}{d}\right)$. Similarly,

$\dfrac{1}{2}\left(\dfrac{a}{b} + \dfrac{c}{d}\right) < \dfrac{c}{d}$, and therefore $0 < \dfrac{a}{b} < \dfrac{1}{2}\left(\dfrac{a}{b} + \dfrac{c}{d}\right) < \dfrac{c}{d}$.

21. We are considering $\dfrac{a}{b}$ and $\dfrac{a+x}{b+x}$ when $a < b$.

$\dfrac{a}{b} < \dfrac{a+x}{b+x}$ because $ab + ax < ab + bx$.

22. (a) $\dfrac{29}{8}$ **(b)** $\dfrac{87}{68}$ **(c)** $\dfrac{25}{144}$ **(d)** 1 (provided that $|x| \neq |y|$)

23. $6\dfrac{7}{18}$ hours

24. (a) $\dfrac{-4}{3}$ **(b)** $\dfrac{-11}{8}$ **(c)** $\dfrac{24}{17}$ **(d)** -3

25. 261/4 hours

26. (a) 3 and 4 **(b)** 4 and 5

Problem Set 6-5

1. $\dfrac{3}{2}$

2. $24\dfrac{1}{2}$ cents

3. (a) 30 **(b)** $-3\dfrac{1}{3}$ **(c)** $23\dfrac{1}{3}$ **(d)** $10\dfrac{1}{2}$

4. $\dfrac{16}{9}$

5. 2469

6. $4.74

7. 270 miles

8. 64

9. 72 minutes for 30 inches

10. (a) 42, 56 **(b)** 24, 32

11. 500 ft. by 900 ft.

12. $14,909.09, $29,918.18, $37,272.73

13. $77 and $99

14. 135

15. $9\dfrac{9}{14}$ days

16. No, the ratio of the prices is proportional to the ratio of the areas.

17. (a) $2:5$. Because the ratio is $2:3$, there are $2x$ boys and $3x$ girls, hence the ratio of boys to all the students is $2x/(2x + 3x) = 2/5$. **(b)** $m : (m + n)$

18. $1\dfrac{1}{3}$ days

19. $13\dfrac{1}{3}$ hours

20. $\dfrac{a}{b} = \dfrac{c}{d}$ implies $ad = bc$, which is equivalent to

$d = \dfrac{bc}{a}$; then, $\dfrac{d}{c} = \dfrac{b}{a}$.

21. We need to prove that if $0 < \dfrac{a}{b} < 1$ and $0 < \dfrac{c}{d} < 1$,

then $\dfrac{a}{b} \cdot \dfrac{c}{d} < \dfrac{a}{b}$ and $\dfrac{a}{b} \cdot \dfrac{c}{d} < \dfrac{c}{d}$. We prove this as follows:

$\dfrac{c}{d} < 1$ and $\dfrac{a}{b} > 0$ implies $\dfrac{c}{d} \cdot \dfrac{a}{b} < 1 \cdot \dfrac{a}{b}$ or $\dfrac{a}{b} \cdot \dfrac{c}{d} < \dfrac{a}{b}$.

Similarly, $\dfrac{a}{b} < 1$ and $\dfrac{c}{d} > 0$ implies $\dfrac{a}{b} \cdot \dfrac{c}{d} < 1 \cdot \dfrac{c}{d}$ or

$\dfrac{a}{b} \cdot \dfrac{c}{d} < \dfrac{c}{d}$.

22. (a) $\dfrac{1}{2}$ **(b)** Let $\dfrac{a}{b} = \dfrac{c}{d} = \dfrac{e}{f} = r$.

Then $a = br$
$c = dr$
$e = fr$
So, $a + c + e = br + dr + fr$,
$a + c + e = r(b + d + f)$,
$\dfrac{a + c + e}{b + d + f} = r$

23. (a) $\frac{a}{b} = \frac{c}{d}$ implies $\frac{a}{b} + 1 = \frac{c}{d} + 1$, which implies $\frac{a+b}{b} = \frac{c+d}{d}$. (b) By inverting (Problem 20), $\frac{b}{a} = \frac{d}{c}$ and by part (a), $\frac{b+a}{a} = \frac{d+c}{c}$. Then inverting again gives $\frac{a}{a+b} = \frac{c}{d+c}$. (c) $\frac{a}{b} = \frac{c}{d}$ implies $\frac{a}{b} - 1 = \frac{c}{d} - 1$, which implies $\frac{a-b}{b} = \frac{c-d}{d}$. From part (a) and this last result we have $\frac{a+b}{b} \div \frac{a-b}{b} = \frac{c+d}{d} \div \frac{c-d}{d}$, which implies $\frac{a+b}{a-b} = \frac{c+d}{c-d}$.

24. $\frac{37}{125}$ of a mile

25. (a) $\frac{-3}{5}, \frac{-2}{5}, 0, \frac{1}{5}, \frac{2}{5}$ (b) $\frac{13}{24}, \frac{7}{12}, \frac{13}{18}$

26. (a) $x \geq \frac{3}{2}$ (b) $x > 3$ (c) $x > \frac{-7}{15}$ (d) $x \leq \frac{-56}{5}$

27. Answers vary. Examples are: (a) $\frac{11}{30}, \frac{12}{30}, \frac{13}{30}$

(b) $\frac{-1}{12}, \frac{-1}{9}, \frac{-5}{36}$

Brain Teaser (p. 317)

Let d be the distance between the houses and v the speed. Then $\dfrac{2d + \frac{3}{8}}{v} = \dfrac{d + \frac{5}{12}}{v}$. Hence $2d + \frac{3}{8} = d + \frac{5}{12}$, $d = \frac{5}{12} - \frac{3}{8} = \frac{1}{24}$ mi.

Problem Set 6-6

1. (a) $\frac{1}{3^{13}}$ (b) 3^{13} (c) 5^{11} (d) 5^{19} (e) $\frac{1}{(-5)^2}$, or $\frac{1}{5^2}$

(f) a^5 (g) a^2 (h) $\frac{1}{a}$

2. (a) $\left(\frac{1}{2}\right)^{10}$ (b) $\left(\frac{1}{2}\right)^3$ (c) $\left(\frac{2}{3}\right)^9$ (d) 1 (e) $\left(\frac{5}{3}\right)^3$

(f) $\left(\frac{5}{6}\right)^{21}$

3. (a) False $2^3 \cdot 2^4 \neq (2 \cdot 2)^{3+4}$ (b) False $2^3 \cdot 2^4 \neq (2 \cdot 2)^{3\cdot4}$ (c) False $2^3 \cdot 2^3 \neq (2 \cdot 2)^{2\cdot3}$ (d) False $a^0 = 1$ if $a \neq 0$ (e) False $(2 + 3)^2 \neq 2^2 + 3^2$ (f) False $(2 + 3)^{-2} \neq \frac{1}{2^2} + \frac{1}{3^2}$ (g) False $a^{mn} = (a^m)^n \neq a^m \cdot a^n$

(h) True $\left(\frac{a}{b}\right)^{-1} = \frac{1}{\left(\frac{a}{b}\right)} = \frac{b}{a}$

4. (a) 5 (b) 6 or -6 (c) -2 (d) -4 (e) 0 (f) 15

5. $2 \cdot 10^{11}$; $2 \cdot 10^5$

6. (a) $x \leq 4$ (b) $x \leq 1$ (c) $x \geq 2$ (d) $x > 0$

7. (a) $\frac{1 - x^2}{x}$ (b) $\frac{x^2 y^2 - 1}{y^2}$ (c) $6x^2 + 4x$ (d) $\frac{1 + y^6}{y^3}$ (e) $(3a - b)^2$ (f) $b/(b + a)$

8. (a) $\left(\frac{1}{2}\right)^3$ (b) $\left(\frac{3}{4}\right)^8$ (c) $\left(\frac{4}{3}\right)^{10}$ (d) $\left(\frac{4}{5}\right)^{10}$ (e) $\left(\frac{4}{3}\right)^{10}$ (f) $\left(\frac{3}{4}\right)^{100}$

9. (a) 10^{10} (b) $10^{10} \cdot (6/5)^2$

10. (a) $3/2, 3/4, 3/8, 3/16, 3/32$ (b) Each of the four ratios is $\frac{1}{2}$ (c) $3/1024$

11. (a) $3/4$ (b) 24 (c) $3/128$ (d) $n = -7$

12. (a) 3^{400} (b) $4^{300} = (4^3)^{100} = 64^{100}$, $3^{400} = (3^4)^{100} = 81^{100}$ and $81^{100} > 64^{100}$

13. (a) 32^{50} because $32^{50} = (2^5)^{50} = 2^{250}$ and $4^{100} = 2^{200}$ (b) $(-3)^{-75}$

14. 216

15. 27

16. (a) $\frac{2}{7}$ (b) $\frac{40}{3}$ (c) $\frac{1}{3^4}$ (d) $\frac{1}{100}$ (e) 9 or -9 (f) $\frac{49}{100}$ (g) $\frac{9}{16}$ (h) $\frac{x}{x+y}$

17. (a) $\frac{-4}{3}$ (b) $\frac{-9}{10}$ (c) $\frac{60}{13}$ (d) $\frac{-9}{4}$ (e) 9 or -9 (f) $\frac{4}{5}$

18. $1\frac{1}{5}$ days

19. It will become greater because $\frac{3x}{8x} < \frac{3x + 2}{8x + 2}$.

20. $\frac{-6}{7}, \frac{-3}{4}, \frac{-2}{3}, \frac{-1}{2}, 0, \frac{7}{9}, \frac{4}{5}, \frac{6}{7}, \frac{9}{7}$

Chapter Test

1. (a) (b)

2. $\frac{10}{12}, \frac{15}{18}, \frac{20}{24}$

3. (a) $\frac{6}{7}$ (b) $\frac{ax}{b}$ (c) $\frac{0}{1}$ (d) $\frac{5}{9}$ (e) b (f) $\frac{2}{27}$

4. (a) $=$ (b) $>$ (c) $>$ (d) $<$

5. (a) $\frac{11}{10}$ (b) $\frac{13}{175}$ (c) $\frac{10}{13}$ (d) $\frac{25}{24}$ (e) $\frac{50}{9}$ (f) $\frac{-26}{27}$

6. (a) $-3, \frac{1}{3}$ (b) $-3\frac{1}{7}, \frac{7}{22}$ (c) $\frac{-5}{6}, \frac{6}{5}$ (d) $\frac{3}{4}, \frac{-4}{3}$

7. $-2\frac{1}{3}, -1\frac{7}{8}, 0, (71/140)^{300}, 69/140, 1/2, 71/140, (74/73)^{300}$

188

8. (a) 6 **(b)** $\frac{5}{4}$ **(c)** $\frac{-1}{4}$

9. (a) $x \le \frac{42}{25}$ **(b)** $x \le \frac{3}{2}$ **(c)** $x = \frac{8}{9}$ **(d)** $x = \frac{3}{2}$

10. $\frac{a}{b} \div \frac{c}{d} = x$ if and only if $\frac{a}{b} = \frac{c}{d} \cdot x$. $x = \frac{d}{c} \cdot \frac{a}{b}$ is the solution of the equation because $\frac{c}{d} \cdot \left(\frac{d}{c} \cdot \frac{a}{b}\right) = \frac{a}{b}$.

11. 9

12. (a) $\frac{1}{2^{11}}$ **(b)** $\frac{1}{5^{20}}$ **(c)** $\left(\frac{3}{2}\right)^{28}$, or $\frac{3^{28}}{2^{28}}$ **(d)** 3^{18}

13. 17 pieces, $\frac{11}{6}$ yards left.

14. (a) 15 **(b)** 15 **(c)** 4

15. 76/100, 78/100 but answers may vary.

16. $70

CHAPTER 7

Problem Set 7-1

1. (a) $0 \cdot 10^0 + 0 \cdot 10^{-1} + 2 \cdot 10^{-2} + 3 \cdot 10^{-3}$
(b) $2 \cdot 10^2 + 0 \cdot 10 + 6 \cdot 10^0 + 0 \cdot 10^{-1} + 6 \cdot 10^{-2}$
(c) $3 \cdot 10^2 + 1 \cdot 10 + 2 \cdot 10^0 + 0 \cdot 10^{-1} + 1 \cdot 10^{-2} + 0 \cdot 10^{-3} + 3 \cdot 10^{-4}$ **(d)** $0 \cdot 10^0 + 0 \cdot 10^{-1} + 0 \cdot 10^{-2} + 0 \cdot 10^{-3} + 1 \cdot 10^{-4} + 3 \cdot 10^{-5} + 2 \cdot 10^{-6}$

2. (a) 4356.78 **(b)** 4000.608 **(c)** 40,000.03 **(d)** 0.204007

3. (a) 536.0076 **(b)** 3.008 **(c)** 0.000436 **(d)** 5,000,000.2

4. (a) 436/1000 **(b)** 2516/100 **(c)** ⁻316,027/1000 **(d)** $\frac{281,902}{10,000}$ **(e)** ⁻43/10 **(f)** ⁻6201/100

5. (a), (b), (c), (d), (e), (f), and (h) can be represented by terminating decimals.

6. (a) 0.8 **(b)** 3.05 **(c)** 0.5 **(d)** 0.03125 **(e)** 0.01152 **(f)** 0.2128 **(h)** 0.08

7. (a) 39.202 **(b)** 168.003 **(c)** ⁻390.6313 **(d)** 1.49093 **(e)** ⁻10.4 **(f)** 4.681

8. (a) 17.702 **(b)** 8.538 **(c)** 0.0272 **(d)** 68

9. $231.24

10. 0.8

11. Lining up the decimal points acts as using place value.

12. (a) 463,000,000 **(b)** 4,000,000 **(c)** 4,630,000,000 **(d)** 46,300,000,000 **(e)** 463,000 **(f)** 4.63

13. (a) 0.000463 **(b)** 0.000004 **(c)** 0.00463 **(d)** 0.00000000463

14. (a) 46,300 **(b)** 400 **(c)** 463,000 **(d)** 0.463

15. (a), (c), and (f)

16. Approximately 0.11 in.

17. 1.679 points

18. (a) 0.077 **(b)** 406

19. Answers may vary.

20. 62.298 lb

21.

8.2	1.9	6.4
3.7	5.5	7.3
4.6	9.1	2.8

22. $8.00

23. (a) 5.4, 6.3, 7.2 **(b)** 1.3, 1.5, 1.7 **(c)** 0.0625, 0.03125, 0.015625 **(d)** 6.7, 8, 9.3

24. The person might divide the entry by 1000.

25. Do a division problem. Depending upon the type of calculator and how many places in the display, the division may have to be done in parts.

26. (a) 91,000,000.1106 **(b)** ⁻90,753086.5318 **(c)** 45,135,802.09496 **(d)** 102,880,657,928.6

27. (a) Dime-a-time **(b)** System B **(c)** 25

28. No

29. Second option; Approximately $4,368,709 better.

30. The number of digits in the terminating decimal is the greater of m or n.

Brain Teaser (p. 342)
One possibility is 77/0.07 = 100.

Problem Set 7-2

1. (a) $0.\overline{4}$ **(b)** $0.\overline{285714}$ **(c)** $0.\overline{27}$ **(d)** $0.0\overline{6}$ **(e)** $0.02\overline{6}$ **(f)** $0.0.\overline{1}$ **(g)** $0.8\overline{3}$ **(h)** $0.\overline{076923}$

2. (a) (i) $0.\overline{142857}$ (ii) $0.\overline{285714}$ (iii) $0.\overline{428571}$ (iv) $0.\overline{571428}$ (v) $0.\overline{714285}$ (vi) $0.\overline{857142}$ **(b)** 6 **(c)** The answers all contain the same digits, 1, 2, 4, 5, 7, and 8. The digits in each answer repeat in the same sequence; that is, in each case a 1 is always followed by a 4, which is always followed by a 2, which is always followed by an 8, and so on. In each of the answers in (i)–(vi), the starting digit is different, but the sequence of numbers is the same.

3. (a) The sum is always 999. **(b)** Yes **(c)** It appears that the sum will be a power of 10 less 1. **(d)** No

4. (a) $0.\overline{076923}$ **(b)** $0.\overline{047619}$ **(c)** $0.\overline{157894736842105263}$

5. (a) 221/90 **(b)** 243/99 **(c)** 243/99 **(d)** 243/990 **(e)** 243/9900 **(f)** ⁻2430/99 **(g)** 4/9 **(h)** 2/3 **(i)** 5/9 **(j)** 34/99 **(k)** ⁻232/99 **(l)** ⁻2/99

6. (a) $3.2\overline{3}$, $3.\overline{23}$, 3.23, 3.22, 3.2 **(b)** ⁻1.45, ⁻1.454, ⁻1.45$\overline{4}$, ⁻1.4$\overline{54}$, ⁻1.$\overline{454}$

7. Answers may vary. (a) 3.23 **(b)** 462.245 **(c)** 462.243 **(d)** 0.02$\overline{9}$

8. (a) 3.25 **(b)** 462.245 **(c)** 0.01515 **(d)** 462.2$\overline{43}$

9. (a) 49736.5281 **(b)** 41235.6789

10. (a) 200 **(b)** 200 **(c)** 204 **(d)** 203.7 **(e)** 203.65

11. 19 mi

12. (a) Okay, it only totals $2.17 **(b)** Don't buy your date a soft drink.

13. $37

14. Estimates may vary. Exact answers are as follows: (a) 122.06 **(b)** 57.31 **(c)** 25.40 **(d)** 136.15

15. 28,000 years
16. (a) $3.325 \cdot 10^3$ (b) $4.632 \cdot 10$ (c) $1.3 \cdot 10^{-4}$
(d) $9.30146 \cdot 10^5$
17. (a) 0.0000000032 (b) 3,200,000,000 (c) 0.42
(d) 620,000
18. (a) $1.27 \cdot 10^7$ (b) $5.797 \cdot 10^6$ (c) $5 \cdot 10^7$
19. (a) 0.0000044 (b) 19,900 (c) 3,000,000,000
20. (a) $4.8 \cdot 10^{28}$ (b) $4 \cdot 10^7$ (c) $2 \cdot 10^2$
21. 1000^5
22. Because $1/99 = 0.0101010101\ldots$, then $51/99 = 51(1/99) = 51 \cdot 0.01010101\ldots = 0.51515151\ldots$
However, $x/99$ behaves differently if $x > 99$.
23. (a) $1.\overline{6}, 2, 2.\overline{3}$ (b) $6/7 = 0.\overline{857142}, 7/8 = 0.875,$
$8/9 = 0.\overline{8}$
24. (a) $0.\overline{446355}; 6$ (b) $1.3\overline{5775}$; yes; 4
25. (a) 21.6 lb (b) 48 lb
26. $22,761.95
27. A fraction in simplest form, a/b, can be written as a terminating decimal if and only if the prime factorization of the denominator contains no primes other than 2 or 5.
28. (a) 1672/100 (b) 3/1000 (c) $^-507/100$
(d) 123/1000

Problem Set 7-3
1. (a) 789% (b) 3.2% (c) 19,310% (d) 20%
(e) $83.\overline{3}\%$ or $83\frac{1}{3}\%$ (f) 15% (g) 12.5%
(h) 37.5% (i) 62.5% (j) $16.\overline{6}\%$ (k) 80% (l) 2.5%
2. (a) $0.\overline{16}$ (b) 0.045 (c) $0.\overline{002}$ (d) $0.00\overline{285714}$
(e) $0.13\overline{6}$ (f) 1.25 (g) $0.00\overline{3}$ (h) 0.0025
3. (a) 4 (b) 2 (c) 25 (d) 200 (e) 12.5
4. Answers may vary.
5. (a) 2.04 (b) 50% (c) 60 (d) 3.43 (e) 400%
(f) 40
6. 63
7. $16,960
8. $14,500
9. $437.50
10. (a) Bill, 221 (b) Joe, 90% (c) Ron, 265
11. 20%
12. 15%
13. Approximately 18.4%
14. Approximately 89.7%
15. 100%
16. $22.40
17. $5.10
18. 50 cups
19. $336
20. 35%
21. $3200
22. 1200
23. $16.\overline{6}\%$
24. $10.37

25. Approximately $82,644.63
26. $11.\overline{1}\%$
27. $440
28. $33.\overline{3}\%$
29. $187.50
30. Approximately $9207.58
31. (a) $3.30 (b) $24 (c) $1.90 (d) $24.50
32. (a) 4% (b) 32% (c) 64%
33. (a) Approximately 4.9%, 34.6%, and 60.5%
(b) Approximately 6.3%, 37.5%, and 56.3%
(c) Approximately 8.2%, 40.8%, and 51%
(d) Approximately 2.7%, 27.8%, and 69.4%
34. (a) $d + 1$ (b) $d + 0.25(n - 7)$
35. 97 days
36. 3321/100
37. $0.\overline{2}$
38. 559/18
39. (a) $3.25 \cdot 10^6$ (b) $1.2 \cdot 10^{-4}$
40. (a) 32.0 (b) 30

Brain Teaser (p. 362)
Let C = amount of crust
P = amount of pie
x = percent of crust to be reduced
C = 25% of P
$C = Cx/100 = (20/100)P$
$x = 20\%$

Problem Set 7-4
1. (a) 6%, 2, 3%, 4, $125.50 (b) 8%, 3, 2%, 12, $268.24
(c) 10%, 5, $0.8\overline{3}\%$, 60, $645.30 (d) 12%, 4, 12/365,
1460, $615.95
2. $5460
3. $24.46
4. 3.5%
5. Approximately $32,040.82
6. $64,800
7. $4416.34
8. $23,720.58
9. $81,628.82
10. $1944
11. The Pay More Bank has a better rate.
12. (iii) 13.2%
13. Approximately $2.53
14. Approximately $5918.41
15. Approximately $3592.89
16. $10,935
17. Approximately 12.78%
18. Approximately 7.3 years

Problem Set 7-5
1. Answers may vary. One answer is
0.232233222333 . . .
2. $0.7\overline{7}, 0.\overline{7}, 0.78, 0.787787778\ldots, 0.\overline{78}, 0.788, 0.7\overline{8}$
= 0.788

190

3. $0.\overline{9}$, $0.9\overline{98}$, $0.\overline{98}$, $0.9\overline{88}$, 0.9, $0.\overline{898}$
4. (a), (d), (e), and (f) represent irrational numbers
5. (a) 15 (b) 15.8 (c) 13 (d) 22.6 (e) Impossible (f) 25
6. (a) 4.12 (b) 2.65 (c) 4.58 (d) 0.11 (e) 4.51 (f) 1.28
7. (a) False, $\sqrt{2} + 0$ (b) False: $^{-}\sqrt{2} + \sqrt{2}$ (c) False: $\sqrt{2} \cdot \sqrt{2}$ (d) False: $\sqrt{2} - \sqrt{2}$
8. False $\sqrt{64 + 36} \neq \sqrt{64} + \sqrt{36}$
9. Answers may vary. For example, $\sqrt{2}$, $\sqrt{3}$, and $\sqrt{5}$
10. Answers may vary. For example, assume the following pattern continues 0.54544544454444 . . .
11. No; 22/7 is a rational number that can be represented by the repeating decimal $3.\overline{142857}$.
12. No; $\sqrt{13}$ is an irrational number, so when it is expressed as a decimal, it is nonterminating and nonrepeating.
13. (a) R (b) ∅ (c) Q (d) ∅ (e) R (f) R
14. (a) $x \leq 8/3$

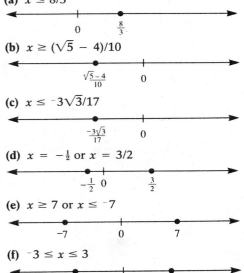

(b) $x \geq (\sqrt{5} - 4)/10$

(c) $x \leq {}^{-}3\sqrt{3}/17$

(d) $x = -\frac{1}{2}$ or $x = 3/2$

(e) $x \geq 7$ or $x \leq {}^{-}7$

(f) $^{-}3 \leq x \leq 3$

15. (a) N, I, Q, R (b) Q, R (c) R (d) N, I, Q, R (e) ∅ (f) Q, R
16. (a) 64 (b) None (c) $^{-}$64 (d) None (e) All real numbers greater than 0 (f) None
17. 6.4 ft
18. (a) 8.98 sec (b) 20.07 sec
19. Suppose $\sqrt{3}$ is rational. $\sqrt{3} = a/b$ where a and b are integers and $b \neq 0$. Therefore, $3 = a^2/b^2$, or $3b^2 = a^2$. a^2 has an even number of 3's in its prime factorization but $3b^2$ has an odd number of 3's in its

prime factorization and this is impossible. Thus, $\sqrt{3}$ is irrational.
20. Suppose $\sqrt{p}$ is rational, where p is a prime. Then $\sqrt{p} = a/b$ where a and b are integers and $b \neq 0$. Thus, $p = a^2/b^2$ or $pb^2 = a^2$. Since b^2 has an even number of p's in its prime factorization, pb^2 has an odd number of p's in its prime factorization and this is impossible. Thus, $\sqrt{p}$ is irrational.
21. (a) m is a perfect square. (b) Use the result of Problem 20.
22. (a) $0.5 + 1/0.5 = 0.5 + 2 = 2.5 \geq 2$ (b) Suppose $x + 1/x < 2$. Then $(x^1 + 1)/x < 2$. Since $x > 0$, $x^2 + 1 < 2x$ so that $x^2 - 2x + 1 < 0$, or $(x - 1)^2 < 0$ which is false. Therefore, $x + 1/x \geq 2$.
23. 3/1250
24. 4.09, $4.09\overline{1}$, 4.099, $4.0\overline{9}$
25. 8/33
26. (a) 203,000 (b) 0.00038
27. $20,274
28. 60%

Problem Set 7.6
1. (a) $6\sqrt{5}$ (b) 23 (c) $11\sqrt{3}$ (d) $6\sqrt{7}$ (e) 13/14 (f) 1/2
2. (a) $^{-}$3 (b) $2\sqrt[5]{3}$ (c) 2 (d) $5\sqrt[3]{2}$ (e) $^{-}$3 (f) $2\sqrt[4]{4}$
3. (a) $2\sqrt{3} + 3\sqrt{2} + 6\sqrt{5}$ (b) $2\sqrt[3]{5}$ (c) $30 + 12\sqrt{6}$ (d) $\sqrt{\frac{1}{2}}$, or $\sqrt{2}/2$ (e) $17\sqrt{2}$ (f) $\sqrt{6}$
4. (a) 4 (b) 9 (c) 32 (d) 9 (e) 1/256 (f) 9 (g) 1/4 (h) 1/9 (i) 4 (j) 32 (k) 10 (l) 8 (m) 16 (n) 1/4 (o) 4
5. No
6. (a) Sometimes (b) Sometimes (if $x = 0$) (c) Always (d) Sometimes (if $a = {}^{-}b$) (e) Always
7. 21
8. (a) 2^{10} (b) 2^{11} (c) 2^{12}
9. $(4/25)^{-1/4}$, $(4/25)^{-1/3} = (25/4)^{1/3}$
10. (a) $\sqrt{3}$ (b) $\sqrt[3]{3}$ (c) $\sqrt{12} + \sqrt{14}$
11. $\sqrt[8]{2^7}$
12. (a) 4 (b) 3/2 (c) $^{-}$4/7 (d) 5/6
13. $\sqrt[3]{1/16}$
14. (a) n is odd (b) When m is even, then n can be any number except 0. When m is odd, then n must also be odd.

Chapter 7 Test
1. (a) $^{-}$0.693 (b) 31.564 (c) 0.2284 (d) 0.032 (e) $^{-}$0.097 (f) 0.00000016
2. (a) $3 \cdot 10 + 2 \cdot 1 + 0 \cdot 10^{-1} + 1 \cdot 10^{-2} + 2 \cdot 10^{-3}$ (b) $0 \cdot 10^{-1} + 0 \cdot 10^{-2} + 1 \cdot 10^{-3} + 0 \cdot 10^{-4} + 3 \cdot 10^{-5}$

3. A fraction in simplest form, a/b, can be written as a terminating decimal if and only if the prime factorization of the denominator contains no primes other than 2 or 5.
4. 8
5. (a) $0.\overline{571428}$ (b) 0.125 (c) $0.\overline{6}$ (d) 0.625
6. (a) 7/25 (b) 1/3 (c) 94/95
7. (a) 307.63 (b) 307.6 (c) 308 (d) 300
8. (a) $x \le 3.\overline{3}$ (b) 0 (c) 20,000 (d) 20 (e) 34 (f) $0.\overline{6}$
9. (a) 25% (b) 192 (c) $56.\overline{6}$ (d) 20%
10. (a) 12.5% (b) 7.5% (c) 627% (d) 1.23% (e) 150%
11. (a) 0.60 (b) $0.00\overline{6}$ (c) 1
12. (a) No; $-\sqrt{2} + \sqrt{2}$ is not an irrational number. (b) No; see part (a). (c) No; $\sqrt{2} \cdot \sqrt{2}$ is not an irrational number. (d) No; $\sqrt{2}/\sqrt{2}$ is not an irrational number.
13. 4.796
14. (a) $4.26 \cdot 10^5$ (b) $2.37 \cdot 10^{-6}$ (c) $3.2 \cdot 10$ (d) $3.25 \cdot 10^{-4}$
15. (a) 3 (b) 3 (c) 2 (d) 3
16. (a) Irrational (b) Irrational (c) Rational (d) Rational (e) Irrational
17. $9280
18. $3.\overline{3}$%
19. 88.6%
20. $5750
21. It makes no difference.
22. $80
23. $15,000
24. $15,110.68
25. (a) $11\sqrt{2}$ (b) $12\sqrt{2}$ (c) $6\sqrt{10}$ (d) $3\sqrt[3]{2}$
26. (a) $1/2^{11}$ (b) $1/5^{20}$ (c) $(3/2)^{28}$ (d) 3^{18}

CHAPTER 8

Problem Set 8-1
1. (a) {1, 2, 3, 4} (b) {Red, Blue} (c) $S = \{(1, \text{Red}),$ (1, Blue), (2, Red), (2, Blue), (3, Red), (3, Blue), (4, Red), (4, Blue)} (d) $S = \{(\text{Red}, 1), (\text{Red}, 2),$ (Red, 3), (Red, 4), (Red, 5), (Red, 6), (Blue, 1), (Blue, 2), (Blue, 3), (Blue, 4), (Blue, 5), (Blue, 6)} (e) $S = \{(1, 1),$ (1, 2), (1, 3), (1, 4), (2, 1), (2, 2), (2, 3), (2, 4), (3, 1), (3, 2), (3, 3), (3, 4), (4, 1), (4, 2), (4, 3), (4, 4)} (f) $S = \{(\text{Red}, \text{Red}), (\text{Red}, \text{Blue}), (\text{Blue}, \text{Red}), (\text{Blue}, \text{Blue})\}$
2. (a) $S = \{0, 1, 2, 3, 4, 5, 6, 7, 8, 9\}$ (b) $A = \{0, 1, 2, 3, 4\}$ (c) $B = \{1, 3, 5, 7, 9\}$ (d) $C = \{0, 1, 3, 4, 5, 6, 7, 8, 9\}$
3. (b) $P(A) = \frac{5}{10}$, or $\frac{1}{2}$ (c) $P(B) = \frac{5}{10}$, or $\frac{1}{2}$
(d) $P(C) = \frac{9}{10}$

4. (a) $P(\text{Red}) = \frac{26}{52}$, or $\frac{1}{2}$ (b) $P(\text{Face Card}) = \frac{12}{52}$, or $\frac{3}{13}$ (c) $P(\text{Red or a 10}) = \frac{28}{52}$ or $\frac{7}{13}$ (d) $P(\text{Queen}) = \frac{4}{52}$, or $\frac{1}{13}$ (e) $P(\text{Not a queen}) = \frac{48}{52}$, or $\frac{12}{13}$ (f) $P(\text{Face card or a club}) = \frac{22}{52}$, or $\frac{11}{26}$ (g) $P(\text{Face card and a club}) = \frac{3}{52}$ (h) $P(\text{Not a face card and not a club}) = \frac{30}{52}$, or $\frac{15}{26}$

5. (a) $P(\text{Brown}) = \frac{4}{12}$, or $\frac{1}{3}$ (b) $P(\text{Either black or green}) = \frac{8}{12}$, or $\frac{2}{3}$ (c) $P(\text{Red}) = \frac{0}{12} = 0$ (d) $P(\text{Not black}) = \frac{6}{12}$, or $\frac{1}{2}$

6. $P(\text{Vowel}) = \frac{5}{26}$; $P(\text{Consonant}) = 1 - \frac{5}{26} = \frac{21}{26}$

7. (a) $P(\text{Win on first roll}) = \frac{8}{36}$, or $\frac{2}{9}$ (b) $P(\text{Lose on first roll}) = \frac{4}{36}$, or $\frac{1}{9}$ (c) $P(\text{Neither winning nor losing on first roll}) = \frac{24}{36}$, or $\frac{2}{3}$ (d) Either 6 or 8 has a probability of $\frac{5}{36}$ of occurring again. (e) $P(1) = 0$. (f) $P(\text{less than 13}) = 1$ (g) 10
8. 70%

9. (a) $P(\text{Black}) = \frac{18}{38}$, or $\frac{9}{19}$ (b) $P(\text{0 or 00}) = \frac{2}{28}$, or $\frac{1}{19}$ (c) $P(\text{not 1–12}) = \frac{26}{38}$, or $\frac{13}{19}$ (d) $P(\text{Odd or green}) = \frac{20}{38}$, or $\frac{10}{19}$

10. 10
11. (a) No (b) Yes (c) Yes (d) Yes (e) No (f) Yes (g) No (h) No
12. $\frac{45}{150}$ or $\frac{3}{10}$
13. (a) $\frac{1}{2}$ (b) $\frac{3}{4}$ (c) $\frac{3}{4}$
14. 0.7
15. No, the sum can't be greater than 1
16. (a) $\frac{45}{80}$ (b) $\frac{10}{80}$ (c) $\frac{60}{80}$ (d) $\frac{30}{80}$
17. $\frac{1}{24}$

Brain Teaser (p. 396)

You should choose your die second, because then you can base your choice on the die that was picked first. The best second choices are given below, along with the probability of the second choice winning.

1st Person's Choice	2nd Person's Choice	Probability 2nd Choice Winning
A	D	$\frac{2}{3}$
B	A	$\frac{2}{3}$
C	B	$\frac{2}{3}$
D	C	$\frac{2}{3}$

This table can be verified by constructing a sample space for the various first and second choices. For more information, see R. Billstein, "A Fun Way to Introduce Probability," *The Arithmetic Teacher* 24 (January 1977): 39–42.

Problem Set 8-2

1. (a) $\frac{1}{216}$ (b) $\frac{1}{120}$
2. (a) $\frac{1}{24}$ (b) $\frac{1}{64}$ (c) $\frac{1}{84}$ (d) $\frac{21}{108}$, or $\frac{7}{36}$
3. $\frac{1}{30}$
4. (a) $P(SOS) = \frac{1}{3}$ using box 1 and $P(SOS) = \frac{1}{5}$ using box 2, so choose box 1. (b) $P(SOS) = \frac{4}{27}$ with both boxes
5. (a) $\frac{64}{75}$ (b) $\frac{11}{75}$
6. She should play Billie-Bobby-Billie; then the probability of winning two in a row is $\frac{3}{5}$.
7. (a) $P(\infty) = \frac{1}{5}$ (b) P(at least one black) $= \frac{4}{5}$ (c) P(at most one black) $= \frac{11}{15}$ (d) $P(\bullet\circ, \circ\bullet) = \frac{8}{15}$
8. P(at least 3 H) $= \frac{5}{16}$
9. $\frac{1}{16}$
10. (a) $\frac{1}{5}$ (b) $\frac{3}{5}$ (c) $\frac{1}{5}$

11. (a) P(3 plums) $= \frac{25}{8000}$, or $\frac{1}{320}$ (b) P(3 oranges) $= \frac{126}{8000}$, or $\frac{63}{4000}$ (c) P(3 lemons) $= 0$ (d) P(no plums) $= \frac{4275}{8000}$, or $\frac{171}{320}$
12. $\frac{1}{32}$
13. 1
14. (a) $\frac{16}{81}$ (b) $\frac{8}{27}$
15. $\frac{1}{256}$
16. $\frac{1152}{39,916,800}$, or $\frac{1}{34,650}$
17. 0.986
18. (a) $\frac{1}{25}$ (b) $\frac{8}{25}$ (c) $\frac{16}{25}$
19. (a) 0.3 (b) 15
20. 0.7
21. $0.08\overline{3}$
22. 0.271
23. 0.4
24. (a) A is the best choice followed by B and then C. (b) No. C is now the best choice. $P(C$ winning$) = \frac{35}{99}$, $P(B$ winning$) = \frac{34}{99}$, $P(A$ winning$) = \frac{30}{99}$.
25. The probabilities of Abe's winning the game are summarized in the table below. Of the 12 possible games, only 8 result in choices with equally likely probabilities.

		Abe's choice			
		HH	HT	TH	TT
Your choice	HH	—	.50	.75	.50
	HT	.50	—	.50	.25
	TH	.25	.50	—	.50
	TT	.50	.75	.50	—

26. (a) (v) (b) (iii) (c) (ii) (d) (i) (e) (iv)
27. (a) $\frac{1}{30}$ (b) 0 (c) $\frac{19}{30}$

Brain Teaser (p. 409)

The probability that at least two people share the same birthday is one minus the probability that no two people share the same birthday. We calculate the latter probability first. Let's pick a first person. Since there are 364 birthdays that a second person can have which are

193

different from the first person's birthday, the probability that the second person's birthday differs from the first is $\frac{364}{365}$. In order for the third person to have a birthday different from the first and the second person, he or she must be born on one of the 363 days which are different from the first two person's birthdays. Thus the probability that the third person's birthday differs from the first and second is $\frac{363}{365}$. Hence the probability that the first three people have different birthdays is $\frac{364}{365} \cdot \frac{363}{365}$. Continuing in this way, we find the probability that all n people have different birthdays in $\frac{364}{365} \cdot \frac{363}{365} \cdot \frac{362}{365} \cdot \ldots \cdot \frac{365 - (n - 1)}{365}$. To find the value of n for which the above product is less than $\frac{1}{2}$, we can use a calculator and try various values of n. For $n = 23$, the above product is slightly less than $\frac{1}{2}$. Hence, if there are 23 people in a room, the probability that no two people share the same birthday is slightly less than $\frac{1}{2}$; therefore the complementary probability that at least 2 people share the same birthday is slightly greater than $\frac{1}{2}$.

Problem Set 8-3

1. (a) $\frac{6}{18}$ or $\frac{1}{3}$ (b) $\frac{2}{11}$

2. $\frac{1}{4}$

3. $\frac{1}{4}$

4. $\frac{3}{51}$

5. $\frac{4}{12}$ or $\frac{1}{3}$

6. 0.0005

7. $\frac{1}{4}$

8. $\frac{4500}{10,000}$, or $\frac{9}{20}$

9. (a) $\frac{3}{12}$ (b) $\frac{27}{132}$ or $\frac{9}{44}$ (c) $\frac{216}{1320}$ or $\frac{9}{55}$

(d) $\frac{1512}{11,880}$ or $\frac{7}{55}$

10. $\frac{69}{3000}$ or $\frac{23}{1000}$

11. (a) $\frac{38}{100}$ or $\frac{19}{50}$ (b) $\frac{10}{100}$ or $\frac{1}{10}$ (c) $\frac{25}{36}$

12. $\frac{10}{30}$ or $\frac{1}{3}$

13. (a) Let the numbers 1, 2, 3, 4, 5, and 6 represent the numbers of the die and ignore the numbers 0, 7, 8, 9. (b) Number the persons 01, 02, 03, . . . , 18, 19, 20. Go to the random digit table and mark off groups of two. The three persons chosen are the first three whose numbers appear. (c) Represent Red by the numbers 0, 1, 2, 3, 4; Green by the numbers 5, 6, 7; Yellow by the number 8; and white by the number 9.

14. 1200 fish

15. $\frac{30}{100}$ or $\frac{3}{10}$

16. Pick a starting spot in the table and count the number of digits it takes before all the numbers 1 through 9 are obtained. Repeat this experiment many times and find the average number of coupons.

17. Let 500 students be represented by the numbers 001, 002, 003, 004, . . . , 500. Pick a starting spot in the table and mark groups at three. The first 30 numbers less than 501 represent the 30 students to be chosen.

18. For example, let the digits 0, 1, 2, 3, 4, 5, 6, 7 represent rain on Monday and the digits 8, 9 represent dry weather on Monday. Based on this result, continue to simulate the rest of the week.

18. Answers may vary.

20. (a) 7 (b) Answers may vary

21. Answers vary, e.g., use a random digit table. Let the digits 1–8 represent a win and the digits 0 and 9 represent losses. Mark off blocks of 3. If only the digits 1–8 appear, then this represents 3 wins in a row.

22. Answers may vary, e.g., mark off blocks of 2 digits and let the digits 00, 01, 02, . . . , 13, 14 represent contracting the disease and 15 to 90 represent no disease. Mark off blocks of 3 digits to represent the 3 children. If at least one of the numbers is 00 to 14, then this represents a child in the 3-child family having strep.

23. Let the 10 ducks be represented by the digits 0, 1, 2, 3, . . . , 8, 9. Then pick a starting point in the table and mark off 10 digits to simulate which ducks the hunters shoot at. Count how many of the digits 0 through 9 are not in the 10 digits and this represents the ducks that escaped. Do this experiment many times and take the average to determine an answer. See how close your simulation comes to the theoretical probability of 3.49.

Problem Set 8-4

1. 12 to 40, or 3 to 10; 40 to 12, or 10 to 3
2. 30 to 6, or 5 to 1
3. 15 to 1

4. (a) $\frac{1}{2}$ **(b)** $\left(\frac{1}{2}\right)^{10}$, or $\frac{1}{1024}$ **(c)** 1023 to 1

5. $\frac{5}{8}$

6. 1 to 1
7. 4 to 6 or 2 to 3
8. 20 to 18 or 10 to 1
9. $0.25
10. $3.50
11. $3.00
12. 3 hours
13. Approximately 8¢
14. $10,000
15. (a) Al gets $75, Betsy gets $25. **(b)** 3 to 1 **(c)** Al gets approximately $89, Betsy gets approximately $11. **(d)** 57 to 7

Problem Set 8-5

1. 224
2. 210
3. 32
4. 10,000
5. 1352; 35,152
6. 180
7. (a) T **(b)** F **(c)** F **(d)** F **(e)** T **(f)** T **(g)** T
8. 8! = 40,320
9. 15
10. (a) 12 **(b)** 210 **(c)** 3360 **(d)** 34,650 **(e)** 3780
11. (a) 24,360 **(b)** 4,060
12. 792
13. 9! = 362,880
14. $\frac{1}{120}$
15. 45
16. 729
17. 1260
18. (a) 6 **(b)** 36
19. 72
20. 378
21. (a) $\frac{1}{13}$ **(b)** $\frac{8}{65}$
22. (a) 10 **(b)** 1 **(c)** 1 **(d)** 3
23. $\frac{4480}{19,683}$, or approximately 0.228
24. 3480
25. 1260
26. 720
27. (a) $\frac{1}{4}$ **(b)** $\frac{1}{52}$ **(c)** $\frac{48}{52}$, or $\frac{12}{13}$ **(d)** $\frac{3}{4}$ **(e)** $\frac{1}{2}$ **(f)** $\frac{1}{52}$

(g) $\frac{4}{13}$ **(h)** 1
28. (a) $\frac{15}{19}$ **(b)** $\frac{56}{361}$ **(c)** $\frac{28}{171}$

Brain Teaser (p. 440)
The probability of a sucessful flight with 2 engines is 0.9999 and with 4 engines is 0.99999901.

Chapter Test
1. (a) S = {Sunday, Monday, Tuesday, Wednesday, Thursday, Friday, Saturday} **(b)** E = {Tuesday, Thursday} **(c)** $P(T) = \frac{2}{7}$
2. (a) $P(A) = 0$ **(b)** $P(A) = 1$ **(c)** $0 \leq P(A) \leq 1$ **(d)** $P(\overline{A}) = 1 - P(A)$
3. (a) $P(\text{Black}) = \frac{5}{12}$ **(b)** $P(\text{Black or white}) = \frac{9}{12}$, or $\frac{3}{4}$
(c) $P(\text{Neither red nor white}) = \frac{5}{12}$ **(d)** $P(\text{Not red}) = \frac{9}{12}$, or $\frac{3}{4}$ **(e)** $P(\text{Black and white}) = 0$ **(f)** $P(\text{Black or white or red}) = 1$
4. (a) $P(\text{Club}) = \frac{13}{52}$, or $\frac{1}{4}$ **(b)** $P(\text{Spade and a 5}) = \frac{1}{52}$
(c) $P(\text{Heart or a face card}) = \frac{22}{52}$, or $\frac{11}{26}$ **(d)** $P(\text{Not a jack}) = \frac{48}{52}$, or $\frac{12}{13}$
5. (a) $P(3W) = \frac{64}{729}$ **(b)** $P(3W) = \frac{204}{504}$, or $\frac{1}{21}$
6. $P(\text{Success}) = \frac{72}{150}$, or $\frac{12}{25}$
7. $P(L) = \frac{6}{25}$
8. $\frac{14}{80}$, or $\frac{7}{40}$
9. $\frac{7}{45}$
10. $\frac{4}{48}$, or $\frac{1}{12}$
11. $\frac{3}{3}$, or $\frac{1}{1}$
12. $\frac{3}{8}$
13. 30¢
14. $33\frac{1}{3}$¢ or 34¢
15. 900
16. 120
17. 24
18. 9900
19. 5040
20. $\frac{2}{20}$, or $\frac{1}{10}$
21. (a) 60 **(b)** $\frac{1}{20}$ **(c)** $\frac{1}{60}$

22. $\frac{15}{36}$

23. $\frac{2}{5}$

24. 0.027

25. (a) $n!$ (b) n

26. $\frac{63}{80}$

27. $\frac{6}{27}$ or $\frac{2}{9}$

28. (a) For example, let the digits 1, 2, 3, 4, 5, 6, represent the numbers on the die, disregard 0, 7, 8 and 9. (b) For example, let the digits 01, 02, 03, . . . , 11, 12 represent the 12 months of the year. Go to the table and mark off blocks of two digits. Disregard 00 and numbers greater than 12. (c) For example, let the digits 1, 2, 3 represent Red, 4, 5, 6 represent white, and 7, 8, 9 represent Blue. Disregard the number 0.

29. $P(A) = \frac{14}{48}$, $P(B) = \frac{20}{48}$, $P(C) = \frac{14}{48}$

30. $\frac{8}{20}$ or $\frac{2}{5}$

CHAPTER 9

Problem Set 9-1

1. (a) 72, 74, 81, 81, 82, 85, 87, 88, 92, 94, 97, 98, 103, 123, 125 (b) 72 lbs. (c) 125 lbs.

2.

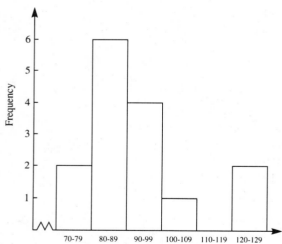

Weights of Students in East Junior
High Algebra I Class

3. Answers may vary.

4.

Home Run Leaders
1976–88

National League		2	2		American League
	9 8 7 7 7 6 1	3	2 2 9 9		
	9 8 8 0 0	4	0 0 1 2 3 5 6 9		
		2	5		

1 | 3 | represents 31 home runs | 3 | 2 represents 32 home runs

5.

Average Ages of Airplanes
as of July 1, 1988

Major U.S. Airlines		7	7		Selected Foreign Airlines
		8	2 7 8		
	5	9	1 6 9		
	8 3 1	10	0 3		
		11			
	1	12			
		13	0		
	9 6	14			
	5 3 1	15			

5 | 9 | represents 5 3 1
9.5 years | 8 | 2 represents 8.2 years

6. (a) November 30 cm (b) October, 15 cm; December 25 cm; January, 10 cm

7. (a)

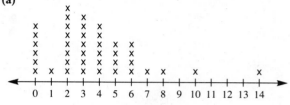

Number of children of U.S. Presidents

(b)

No. of Children	Tally	Frequency
0	⦀⦀		6
1		1
2	⦀⦀ ⦀⦀⦀	8
3	⦀⦀ ⦀⦀	7
4	⦀⦀		6
5	⦀⦀⦀⦀	4
6	⦀⦀⦀⦀	4
7			1
8			1
9		0
10			1
11		0
12		0
13		0
14			1
		40

(c) 2

8.

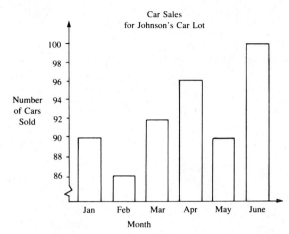

Car Sales
for Johnson's Car Lot

Number of Cars Sold

Month

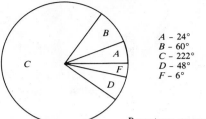

(b) Course Grades For Elementary Teachers

A – 24°
B – 60°
C – 222°
D – 48°
F – 6°

Percentages are approximate

9. (a)

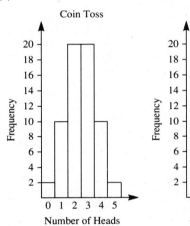

Coin Toss

Frequency

Number of Heads

(b)

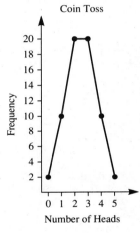

Coin Toss

Frequency

Number of Heads

11. (a) Fall Text Book Costs

```
1
*   6
2   3 3
*   .
3   0 3
*   5 7 7 9 9
4   0 1 2 2
*   5 8 9
5   0 0 1 3     2 | 3  represents
*   8                  $23
6   0 2 2
```

(b) Fall Textbook Costs

Classes	Tally	Frequency	Classes	Tally	Frequency
$15–19	|	1	$45–49	|||	3
$20–24	||	2	$50–54	||||	4
$25–29		0	$55–59	|	1
$30–34	||	2	$60–64	|||	3
$35–39	||||	5			25
$40–44	||||	4			

(c) (d) Frequency polygon and histogram on same graph.

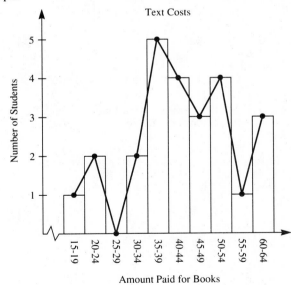

Text Costs

Number of Students

Amount Paid for Books

10. (a)

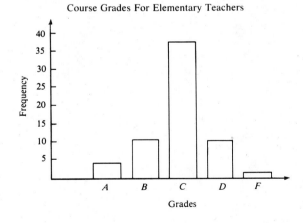

Course Grades For Elementary Teachers

Frequency

Grades

197

12.

	Glasses of Lemonade Sold
Friday	🥤
Thursday	🥤
Wednesday	🥤 🥤 🥤
Tuesday	🥤 🥤
Monday	🥤 🥤

🥤 represents 10 glasses

13. Answers may vary.
14. Answers may vary.
15. The line graph is more helpful, since we can approximate the point midway between 8:00 and 12:00 noon and then draw a vertical line upward until it hits the line graph. An approximation for the 10:00 temperature can then be obtained from the vertical axis.
16. Answers may vary.

Problem Set 9-2
1. (a) Mean $= 6.625$, median $= 7.5$, mode $= 8$
(b) Mean $= 13.\overline{4}$, median $= 12$, mode $= 12$
(c) Mean $\doteq 19.9$, median $= 18$, modes $= 18$ and 22
(d) Mean $= 81.4$, median $= 80$, mode $= 80$
(e) Mean $= 5.8\overline{3}$, median $= 5$, mode $= 5$
2. (a) The mean, median and mode are all 80.
(b) Answers may vary.
3. 1500
4. 150 pounds
5. $78.\overline{3}$
6. (a) $\overline{x} = 18.4$ years **(b)** 23.4 years **(c)** 28.4 years
(d) The mean in (b) is equal to the mean in (a) plus 5 years. The mean in (c) is equal to the mean in (a) plus 10 years or the mean in (b) plus 5 years.
7. Mean $= \$22,700$, median $= \$20,000$, mode $= \$20,000$
8. Mode
9. Approximately 2.59
10. 215.45 pounds
11. $320
12. $1880
13. (a) $41,275 **(b)** $38,000 **(c)** $38,000
14. $s \doteq 7.3$ cm
15. The mean increases by the number which has been added. The standard deviation remains the same.
16. (a) $s = 0$ **(b)** Yes
17. (a) Approximately 76.81 **(b)** 76 **(c)** 71
(d) Approximately 156.82 **(e)** Approximately 12.52
18. 91
19. 96, 90; and 90
20. 2

21. No, to find the average speed we divide the distance traveled by the time it takes to drive it. The first part of the trip took $\frac{5}{30}$ or $\frac{1}{6}$ of an hour. The second part of the trip took $\frac{5}{50}$ or $\frac{1}{10}$ of an hour. Therefore, to find the average speed we compute $\frac{10}{\frac{1}{6} + \frac{1}{10}}$ to obtain 37.5 mph.

22.

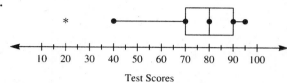

Test Scores

23.
(a)

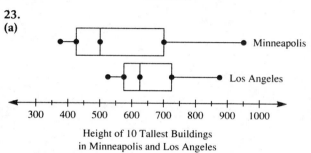

Height of 10 Tallest Buildings in Minneapolis and Los Angeles

(b) There are no outliers
24. (a) (i) Increase by $1000 **(ii)** Increase by $1000 **(iii)** Increase by $1000 **(iv)** Increase by $1000 **(v)** Stays the same **(b) (i)** Increase by 5% **(ii)** Increase by 5%
25. (a) (i) $\overline{x} = 5$, $m = 5$ **(ii)** $\overline{x} = 100$, $m = 100$ **(iii)** $\overline{x} = 307$, $m = 307$ **(b)** The mean and median of an arithmetic sequence are the same.
26.

$$v = \frac{(x_1 - \overline{x})^2 + (x_2 - \overline{x})^2 + \cdots + (x_n - \overline{x})^2}{n}$$

$$= \frac{(x_1^2 - 2\overline{x}x_1 + \overline{x}^2) + (x_2^2 - 2\overline{x}x_2 + \overline{x}^2) + \cdots + (x_n^2 - 2\overline{x}x_n + \overline{x}^2)}{n}$$

$$= \frac{(x_1^2 + x_2^2 + \cdots + x_n^2) - 2\overline{x}(x_1 + x_2 + \cdots + x_n) + n\overline{x}^2}{n}$$

$$= \frac{x_1^2 + x_2^2 + \cdots + x_n^2}{n} - \frac{2\overline{x}(x_1 + x_2 + \cdots + x_n)}{n} + \frac{n\overline{x}^2}{n}$$

$$= \frac{x_1^2 + x_2^2 + \cdots + x_n^2}{n} - 2\overline{x}^2 + \overline{x}^2$$

$$= \frac{x_1^2 + x_2^2 + \cdots + x_n^2}{n} - \overline{x}^2$$

27. (a)

History Test Scores

```
5 | 5
6 | 4 8
7 | 2 3 3 4 6 7 9
8 | 0 2 5 5 5 6 7 8 8 9
9 | 0 0 3 4 6
```

7 | 2 represents a score of 72

History Test Scores

(b)

Classes	Tallies	Frequency
55–59		1
60–64		1
65–69		1
70–74		4
75–79		3
80–84		2
85–89		8
90–94		4
95–99		1

(c)

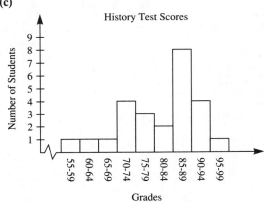

(d)

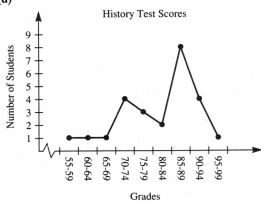

(e) Approximately 115°

Brain Teaser (p. 476)

The mean speed for the total 6-mile run is 6 divided by the total time it took to drive 6 miles. The total time is the sum of the times spent on the first 3 miles, the next $1\frac{1}{2}$ miles, and the last $1\frac{1}{2}$ miles. On the first 3 miles, he averaged 140 miles per hour. Thus his time was $\frac{3}{140}$ hours. Similarly, the times on the next two segments were $\frac{1.5}{168}$ hours and $\frac{1.5}{210}$ hours. His total time was therefore $\frac{3}{140} + \frac{1.5}{168} + \frac{1.5}{210} = 0.0375$ hours. Consequently, the mean speed was $\frac{6}{0.375} = 160$ miles per hour.

Problem Set 9-3

1. (a) 1020 **(b)** 1425 **(c)** 1.5
2. 97.5%
3. 0.68
4. (a) verbal; 0.6; quantitative, $0.8\overline{3}$; logical reasoning, 1 **(b)** (i) Logical reasoning (ii) verbal (iii) Holly has a composite score of $0.8\overline{1}$.
5. (a) $Q_2 = P_{50} = 65$ **(b)** $P_{16} = 53$ **(c)** $P_{84} = 77$
6. They are the same.
7. (a) Cum/n

```
   0
   2.5
   2.5
  10.3
  15.4
  30.8
  43.6
  61.5
  74.4
  94.9
 100
```

(b)

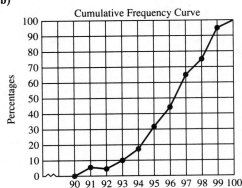

(c) Yes; the curves should always slope up to 100%.

199

8. (a) 1.07% **(b)** 95.54% **(c)** 2.27%
9. 1.4%
10. Nathan, Jill has a percentile rank of 40.
11. 0 percentile
12. 90
13. Between 59 in. and 69 in.
14. 50
15. 1600
16. (a) 74.17 **(b)** 75 **(c)** 65 **(d)** 237.97 **(e)** 15.43

(f)

Score	Frequency
98	1
91	2
84	1
82	1
77	1
73	1
65	3
56	1
43	1
Total	12

(g)

Frequency of Scores

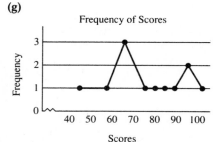

Scores

17. 27.74
18. 76.6̄
19.

Men's Olympic
100 meter Run Times
1896–1964

```
1 0 | 0 2 3 3 3 4
  * | 5 6 8 8 8 8
1 1 | 0 0
  * |                    10 | 0 represents
1 2 | 0                  10.0 seconds
```

Problem Set 9-4
1. Answers vary.
2. Answers may vary. One possibility is that the temperature is always 25°C.
3. She could have taken a different number of quizzes during the first part of the quarter than the second part.
4. When the radius of a circle is doubled, the area is quadrupled, which is misleading since the population has only doubled.
5. The horizontal axis does not have uniformly-sized intervals and both the horizontal axis and the graph are not labeled.
6. Answers vary.
7. There were more scores above the mean than below, but the mean was affected more by low scores.
8. It could very well be that most of the pickups sold in the past 10 years were actually sold during the last 2 years. In such a case most of the pickups have been on the road for only 2 years, and therefore the given information would not imply that the average life of a pickup is around ten years.
9. Answers vary; however, he is assuming that there are no deep holes in the river where he crosses.
10. The three-dimensional drawing distorts the graph. The result of doubling the radius and the height of the can are to increase the volume by a factor of 8.

Chapter Test
1. If the average is 2.41 children, then the *mean* is being used. If the average is 2.5, then the *mean* or the median might have been used.
2. 23
3. (a) Mean = 30, median = 30, mode = 10
(b) Mean = 5, median = 5, modes = 3, 5, 6
4. (a) Range = 50, variance $\doteq$ 371.42, standard deviation $\doteq$ 19.27 **(b)** Range = 8, variance = 5.2, standard deviation = 2.28

5. (a)

Miss Rider's Class
Masses in Kilograms

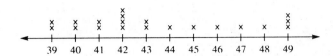

(b)

Miss Rider's Class
Masses in Kilograms

```
3 |
* | 9 9
4 | 0 0 1 1 2 2 2 2 3 3 4
* | 5 6 7 8 9 9 9          4 | 0 represents
                                 40 kg
```

(c)

Miss Rider's Class
Masses in Kilograms

Mass	Tally	Frequency
39	||	2
40	||	2
41	||	2
42	||||	4
43	||	2
44	|	1
45	|	1
46	|	1
47	|	1
48	|	1
49	|||	3
		20

(d)

Miss Rider's Class
Masses in Kilograms

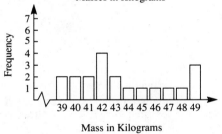

Mass in Kilograms

6. (a)

Test Grades

Class	Tally	Frequency
61–70	⊬⊢ |	6
71–80	⊬⊢ ⊬⊢ |	11
81–90	⊬⊢ ||	7
91–100	⊬⊢ |	6
		30

(b) and **(c)** are shown on the same graph.

Grade Distribution

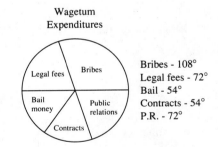

7.

Wagetum
Expenditures

Bribes - 108°
Legal fees - 72°
Bail - 54°
Contracts - 54°
P.R. - 72°

201

8. The widths of the bars are not uniform and the graph has no title.
9. $2840
10. 150 mph
11. (a)

Life Expectancy for Males and Females

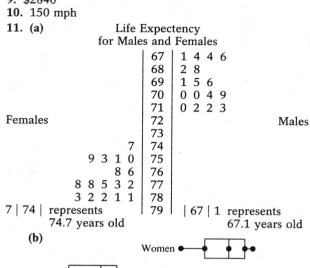

```
Females                                    Males
              67 | 1 4 4 6
              68 | 2 8
              69 | 1 5 6
              70 | 0 0 4 9
              71 | 0 2 2 3
              72
              73
          7 | 74 |
     9 3 1 0 | 75 |
         8 6 | 76 |
   8 8 5 3 2 | 77 |
   3 2 2 1 1 | 78 |
              79 |
```

7 | 74 | represents | 67 | 1 represents
74.7 years old   67.1 years old

(b)

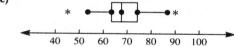

```
Women  •——•  ▭•▭  •——•
Men  •——▭•▭——•
      67 68 69 70 71 72 73 74 75 76 77 78 79 80
```

12. Larry was correct because his average was $2.\overline{6}$ while Moe's was $2.7\overline{3}$

13. (a) 360 (b) none (c) 350 (d) $5 \doteq 108.21$
14. (a) 67 (b) $UQ = 74$, $LQ = 64$
(c)

```
   *  •——▭•▭——•  *
      40  50  60  70  80  90  100
```

(d) 50% (e) 30% (f) No, there are less speeds close to 67 in the 3rd quartile than in the 2nd quartile.
15. (a) 25 (b) 475
16. 475
17. (a) 525 (b) 600 (c) 675
18. 1.6
19. Approximately 50th.
20. (a) Answers vary. (b) They show very popular shows during the ratings sweeps. Answers vary.
21. Answers vary.

CHAPTER 10

Problem Set 10-1
1. (a) {C} (b) ∅ (c) {C} (d) {C} (e) $\overline{CE}$ (f) $\overrightarrow{AB}$
(g) $\overrightarrow{BA}$ (h) $\overleftrightarrow{AD}$
2. No. The symbol is a finite collection of points.

3. (a) ∅ (b) ∠E-BD-A (c) {C} (d) {A} (e) {A}
(f) {A} (g) Answers vary. (h) $\overleftrightarrow{AC}$ and $\overrightarrow{DE}$ (i) Plane BCD
4. (a) True (b) True (c) False (d) False (e) True
(f) True (g) False (h) False (i) False (j) True
(k) True (l) True
5. Answers vary
6. (a) Infinitely many (b) One
7. (a) None (b) One
8. Answers vary
9. (a) 54′ (b) 15°7′48″
10. (a) Yes; otherwise a point of intersection of the two lines would also be a point of intersection of the two parallel planes. (b) No; an example may be seen in the drawing in Problem 3. (c) Yes; if the planes were not parallel, they would intersect in a line m and at least one of the given lines would intersect m and would then intersect plane α, which contradicts the fact that the given lines are parallel to α.
11. (a) Approximately 44° (b) Approximately 120°
12. (a) 41°31′10″ (b) 79°48′47″
13. (a) 4 (b) 6 (c) 8 (d) $2(n - 1)$
14. (a) 3 (b) 6 (c) 10 (d) $1 + 2 + 3 + \cdots + (n - 1) = n(n - 1)/2$
15. (a)

Number of Intersection Points

Number of Lines	0	1	2	3	4	5
2	⇄	✕	Not Possible	Not Possible	Not Possible	Not Possible
3	⇛	⋇	⋇	✕	Not Possible	Not Possible
4	⇛	⋇	Not Possible	⋇	⋇	Not Possible
5	⇛	⋇	Not Possible	Not Possible	⋇	⋇
6	⇛	⋇	Not Possible	Not Possible	Not Possible	⋇

(b) $n(n - 1)/2$

16. Three points determine a single plane, and a plane determines a level surface. Four points may not all lie in a plane and hence may not determine a level surface.
17. (a) No; if ∠BDC were a right angle, then both $\overleftrightarrow{BD}$ and $\overleftrightarrow{BC}$ would be perpendicular to $\overleftrightarrow{DC}$ and thus be parallel. (b) No; the angle formed by $\overrightarrow{PD}$ and $\overrightarrow{PC}$ must have measure less than a right angle. Otherwise, $\overrightarrow{DP}$ would be parallel to either $\overleftrightarrow{DC}$ or $\overleftrightarrow{PC}$. This is impossible (c) Yes; use the definition of perpendicular planes.
18. (a) Yes (b) Yes (c) Yes
19. Answers may vary.
20. (a) The line must contain 2 distinct points. These two points with the point not on the line are 3 distinct noncollinear points that determine a plane. (b) One line is determined by 2 distinct points. The other line may be determined by one of these points and another point. Thus, we have 3 distinct noncollinear points that determine a plane.

21. Suppose $\alpha \parallel \beta$, and γ intersects α in $\overleftrightarrow{AB}$, and γ intersect β in $\overleftrightarrow{CD}$. If $\overleftrightarrow{AB} \cap \overleftrightarrow{CD}$ is point Q, then Q is a point of both plane α and plane β. This cannot happen so $\overleftrightarrow{AB} \parallel \overleftrightarrow{CD}$.

22. Answers may vary.

(a)
```
TO ANGLE :SIZE
   FD 100 BK 100
   RT :SIZE FD 100
   BK 100 LT :SIZE
END
```

(b)
```
TO SEGMENT :LENGTH
   FD :LENGTH BK :LENGTH
END
```

(c)
```
TO PERPENDICULAR :LENGTH1
      :LENGTH2
   FD :LENGTH1 BK :LENGTH1/2
   RT 90 FD :LENGTH2
   BK :LENGTH2 LT 90
   BK :LENGTH1/2
END
```

(d)
```
TO PARALLEL :LENGTH1 :LENGTH2
   DRAW
   FD :LENGTH1 PENUP
   RT 90 FD 10 RT 90
   PENDOWN FD :LENGTH2
   PENUP HOME
   RT 180 PENDOWN
END
```

(In Apple Logo II, replace DRAW with CLEARSCREEN).

Problem Set 10-2

1. (a) 1, 2, 3, 6, 7, 8, 9, 11, 12 **(b)** 1, 2, 7, 8, 9, 11
(c) 1, 2, 7, 8, 9, 11 **(d)** 1, 2, 7, 8, 9, 11 **(e)** 7, 8
(f) 1, 2, 9, 11
2. (a)

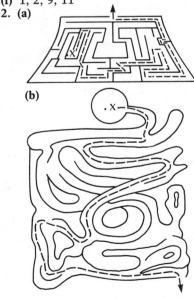

(b)

3. (a) Outside **(b)** Outside
4. (a) Yes **(b)** No
5. (a) $\{E, G\}$ **(b)** $\overleftrightarrow{EG}$ **(c)** $\overrightarrow{EH} \cup \overrightarrow{GK}$ **(d)** $\{F\}$
6. 6
7. (a) and **(c)** are convex; **(b)** and **(d)** are concave.
8. Answers may vary.
9. (d), **(e)** and **(f)** are impossible because the measure of each angle of an equilateral triangle has measure 60°.
10. (a) 35 **(b)** 170 **(c)** 4850
11. (a) 12 **(b)** 18
12. (a) Isosceles and equilateral **(b)** Isosceles
(c) Scalene **(d)** Isosceles and equilateral
13. 14
14. Answers may vary.
15. (a) False. To be isosceles, the triangle may have only 2 congruent sides, not necessarily 3. **(b)** True
(c) True **(d)** True **(e)** True **(f)** False. To be a regular quadrilateral, a rhombus would have to be a square. Not all rhombii are squares. **(g)** True **(h)** False. A scalene triangle has no two sides congruent. **(i)** True **(j)** True
(k) False. All squares are rectangles. **(l)** False. Some trapezoids are parallelograms, because the set of parallelograms is a proper subset of the set of trapezoids. **(m)** True **(n)** False. An isosceles trapezoid that is a square is also a kite. **(o)** False. See (n).
16. Answers may vary.
17. (a) Answers may vary.
```
TO SQUARE :SIDE
   REPEAT 4 [FD :SIDE RT 90]
END
```
(b) Answers may vary.
```
TO RECTANGLE :WIDTH :LENGTH
   REPEAT 2 [FD :WIDTH RT 90 FD
      :LENGTH RT 90]
END
```
18. (a) 45 **(b)** $n(n-1)/2$
19. (a) Answers may vary. **(b)** $\overrightarrow{BE}$ **(c)** $\{B\}$
(d) $\angle EBC$ **(e)** No
20. $\varnothing$, 1 point, 2 points, ray
21. (a) $\{C\}$ **(b)** $\overleftrightarrow{BD}$ **(c)** $\overline{AB}$, $\overline{AC}$, and $\overline{AD}$ **(d)** $\{D\}$
22. (a) False. A ray has only one endpoint. **(b)** True
(c) False. Skew lines cannot be contained in the single plane. **(d)** False. $\overrightarrow{MN}$ has a endpoint M and extends in the direction of point N; $\overrightarrow{NM}$ has endpoint N and extends in the direction of point M. **(e)** True **(f)** False. Their intersection is a line.
23.

$$\overline{A} \qquad \overline{B} \quad \overline{C} \qquad \overline{D}$$

Brain Teaser (p. 530)
No

Brain Teaser (p. 538)
180 degrees; 180 degrees

Problem Set 10-3

1. **(a)** $\angle 1$ and $\angle 2$ are adjacent angles; $\angle 3$ and $\angle 4$ are vertical angles. **(b)** $\angle 1$ and $\angle 2$ are vertical angles; $\angle 3$ and $\angle 4$ are adjacent angles. **(c)** $\angle 1$ and $\angle 2$ are neither vertical nor adjacent angles. **(d)** $\angle 1$ and $\angle 2$ are adjacent angles.

2. **(a)** $m(\angle 2) = 130°$ **(b)** $m(\angle 3) = 50°$ **(c)** $m(\angle 4) = 130°$

3. Answers may vary.

4. Answers may vary.

5. 14 pairs

6. 13 pairs

7. **(a)** $60°$ **(b)** $45°$ **(c)** $60°$ **(d)** $60°$

8. **(a)** Yes; a pair of corresponding angles are $50°$ each. **(b)** Yes; a pair of corresponding angles are $70°$ each. **(c)** Yes; a pair of alternate interior angles are $40°$ each. **(d)** Yes; a pair of corresponding angles are $90°$ each.

9. **(a)** No. Two or more obtuse angles will produce a sum of more than $180°$. **(b)** Yes. For example, each angle may have measure $60°$. **(c)** No. The sum of the measures of the three angles would be more than $180°$. **(d)** No. It may have an obtuse or a right angle as well.

10. **(a)** $70°$ **(b)** $70°$ **(c)** $65°$ **(d)** $45°$

11. **(a)** $x = 40°$ and $y = 50°$ **(b)** $x = 50°$ and $y = 60°$

12. $60°$

13. $90°$

14. $60°$

15. **(a)** $360°$ **(b)** $360°$ **(c)** $360°$

16. If the two distinct lines are both perpendicular, then the measures of $\angle B$ and $\angle C$ are both $90°$. This would force the sum of the measures of the angles of $\triangle ABC$ to be greater than $180°$, which is impossible.

17. **(a)** 20 **(b)** $150°$

18. **(a)** $5 \cdot 180° - 360° = 540°$ **(b)** The sum of the measures of the angles in all n triangles is $180n$ degrees. Subtracting the measures of all nonoverlapping angles whose vertex is P, we obtain $180n - 360° = (n - 2)180°$.

19. **(a)** There are $5 - 2$ triangles which can be drawn from any vertex of the pentagon. Hence, there are $(5 - 2)180$ degrees in the sum of the angle measures of the interior angles of any convex pentagon. **(b)** There are $n - 2$ triangles which can be drawn from any vertex of the n-gon. Hence, there are $(n - 2)180$ degrees in the sum of the angle measures of the interior angles of any convex polygon.

20. **(a)** True **(b)** False **(c)** False **(d)** True **(e)** False **(f)** True

21. **(a)** Equal

(b) $m(\angle 4) = 180° - m(\angle 3)$ (Straight angle)
$= 180° - [180° - m(\angle 1) - m(\angle 2)]$
$= m(\angle 1) + m(\angle 2)$

22. $60, 84, 108, 132, 156$

23. Theorem 10-1(a) Supplements of the same angle, or congruent angles, are congruent.

Proof: (a) Let both $\angle 2$ and $\angle 3$ be supplements of $\angle 1$.
$m(\angle 2) + m(\angle 1) = 180$
$m(\angle 3) + m(\angle 1) = 180$
$m(\angle 2) + m(\angle 1) = m(\angle 3) + m(\angle 1)$
$m(\angle 2) = m(\angle 3)$
$\angle 2 \cong \angle 3$

(b) Let $\angle 3$ be the supplement of $\angle 1$, and $\angle 4$ be the supplement of $\angle 2$, and $\angle 1 \cong \angle 2$.
$m(\angle 3) + m(\angle 1) = 180$
$m(\angle 4) + m(\angle 2) = 180$
$m(\angle 3) + m(\angle 1) = m(\angle 4) + m(\angle 2)$
$\angle 1 \cong \angle 2$ implies $m(\angle 1) = m(\angle 2)$
$m(\angle 3) + m(\angle 2) = m(\angle 4) + m(\angle 2)$
$m(\angle 3) = m(\angle 4)$
$\angle 3 \cong \angle 4$

Theorem 10-1(b) Complements of the same angle, or congruent angles, are congruent.

Proof: Proof is similar to the above.

24. If two lines are perpendicular to the same line, then congruent corresponding angles of $90°$ each are formed, and hence the lines are parallel.

25. If two lines are perpendicular to the same line, then congruent corresponding angles of $90°$ each are formed, and hence the lines are parallel.

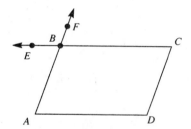

(a)
$$m(\angle A) = m(\angle FBC)$$
(corresponding angles)
$$m(\angle FBE) + m(\angle FBC) = 180°$$
(supplementary angles)
$$m(\angle FBE) = m(\angle ABC)$$
(vertical angles)

Thus,
$$m(\angle ABC) + m(\angle A) = 180° \quad \text{(substitution)}$$

(b)
$$m(\angle A) = m(\angle ABE)$$
(alternate interior angles)
$$m(\angle ABE) = m(\angle C)$$
(corresponding angles)

Hence,
$$m(\angle A) = m(\angle C).$$
Likewise $m(\angle B) = m(\angle D)$.

26. This follows directly from Problem 25.

27. Let *ABCD* be a quadrilateral with $m(\angle 1) = m(\angle 3)$ and $m(\angle 2) = m(\angle 4)$.

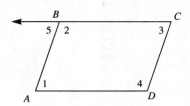

We are given that $m(\angle 1) = m(\angle 3)$ and $m(\angle 2) = m(\angle 4)$. Also, we know $m(\angle 1) + m(\angle 2) + m(\angle 3) + m(\angle 4) = 360°$. Substituting, we have $m(\angle 1) + m(\angle 2) + m(\angle 1) + m(\angle 2) = 360°$. Thus $2m(\angle 1) + 2m(\angle 2) = 360°$, or $2[m(\angle 1) + m(\angle 2)] = 360°$, and so $m(\angle 1) + m(\angle 2) = 180°$. Because $m(\angle 5) + m(\angle 2) = 180°$, then $m(\angle 1) + m(\angle 2) = m(\angle 5) + m(\angle 2)$. Subtracting $m(\angle 2)$ from both sides, we have $m(\angle 1) = m(\angle 5)$. Now, because alternate interior angles are congruent, we have $\overleftrightarrow{AD} \parallel \overleftrightarrow{BC}$. Similarly, it can be shown that $\overleftrightarrow{AB} \parallel \overleftrightarrow{DC}$.

28. 83.5° or 83°30′

29. Answers may vary.
  (a) TO PARALLELOGRAM :L :W :A
      REPEAT 2[FD :L RT 180-:A FD
       :W RT :A]
      END
  (b) TO RECTANGLE :L :W
      PARALLELOGRAM :L :W 90
      END
  (c) TO RHOMBUS :L :A
      PARALLELOGRAM :L :L :A
      END
  (d) Execute PARALLELOGRAM 50 50 90.
  (e) Execute RHOMBUS 50 90.

30. 6

31. No, the union of two rays will always extend infinitely in at least one direction.

32. Answers may vary.

33. Answers may vary.

34. Answers may vary.

35. Sketches may vary, but the possibilities are the empty set, a single point, a segment, a quadrilateral, a pentagon, and a hexagon. There are various types of quadrilaterals possible.

36. **(a)** A hexagon **(b)** A pentagon **(c)** Two intersecting segments or lines **(d)** A rectangle **(e)** A rhombus or square

37. **(a)** All angles must be right angles and all diagonals are the same length. **(b)** All sides are the same length and all angles are right angles. **(c)** Impossible because all squares are parallelograms.

Problem Set 10-4

1. **(a)** Quadrilateral pyramid **(b)** Quadrilateral prism; possibly a trapezoidal prism **(c)** Pentagonal pyramid

2. **(a)** *A, D, R, W* **(b)** $\overline{AR}, \overline{RD}, \overline{AD}, \overline{AW}, \overline{WR}, \overline{WD}$ **(c)** $\triangle ARD, \triangle AWD, \triangle AWR, \triangle WDR$ **(d)** {*R*}

3. Answers may vary.

4. **(a)** 5 **(b)** 4 **(c)** 4

5. **(a)** True **(b)** False **(c)** True **(d)** False **(e)** False **(f)** False **(g)** False **(h)** True

6. 3; Each pair of parallel faces could be considered as bases.

7. Answers may vary.

8. Drawings may vary, but the statement is true.

9. All are possible.

10. **(a)**  **(b)**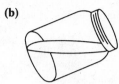

  (c)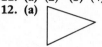

11. **(a)** (2) **(b)** (4)

12. **(a)**

  (b)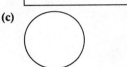

  (c)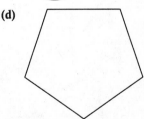

  (d)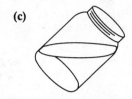

  (e)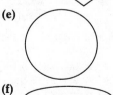

  (f)

205

13. Answers may vary.
14. (a) $5 + 5 - 8 = 2$ (b) $6 + 8 - 12 = 2$
(c) $6 + 6 - 10 = 2$
15.   Pyramid   Prism
   (a) $n + 1$ $n + 2$
   (b) $n + 1$ $2n$
   (c) $2n$ $3n$
   (d) $(n + 1) + (n + 1) - 2n = 2$
         $(n + 2) + 2n - 3n = 2$
16. (a) 6 (b) 48 (c) 11
17. (a) A cone might be described as a many-sided pyramid. (b) A cylinder might be described as a many-sided prism.
18. (a) Yes (b) Yes (c) No
19. (a) Yes; It is also a rectangle because the opposite sides are parallel and congruent and plane ABE is perpendicular to plane ADE making $\angle ABF$ a right angle. A parallelogram with a right angle is a rectangle.
(b) Planes ABG, BFE, GFE, FEC, BCD, and GCD
(c) Yes; If $\overleftrightarrow{CD}$ intersects the plane ABF, it must intersect it along $\overleftrightarrow{AB}$, since $\overleftrightarrow{CD}$ is in the plane determined by ABC and any point common to both planes is on $\overleftrightarrow{AB}$. This is a contradiction because $\overleftrightarrow{AB}$ and $\overleftrightarrow{CD}$ are parallel.
20. $m(\angle BCD) = 60°$
21. $140°$
22. (a) True (b) True (c) False; The triangle coud be equilateral and have three acute angles.
23. (a) Right (b) The sum of the measures of complementary angles is 90°; hence the measures of the third angle must be 90°, and the triangle is a right triangle.
24. The two lines intersect on the same side of the transversal where the interior angles have angle measure sum less than 180°.
25. Parallelogram

Brain Teaser (p. 552)
Read Hoffer's article listed.

Problem Set 10-5
1. (a), (b), (c), (e), (g), (h), and (j) are traversable.
   (a)   (b)

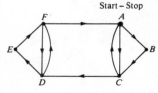

Path:
ABCACDEFDFA;
any point can be a
starting point.

Path:
ABACBCDCDA; any
point can be a
starting point.

(c)

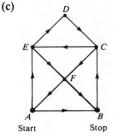

Start   Stop

Path:
ABCFAEDCEFB;
only points A and B
can be starting
points.

(e)

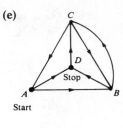

Start

Path: *ABCBDCAD*;
only points A and D
can be starting
points.

(g)

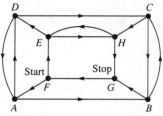

Path:
FADABCBGFEDCHEHG;
only points F and G
can be starting
points.

(h)

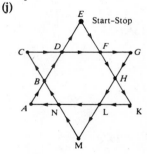

Path: *ACBCDCDAB*;
only points A and B
can be starting
points.

(j)

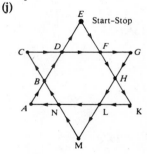

Path:
EFHKLNABDFGHLMNBCDE;
any point can be a starting point.

2. All are possible if the starting and stopping points are not the same. If the traveling salesperson must start and return home, then it depends upon where home is.

206

3.

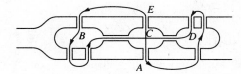

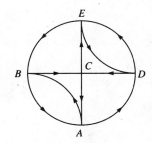

Path: *CEBABCADEDC*; any point can be a starting point.

4. (a)

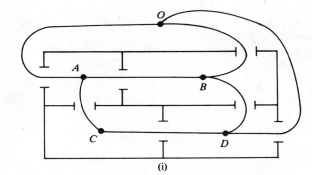

(i)

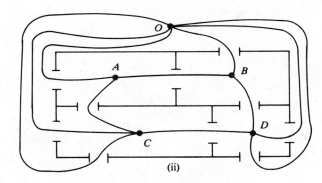

(ii)

(b) Network (i) is not traversable, since it has four odd vertices. Network (ii) has two odd vertices, so it is traversable, as shown.

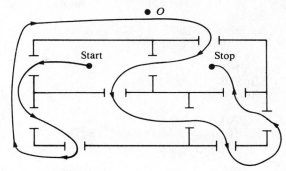

5. Yes. See figure.

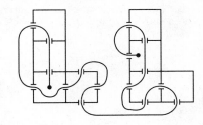

6. It is not possible.

7.

Network	R	V	A	V − A + F
(a)	6	6	10	2
(b)	7	4	9	2
(c)	6	6	10	2
(d)	4	4	6	2
(e)	5	4	7	2
(f)	8	8	14	2
(g)	9	8	15	2
(h)	6	4	8	2
(i)	7	7	12	2
(j)	8	12	18	2

8.

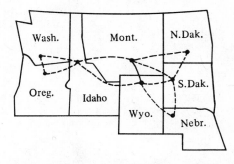

Since all vertices are even, the trip is possible. It makes no difference where she starts.

9. (a) Yes **(b)** No **(c)** Yes **(d)** Yes **(e)** Yes **(f)** No

207

*Problem Set 10-6

1. (a) TO RECTANGLE :LENGTH :WIDTH
       PARALLELOGRAM :LENGTH
         :WIDTH 90
     END
   (b) TO RHOMBUS :SIDE :ANGLE
       PARALLELOGRAM :SIDE :SIDE
         :ANGLE
     END

2. TO SQUARE :SIDE
     RHOMBUS :SIDE 90
   END

3. TO CUBE :SIDE
     REPEAT 3 [RHOMBUS :SIDE 60 RIGHT
     120]
   END

4. (a) 60° (b) (360/7)° (c) 45° (d) 30°

5. Execute on the computer.

6. No; the methods of this section yield an equilateral triangle if a 6-pointed star is attempted.

7. Answers may vary.
   (a) TO HEXSTACK :SIDE
       REPEAT 3 [LEFT 30 HEXAGON
         :SIDE FD :SIDE RT 60 FD
         :SIDE LT 60]
     END
     TO HEXAGON :SIDE
       REPEAT 6 [FD :SIDE RIGHT 60]
     END
   (b) TO HONEYCOMB :SIDE
       REPEAT 3 [HEXAGON :SIDE RT 120]
     END

8. Answers may vary.
   TO THIRTY
     FD 100 BK 100 RT 30
     FD 100 BK 100 LT 30
   END

9. Answers may vary.
   (a) TO SEG
         RT 45 FD 50 BK 100
         FD 50 LT 45
       END
   (b) TO PAR
         PENUP FD 50 PENDOWN
         SEG
       END

10. Answers may vary.
    TO COUNT.ANGLES :NUMBER
      IF :NUMBER = 1 OUTPUT 0 STOP
      OUTPUT :NUMBER - 1 +
        COUNT.ANGLES :NUMBER - 1
    END
    (In Apple Logo II, replace IF :NUMBER = 1 OUTPUT 0 STOP with IF :NUMBER = 1 [OUTPUT 0 STOP].)

Chapter 10 Test

1. Answers may vary.

2. (a) $\overleftrightarrow{AB}$, $\overleftrightarrow{BC}$ and $\overleftrightarrow{AC}$ (b) $\overrightarrow{BA}$ and $\overrightarrow{BC}$ (c) $\overline{AB}$ (d) $\overrightarrow{AB}$ (e) $\overline{AB}$

3. (a) Answers may vary. (b) Planes APQ and BPQ (c) $\overrightarrow{AQ}$ (d) No. $\overleftrightarrow{PQ}$ and $\overleftrightarrow{AB}$ are skew lines so that no single plane contains them.

4. Answers may vary.

5. Answers may vary.

6. (a) No. The sum of the measures of two obtuse angles is greater than 180°, which is the sum of the measures of the angles of any triangle. (b) No. The sum of the measures of the four angles in a parallelogram must be 360°. If all the angles are acute, the sum would be less than 360°.

7. 18°, 36°, 126°.

8. (a) Given any convex n-gon, pick any vertex and draw all possible diagonals from this vertex. This will determine $n - 2$ triangles. Because the sum of the measures of the angles in each triangle is 180°, the sum of the measures of the angles in the n-gon is $(n - 2)180°$. (b) 90

9. (a) Answers may vary. (b) Euler's formula holds.

10. Answers may vary.

11. Answers may vary, but the possibilities are a point, a segment, a triangle, or a quadrilateral.

12. 6

13. 35°8'35"

14. (a) 60° (b) 120° (c) 120°

15. 8

16. 48°

17. (a) (i), (ii), and (iv) are traversable.
    (b) (i)
    Path: *ABCDEFACEA*; any point can be used as a starting point.
    (ii)
    Path: *ABCDAEDBE*; points A and E are possible starting points.
    (iv)
    Path: *ACDEACDEABC*; points A or C are possible starting points.

18. Answers may vary.
    TO PERPENDICULAR :SEG1 :SEG2
      FD :SEG1 RT 90
      FD :SEG2
    END

19. Answers may vary.
```
TO ISOS :LEG :ANGLE
  FD :LEG
  RT 180 - :ANGLE
  FD :LEG
  RT 90 + :ANGLE/2
END
```

CHAPTER 11

Problem Set 11-1

1. (a) $\overline{BC} > \overline{AC}$ (b) $m(\angle A) > m(\angle B)$ (c) The side of greater length is opposite the angle of greater measure.
2. (c) Right (d) No triangle is possible.
3. (b) The triangle is unique by *SSS*. (c) The triangle is unique by *SSS*. (d) There is no triangle because of the Triangle Inequality. (e) The triangle is unique by *SSS*. (f) The triangle is unique by *SAS*. (g) The triangle is not unique. (h) The triangle is unique by *SAS*. (i) The triangle is unique by *SAS*.
4. 22
5. (a) Yes; *SAS* (b) Yes; *SSS* (c) No
6. (a) Yes; *SSS* (b) Yes; *SSS* since $AC = DE = 3 + DC$ (c) It is impossible to determine from the information given. (d) Yes; *SAS* (e) Yes; *SAS* (f) Yes; *SAS*
7. (a) $\triangle AEC \cong \triangle ADB$ by *SAS* (b) $\triangle ABC \cong \triangle ADC$ by *SSS* (c) $\triangle BDA \cong \triangle BEC$ by *SAS*
8. The purpose of the diagonals is to form congruent triangles. Triangles are rigid structures and hence make the gate stronger.
9. The lengths of the wires must be the same because they are congruent parts of congruent triangles formed.
10. Such a construction tells us that $\triangle BDC \cong \triangle BAC$ by *SAS*. Therefore, $BD = AB$. By measuring BD, we know AB.
11. Construction
12. Construction
13. (a) $\triangle ABC \cong \triangle ABC$; $\triangle ACB \cong \triangle ABC$; $\triangle BAC \cong \triangle ABC$; $\triangle BCA \cong \triangle ABC$; $\triangle CAB \cong \triangle ABC$; $\triangle CBA \cong \triangle ABC$ (b) Consider $\triangle ACB \cong \triangle ABC$. Because $\triangle ABC$ is equilateral, it is also isosceles. We also know that the base angles of an isosceles triangle are congruent. Suppose $\angle A \cong \angle B$. Then by the triangle congruence, we have $\angle B \cong \angle C$. Hence $\angle A \cong \angle B \cong \angle C$, and the triangle is equiangular.
14. (a) $\overline{AD} \cong \overline{CD}$ (b) $\angle ABD \cong \angle CBD$; definition of angle bisector $\overline{AB} \cong \overline{BC}$; given; $\overline{BD} \cong \overline{BD}$; $\triangle ABD \cong \triangle CBD$; *SAS*; $\overline{AD} \cong \overline{CD}$; *CPCTC* (c) 90° (d) $\angle ADB$ and $\angle CDB$ are congruent by *CPCTC* (using part (b)); $\angle ADB$ and $\angle CDB$ are congruent adjacent supplementary angles, and therefore, each must have a measure of 90°.

15. (a) F is the midpoint of both diagonals. (b) We can show $\triangle ABD \cong \triangle CBD$ by *SSS* and, then $\angle BDC \cong \angle BDA$ by *CPCTC*. $\triangle AFD \cong \triangle CFD$ by *SAS*, so $\overline{AF} \cong \overline{FC}$, thus F is the midpoint of $\overline{AC}$. A similar argument will show $\overline{BF} \cong \overline{FD}$. (c) 90° (d) From part (b), $\angle AFD \cong \angle DFC$ by *CPCTC*, but are also supplementary. Hence, $m(\angle AFD) = 90°$. A similar argument is used for $\angle BFA$ and $\angle BFC$.
16. (a) A parallelogram (b) Let $ABCD$ be the quadrilateral, with E the intersection point of its diagonals. Show that $\triangle AED \cong \triangle CEB$ and that $\triangle BEA \cong \triangle DEC$. Use congruent alternate interior angles to show $\overline{BC} \parallel \overline{AD}$ and $\overline{AB} \parallel \overline{CD}$.

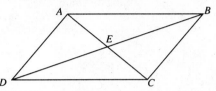

17. (a) The angles formed by the diagonals of a rhombus are right angles. (b) First show that $\triangle ABO \cong \triangle CDO$ and conclude that $\overline{AO} \cong \overline{OC}$. Then show that $\triangle ABO \cong \triangle CBO$ by *SSS*. Hence, conclude that $\angle AOB \cong \angle COB$ and consequently that each angle is a right angle.

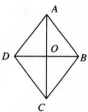

18. (a) A parallelogram. (b) Let $\overline{AB} \cong \overline{CD}$ and $\overline{BC} \cong \overline{AD}$. Prove that $\triangle ABC \cong \triangle CDA$ and conclude that $\overline{BC} \parallel \overline{AD}$. Similarly show $\triangle ABD \cong \triangle DCB$ and conclude that $\overline{AB} \parallel \overline{DC}$.

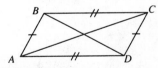

19. $\triangle BAC \cong \triangle CAB$; *SAS*. $\angle ABC \cong \angle ACB$ by *CPCTC*
20. Answers may vary.
```
TO EQUITRI :SIDE
  REPEAT 3 [FD :SIDE RT 120]
END
```
21. Execute the procedure.
22. They produce basically the same result.

23. (a) A triangle is constructed because the computer does not know the difference in an angle measure and a compass heading. **(b)** In reality, no because no triangle has one angle with measure 190°. **(c)** Add the following:

```
IF NOT (:ANGLE < 180) PRINT [NO
TRIANGLE IS POSSIBLE.] STOP
```

(In Apple Logo II, use the following line:

```
IF NOT (:ANGLE < 180) [PRINT [NO
TRIANGLE IS POSSIBLE.] STOP].)
```

Problem Set 11-2

1. (d) Infinitely many triangles are possible.
2. (a) No; By *ASA*, the triangle is unique. **(b)** No; By *AAS*, the triangle is unique. **(c)** No; By *ASA*, the triangle is unique. **(d)** Yes; *AAA* does not determine a unique triangle.
3. (a) Yes; *ASA* **(b)** Yes; *AAS* **(c)** No **(d)** No
4. (a) Yes; *ASA* **(b)** Yes; *AAS*
5. The triangles are all congruent. This can be proved in a variety of ways. One can determine the measures of all the angles and use *ASA*.
6. (a) Parallelogram **(b)** None **(c)** None
(d) Rectangle **(e)** Rhombus **(f)** Square
(g) Parallelogram
7. (a) True **(b)** True **(c)** True **(d)** True **(e)** True
(f) False, A counterexample can be seen in a trapezoid in which two consecutive angles are right angles but the other two are not. **(g)** True **(h)** False; A square is both a rectangle and a rhombus. **(i)** False; A square can be a trapezoid. **(j)** True
8. (a) Answers may vary. **(b)** If a quadrilateral had three right angles, then the fourth must also be a right angle. **(c)** No; any parallelogram with a pair of right angles must have right angles as its other pair of angles and hence be a rectangle.
9. (a) $\overline{OP} \cong \overline{QO}$ **(b)** $\angle PDO \cong \angle QBO$; alternate interior angles formed by the transversal $\overleftrightarrow{DB}$ and parallel lines $\overleftrightarrow{DC}$ and $\overleftrightarrow{AB}$. $\angle DPO \cong \angle BQO$ because $\overleftrightarrow{PQ}$ is a transversal of $\overleftrightarrow{CD}$ and $\overleftrightarrow{AB}$. $\overline{DO} \cong \overline{BO}$; diagonals of a parallelogram bisect each other. $\triangle POD \cong \triangle QOB$; *AAS*. $\overline{PO} \cong \overline{QO}$; *CPCTC*.
10. (a) $\triangle ABC \cong \triangle ADC$ by *SSS*. Hence $\angle BAC \cong \angle DAC$ and $\angle BCM \cong \angle DCM$ by *CPCTC*. Therefore, $\overleftrightarrow{AC}$ bisects $\angle A$ and $\angle C$. **(b)** The angles formed are right angles. By part (a), $\angle BAM \cong \angle DAM$. Hence $\triangle ABM \cong \triangle ADM$ by *SAS*. $\angle BMA \cong \angle DMA$ by *CPCTC*. Since $\angle BMA$ and $\angle DMA$ are adjacent congruent supplementary angles, each must be a right angle. Since vertical angles formed are congruent, all four angles formed by the diagonals are right angles. **(c)** By part (b), $\overline{BM} \cong \overline{MD}$; *CPCTC*
11. (a) They are congruent. **(b)** Show that $\triangle ABC \cong \triangle BCD \cong \triangle CDE \cong \triangle DEA \cong \triangle EAB$.

12. (a) The sides opposite congruent angles in an isosceles trapezoid are congruent. **(b)** The diagonals are congruent. **(c)** In isosceles trapezoid *ABCD*, draw $\overline{BX}$ and $\overline{CY}$ perpendicular to $\overline{AD}$. *BCYX* is a rectangle. (Why?) $\overline{BX} \cong \overline{CY}$; opposite sides of a rectangle are congruent. $\triangle BAX \cong \triangle CDY$; *AAS*. $\overline{AB} \cong \overline{DC}$; *CPCTC*. $\triangle ABD \cong \triangle DCA$; *SAS*. $\overline{AC} \cong \overline{DB}$; *CPCTC*.
13. (a) Rhombus **(b)** Use *SAS* to prove that $\triangle ECF \cong \triangle GBF \cong \triangle EDH \cong \triangle GAH$. **(c)** Parallelogram
(d) Suppose *ADCB* in part (a) is a parallelogram. Use *SAS* to show that $\triangle EDH \cong \triangle GBF$ and conclude that $\overline{EH} \cong \overline{GF}$. Similarly, show that $\triangle ECF \cong \triangle GAH$ and hence that $\overline{EF} \cong \overline{GH}$. Next use *SSS* to prove that $\triangle EFG \cong \triangle GHE$. Now conclude that $\angle GEH \cong \angle EGF$ and consequently that $\overline{FG} \parallel \overline{EH}$. Similarly, show that $\overline{EF} \parallel \overline{HG}$. **(e)** Parallelogram
14. (a) Prove that $\triangle ABD \cong \triangle CDB$ and $\triangle ADC \cong \triangle CBA$. **(b)** Use a pair of triangles from (a). **(c)** Prove that $\triangle ABF \cong \triangle CDF$. **(d)** Extend *AB* and look for corresponding angles.
15. (a) Use *ASA* to prove that $\triangle ABF \cong \triangle CDF$ and consequently that $\overline{BF} \cong \overline{FD}$ and $\overline{AF} \cong \overline{FC}$. **(b)** Show that $\triangle ABD \cong \triangle DCA$ and conclude that $\overline{BD} \cong \overline{CA}$.
16. Joachim needs to use the lengths of the sides and one 90° angle.
17. (a) The lengths of one side of each square must be equal. **(b)** The lengths of the sides of two perpendicular sides of the rectangles. **(c)** Answers vary. One solution is the lengths of two adjacent sides of the parallelograms and the angles between them.
18. (b) (i) Two intersecting line segments (ii) Three segments that do not close into a triangle.
(c) Add the following line:

```
IF NOT (ALLOF (:ANGLE1 +
:ANGLE2 < 180) (:ANGLE1 > 0)
(:ANGLE 2 > 0)) PRINT [NO
TRIANGLE IS POSSIBLE.] STOP
```

(In Apple Logo II, use the following line:

```
IF NOT (AND (:ANGLE1 + :ANGLE2
< 180) (:ANGLE1 > 0)
(:ANGLE2 > 0)) [PRINT [NO
TRIANGLE IS POSSIBLE.] STOP])
```

19. (a) Answers may vary.

```
TO RHOMBUS :SIDE :ANGLE
  REPEAT 2 [FD :SIDE RT (180-
    :ANGLE) FD :SIDE RT :ANGLE]
END
```

(b) They are congruent.
(c)
```
TO SQ.RHOM :SIDE
  RHOMBUS :SIDE 90
END
```

20. Construction
21. Construction
22. (a) Yes; *SAS* **(b)** Yes; *SSS* **(c)** No

Since the treasure is equidistant from two roads, it must lie on the angle bisector of the angle formed by the roads. Since it is also equidistant from Long John's Bay and Bottle O'Rum Inn, it must be on the perpendicular bisector of the segment joining these two points. Hence, the treasure is located at the intersection of the mentioned angle bisector and perpendicular bisector.

Problem Set 11-3
1.–4. Constructions
5. (d) The lines containing the altitudes meet at a point inside the triangle. **(e)** The lines containing the altitudes meet at the vertex of the right angle. **(f)** The lines containing the altitudes meet outside the triangle.
6. (a) The perpendicular bisectors meet at a point inside the triangle. **(b)** The perpendicular bisectors meet at a point outside the triangle. **(c)** The perpendicular bisectors meet at the midpoint of the hypotenuse of the right triangle.
7. Draw triangle ABC. The intersection of the perpendicular bisectors of the sides of this triangle should be the point to locate the airport.
8. (a) The perpendicular bisectors of a chord of a circle contains the center of the circle. **(b)** Choose an arbitrary chord $\overline{AB}$ on the circle with center O. Then $\overline{OA} \cong \overline{OB}$ since both are radii. Construct the angle bisector of $\angle AOB$ and let P be the point of intersection with chord $\overline{AB}$. Then $\triangle AOP \cong \triangle BOP$ by SAS, and $\angle OPB$ is a right angle since it is both congruent and supplementary to $\angle OPA$. Since $\overline{AP} \cong \overline{PB}$ and $\angle OPB$ is a right angle, $\overline{OP}$ is the perpendicular bisector of $\overline{AB}$, and therefore the perpendicular bisector of an arbitrary chord contains point O.

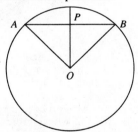

(c) Hint: Construct two non-parallel chords and find their perpendicular bisectors. The intersection of the perpendicular bisectors is the center of the circle.
9.–11. Constructions
12. (a) $\overleftrightarrow{PQ}$ is the perpendicular bisector of $\overline{AB}$. **(b)** Q is on the perpendicular bisector of $\overline{AB}$ because $\overline{AQ} \cong \overline{QB}$. Similarly, P is on the perpendicular bisector of $\overline{AB}$. Because a unique line contains two points, the perpendicular bisector contains $\overleftrightarrow{PQ}$. **(c)** $\overrightarrow{PQ}$ is the angle bisector of $\angle APB$; $\overrightarrow{QC}$ is the angle bisector of $\angle AQB$. **(d)** Show that $\triangle APQ \cong \triangle BPQ$ by SSS; then $\angle APQ \cong \angle BPQ$ by $CPCTC$. Show that $\triangle AQC \cong \triangle BQC$ and conclude that $\angle AQC \cong \angle BQC$.

13. (b) Construct two perpendicular segments bisecting each other and congruent to the given diagonal. **(c)** There is no unique rectangle. The endpoints of two segments bisecting each other and congruent to the given diagonal determine a rectangle. Since the segments may intersect at any angle, there are infinitely many such rectangles. **(d)** Without the angle between the sides being given, there is no unique parallelogram. **(e)** Construct two perpendicular segments bisecting each other and congruent to the given diagonals. **(f)** This is impossible because the sum of the measures of the angles would be greater than 180°. **(g)** This is impossible because the fourth angle must be a right angle also. **(h)** The kite would not be unique without knowing lengths of some sides. **(i)** The kite would not be unique but would be a square. **(j)** Consider $\triangle ABC$ and the angle bisector $\overrightarrow{CD}$. Since $\overline{AC} \cong \overline{BC}$, then $\overline{CD} \perp \overline{AB}$. It is possible to construct $\triangle ADC$, since AD is half as long as the base and $m(\angle DAC) = 90° - \tfrac{1}{2}m(\angle ACB)$.

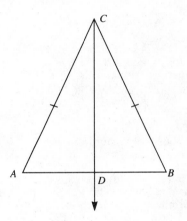

(k) There is no unique trapezoid unless two sides are designated as parallel; if this is the case, consider the trapezoid $ABCD$. Through B, construct $\overline{BE} \parallel \overline{CD}$. It follows that $BE = CD$. (Why?) Also, $AE = AD - ED = AD - BC$. Hence, $\triangle ABE$ can be constructed by SSS. Now extend $\overline{AE}$ so that $\overline{ED} \cong \overline{BC}$, and through B, draw $\overline{BC}$ parallel to $\overline{AE}$.

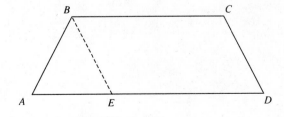

14.–16. Constructions.

17. Answers may vary.
```
TO ALTITUDES
  REPEAT 3 [RT 30 FD 60 RT 90 FD
     110 BK 130 FD 20 LT 90 FD 60
     RT 90]
END
```
18. Answers may vary.
(a)
```
TO ANGBIS :MEAS
   REPEAT 3 [FD 75 BK 75 RT
     :MEAS/2]
   END
```
(b)
```
TO PERBIS :SIZE
   FD :SIZE/2 RT 90 FD :SIZE BK
   :SIZE/2 FD :SIZE RT 90 FD
   :SIZE/2
   END
```
(c)
```
TO PARALLEL :SEG1 :SEG2
   FD :SEG1 PENUP RT 90
   FD 20 RT 90 PENDOWN
   FD :SEG2
   END
```
19. (a) Yes; *SAS* **(b)** Yes; *SAS* **(c)** Yes; *SSS* **(d)** Yes; *ASA*

20. $\triangle ABC \cong \triangle DEC$ by ASA. ($\overline{BD} \cong \overline{CE}$, $\angle ACD \cong \angle ECD$ as vertical angles, and $\angle B \cong \angle E$ as alternate interior angles formed by the parallels $\overline{AB}$ and $\overline{ED}$ and the transversal $\overleftrightarrow{EB}$.) $\overline{AC} \cong \overline{DC}$ by *CPCTC*.

21. Construction

Problem Set 11-4
1. The diameter is the longest chord of a circle.
2. Isosceles triangle; two sides are radii.
3. Right triangle
4. (a) 90° **(b)** 90° **(c)** 90° **(d)** An angle whose vertex is on a circle and whose sides intersect the circle in two points (determining a diameter) is a right angle. **(e)** In the drawing below, $\triangle AOC$ and $\triangle BOC$ are isosceles. (Why?) $\angle OAC \cong \angle OCA$ and $\angle OCB \cong \angle OBC$; base angles of an isosceles triangle are congruent. Therefore, $m(\angle OAC) + m(\angle OCA) + m(\angle OCB) + m(\angle OBC) = 2m(\angle OAC) + 2m(\angle OBC) = 180°$. Thus, $m(\angle OAC) + m(\angle OBC) = 90°$. Hence $m(\angle ACB) = 90°$.

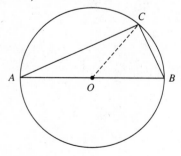

5. Construction

6. No; The tangent line will intersect one circle in two points.
7. Construction
8. Hint: First inscribe a regular hexagon in the given circle.
9. Hint: First inscribe a square in the given circle.
10. (c) Opposite angles are supplementary.
11. Hint: The center of the circle is at the intersection point of the diagonals.
12. No; it is only possible if the sides are equidistant from some point.
13. Hint: Draw a perpendicular from O to ℓ to obtain the radius of the circle.
14. Hint: Bisect the interior angles on the same side of the transversal. The center of the circle is the point of intersection of the angle bisectors.
15. (a) Isosceles **(b)** $m(\angle 1 + m(\angle 2) = m (\angle 3)$ **(c)** $m(\angle 1) = \frac{1}{2}m(\angle 3)$ **(d)** $\alpha = \frac{1}{2}\beta$ **(e)** $m(\angle 1) = m(\angle 2) = m(\angle 3)$
16. (a) 0, 1 or 2 depending on how the line is chosen. **(b)** 0, 1, or infinitely many depending on how the plane is chosen.
17. Given that $\overline{AB} \cong \overline{CD}$ (see the figure), prove that $\overline{OM} \cong \overline{ON}$. First prove that $\overline{AM} \cong \overline{MB}$ and $\overline{CN} \cong \overline{ND}$. Then show that $\triangle ABO \cong \triangle COD$. Hence, conclude that $\angle A \cong \angle C$. Now prove that $\triangle AMO \cong \triangle CNO$ (by *SAS*). Consequently $\overline{OM} \cong \overline{ON}$.

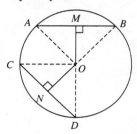

18. The radius r of the circle is half the distance between the parallel lines. The center of the circle is on line n parallel to the given lines and equidistant from these lines. The center of the required circle can be obtained by finding the point of intersection of line n with the circle whose center is at P and whose radius is r.
19. Answers may vary. Newer versions of Logo have a FILL primitive.
```
TO FILL.CIRCLE :RADIUS
  REPEAT 360 [FD :RADIUS BK
     :RADIUS RT 1]
END
```
20. Answers may vary.
```
TO DIAMETER
  REPEAT 360 [FD 1 RT 1]
  RT 90 FD 100
END
```
21. $\overline{AB}$

22. $\angle ABC$

23. The triangles are congruent by *AAS*. Sometimes this result is called Hypotenuse-Acute Angle or HA.

24. (a) It also bisects the opposite angle. **(b)** Yes; Use vertical angles to show this result.

Problem Set 11-5

1. 3

2. (a) Yes; *AAA* **(b)** Yes; sides are proportional and angles are congruent. **(c)** No **(d)** No **(e)** Yes; radii are proportional. **(f)** No **(g)** Yes; sides are proportional and angles are congruent.

3. This illustration is one possibility.

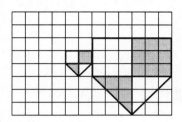

(a)

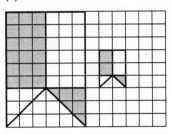

(b)

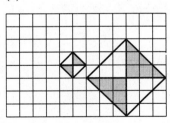

(c)

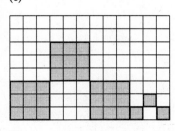

(d)

4. Yes; The scale factor is 1 and the angles are congruent.

5. (c) The triangles are similar if the corresponding sides are proportional.

6. (c) The triangles are similar if, for example, in $\triangle ABC$ and $\triangle DEF$, we have $AB/DE = AC/DF$ and $\angle A \cong \angle D$.

7. Answers may vary. **(a)** Two rectangles, one of which is a square and the other is not. **(b)** Two rhombuses, one of which is a square and the other is not but the sides are all the same length.

8. The ratio of the perimeters is the same as the ratio of the sides.

9. (a) (i) $\triangle ABC \sim \triangle DEF$ by *AA* (ii) $\triangle ABC \sim \triangle EDA$ by *AA* (iii) $\triangle ACD \sim \triangle ABE$ by *AA* (iv) $\triangle ABE \sim \triangle DCB$ by *AA* **(b)** (i) 2/3 (ii) 1/2 (iii) 3/4 (iv) 3/4

10. (a) 7 **(b)** 24/7 **(c)** 15/2 **(d)** 10 m

11. (a) 9 **(b)** 14/3 **(c)** 15/2 **(d)** 29/3

12. Construction.

13. (a) Polly is incorrect. 8/6 = 5/3; sides are not proportional. **(b)** Polly is correct. In the triangle on the left, $\alpha + 2\alpha = 180° - 90°$. Thus, $3\alpha = 90°$, or $\alpha = 30°$. The triangles are similar by *AA*. **(c)** Polly is correct. The triangles are similar by *AA*.

14. (a) (1) $\triangle ABC \sim \triangle ACD$ by *AA* since $\angle ADC$ and $\angle ACB$ are right angles, and $\angle A$ is common to both. (2) $\triangle ABC \sim \triangle CBD$ by *AA* since $\angle CDB$ and $\angle ACB$ are right angles and $\angle B$ is common to both. (3) Using (1) and (2), $\triangle ACD \sim \triangle CBD$ by the transitive property. **(b)** (1) $AC/AB = CD/BC = AD/AC$ (2) $BC/BA = CD/AC = BD/BC$ (3) $AC/CB = CD/BD = AD/CD$

15. No; The maps are similar and even though the scales may change, the actual distances do not.

16. Construction

17. 15 m

18. 9 m

19. (a) $\triangle ABC \sim \triangle BDC$ **(b)** $m(\angle ABC) = m(\angle ACB)$; base angles of an isosceles triangle are congruent and have the same measure.
$$m(\angle ABC) + m(\angle ACB) + 36° = 180°$$
$$2m(\angle ABC) = 144°$$
$$m(\angle ABC) = 72°$$
$$\tfrac{1}{2}m(\angle ABC) = m(\angle DBC) = 36°$$
$$\triangle ABC \sim \triangle BDC \text{ by } AA$$

20. $\angle CDE \cong \angle DFA$; They are alternate interior angles formed when parallel lines $\overleftrightarrow{AB}$ and $\overleftrightarrow{DC}$ are cut by a transversal. $\angle FEB \cong \angle DEC$; vertical angles are congruent. $\triangle BFE \cong \triangle CDE$; *AA*

21. (a) $\angle C \cong \angle ADG$ because both are right angles. $\angle CGF$ and $\angle AGD$ are complementary, as are $\angle AGD$ and $\angle GAD$. Thus $\angle CGF \cong \angle GAD$ and $\triangle GCF \sim \triangle ADG$ by *AA*. **(b)** No. $\overline{GF}$ is the hypotenuse of $\triangle GCF$ and congruent leg of $\triangle ADG$. They are not corresponding sides, and the hypotenuse $\overline{AG}$ of $\triangle ADG$ must be longer than GF.

22. 10 cm

23. Answers may vary.

(a) TO RECTANGLE :LEN :WID
    REPEAT 2 [FD :LEN RT 90 FD
     :WID RT 90]
    END
    TO SIM.RECT :LEN :WID
    RECTANGLE :LEN*2 :WID*2
    END

(b) TO SIM.RECTANGLE :LEN :WID
     :SCALE
    RECTANGLE :LEN*:SCALE
     :WID*:SCALE
    END

(c) TO PARALLELOGRAM :LEN :WID
     :ANGLE
    REPEAT 2 [FD :LEN RT 180-
     :ANGLE FD :WID RT :ANGLE]
    END
    TO SIM.PAR :LEN :WID :ANGLE
     :SCALE
    PARALLELOGRAM :LEN*:SCALE
     :WID*:SCALE :ANGLE
    END

24. Answers may vary.

(a) TO TRISECT :LEN
    REPEAT 3 [MARK FD :LEN/3]
    END
    TO MARK
    RT 90 FD 5
    BK 5 LT 90
    END

(b) TO PARTITION :LEN :NUM
    REPEAT :NUM [MARK FD
     :LEN/:NUM]
    END

25. No; the image is two-dimensional while the original person is three-dimensional.

26. Construction

Brain Teaser (p. 620)

Construct $\overline{BP}$ perpendicular to $\overline{CF}$ as shown. $\triangle CBP \cong \triangle DFE$ by AAS because $\overline{BC} \cong \overline{FD}$ (opposite sides in a rectangle), $\angle DEF \cong \angle CPB$ (right angles) and from $\angle FDE \cong \angle CFD$ (alternate interior angles between the parallels $\overleftrightarrow{CF}$ and $\overleftrightarrow{DE}$ and the transversal $\overleftrightarrow{DF}$) and $\angle CFD \cong \angle BCP$ (alternate interior angles between $\overleftrightarrow{FD} \parallel \overleftrightarrow{BC}$ and the tranversal $\overleftrightarrow{CF}$) it follows that $\angle FDE \cong \angle BCP$. By CPCTC, $\overline{CP} \cong \overline{DE}$ and hence $CP = DE = 4$ m. We have $CF = PF + CP$. Because $ABPF$ is a rectangle $PF = BA = 9$ m and hence $CF = 9 + 4 = 13$ m. Now $AF = BP$ ($ABPF$ is a rectangle), $\overline{FE} \cong \overline{BP}$ (CPCTC in $\triangle CBP$ and $\triangle DFE$) and hence $FE = BP$. Consequently $AF = FE$. Next show that $\triangle ABF \sim \triangle EFD$ (by AA since $\angle AFB$ and $\triangle FDE$ are complements of $\angle DFE$ and each triangle has a right angle.) Consequently $AB/EF = AF/ED$ or $9/ED = AF/4$ or $EF \cdot AF = 36$. Because $EF = AF$, we have $(EF)^2 = 36$ or $EF = 6$. Because $AE = 2EF$, $AE = 12$ m.

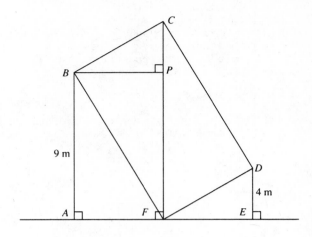

Problem Set 11-6

Answers for the entire section may vary. Procedures are written only as possible answers.

1. TO SIMSQ :SIDE :K
    SQUARE :SIDE
    LEFT 90
    PENUP FD 50 PENDOWN
    SQUARE :SIDE*:K
    END
    TO SQUARE :SIDE
    REPEAT 4 [FD :SIDE RT 90]
    END

2. TO RTISOS :HYPOT
    DRAW
    FD :HYPOR RT 135
    CHECK
    END

(In Apple Logo II, replace DRAW with CLEARSCREEN.)

    TO CHECK
    FORWARD 1
    SETHEADING TOWARDS 00
    IF ABS (HEADING - 225) < 2
     HOME STOP
    SETHEADING -135
    CHECK
    END

(In Apple Logo II, replace SETHEADING TOWARDS 00 with SETHEADING TOWARDS [0 0] and IF ABS (HEADING-225)<2 HOME STOP with IF ABS (HEADING-225<2) [HOME STOP].)

    TO ABS :VALUE
    IF :VALUE<0 OUTPUT-:VALUE ELSE
     OUTPUT :VALUE
    END

(In Apple Logo II, replace IF :VALUE<0 OUTPUT -:VALUE ELSE OUTPUT :VALUE with IF :VALUE <0 [OUTPUT -:VALUE] [OUTPUT :VALUE].)

214

3. ```
TO TR130 :HYPOT
  DRAW
  FD :HYPOT/2 RT 120
  FD :HYPOT RT 120
  HOME
END
```
*(In Apple Logo II, replace DRAW with CLEARSCREEN.)*

4. ```
TO STAR :SIDE
  HEXAGON :SIDE
  REPEAT 6 [LT 60 FD :SIDE RT 120
    FD :SIDE]
END
TO HEXAGON :SIDE
  REPEAT 6 [FD :SIDE RT 60]
END
```

5. ```
TO ISOSCELES3 :ANGLE :HEIGHT
  DRAW
  PENUP FD :HEIGHT
  PENDOWN RT 90
  CHECKHEADR :ANGLE
  HOME
  PENUP FD :HEIGHT
  PENDOWN LT 90
  CHECKHEADL :ANGLE
END
```
*(In Apple Logo II, replace DRAW with CLEARSCREEN.)*
```
TO CHECKHEADR :ANGLE
  SETHEADING TOWARDS 0 0
  IF ABS (HEADING-(180+:ANGLE))<2
    HOME STOP
  SETHEADING 90 FD 1
    CHECKHEADR :ANGLE
END
```
*(In Apple Logo II, replace SETHEADING TOWARDS 0 0 with SETHEADING TOWARDS [0 0] and IF ABS (HEADING-(180+:ANGLE))<2 HOME STOP with IF (ABS HEADING-(180+:ANGLE))<2 [HOME STOP].)*
```
TO CHECKHEADL :ANGLE
  SETHEADING TOWARDS 0 0
  IF ABS (HEADING-(90+:ANGLE))<2
    HOME STOP
  SETHEADING -90 FD 1
    CHECKHEADL :ANGLE
END
```
*(In Apple Logo II, replace SETHEADING TOWARDS 0 0 with SETHEADING TOWARDS [0 0] and IF ABS (HEADING-(90+:ANGLE))<2 HOME STOP with IF (ABS HEADING-(90+:ANGLE))<2 [HOME STOP].)*
```
TO ABS :VALUE
  IF :VALUE<0 OUTPUT-:VALUE ELSE
    OUTPUT :VALUE
END
```
*(In Apple Logo II, replace IF :VALUE<0 OUTPUT-:VALUE ELSE OUTPUT :VALUE with IF :VALUE <0 [OUTPUT -:VALUE] [OUTPUT :VALUE].)*

**Chapter 11 Test**

1. (a) $\triangle ABD \cong \triangle CBD$ by *SAS* (b) $\triangle AGC \cong \triangle DEB$ by *SAS* (c) $\triangle ABC \cong \triangle EDC$ by *AAS* (d) $\triangle ADB \cong \triangle ACE$ by *ASA* (e) $\triangle ABD \cong \triangle CBD$ by either *SAS* or *ASA* (f) $\triangle ABD \cong \triangle CBD$ by *SAS* (g) $\triangle ABD \cong \triangle CBE$ by *SSS* (h) $\triangle ABC \cong \triangle ADC$ by *SSS*

2. A parallelogram. $\triangle ADE \cong \triangle CBF$ by *SAS*. Hence, $\angle DEA \cong \angle CFB$. Since $\angle DEA \cong \angle EAF$ (alternate interior angles between the parallels $\overleftrightarrow{DC}$ and $\overleftrightarrow{AB}$ and the transversal $\overleftrightarrow{AE}$), it follows that $\angle EAF \cong \angle CFB$. Consequently, $\overline{AE} \parallel \overline{CF}$. Also, $\overline{EC} \parallel \overline{AF}$ (Why?), and therefore *AECF* is a parallelogram.

3. Construction

4. (a) $x = 8$; $y = 5$ (b) $x = 6$

5. Construction

6. $a/b = c/d$ because $a/b = x/y$ and $x/y = c/d$.

7. Hint: Find the intersection of the perpendicular bisector of *AB* and line $\ell$.

8. (a) $\triangle ACB \sim \triangle DEB$ by *AA*. $x = 24/5$ (b) $\triangle ADE \sim \triangle ACB$ by *AA*. $x = 55/6$ and $y = 4/3$.

9. (a) False; A chord has its endpoints on the circle. (b) False; A diameter intersects a circle in two points, and a tangent intersects it in only one point. (c) True (d) True (e) True

10. 12 m

11. (a) (iii) and (iv) (b) Any regular convex polygon can be inscribed in a circle.

12. 6 m

13. 256/5 m

## CHAPTER 12

**Problem Set 12-1**

1. (a) A translation (b) A translation

2. (a) (b)

3. (a) (b)
```

4. Construction

5. Answers may vary.

6. Answers may vary.

7.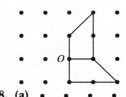

8. (a) 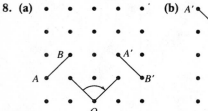 (b)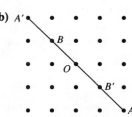

9. Construction

10. Hint: Find the image of the center, *M*, and one point on the circumference of the circle. Use these to find the image of the circle.

11. Construction

12. Construction

13. Hint: Find the midpoint of $\overline{PP'}$. This is the center of the half-turn.

14. Hint: Find the image *m'*, of line *m* under a half-turn with center *P*. This intersection of *m'* and line *l* is point *A*.

15. (b) A rotation with center *O* through β − α (c) No (d) Yes

16. Hint: Find the image, circle *O'*, of circle *O* under a half-turn with point *P* as center. The intersection of circle *O'* and circle *Q* will determine point *B* if it exists. (It may be possible to find two points on circle *Q* such that either may be point *B*.)

17. Hint: Pick any point, *P*, on the smaller circle. Rotate the middle circle 60 degrees using point *P* as the center. The intersection of the image of the middle circle and the larger circle will determine a vertex of the required triangle.

18.
```
   TO SLIDE :DIRECTION
        :DISTANCE :SIDE
      EQUILATERAL :SIDE
      SETHEADING :DIRECTION
      FORWARD :DISTANCE
      PENDOWN
      SETHEADING 0
      EQUILATERAL :SIDE
   END
   TO EQUILATERAL :SIDE
      REPEAT 3[FORWARD :SIDE RIGHT
        120]
   END
```

19.
```
   TO ROTATE :A :SIDE
      SQUARE :SIDE
      RIGHT :A
      SQUARE :SIDE
   END
   TO SQUARE :SIDE
      REPEAT 4[FORWARD :SIDE RIGHT
        90]
   END
```

20. (a)
```
   TO TURN.CIRCLE :A
      CIRCLE
      LEFT :A
      CIRCLE
   END
   TO CIRCLE
      REPEAT 360[FORWARD 1 RT 1]
   END
```
To produce the desired transformation, execute `TURN.CIRCLE 180`. (b) To produce the desired transformation, execute `TURN.CIRCLE 90`.

Problem Set 12-2

1. (a)   (b)

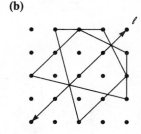

2. Construction

3. (b) Yes. Find *A'* and *C'*, the images of *A* and *C*. Label the point of intersection of $\overline{AB}$ and line *l* as point *P*; label the point of intersection of $\overline{BC}$ and line *l* as point *Q*. Draw $\overleftrightarrow{A'P}$ and $\overleftrightarrow{C'Q}$. The intersection of these lines is *B'*.

4. Hint: Find the image of the center of the circle and one point on the circumference of the circle to determine the image of the circle.

5. (a) Yes, there are infinitely many such lines all of which contain the center of the circle. (b) Yes, there are two: the reflecting line is the perpendicular bisector of the segment, and the reflecting line is the line containing the segment. (c) Yes, the reflecting line is the line containing the ray. (d) Yes, there are four such lines: the perpendicular bisectors of the pairs of parallel sides, and the diagonals. (e) Yes, there are two such lines: the perpendicular bisectors of the pairs of parallel sides. (f) There are none. (g) Yes, there is one such line in a general isosceles triangle: the line that is the perpendicular bisector of the side that is not congruent to the other two. (h) Yes, there are three such lines: the perpendicular bisectors of each of the sides.

216

(i) There are none. (j) Yes, there is one such line in a general isosceles trapezoid; the line that is the perpendicular bisector of the parallel sides. (k) Yes, there is one such line; the line that is the perpendicular bisector of the chord determined by the endpoints of the arc. (l) Yes, there is one in a general kite: it is the diagonal determined by the vertices of the noncongruent angles. (m) Yes, there are two, the diagonals. (n) Yes, there are six such lines: the perpendicular bisectors of the parallel sides and the three diameters determined by the vertices on the circumscribed circle. (o) Yes, there are *n* such lines.

6. Construction
7. Construction
8. The final image is the same as the original.
9. The images are congruent. No; unless *m* and ℓ are the same line.
10. Construction
11. The images are congruent, but not the same.
12. Construction
13. (a) The images are the same. (b) Yes
14. 1 to 2 is a rotation: 1 to 3 is a rotation; 1 to 4 is a translation; 1 to 5 is a rotation; 1 to 6 is a translation; 1 to 7 is a translation.
15. Construction
16. Reflect *A* in road 1 and *B* in road 2. Connect the images by a straight line. The intersection points with road 1 and road 2 are the desired locations for *P* and *Q*.
17. Reflect *B* in the line that contains side 1 to point *B′*, then reflect *B′* in the line that contains side 2 to point *B″*. Next reflect *B″* in the line that contains side 3, to point *B‴*. If the ball at *A* is shot at point *B‴*, it will bounce as desired and hit the ball at *B*. (Why?)

B‴ •

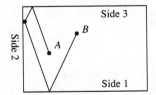

B″ •   •*B′*

18. (a) 150 degree rotation about the turtle's starting point. (b) Reflection about a vertical line containing the turtle's starting point. (c) 45 degree rotation and slide.
19. (a) Answers may vary. (b) The drawing produced in FIG2 is a reflection of the drawing produced by FIG1 through a horizontal line that contains the starting point of the turtle. (c) The drawing produced by FIG3 is a reflection to the drawing produced by FIG1 through a vertical line that contains the starting point of the turtle.
20. (a) TO EQTRI :SIDE
       REPEAT 3[FORWARD :SIDE RIGHT
         120]
     END
   (b) TO EQTR12 :SIDE
       REPEAT 3[FORWARD :SIDE LEFT
         120]
     END
(c) A reflection in a vertical line through the turtle's home. (d) A half-turn with the turtle's home as center.
21. *H, I, N, O S X,* and *Z*
22. *H, I, N, O, S, X,* and *Z*
23. Half-turn about the center of the letter *O*
24. (a) Infinitely many with the center of the circle as the center of the rotations (b) Infinitely many reflections in lines containing diameters.

Brain Teaser (p. 657)
Translate *B* towards *A* in the direction perpendicular to the banks of the river along the distance equal to the width of the river. Connect *A* with the image *B′*. The point *P* where $\overline{AB'}$ intersects the far bank is the point where the bridge should be built.

Problem Set 12-3
1. (a) The images are congruent, but not the same. The directions of the translations are opposite. (b) The images are congruent, but not the same. The rotations are in opposite directions.
2. (a) A translation determined by slide arrow $\overrightarrow{NM}$.
(b) A rotation of 75 degrees with center *O* in a counterclockwise direction. (c) A rotation of 45 degrees with center *A* in a clockwise direction. (d) A glide reflection that is the composition of a reflection in line *m* and a translation that takes *B* to *A*. (e) A reflection in line *n*.
3. (a) A half-turn with center the point of intersection of the perpendicular lines. (b) A rotation of 100 degrees clockwise with the same center as the given rotations. (c) A rotation of 50 degrees counterclockwise with the same center as the given rotations. (d) A translation of 15 cm along the same line and in the same direction as the given translations. (e) A translation of 5 cm along the same line but in the direction of the 15 cm translation. (f) A single reflection in a line parallel to the other three lines. (g) A single reflection in a line concurrent with the other three lines.

4. Answers may vary.

5. (c) C is the midpoint of the segment connecting the images.

6. (a) Point P **(b)** Point O **(c)** The final image of any point when it is reflected in A, B, C, A, B, and C where A, B, and C are the vertices of a triangle is the point itself.

7. Straight up; the transformation is a translation, the composition of two half-turns where the centers are each of the quarters.

8. Answers may vary, but the image is determined by two reflections.

9. (a) Yes **(b)** Yes **(c)** No **(d)** Yes

10. (a) (2,1) **(b)** (6,3) **(c)** (7,4) **(d)** (6,4)

11.

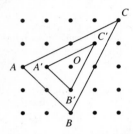

12. Answers may vary, but one possibility is that the similarity is the composition of a rotation that takes D to D', C to a point on $\overrightarrow{D'C'}$ and D to a point on $\overrightarrow{D'A'}$ and a size transformation with scale factor $D'C'/DC$.

13. Answers may vary.

Problem Set 12-4

1. (a) Line, rotational and point symmetry **(b)** Line symmetry **(c)** Line symmetry **(d)** Line symmetry

2. Answers may vary.

3. (a)

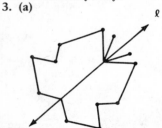

(b)

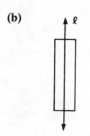

4. (a) (i) 4 (ii) None (iii) 2 (iv) 1
(b)

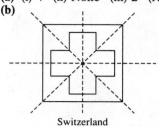

Switzerland

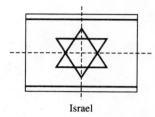

Israel

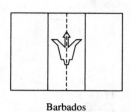

Barbados

5. (a) 1 vertical **(b)** 1 vertical **(c)** None **(d)** 1 vertical **(e)** 5 lines **(f)** 1 vertical

6. Sketches may vary. **(a)** Any scalene triangle **(b)** A nonequilateral isosceles triangle **(c)** Not possible **(d)** Any equilateral triangle

7. Sketches may vary.

8. (a) Yes, a figure with point symmetry has 180 degree rotational symmetry. **(b)** Not necessarily. Counterexamples may vary. **(c)** Yes, figures may vary. **(d)** No to both questions. Counterexamples may vary. **(e)** Yes, see part (a).

9. (a)

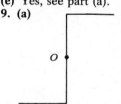

(b)

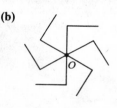

10. (a) 7 **(b)** 2 **(c)** 7 **(d)** 33

11. All definitions are concerned with lines of symmetry and not properties of sides and angles as defined earlier. They are equivalent unless they imply exactly the number of lines of symmetry indicated. If that is the case, then there are several differences.

12.
```
TO TURN.SYM :S :N :A
  REPEAT :N[SQUARE :S RIGHT :A]
END
TO SQUARE :S
  REPEAT 4[FORWARD :S RIGHT 90]
END
```
(a) Execute TURN.SYM 50 6 60
(b) Execute TURN.SYM 50 3 120
(c) Execute TURN.SYM 50 2 180
(d) Execute TURN.SYM 50 3 240
(e) Execute TURN.SYM 50 6 300

```
13. TO TURN.SY :S :N :A
      REPEAT :N[EQTRI :S RIGHT :A]
    END
    TO EQTRI :S
      REPEAT 3[FORWARD :S RIGHT 120]
    END
```
(a) Execute TURN.SY 50 6 60
(b) Execute TURN.SY 50 3 120
(c) Execute TURN.SY 50 3 240
(d) Execute TURN.SY 50 6 300

14. Construction
15. Construction

Problem Set 12-5

1. (a)

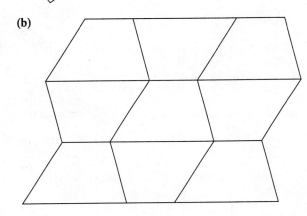

(b)

```
    TO SQUARE :SIDE
      REPEAT 4[FORWARD :SIDE RIGHT
        90]
    END
(b) TO TESSELTRI
      PENUP BACK 70 PENDOWN
      REPEAT 9[TRIANGLE 20 FORWARD
        20]
      PENUP BACK 180 RIGHT 60
      FORWARD 20 LEFT 60 PENDOWN
      REPEAT 9[TRIANGLE 20 FORWARD
        20]
    END
    TO TRIANGLE :SIDE
      REPEAT 3[FORWARD :SIDE RIGHT
        120]
    END
(c) TO TESSELHEX
      PENUP BACK 70 LEFT 90 PENDOWN
      REPEAT 4[HEXAGON 20 RIGHT
        120 FORWARD 20 LEFT 60
      HEXAGON 20 FORWARD 20 LEFT
        60]
    END
    TO HEXAGON :SIDE
      REPEAT 6[FORWARD :SIDE RIGHT
        60]
    END
7. TO TILESTRIP :S
     REPEAT 4[TILE :S PENUP RIGHT
       180 FORWARD 3*:S PENDOWN]
   END
   TO TILE :S
     RIGHT 180
     REPEAT 3 [REPEAT 4[FORWARD :S
       LEFT 60] RIGHT 120]
   END
```

2. (a) Rotate the quadrilateral 180 degrees about the midpoint of each side. Repeat the process for each quadrilateral constructed in this way. (b) Yes
3. (a), (c), and (d) tessellate the plane.
4. (a) The dual is also a tessellation of squares. (b) The dual is a tessellation of triangles. (c) The dual is a tessellation of equilateral triangles.
5. Answers may vary.
6. (a)
```
    TO TESSELSQUARE
      PENUP BACK 70 PENDOWN
      REPEAT 9[SQUARE 20 FORWARD
        20]
      PENUP BACK 180 RIGHT 90
      FORWARD 20 LEFT 90 PENDOWN
      REPEAT 9[SQUARE 20 FORWARD
        20]
    END
```

Problem Set 12-6

1.
```
   TO WALL3 :XPT :YPT :SIDE
     DRAW
     SETUP :XPT :YPT
     WALLPAPER3 :YPT :SIDE
   END
```
(In Apple Logo II, replace DRAW with CLEARSCREEN.)
```
   TO SETUP :XPT :YPT
     PENUP
     SETXY :XPT :YPT
     PENDOWN
   END
```
(In Apple Logo II, replace SETXY :XPT :YPT with SETPOS (LIST :XPT :YPT.)

219

```
TO WALLPAPER3 :YPT :SIDE
 TRISTRIP :SIDE
 PENUP
 SETUP (:XPT+:SIDE*(SORT 3)/2 :YPT
 PENDOWN
 WALLPAPER3 :YPT :SIDE
END
TO TRISTRIP :SIDE
 IF XCOR+:SIDE>120 TOPLEVEL
 IF (ANYOF (XCOR<-120)
  (XCOR+:SIDE*(SQRT 3)/2>120)
  (YCOR<-100)(YCOR+:SIDE>100))
  STOP
 TRIANGLE :SIDE
 FORWARD :SIDE
 RIGHT 60
 TRIANGLE :SIDE
 LEFT 60
 TRISTRIP :SIDE
END
```

*(In Apple Logo II, replace IF XCOR+:SIDE
>120 TOPLEVEL with IF
XCOR+:SIDE>120 [THROW "TOPLEVEL].
Also replace IF (ANYOF (XCOR<-120)
(XCOR+:SIDE*(SQRT 3)/2>120)
(YCOR<-100) (YCOR+:SIDE>100))
STOP with IF (OR (XCOR<-120)
(XCOR+:SIDE*(SQRT 3)/2>120) (YCOR
<-100) (YCOR+:SIDE>100)) [THROW
"TOPLEVEL].)*

```
TO TRIANGLE :SIDE
 REPEAT 3[FORWARD :SIDE RIGHT
 120]
END
```

2. The conditions are to keep the turtle from drawing off the screen. It forces the boundaries to be as follows: $-120 < x < 120$ and $-100 < y < 100$.

3.
```
TO WALL4 :XPT :YPT :SIDE
 DRAW
 SETUP :XPT :YPT
 WALLPAPER4 :YPT :SIDE
END
```

*(In Apple Logo II, replace DRAW with
CLEARSCREEN.)*
```
TO SETUP :XPT :YPT
 PENUP
 SETXY :XPT :YPT
 PENDOWN
END
```

*(In Apple Logo II, replace SETXY :XPT :YPT
with SETPOS (LIST :XPT :YPT.)*
```
 TO WALLPAPER4 :YPT :SIDE
 MAKE "X XCOR
 HEXSTRIP :SIDE
 PENUP
```

```
 SETUP (XCOR+:SIDE*(SQRT 3)) :YPT
 PENDOWN
 WALLPAPER4 :YPT :SIDE
END
TO HEXSTRIP :SIDE
 IF XCOR+:SIDE>120 TOPLEVEL
 IF (ANYOF (XCOR<-120) (XCOR+
 :SIDE*(SQRT 3))>120) (YCOR<
 -100) (YCOR+:SIDE*3>100)) STOP
 HEXAGON :SIDE
 FORWARD :SIDE RIGHT 60 FORWARD
 :SIDE LEFT 60
 HEXSTRIP :SIDE
END
```

*(In Apple Logo II, replace IF XCOR+:SIDE
>120 TOPLEVEL with IF
XCOR+:SIDE>120 [THROW "TOPLEVEL].
Also replace IF (ANYOF (XCOR<-120)
(XCOR+:SIDE*(SQRT 3))>120)
(YCOR<-100) (YCOR+:SIDE*3>100))
STOP with IF (OR (XCOR<-120)
(XCOR+:SIDE*(SQRT 3))>120) (YCOR
<-100) (YCOR+:SIDE*3>100))
[STOP].)*

```
TO HEXAGON :SIDE
 REPEAT 6[FORWARD :SIDE RIGHT 60]
END
```

4. Answers may vary.

5. Yes; once the figures fit between two parallel lines, then one could make a rubber stamp of the parallel lines and the drawings between them and stamp them all across the plane.

6.
```
TO WALL5 :XPT :YPT :SIDE1 :SIDE2
 DRAW
 SETUP :XPT :YPT
 WALLPAPER5 :YT :SIDE1 :SIDE2
END
```

*(In Apple Logo II, replace DRAW with
CLEARSCREEN.)*
```
TO SETUP :XPT :YPT
 PENUP
 SETXY :XPT :YPT
 PENDOWN
END
```

*(In Apple Logo II, replace SETXY :XPT :YPT
with SETPOS (LIST :XPT :YPT.)*
```
 TO WALLPAPER5 :YPT :SIDE1
 :SIDE2
 RECTANGLESTRIP :SIDE1 :SIDE2
 PENUP
 SETUP (XCOR+:SIDE2) :YPT
 PENDOWN
 WALLPAPER5 :YPT :SIDE1 :SIDE2
END
```

220

```
TO RECTANGLESTRIP :SIDE1 :SIDE2
 IF XCOR+:SIDE2>120 TOPLEVEL
 IF (ANYOF (XCOR<-120)
  (XCOR+:SIDE2>120) (YCOR<-100)
  (YCOR+:SIDE1>100)) STOP
 RECTANGLE :SIDE1 :SIDE2
 FORWARD :SIDE1
 RECTANGLESTRIP :SIDE1 :SIDE2
END
```

*(In Apple Logo II, replace IF XCOR+:SIDE2
>120 TOPLEVEL with IF
XCOR+:SIDE2>120 [THROW
"TOPLEVEL]. Also replace IF (ANYOF
(XCOR<-120) (XCOR+:SIDE2>120)
(YCOR<-100) (YCOR+:SIDE1>100))
STOP with IF (OR (XCOR<-120)
(XCOR+:SIDE2>120) (YCOR <-100)
(YCOR+:SIDE1>100)) [STOP].)*

```
TO RECTANGLE :SIDE1 SIDE2
 REPEAT 2[FORWARD :SIDE1 RIGHT 90
   FORWARD :SIDE2 RIGHT 90]
END
```

```
7. TO WALL6 :XPT :YPT :SIDE
 DRAW
 SETUP :XPT :YPT
 WALLPAPER6 :YPT :SIDE
END
```

*(In Apple Logo II, replace DRAW with
CLEARSCREEN.)*

```
TO SETUP :XPT :YPT
 PENUP
 SETXY :XPT :YPT
 PENDOWN
END
```

*(In Apple Logo II, replace SETXY :XPT :YPT
with SETPOS (LIST :XPT :YPT).)*

```
 TO WALLPAPER6 :YPT :SIDE
  CHEVRONSTRIP :SIDE
  PENUP
  SETUP (XCOR+:SIDE) :YPT
  PENDOWN
  WALLPAPER6 :YPT :SIDE
END
 TO CHEVRONSTRIP :SIDE
  IF XCOR+:SIDE>120 TOPLEVEL
  IF (ANYOF (XCOR-:SIDE<-120)
  (XCOR+:SIDE>120)
  (YCOR-:SIDE*(SQRT 2)/2<-100)
  (YCOR+:SIDE>100)) STOP
 CHEVRON :SIDE
 FORWARD :SIDE
 CHEVRONSTRIP :SIDE
END
```

*(In Apple Logo II, replace IF XCOR+:SIDE
>120 TOPLEVEL, with IF
XCOR+:SIDE>120 [THROW "TOPLEVEL],
and replace IF (ANYOF (XCOR-:SIDE<-
120) (XCOR+:SIDE>120) (YCOR-
:SIDE*(SQRT 2)/2<-100)
(YCOR+:SIDE>100)) STOP with IF (OR
(XCOR-:SIDE<-120)
(XCOR+:SIDE>120) (YCOR-
:SIDE*(SQRT 2)/2<-100)
(YCOR+:SIDE>100)) [STOP].)*

```
TO CHEVRON :SIDE
 FORWARD :SIDE RIGHT 135
 FORWARD :SIDE*(SQRT 2)/2 LEFT 90
 FORWARD :SIDE*(SQRT 2)/2
  RIGHT 135
 FORWARD :SIDE RIGHT 45
 FORWARD :SIDE*(SQRT 2)/2
  RIGHT 90
 FORWARD :SIDE*(SQRT 2)/2
  RIGHT 45
END
```

Chapter 12 Test
1. (a)

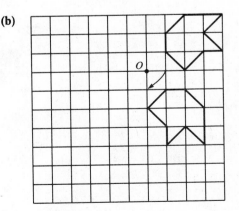

(b)

(c)

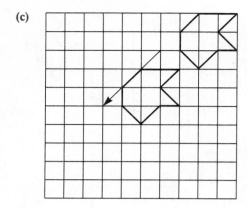

2. Construction
3. (a) 4 (b) 1 (c) 1 (d) None (e) 2 (f) 2
4. (a) Line and rotational (b) Line, rotational, and point (c) Line
5. (a) Infinitely many (b) Infinitely many (c) 3 (d) 9
6. (a) Reflection (b) Rotation (c) Glide reflection (d) Translation
7. (a) 1 (b) 2 (c) 3 (d) 2
8. This answer depends totally upon how the letters are made, but generally we have the following: *c* has line symmetry; *i* has line symmetry; *o* has line, rotational, and point symmetry; *s* has rotational and point symmetry; *t* has line symmetry; *v* has line symmetry; *w* has line symmetry; *x* has line, rotational, and point symmetry; *z* has rotational and point symmetry.
9. Answers may vary, but a circle can be transformed into itself by all the transformations.
10. Hint: Construct the perpendicular bisector of $\overline{AB}$.
11. Hint: $\overline{BC}$ formed by the midpoints of $\overline{A'B'}$ and $\overline{A'C'}$.
12.
```
TO RHOMSTRIP :SIDE :ANGLE
   IF (ANYOF (XCOR-:SIDE<-120)
   (XCOR+:SIDE*2>120)
   (YCOR-:SIDE<-100)
   (YCOR+:SIDE*2>100)) STOP
   RHOMBUS :SIDE :ANGLE
   FORWARD :SIDE
   RHOMSTRIP :SIDE :ANGLE
END
```

*(In Apple Logo II, replace IF (ANYOF (XCOR-:SIDE<-120) (XCOR+:SIDE*2>120) (YCOR-:SIDE<-100) (YCOR+:SIDE*2>100) STOP with IF (OR (XCOR-:SIDE<-120) (XCOR+:SIDE*2>120) (YCOR-:SIDE<-100) (YCOR+:SIDE*2>100)) [STOP].)*

```
TO RHOMBUS :SIDE :ANGLE
   REPEAT 2[FORWARD :SIDE RIGHT
   180-:ANGLE FORWARD :SIDE
   RIGHT :ANGLE]
END
```

CHAPTER 13

Problem Set 13-1
1. (a) 2.78 (b) 14,400 (c) 100 (d) 0.48 (e) 31 (f) 418,880
2. (a) 20; 2 (b) 36; 3.6 (c) 45; 4.5 (d) 5; 50 (e) 6.2; 62 (f) 7.9; 79 (g) 93; 9.3
3. Answers vary.
4. (a) 98 (b) 9.8
5. (a) centimeters (b) millimeters (c) centimeters (d) centimeters (e) centimeters (f) meters (g) centimeters (h) centimeters
6. (a) inches (b) inches (c) feet (d) inches (e) inches (f) yards (g) feet (h) inches
7. (a) 3.5; 3500 (b) 163; 1630 (c) 0.035; 3.5 (d) 0.1; 10 (e) 200; 2000
8. (a) 10.00 (b) 0.77 (c) 10.0 (d) 15.5 (e) 195.0 (f) 8.1 (g) 40.0
9. 6 m, 5218 mm, 245 cm, 700 mm, 91 mm, 8 cm
10. (a) 1724 (b) 106 (c) 316
11. (a) 8 cm (b) 12 cm (c) 9 cm (d) 20 cm
12. (a) 1.0 (b) 0.17 (c) 0.262 (d) 3000 (e) 0.03 (f) 170 (g) 3500 (h) 0.359 (i) 0.1 (j) 64.7 (k) 1 (l) 5000 (m) 5130
13. (a) $AB + BC > AC$ (b) $BC + CA > AB$ (c) $AB + CA > BC$
14. (b) and (c)
15. (a) 13 cm (b) $(a + b + c)$ cm (c) $3s$ (d) $4s$ (e) $2l + 2w$ (f) ns
16. (a) answers vary (b) 8 (c) 20
17. (a) 6 cm (b) $\dfrac{3}{\pi}$ m (c) $\dfrac{0.335}{\pi}$ m (d) 46 cm
18. (a) 6π cm (b) 6π cm (c) 4 cm (d) $6\pi^2$ cm
19. The circumference is doubled.
20. πr
21. If the radius of each ball is r, then the height of the can is 3 times the diameter that is, $6r$. The perimeter at the top is $2\pi r$ and $2\pi r > 6r$.
22. (a) 2 : 1 (b) The ratio of the perimeters of two similar triangles is the same as the ratio of corresponding sides. (c) If $\triangle ABC \sim \triangle A'B'C'$, with $\dfrac{A'B'}{AB} = r$, then, $\dfrac{\text{perimeter } \triangle A'B'C'}{\text{perimeter } \triangle ABC} = \dfrac{rAB + rBC + rAC}{AB + BC + AC} = \dfrac{r(AB + BC + AC)}{AB + BC + AC} = r$.
23. (a) about $9.5 \cdot 10^{12}$ km (b) about $4.1 \cdot 10^{13}$ km (c) about $6.9 \cdot 10^8$ h, or about 78000 years (d) 2495 h, or about 104 days
24. (a) 3096 (b) 1032 (c) March 4.04

Brain Teaser (p. 705)
The tallest person on earth could walk under the wire. Suppose the two concentric circles below represented the earth and the lengthened wire.

$\overline{OA}$ and $\overline{OB}$ are the radii of the respective circles and have lengths r and $r + x$. Since the circumference of the earth plus 20 m equals the circumference of the lengthened wire, we have $2\pi r + 20 = 2\pi(r + x)$.

Consequently, $x = \dfrac{10}{\pi}$, or approximately 3.18 m.

Problem Set 13-2
1. **(a)** cm²; in² **(b)** cm²; in² **(c)** cm²; in² **(d)** m²; ft²
(e) m²; ft² **(f)** km²; yd²
2. Answers may vary.
3.

m²	cm,²	mm²
0.0588	588	58,800
0.000192	1.92	192
1.5	15,000	1,500,000
0.01	100	10,000
0.0005	5	500

4. A 2-m square is a square that has measure 2 m on a side, and hence an area of 4 m². Two square meters is the area of any shape that occupies 2 m².
5. **(a)** 444.4 **(b)** 0.32 **(c)** 6400 **(d)** 130680
6. **(a)** 20 cm² **(b)** 900 cm² or 0.09 m² **(c)** 7.5 m²
(d) 39 cm² **(e)** 600 cm² **(f)** 60 cm²
7. **(a)** 9 cm² **(b)** 96 cm² **(c)** 64 cm² **(d)** 20 cm²
(e) 84 cm² **(f)** 105 cm²
8. **(a)** 4900 m² **(b)** 98 **(c)** 0.98
9. The area of each triangle is 10 cm², since they all have the same base, $\overline{AB}$, and the same height.
10. **(a)** 1.95 km², 195 ha **(b)** 1,950,000 square yards; approximately 0.63 square miles; approximately 403 acres. The comparable problem in (a) is much easier since the conversions in (b) from square yards to square miles and then to acres involve complicated conversion factors.
11. **(a)** $24\sqrt{3}$ cm² **(b)** $9\sqrt{3}$ cm²
12. **(a)** $1\frac{1}{2}$ **(b)** 2 **(c)** 3 **(d)** $3\frac{1}{2}$ **(e)** $5\frac{1}{2}$ **(f)** 3 **(g)** 3
(h) 2 **(i)** 5 **(j)** 6 **(k)** 4 1/2
13. Pick's theorem holds for all polygons in problem 12; for example, in (d), $I + \frac{1}{2}B - 1 = 1 + \frac{1}{2}(7) - 1 = 3\frac{1}{2}$.

14. **(a)**
15. **(a)** 75 cm² **(b)** Dropping perpendiculars to the lower base from the endpoints of the upper base forms isoceles right triangles whose legs are $\dfrac{a - b}{2}$. So, $h = \dfrac{a - b}{2}$. Then, using the formula for the area of a trapezoid, $A = \dfrac{1}{2} \cdot (a + b) \cdot \dfrac{a - b}{2} = \dfrac{a^2 - b^2}{4}$.
16. $\dfrac{ab}{2}$
17. **(a)** 25π cm² **(b)** $\dfrac{8}{3}\pi$ cm² **(c)** 3.6π cm²
(d) 4.5π cm²
18. **(a)** 16π cm² **(b)** $r = \dfrac{s}{\sqrt{\pi}}$
19. **(a)** 2π cm² **(b)** $\left(2 + \dfrac{\pi}{2}\right)$ cm² **(c)** 2π cm²
(d) $50\pi - 100$
20. **(a)** \$405.11 **(b)** \$550
21. **(a)** $\dfrac{1}{4}\pi r^2$ **(b)** $\dfrac{1}{8}\pi r^2$ **(c)** $\dfrac{1}{16}\pi r^2$
22. $x = \dfrac{20}{3}$
23. 7π m²
24. 1200
25. 8
26. **(a)** (i) 12; 10; (ii) 14; 10, (iii) 62; 22 **(b)** (i) 9; 5;
(ii) 42; 12 **(c)** $2(n + 1)$ **(d)** $n - 1$
27. **(a)** Rotate the shaded region 180° clockwise about point E. The area of the triangle is the same as the area of the parallelogram. Thus, $A = \dfrac{h}{2} \cdot b$.
28. **(a)** $400 - 100\pi$ cm² **(b)** $\dfrac{100}{3}\pi + 50\sqrt{3}$ cm²
29. **(a)** $4:9$. Justification: $\dfrac{A_1}{A_2} = \dfrac{s_1^2}{s_2^2}$, and $\dfrac{s_1}{s_2} = \dfrac{2}{3}$, hence $\dfrac{A_1}{A_2} = \left(\dfrac{2}{3}\right)^2 = \dfrac{4}{9}$. **(b)** $4:9$ (Hint: $A = d^2/2$, where d is the length of a diagonal.)
30. **(a)** $4:1$ **(b)** If r is the ratio of corresponding sides, then r^2 is the ratio of their areas. **(c)** Given $\triangle ABC \sim \triangle A'B'C'$, with $\dfrac{AB}{A'B'} = r$. From $\triangle ABD \sim \triangle A'B'D'$ (AA), we have $\dfrac{BD}{B'D'} = r$. Hence, the ratio of the areas is $\dfrac{\frac{1}{2}AC \cdot BD}{\frac{1}{2}A'C' \cdot B'D'} = \dfrac{AC}{A'C'} \cdot \dfrac{BD}{B'D'} = r \cdot r = r^2$.

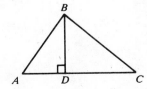
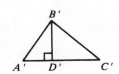

223

31. (a) The 27-in. set is the better buy. The ratio of the areas of similar rectangles is the square of the ratio of the sides. In this case, $(20/27)^2 = 0.548$, so the 20-in. set has an area which is about 55% the area of the 27-in. set, yet, you pay 66% the price of the larger set. **(b)** 28.3 in.

32. A rectangle. The area is the same, so $A = b \cdot h$.

33. The new figure is a parallelogram that has twice the area of the trapezoid. The area of the parallelogram is $\frac{1}{2}(AB + CD) \cdot h$, where h is the height of the parallelogram. Thus the area of the trapezoid is $\frac{1}{2}(AB + CD) \cdot h$.

34. P should be connected to the point that is 2 units above P and $1\frac{1}{2}$ units to the right of P.

35. Construct perpendicular diameters. Draw four arcs, whose radii are equal to that of the circle, and whose centers are the endpoints of the diameters.

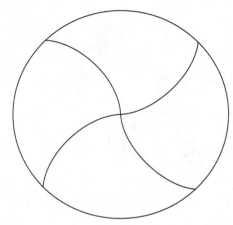

36. (a) 21.46% **(b)** same as in (a). **(c)** same as in (a).

37. Draw altitudes $\overline{BE}$ and $\overline{DF}$ of triangles BCP and DCP, respectively. $\triangle ABE \cong \triangle CDP$ by AAS. Thus $\overline{BE} \cong \overline{DF}$. Because $\overline{CP}$ is a base of $\triangle BCP$ and $\triangle DCP$, and because the heights are the same, the area must be the same.

38. (a) 10 **(b)** 104 **(c)** 0.35 **(d)** 40 **(e)** 8000 **(f)** 6.504

39. (a) $(2\pi + 4)$ cm **(b)** $(6 + 5\pi)$ mm

Brain Teaser

(1) 64 **(2)** 65 **(3)** Although the pieces look like they should fit together, they do not really. To see this, assume the pieces do fit. We then obtain the figure.

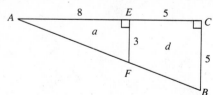

Since $\triangle AEF \sim \triangle ACB$, we have $\frac{8}{13} = \frac{3}{5}$, which is a contradiction. This implies that pieces like those in the figure cannot fit together in order to form a triangle. In order for the pieces to fit together, the measure of $\overline{EF}$ must be given as: $\frac{8}{13} = \frac{EF}{5}$; hence $EF = \frac{40}{13} = 3\frac{1}{13}$. Since $3\frac{1}{13}$ is close to 3, the discrepancy is small and the pieces only appear to fit. Other pieces which appear to fit should be analyzed.

Problem Set 13-3

1. (a) 6 **(b)** $\sqrt{2}$ **(c)** 5a **(d)** 12 **(e)** $\sqrt{3}s$ **(f)** $\sqrt{2}$ **(g)** 9 **(h)** 13 **(i)** $\frac{\sqrt{32}}{2}$, or $2\sqrt{2}$ **(j)** $\sqrt{45}$, or $3\sqrt{5}$ **(k)** $3\sqrt{3}$

2. One leg has length $6\sqrt{5}$ cm and the other $12\sqrt{5}$ cm or about 13.4 cm and 26.8 cm respectively.

3. (a) No **(b)** Yes **(c)** Yes **(d)** Yes **(e)** Yes **(f)** Yes

4. $\sqrt{450}$, or $15\sqrt{2}$ cm

5. (a) $x = 8$, $y = 2\sqrt{3}$ **(b)** $x = 4$, $y = 2$

6. $\sqrt{5200}$ km, or $20\sqrt{13}$ km, or approximately 72.1 km

7. About 2622 mi.

8. $\sqrt{125}$ mi. or about 11.2 mi.

9. Yes, the other legs must also be congruent by the Pythagorean theorem, and then the two triangles are congruent by SSS.

10. $\sqrt{216}$ feet, or $6\sqrt{6}$ feet, or about 14.7 feet.

11. (a) $37.5\sqrt{3}$ cm² **(b)** $\frac{3}{2}\sqrt{3}r^2$ cm²

12. $\left(143 + \frac{73}{2}\pi\right)$ m²

13. 9.8 m

14. (a) $\frac{\sqrt{3}s^2}{4}$ **(b)** $\frac{s^2}{2}$

15. 1.5 m

16. 12.5 cm; 15 cm

17. 25 cm

18. (a)

Draw $\triangle DCB \cong \triangle ABC$. Since all the interior angles in $\triangle ABD$ are 60°, the triangle is equilateral. Hence, $AB = BD = AD$. Since $AC = CD$, it follows that $AC = \frac{1}{2}AD$, and hence $AC = \frac{1}{2}AB$. **(b)** $\frac{\sqrt{3}c}{2}$

19. $\dfrac{c}{\sqrt{2}}$, or $\dfrac{\sqrt{2}c}{2}$

20. $\dfrac{5}{3}$ m

21. (a) Draw a diagonal. The pythagorean theorem ensures that the area of the square whose side is the diagonal will be twice the area of the original square.

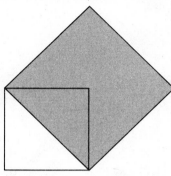

(b) Draw both diagonals. From adjacent vertices, draw lines parallel to the diagonals. The resulting square will have an area half the area of the original square.

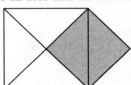

22. (a)

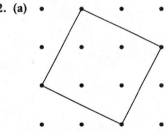

(b) not possible
(c)

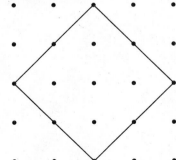

(d) not possible
(e) not possible

23. $\triangle ACD \sim \triangle ABC$. Thus, $\dfrac{b}{x} = \dfrac{c}{b}$ implies $b^2 = cx$.

$\triangle BCD \sim \triangle BAC$. Thus, $\dfrac{a}{y} = \dfrac{c}{a}$ implies $a^2 = cy$.

Consequently, $a^2 + b^2 = cx + cy = c(x + y) = c^2$.

24. The area of the trapezoid is equal to the sum of the areas of the three triangles. Thus,

$$\frac{1}{2}(a + b)(a + b) = \frac{1}{2}ab + \frac{1}{2}ab + \frac{1}{2}c^2$$

$$\frac{1}{2}(a^2 + 2ab + b^2) = ab + \frac{1}{2}c^2$$

$$\frac{a^2}{2} + ab + \frac{b^2}{2} = ab + \frac{c^2}{2}$$

Subtracting ab from both sides and multiplying both sides by 2, we have $a^2 + b^2 = c^2$. The reader should also verify that the angle formed by the two sides of length c has measure 90°.

25. Yes

26. Yes. Let a right triangle have legs of lengths a and b and hypotenuse of length c. Because an equilateral triangle with base of length x has height $\dfrac{\sqrt{3}}{2}x$, its area is $\dfrac{\sqrt{3}}{4}x^2$. Thus, the sum of the areas of the equilateral triangles constructed on the legs is $\dfrac{\sqrt{3}}{4}a^2 + \dfrac{\sqrt{3}}{4}b^2$, or $\dfrac{\sqrt{3}}{4}(a^2 + b^2)$. The area of the equilateral triangle constructed on the hypotenuse is $\dfrac{\sqrt{3}}{4}c^2$. By the Pythagorean Theorem, $c^2 = a^2 + b^2$, and hence $\dfrac{\sqrt{3}}{4}(a^2 + b^2) = \dfrac{\sqrt{3}}{4}c^2$.

27. The area of the large square is equal to the sum of the areas of the smaller square and the four triangles. Thus,

$$(a + b)^2 = c^2 + 4\left(\frac{ab}{2}\right)$$

$$a^2 + 2ab + b^2 = c^2 + 2ab$$

$$a^2 + b^2 = c^2$$

28. 0.032 km, 322 cm, 3.2 m, 3.020 cm

29. (a) 3325 mm², or 33.25 cm² **(b)** 30 cm²
(c) 32 m²

30. $\dfrac{25}{\pi}$ m²

31. (a) 10 cm; 10π cm; 25π cm² **(b)** 12 cm; 24π cm; 144π cm² **(c)** $\sqrt{17}$ m; $2\sqrt{17}$ m; $2\pi\sqrt{17}$ m
(d) 10 cm; 20 cm; 100π cm²

Brain Teaser (p. 732)
The room can be thought of as a box, which can be opened up so that A and C lie on the same plane. Then

225

the shortest path is the line segment connecting A and C. Thus $AC = \sqrt{2^2 + 6^2} = \sqrt{40} = 2\sqrt{10}$ m

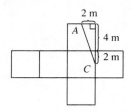

Problem Set 13-4
1. **(a)** 96 cm² **(b)** 216π cm² **(c)** 236 cm²
(d) 64π cm² **(e)** 24π cm² **(f)** 90 cm² **(g)** 5600 sq. ft.
(h) 1500π sq. ft. **(i)** $32\pi + 16\sqrt{5}$ cm²
2. 2.5 L
3. 2688π mm²
4. 162,307,600π km²
5. $\dfrac{16}{36}$, or $\dfrac{4}{9}$
6. **(a)** They are the same. **(b)** The one with radius 6 m.
7. $(108\sqrt{21} + 216\sqrt{3})$ m²
8. **(a)** The area is nine times the original. **(b)** It is doubled.
9. **(a)** The surface area is multiplied by 4. **(b)** The surface area is multiplied by 9. **(c)** The surface area is multiplied by k^2.
10. **(a)** It is tripled. **(b)** It is tripled. **(c)** It is nine times the original area.
11. **(a)** 1.5π m² **(b)** 2.5π m²
12. **(a)** 64.5π cm² **(b)** 7.07 cm
13. Let the radius of the sphere be r and the height of the cylinder h. The area of the sphere is $4\pi r^2$. The lateral surface area of the cylinder is $2\pi rh$. Since $h = 2r$, $2\pi rh = 2\pi r \cdot 2r = 4\pi r^2$.
14. Let x be longer side and y the shorter side of the field. Then because it takes 27 rounds to mow the lawn, $y = 2 \cdot 27 \cdot 3 = 162$ ft. After 12 rounds the dimensions of the remaining uncut rectangular field are $x - 2 \cdot 12 \cdot 3$ by 90. Hence, $\frac{1}{2} \cdot 162 \cdot x = (x - 72) \cdot 90$. Thus $x = 720$ ft. and $y = 162$ ft.
15. $(100\sqrt{17} + 100)$ cm² or approximately 512.3 cm²
16.

(a)   **(b)**
SA = $100\pi(\sqrt{5} + 1)$ cm² $\doteq$ SA = 1350π cm²
323.6π cm²
17. **(a)** Approximately 42.1 cm **(b)** Approximately 73 cm
18. 15.2 cm
19. $(6400\sqrt{2}\pi + 13,600\pi)$ cm²
20. 375π cm²

21. **(a)** 100,000 **(b)** 1.368 **(c)** 500 **(d)** 2,000,000
(e) 1 **(f)** 1,000,000
22. $10\sqrt{5}$ cm
23. $20\sqrt{5}$ cm
24. **(a)** 240 cm, or 2.4 m; 2400 cm², or 0.24 m²
(b) $30 + 10\sqrt{2}$ cm, 75 cm² **(c)** 44 cm, 104 cm²
(d) $(1 + 3\sqrt{5} + 2\sqrt{13})$ cm, 9 cm²
25. The length of the side is 25 cm. The length of the diagonal $\overline{AD}$ is 30 cm.

Brain Teaser (p. 741)
The cone and the flattend region obtained by slitting the cone along a slant height are shown below.

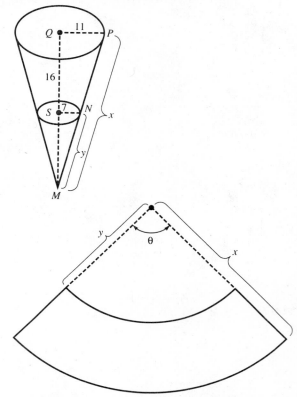

To construct the flattend ring we need to find x, y and θ.
Because $\triangle MQP \sim \triangle MSN$ we have $\dfrac{16 + MS}{MS} = \dfrac{11}{7}$.
Hence $MS = 28$ cm. In $\triangle MSN$ we have $28^2 + 7^2 = y^2$ or $y \doteq 28.86$. In $\triangle PQM$: $x^2 = 11^2 + 44^2$ or $x \doteq 45.35$ cm.

To find θ we roll the sector with radius y and central angle θ into the cone whose base is 7 cm and whose slant height is y. Hence $2\pi y \cdot \dfrac{\theta}{360} = 2\pi \cdot 7$ or $\theta = \dfrac{7 \cdot 360}{28.86} \doteq 87°19'$.

Problem Set 13-5
1. (a) 8000 (b) 0.0005 (c) 0.000675 (d) 3,000,000
(e) 7 (f) 2,000 (g) $8.57 \cdot 10^{-3}$ (h) 675 (i) 345.6
(j) 0.69
2. Spheres will not fill space. They have gaps.
3. (a) 64 cm³ (b) 120 cm³ (c) 216 cm³ (d) 14 cm³
(e) 50 cm³ (f) 21π cm³
(g) 432π cm³ (h) $\dfrac{4000}{3}\pi$ cm³

4. (a) 22,800 cubic feet (b) $\dfrac{20,000}{3}\pi$ cubic feet

(c) 76,200 cubic feet (d) $\dfrac{256\pi}{3}$ cm³

5.

	(a)	(b)	(c)	(d)	(e)	(f)
cm³	2000	500	1500	5000	750	4800
dm³	2	0.5	1.5	5	0.750	4.8
L	2	0.5	1.5	5	0.750	4.8
mL	2000	500	1500	5000	750	4800

6. (a) 200.0 mL (b) 0.320 L (c) 1.0 L (d) 5.00 mL
7. 1680π mm³
8. $\dfrac{64}{216}$, or $\dfrac{8}{27}$
9. It is multiplied by 8.

10.

	(a)	(b)	(c)	(d)
Height	10 cm	3 dm	20 cm	25 cm
cm³	2000	6000	4000	7500
dm³	2	6	4	7.5
L	2	6	4	7.5

11. $253,500\pi$ L
12. 64 to 1
13. 1.62 L
14. 2,500,000 L
15. 32.4 L
16. π mL
17. (a) 25π L (b) 127.32 km

18. No, the customer pays $\dfrac{1}{2}$ as much for $\dfrac{1}{3}$ of the
popcorn.
19. 6-cm grapefruit
20. The larger melon is the better buy. The volume of the larger melon is 1.728 times the volume of the
smaller, but is only $11\dfrac{1}{2}$ times as expensive.

21. 16 m³
22. They are the same.
23. Approximately 2.2 cm
24. Approximately 21.5%

25. (a) For example: $s = 10$ m, $h = 3$ m (b) An
infinite number. Because $V = 100 = \dfrac{1}{3}a^2h$, where a is
the side of the square base, then $300 = a^2h$. This equation has an infinite number of real solutions; we may choose any number for a and find the corresponding value for h or vice versa.

26. $\dfrac{2}{3}\sqrt{\dfrac{2}{5\sqrt{5}}}$ m² $\doteq$ 0.28 m²

27. (a) 512,000 cm³ (b) $V(x) = (y - 2x)^2 \cdot x$
28. Let two square pyramids have sides and heights of s, h, and s_1 and h_1. If pyramids are similar, then

$$\frac{s}{s_1} = \frac{h}{h_1} = r. \text{ Hence } \frac{V}{V_1} = \frac{\frac{1}{3}s^2h}{\frac{1}{3}s_1^2h_1} = \left(\frac{s}{s_1}\right)^2 \cdot \frac{h}{h_1} =$$

$$r^2 \cdot r = r^3$$

29. (a) 15,600 cm² (b) $(100 + 200\sqrt{2})$ cm²
(c) $\left(1649 + \dfrac{81\sqrt{3}}{2}\right)$ m² or about 1719.1 m²

30. (a) 340 cm (b) 6000 cm²
31. $2\sqrt{2}$ m²
32. 62 cm

Problem Set 13-6
1. (a) Tons or kilograms (b) Kilograms (c) Grams
(d) Tons (e) Grams (f) Grams (g) Tons
(h) Kilograms or grams (i) Kilograms or grams
2. (a) milligrams (b) kilograms (c) milligrams
(d) grams (e) grams (f) milligrams
3. (a) 15 (b) 8 (c) 36 (d) 0.072 (e) 4.230
(f) 3.007 (g) 5750 (h) 5.750 (i) 30 (j) 30,000
(k) 41.6 (l) 1.56 (m) 3.1 (n) 60.8
4. (a) No (1 t) (b) No (100 kg) (c) Yes (10 kg)
(d) Yes (1 kg) (e) Yes (0.1 kg)
5. 16,000 g, or 16 kg
6. $2.32
7. $0.02
8. Abel (1 kg for $9)
9. (a) ⁻12°C (b) ⁻18°C (c) ⁻1°C (d) 38°C
(e) 100°C (f) ⁻40°C
10. (a) No (b) No (c) No (d) Yes (e) No (f) Yes
(g) Yes (h) Chilly (i) Hot
11. (a) 50°F (b) 32°F (c) 86°F (d) 212°F (e) 414°F
(f) ⁻40°F
12. (a) $(6\pi + 20)$ cm; $(48 + 18\pi)$ cm² (b) 40π cm;
100π cm² (c) 50 m; 80 m²
13. (a) 35 (b) 0.16 (c) 400,000 (d) 5,200,000
(e) 5,200 (f) 0.0035
14. (a) Yes (b) No (c) Yes
15. $\sqrt{61}$ km
16. (a) $12,000\pi$ cm³; 2400π cm² (b) 42,900 cm³;
$(6065 + 40\sqrt{5314})$ cm²

Problem Set 13-7

1. **(a)** It draws a circle five times. The circumference is $\frac{1}{5}$ of the circumference of CIRCLE1. **(b)** It draws the same size circle as CIRCLE1 but draws it to the left.

2. ```
TO FCIRCLE :N :S
  REPEAT :N [FD :S RT 360/:N]
END
```

3. **(a)**
```
TO ARC :S :D
   REPEAT :D [FD :S RT 1]
   END
```
**(b)**
```
TO ARCRAD :R :D
   REPEAT :D [FD :R*.01745 RT 1]
   END
```

4. Answers vary.

5. Answers may vary. For example:
```
TO FILL.CIRCLE :S
  REPEAT 360 [FD :S BK :S RT 1]
END
```

6. **(a)**
```
TO CIRCS :RAD
   HT
   CIRCLE :RAD
   ARCRAD :RAD/2 180
   LARCRAD :RAD/2 180
   END

   TO CIRCLE :R
   VCIRCLE :R * 0.01745
   END

   TO VCIRCLE :S
   REPEAT 360 [FD :S RT 1]
   END

   TO ARCRAD :R :D
   REPEAT :D [FD :R*.01745 RT 1]
   END

   TO LARCRAD :R :D
   REPEAT :D [FD :R*.01745 LT
   1]
   END
```
**(b)**
```
TO EYES :RAD
   HT
   CIRCLE : RAD
   CIRCLE :RAD/2
   CIRCLE :RAD/4
   LCIRCLE :RAD
   LCIRCLE :RAD/2
   LCIRCLE :RAD/4
   ARCRAD (:RAD + 0.6 * :RAD) 90
   LT 180
   LARCRAD (:RAD + 0.6 * :RAD) 90
   RT 180
   LARCRAD (:RAD + 0.6 * :RAD) 90
   HT
   END
```

```
TO LCIRCLE :RAD
   LVCIRCLE :RAD * 0.01745
END
TO LVCIRCLE :S
   REPEAT 360 [FD :S LT 1]
END
```
**(c)**
```
TO SEMIS :R
   ARCRAD :R 180
   RT 90 FD :R * 2 RT 90
   ARCRAD :R/2 180
   RT 180
   ARCRAD :R/2 180
   END

   TO ARCRAD :R :D
   REPEAT :D[FD :R*.01745 RT 1]
   END
```
**(d)**
```
TO CONCIRC :R
   HT CIRCE :R
   PU LT 90 FD :R/2 RT 90 PD
   CIRCLE :R + :R/2
   PU LT 90 FD :R/2 RT 90 PD
   CIRCLE :R * 2
   END

   TO CIRCLE :R
   VCIRCLE :R * 0.01745
   END

   TO VCIRCLE :S
   REPEAT 360 [FD :S RT 1]
   END
```
**(e)**
```
TO FRAME :SIZE
   SQUARE :SIZE
   FD :SIZE/2
   CIRCLE :SIZE/2
   END
```

7. ```
TO SYMBOL :R
   PU LT 90 FD 140 RT 90 PD
   REPEAT 3 [CIRCLE :R PU RT 90 FD
   9*:R/4 LT 90 PD]
   PU LT 90 FD :R * 45/8 LT 90
   REPEAT 2 [CIRCLE :R PU RT 90 FD
   9*:R/4 LT 90 PD]
   HIDETURTLE
END

TO CIRCLE :R
   HT
   VCIRCLE 0.01745 * :R
   ST
END

TO VCIRCLE :S
   REPEAT 360 [FD :S RT 1]
END
```

228

```
8. TO FLOWER :RAD :DEG
     REPEAT 6 [PETAL :RAD :DEG RT 60]
   END
   TO PETAL :RAD :DEG
     HT ARCRAD :RAD :DEG
     RT 180 - :DEG
     ARCRAD :RAD :DEG
     RT 180 - :DEG
     ST
   END
   TO ARCRAD :R :D
     REPEAT :D [FD :R*.01745 RT 1]
   END
9. TO DIAMCIRC :R
     REPEAT 360 [FD :R *0.0A745 RT 1]
     RT 90
     FD 2*:R
   END
```

Chapter Test

1. (a) 50,000; 5000; 50 (b) 3200; 3.2; 0.0032
(c) 26,000,000; 260,000; 260 (d) 190,000; 19,000; 0.19
2. (a) millimeters (b) centimeters (c) millimeters
(d) kilometers (e) centimeters (f) meters
3. (a) Find the area of $\triangle ADC$ and double it;
$A = 2(\frac{1}{2} \cdot DE \cdot AC)$. (b) $A = b \cdot h = DC \cdot FB$
4. 16
5. (a) $8\frac{1}{2}$ cm² (b) 6.5 cm² (c) 7 cm²
6. 252 cm²
7. The area of the trapezoid is equal to the area of the rectangle constructed from its component parts. The

area of the rectangle is $\frac{h}{2}(b_1 + b_2)$, which is the

formula for the area of a trapezoid.
8. (a) $54\sqrt{3}$ cm² (b) 36π cm²
9. (a) 12π cm² (b) $(12 + 4.5\pi)$ cm² (c) 24 cm²
(d) 64.5 cm² (e) 178.5 m² (f) 4π cm²
10. (a) Yes, $13^2 = 12^2 + 5^2$ (b) No, $104^2 \neq 40^2 + 60^2$
11. (a) S.A. $= 32(2 + \sqrt{13})$ cm², $V = 128$ cm³
(b) S.A. $= 96\pi$ cm², $V = 96\pi$ cm³ (c) S.A. $= 100\pi$ m², $V = \frac{500}{3}\pi$ m³ (d) S.A. $= 54\pi$ cm²,
$V = 54\pi$ cm³ (e) S.A. $= 304$ m², $V = 320$ m³
12. (a) 65π cm² (b) 138.46°

13. (a) Metric tones (b) 1 cm³, or 1 mL (c) 1 g
(d) Same volume (e) 25 (f) 2000 (g) 51,800
(h) 10,000,000 (i) 50,000 (j) 5.830 (k) 25,000
(l) 75,000 (m) 52.813 (n) 4.8
14. (a) 16.7 (b) 0.54 (c) 1089 (d) 2176 (e) 486
(f) 1382.4 (g) 60.8 (h) 3.06 (i) 82.4 (j) 35
15. $V_1/V_2 = (h_1/h_2)^3$

16. (a) 6000 kg (b) 5.7 cm (c) $r = \sqrt[3]{\dfrac{9}{4\pi}}$ m

17. (a) L (b) kg (c) g (d) g (e) kg (f) t (g) mL
18. (a) Unlikely (b) Likely (c) Unlikely
(d) Unlikely (e) Unlikely
19. (a) 2000 (b) 1000 (c) 3 (d) 0.0042 (e) 0.0002

CHAPTER 14

Problem Set 14-1

1. (a) $A(2, 2)$; $B(5, 0)$; $C(4, {}^-3)$; $D(0, {}^-3)$; $E({}^-2, {}^-3)$;
$F({}^-4, 0)$; $G({}^-4, 3)$; $H(0, 3)$ (b) $(2, {}^-3)$; answers may vary.
2. (a) I (b) III (c) II (d) IV (e) Between I and II
3. Quadrant II $= \{(x, y) \mid x < 0 \text{ and } y > 0\}$ Quadrant III $= \{(x, y) \mid x < 0 \text{ and } y < 0\}$ Quadrant IV $= \{(x, y) \mid x > 0 \text{ and } y < 0\}$
4. Answers vary
5. (a) $x = {}^-2$; y is any real number. (b) x is any real number; $y = 1$. (c) $x > 0$ and $y < 0$; x and y are real numbers.
6. Area is 8 square units. Perimeter is 12 units.
7. D has coordinate $(4, {}^-2)$.
8.

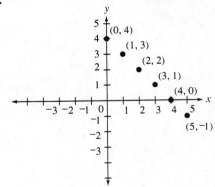

9. (a) $x = {}^-3$

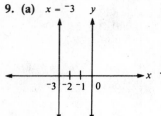

(b)

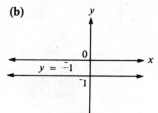

13. (a)

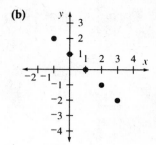

(b)

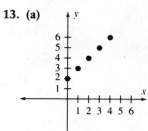

(c)

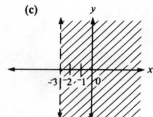

(d)

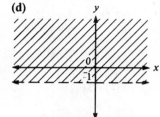

(c)

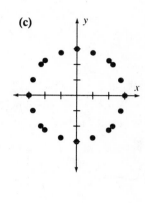

(d)

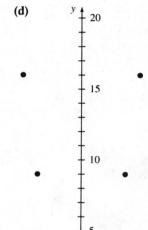

(e)

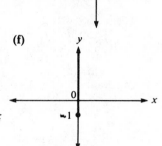

(f)

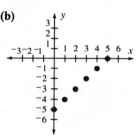

10. (a) $x = 3$ **(b)** $y = {}^-2$ **(c)** $y = 5$ **(d)** $x = {}^-4$

11. (a) $P(3, 4)$; $Q(6, 1)$ **(b)** $N({}^-1, 4)$; $M({}^-1, {}^-1)$

(c) $x = 3$ **(d)** $y = 1$

12. (a)

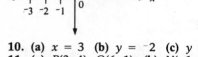

(b)

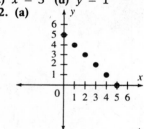

(c)

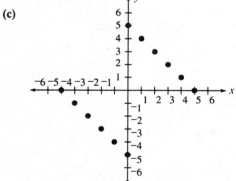

(e)

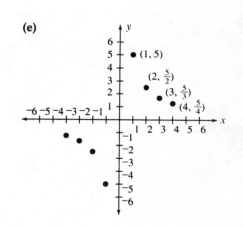

230

14. (a) $\{(x, y) \mid -1 \le x \le 1 \text{ and } -1 \le y \le 1\}$
(b) $\{(x, y) \mid x \le 1 \text{ and } y \le 1\}$ **(c)** $\{(x, y) \mid -1 \le x \le 2$ and $-1 \le y \le 1\}$ **(d)** $\{(x, y) \mid x \ge 0 \text{ and } y \le 1\}$
15. (a) $P'(2, {}^-2)$; $Q'(2, {}^-5)$, $R'(4, {}^-2)$ **(b)** $P'({}^-2, 2)$; $Q({}^-5, 2)$; $R({}^-2, 4)$
16. (a) $(0, {}^-1)$, $(1, 0)$, $(2, {}^-4)$, $({}^-2, {}^-4)$, $({}^-2, 4)$, $(2, 4)$
(b) $(0, 1)$, $({}^-1, 0)$, $({}^-2, 4)$, $(2, 4)$, $(2, {}^-4)$, $({}^-2, {}^-4)$
(c) $({}^-1, 0)$, $(0, 1)$, $({}^-4, 2)$, $({}^-4, {}^-2)$, $(4, {}^-2)$, $(4, 2)$
(d) $(0, {}^-1)$, $({}^-1, 0)$, $({}^-2, {}^-4)$, $(2, {}^-4)$, $(2, 4)$, $({}^-2, 4)$
(e) $(0, {}^-3)$, $(1, {}^-4)$, $(2, 0)$, $({}^-2, 0)$, $({}^-2, {}^-8)$, $(2, {}^-8)$
17. (a) $A'({}^-2, {}^-5)$; $B'(2, {}^-6)$; $C'(5, {}^-1)$ **(b)** $A'(2, 5)$; $B'({}^-2, 6)$; $C'({}^-5, 1)$ **(c)** $A'(2, {}^-5)$; $B'({}^-2, {}^-6)$; $C'({}^-5, {}^-1)$
18. (a) $({}^-2, {}^-4)$ **(b)** $({}^-a, {}^-b)$ **(c)** Yes; a half-turn about $(0, 0)$.
19. (a) $x = 3$ **(b)** $x = {}^-3$ **(c)** $y = 3$
20. (a) $A'(0, 1)$, $B'(2, 2)$, $C'(1, 3)$, $D'({}^-1, 3)$, $E'(b, a)$
21. (a) $(a - b, 0)$ **(b)** $({}^-b, a)$

Problem Set 14-2

1.

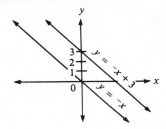

2.

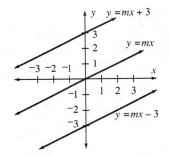

3. (a)

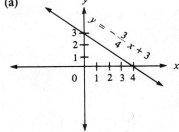

(b)

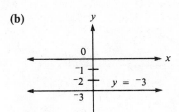

(c)

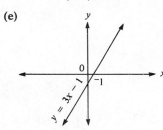

(d)

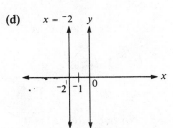

(e)

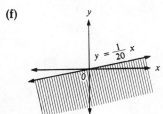

(f)

4.

	x-intercept	y-intercept
(a)	4	3
(b)	None	${}^-3$
(d)	${}^-2$	None
(e)	$\dfrac{1}{3}$	${}^-1$

231

5. (a)

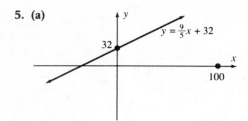

(b)

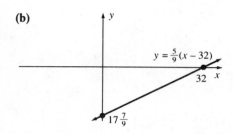

(c) Each line is the reflection of the other in the line $y = x$.

6. (a) $y = \frac{1}{3}x$ **(b)** $y = {}^-x + 3$ **(c)** $y = \frac{{}^-4}{3}x + 4$

(d) $y = \frac{3}{4}x + \frac{7}{4}$ **(e)** $y = \frac{1}{3}x$ **(f)** $y = x$

7. (a) $\frac{1}{3}$ **(b)** $\frac{1}{9}$ **(c)** 0 **(d)** No slope **(e)** 20,000

(f) 1 if $a \neq b$

8. (a) $y = {}^-x - 1$ **(b)** $y = \frac{1}{2}x$ **(c)** $y = 1$

(d) $y = 0 \cdot x + 1$ or $y = 0$ **(e)** $y = x - \frac{1}{2}$

(f) $y = 0$

9. (a) Parallel **(b)** Parallel **(c)** Parallel **(d)** Not parallel

10. (a) $y = {}^-2x - 1$ **(b)** $y = \frac{{}^-2}{3}x + \frac{5}{3}$ **(c)** $x = {}^-2$

(d) $y = 3$ **(e)** $x = {}^-2$ **(f)** $y = 3$ **(g)** $y + x = 1$

(h) $\frac{y}{3} + \frac{x}{2} = 0$

11. (a) $\frac{1}{2}$ **(b)** $\frac{{}^-1}{2}$ **(c)** 0 **(d)** Undefined—no slope

12. (a) $m_l = \frac{2}{1} = 2$ $m_k = \frac{1}{2} = m_n = \frac{{}^-2}{1} = {}^-2$

(b) $m_k = \frac{3}{1} = 3$ $m_l = \frac{{}^-3}{1} = {}^-3$ $m_n = \frac{{}^-2}{2} = {}^-1$

13. $\sqrt{1616}$ feet, or $\sqrt{101}$ feet

14. (a) The equation of ℓ is $y = mx$; the equation of n is $x = 1$. The point of intersection can be found by substituting 1 for x in $y = mx$. Thus, $y = m \cdot 1 = m$, so the point of intersection of ℓ and m is $(1, m)$.

(b) The equation for ℓ is $y = mx + b$; the equation for n is $x = 1$. Substituting 1 for x in $y = mx + b$ yields $y = m \cdot 1 + b$, or $y = m + b$. Thus the y-coordinate of P is $m + b$.

15. The slopes of $\overline{BC}$ and $\overline{DA}$ are each $\frac{1}{2}$, which implies $\overline{BC} \| \overline{DA}$. The slopes of $\overline{CD}$ and $\overline{BA}$ are each 4, which implies $\overline{CD} \| \overline{BA}$. Thus, $ABCD$ is a parallelogram.

16. Let A, B, and C have coordinates $(0, {}^-1)$, $(1, 2)$, and $({}^-1, {}^-4)$, respectively. The slope of $\overline{AB}$ is 3; the slope of $\overline{BC}$ is 3. Hence, A, B, and C are collinear.

17. (a) $y = \frac{{}^-1}{2}x - \frac{3}{2}$ **(b)** $y = \frac{2}{3}x - \frac{11}{3}$

(c) $y = -3$ **(d)** $y = \frac{{}^-5}{7}x - \frac{40}{7}$

18. The x-intercept is a; the y-intercept is b.

19. (a) $y = {}^-3x - 1$ **(b)** $y = {}^-3x + 1$

(c) $y = \frac{1}{3}x - \frac{1}{3}$

20. (a) $y = -x$ **(b)** $y - 2 = (-2/3)(x - 1)$

21. (a) yes **(b)** no

22. (a) perpendicular **(b)** parallel **(c)** perpendicular **(d)** neither

23. $m_{OB} = (a - 0)/(a - 0) = a/a = 1$ $m_{AC} = (a - 0)/(0 - a) = a/-a = -1$ $(m_{OB})(m_{AC}) = 1 \cdot (-1) = -1$, and so the diagonals are perpendicular to each other.

24. (a)

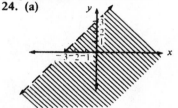

(b)

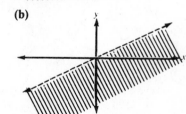

(c) **(d)**

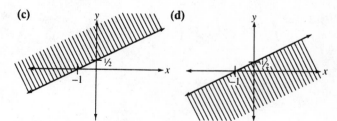

232

25. (a)

(e)

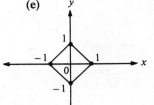

(f)

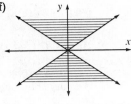

(b)

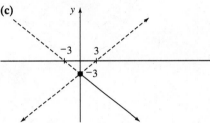

(g)

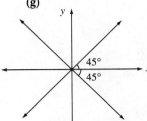

(h)

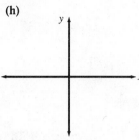

(c)

29. (a) $y = {}^-8$ **(b)** $x = {}^-7$

30. (a) Answers may vary; $(3, {}^-2)$ and $(7, {}^-2)$.
(b) Answers may vary; $({}^-2, {}^-2)$ and $(8, 10)$.
31. There are three possible locations for D: $(4, -8)$, $(12, 0)$ or $(0, 12)$.

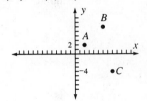

26. (a) $y = {}^-x$ **(b)** $y = {}^-x$ **(c)** $x = 0$ **(d)** $y = {}^-x$
(e) $y = x$ **(f)** $y = x - 3$ **(g)** $y = x + 3$ **(h)** one is
the reflection of the other in the x-axis **(i)** same as (h)
27. (a) $y = {}^-x + 1$ **(b)** $y = {}^-x - 1$ **(c)** $y = x + 1$
(d) $y = x + 1$
28. (a)

32. (a) $1\frac{1}{2}$ square units **(b)** 15 square units **(c)** $7\frac{1}{2}$
square units **(d)** 12 square units **(e)** 3 square units

Problem Set 14-3
1. (a) $\left(0, \frac{-5}{3}\right); \left(\frac{5}{2}, 0\right); (1, {}^-1); \left(2, \frac{-1}{3}\right)$. Answers may
vary.

28. (a)

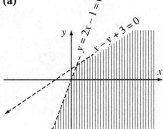

(b)

(c)

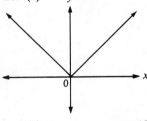

(d)

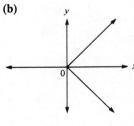

(b)

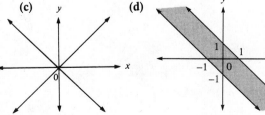

(c)

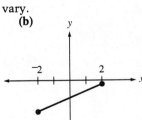

2. (a) $(2, 5)$, unique solution **(b)** No solution
(c) $(1, {}^-5)$, unique solution **(d)** No solution **(c)** $(0, 0)$,
unique solution **(f)** $\left(\frac{4}{11}, \frac{1}{11}\right)$, unique solution

3. (a) $(-11, -8)$ (b) $\left(\dfrac{-30}{1}, \dfrac{-84}{11}\right)$ (c) $\left(\dfrac{13}{3}, \dfrac{43}{12}\right)$

(d) $(0, 0)$ (e) $(-1 + 3\sqrt{2}, 3 - \sqrt{2})$ (f) $\left(\dfrac{-6}{5}, \dfrac{-4}{5}\right)$

4. (a) Unique solution (b) No solution (c) Same line; infinitely many solutions (d) Unique solution

5. The equations of the medians are $y = \dfrac{1}{2}x$; $y = 8x - 40$; and $y = \dfrac{-4}{7}x + \dfrac{40}{7}$. They intersect at $\left(\dfrac{16}{3}, \dfrac{8}{3}\right)$.

6. $y = \dfrac{-1}{2}x - 4$ and $y = \dfrac{1}{3}x - 4$.

7. $8\dfrac{1}{6}$ square units

8. $\dfrac{162}{85}$ sq. units

9. (a) $\left(\dfrac{17}{7}, \dfrac{17}{7}\right)$ (b) The slope of line AB is $\dfrac{5}{2}$. Then the equation of the line perpendicular to line AB and through point C is $y - 1 = \dfrac{-2}{5}(x - 6)$. Substituting $x = \dfrac{17}{7}$ gives $y = \dfrac{17}{7}$ and so the third altitude does pass through point P.

10. $\dfrac{55}{72}$ and $\dfrac{-1}{72}$

11. 4000 gallons of gasoline and 1000 gallons of kerosene.

12. $133\dfrac{1}{3}$ pounds of cashew nut granola and $66\dfrac{2}{3}$ pounds of golden granola.

13. 100 L of the 90% solution and 50 L of the 60% solution.

14. $20,000 and $60,000, respectively.

15. (a) $2,000 (b) 6% annual interest or 0.5% per month.

16. Width 60 inches; length 75 inches.

17. 17 quarters and 10 dimes

18. (a) The answers are all $(-1, 2)$.
(b) $13x + 14y = 15$
$16x + 17y = 18$. The solution is $(-1, 2)$.
(c) $ax + (a + 1)y = a + 2$
$(a + 3)x + (a + 4)y = a + 5$. The solution is $(-1, 2)$ because $x = -1$, $y = 2$ satisfy each equation.

19.

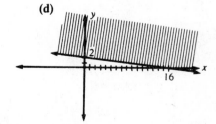

The altitudes $\overline{AU}$ and $\overline{BV}$ intersect at P as shown. Note that $m_{AU} = -1/m_{BC} = -(b - a)/c$. Hence the equation of $\overleftrightarrow{AU}$ is $y = -\dfrac{b - a}{c}x$. Because $\overleftrightarrow{BV}$ is a vertical line which goes through B its equation is $x = b$. Solving these two equations simultanously, we get $x = b$, $y = -\dfrac{b - a}{c}b$ as the coordinates of P. To show that the altitudes are concurrent we find the equation of the line containing the altitude through C perpendicular to $\overline{AB}$. The slope of $\overline{AB}$ is c/b. Hence the equation of the line containing the altitude is $y = (-b/c)(x - a)$. This altitude goes through P because the coordinates of P, $x = b$, $y = -\dfrac{b - a}{c}b$ satisfy the equation $y = -(b/c)(x - a)$.

20. (b) and (c) are not equations of lines.

21.

	Slope	y-intercept
(a)	$\dfrac{-5}{6}$	$\dfrac{7}{6}$
(b)	$\dfrac{-4}{3}$	$\dfrac{2}{5}$
(c)	3.75	1.85
(d)	0	4

22. $y = \dfrac{9}{10}x + \dfrac{17}{5}$ (b) $y = \dfrac{5}{3}x + \dfrac{1}{3}$ (c) $y = -8$

23. (a)

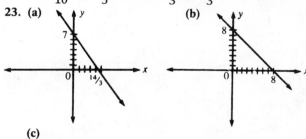

(b)

(c)

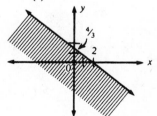

(d)

Let x be the number of minute divisions the hour hand has crossed since 3:00 P.M. and y be the number of minutes the minute hand moved since 3:00 P.M. Since the minute hand is 12 times faster than the hour hand, we have $y = 12x$. Since the position of the hands is reversed at the end of the meetings, the minute hand moved $15 + x$ minutes after 6:00 P.M., and the hour hand passed across $y - 30$ minute divisions. Consequently, we have $15 + x = 12(y - 30)$. The solution to the two equations is $\left(\dfrac{375}{143}, \dfrac{12 \cdot 375}{143}\right)$, which translates into approximately 28 seconds past 3:31 P.M. for the starting time and approximately 37 seconds after 6:17 P.M. for the ending time.

Problem Set 14-4

1. (a) 4 (b) 4 (c) 5 (d) 5 (e) $\sqrt{52}$, or $2\sqrt{13}$ (f) 5
(g) $\dfrac{\sqrt{365}}{4}$, or approximately 4.78 (h) Approximately 3.89 (i) 5 (j) $\sqrt{68}$, or $2\sqrt{17}$

2. $10 + \sqrt{10}$

3. The sides have lengths $\sqrt{45}$, $\sqrt{180}$, and $\sqrt{225}$. Since $(\sqrt{45})^2 + (\sqrt{180})^2 = (\sqrt{225})^2$, the triangle is a right triangle.

4. $AB = 5 = BC$

5. $x = 9$ or $x = {}^-7$

6. (a) $(0, 5)$ (b) $\left(\dfrac{9}{2}, {}^-2\right)$ (c) $(2, {}^-1.2)$ (d) $(1, 0)$

7. $({}^-7, 11)$

8. (a) $({}^-2, 3), (0, 4), (2, 1)$ (b) $\sqrt{37}, 4, \sqrt{61}$

9. (a) $(x - 3)^2 + (y + 2)^2 = 4$ (b) $(x + 3)^2 + (y + 4)^2 = 25$ (c) $(x + 1)^2 + y^2 = 4$
(d) $x^2 + y^2 = 9$

10. (a) Exterior (b) Interior (c) Exterior
(d) Exterior (e) Exterior (f) Interior (g) Exterior
(h) on the circle

11. $x^2 + y^2 = 34$

12. (a) $(x - 4)^2 + (y + 3)^2 = 25$ (b) $(x - 4)^2 + (y + 3)^2 = 2$

13. $(x + 2)^2 + (y + 2)^2 = 52$

14. (a)   (b)

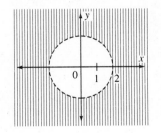

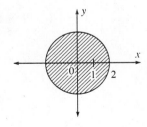

(c)

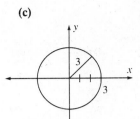

(d)

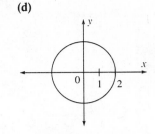

(e) This equation has no graph or the graph is the empty set. (f) Same as (d)

15. $\left(x - \dfrac{29}{10}\right)^2 + y^2 = \left(\dfrac{29}{10}\right)^2$

16. Yes; center $(0, 0)$, radius $\sqrt{\dfrac{1}{2}}$

17. (a) $(5/2, 3/2)$ (b) The equation of the third perpendicular is: $y - 2 = x - 3$. The point in (a) is on the perpendicular bisector because $(3/2) - 2 = (5/2) - 3$. (c) $PO = \sqrt{(5/2 - 0)^2 + (3/2 - 0)^2} = 3$ $PB = \sqrt{(5/2 - 1)^2 + (3/2 - 4)^2)} = 3$ $PC = \sqrt{(5/2 - 5)^2 + (3/2 - 0)^2} = 3$ (d) $(x - (5/2))^2 + (y - (3/2))^2 = 9$

18. $(3/2, 3/2)$

19. $\dfrac{2}{5}\sqrt{5}$

20. $\dfrac{2}{5}\sqrt{5}$

21. (a) $(5, 3)$ (b) $(3, 8)$ (c) no point of intersection
(d) $\sqrt{13}$ (e) 7 (f) 10 (g) $\sqrt{98}$ (h) $\sqrt{29}$
(i) $\sqrt{x_1^2 + y_1^2 + z_1^2}$
(j) $\sqrt{(x_1 - x_2)^2 + (y_1 - y_2)^2 + (z_1 - z_2)^2}$

22.

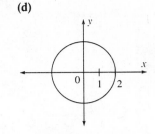

23. (a) $(9, 4)$ (b) $({}^-3, 12)$ (c) $(1, {}^-4)$

24. Let A, B, and C have coordinates $({}^-1, 5), (0, 2)$ and and $(1, {}^-1)$. $AB = \sqrt{10}$; $BC = \sqrt{10}$; $AC = \sqrt{40} = 2\sqrt{10}$, so $AB + BC = AC$, since $\sqrt{10} + \sqrt{10} = 2\sqrt{10}$. Consequently, A, B, and C are collinear.

25. M has coordinates $\left(\dfrac{a}{2}, \dfrac{b}{2}\right)$.

$$BM = \sqrt{\left(\frac{a}{2}\right)^2 + \left(\frac{b}{2} - b\right)^2} = \sqrt{\frac{a^2}{4} + \frac{b^2}{4}}$$

$$AM = \sqrt{\left(\frac{a}{2} - a\right)^2 + \left(\frac{b}{2} - 0\right)^2} = \sqrt{\frac{a^2}{4} + \frac{b^2}{4}}$$

26. (a) The median from C: $y = \dfrac{2b}{2a - 1}\left(x - \dfrac{1}{2}\right)$

The median from B: $y = \dfrac{b}{a - 2}(x - 1)$

The median from A: $y = \dfrac{b}{a + 1}x$

(b) Solve any two equations and check that the solution satisfies the third equation. The medians intersect at $\left(\dfrac{a + 1}{3b}, \dfrac{b}{3}\right)$. **(c)** Use the distance formula to find the ratios.

27. Label the vertices of the parallelogram as shown. It is sufficient to show that the midpoint of one diagonal is the same as the midpoint of the second diagonal. The midpoint of $\overline{PR}$ is at $\left(\dfrac{c}{2}, \dfrac{b}{2}\right)$ and the midpoint of $\overline{QS}$ is at $\left(\dfrac{a + d}{2}, \dfrac{b}{2}\right)$. The midpoints will be identical if and only if $\dfrac{a + d}{2} = \dfrac{c}{2}$ or $a + d = c$. Because the opposite sides of a parallelogram are congruent we have $PS = QR$. However $PS = d$ and $QR = c - a$. Consequently $d = c - a$ or $c = a + d$.

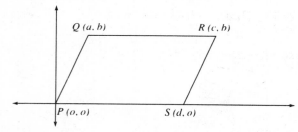

28. H, at home
29. $y = 2$

30. (a) $x = \dfrac{-1}{3}, y = \dfrac{1}{3}$ **(b)** No solution

31. (a) $y < \dfrac{3}{4}x + 5$ **(b)** $x + y + 5 \geq 0$ and $x \leq 0$ and $y \leq 0$

Brain Teaser (p. 819)
Choose a coordinate system as follows: Let the x-axis contain the pine and oak trees, P and O, respectively. Let the y-axis be the perpendicular bisector of $\overline{PO}$.

Assign coordinates of $(1, 0)$, $(^-1, 0)$ and (a, b) to P, O, and G (the gallows), respectively, as shown. Let A and B be the two spikes.

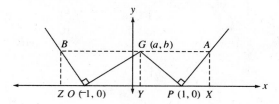

Drop perpendiculars from G, A, and B to the x-axis, obtaining points Y, X, and Z. Now $\triangle AXP \cong \triangle PYG$ and $\triangle GYO \cong \triangle OZB$. (Why?) Thus, $PY = AX = 1 - a$, and $GY = OB = b$, so that the coordinates of A are $(1 + b, 1 - a)$. Similarly, from the second congruence the coordinates of B are $(^-1 - b, 1 + a)$. Thus, the midpoint of $\overline{AB}$—where the treasure is buried—is $(0, 1)$, on the y-axis. Thus, the treasure is on the perpendicular bisector of $\overline{OP}$ and $\frac{1}{2}$ the length of $\overline{OP}$ from $\overline{OP}$.

Problem Set 14-5
1. This answer will vary depending on the version of Logo used.
2. The figures generated by the MEDIAL.TRI procedure are similar.
3.
```
TO AXES
    SETXY 0 120
    SETXY 0 (-120)
    SETXY 0 0
    SETXY 130 0
    SETXY -130 0
    SETXY 0 0
END
```
(In Apple Logo use SETPOS *instead of* SETXY*)*
4. There are three possible squares that can be constructed.
5.
```
TO FILL.RECT
    REPEAT 50 [SETY 30 SETY 0 RT 90
    FD 1 LT 90]
END
```
6.
```
TO CCIRCLE :XCEN :YCEN :RAD
    PU
    SEXTY :XCEN :YCEN
    FD :RAD RT 90
    PD
    CIRCLE :RAD
END

TO CIRCLE :R
    VCIRCLE: R*0.01745
END

TO VCIRCLE :S
    REPEAT 360 [FD :S RT 1]
END
```

```
7. TO QUAD :X1 :Y1 :X2 :Y2 :X3 :Y3
      :X4 :Y4
   PU SETXY :X1 :Y1 PD
   SETXY :X2 :Y2
   SETXY :X3 :Y3
   SETXY :X4 :Y4
   SETXY :X1 :Y1
   END
```

8. (a) Use the QUAD procedure from problem 7 and the following.

```
   TO MEDIAL.QUAD :X1 :Y1 :X2 :Y2
      :Y3 :Y3 :X4 :Y4
   QUAD :X1 :Y1 :X2 :Y2 :X3 :Y3
      :X4 :Y4
   MIDPOINT :X1 :Y1 :X2 :Y2
   MIDPOINT :X2 :Y2 :X3 :Y3
   MIDPOINT :X3 :Y3 :X4 :Y4
   MIDPOINT :X4 :Y4 :X1 :Y1
   MIDPOINT :X1 :Y1 :X2 :Y2
   END

   TO MIDPOINT :X1 :Y1 :X2 :Y2
   SETXY (:X1 + :X2)/2 (:Y1 +
      :Y2)/2
   END
```

(b) The medial quadrilateral is a parallelogram.

9. Use the QUAD procedure from problem 7 and the following.

```
   TO MEDIAL.QUADS :NUM :X1 :Y1 :X2
   :Y2 :X3 :Y3 :X4 :Y4
   IF :NUM=0 STOP
   QUAD :X1 :Y1 :X2 :Y2 :X3 :Y3 :X4
      :Y4
   MEDIAL.QUADS :NUM-1 (:X1 +
      :X2)/2 (:Y1 + :Y2)/2 (:X2 +
      :X3)/2 (:Y2 + :Y3)/2 (:X3 +
      :X4)/2 (:Y3 + :Y4)/2(:X4 +
      :X1)/2 (:Y4 + :Y1)/2
   END
```

```
10. TO SAS :S1 :A :S2
    BK :S1
    RT :A
    FD :S2
    HOME
    END
```

```
11. TO R.ISOS.TRI :LEN
    FD :LEN
    RT 90
    FD :LEN
    RT 135
    FD (SQRT 2) * :LEN
    END
```

```
12. TO CIRC50
    PU
    SETXY (-20) (-40)
    PD
    REPEAT 360 [FD 3.141*50/180 RT
    1]
    END
```

```
13. TO GENCIRC :X :Y :R
    PU
    SETXY :X :Y
    PD
    REPEAT 360 [FD 3.141*:R/180 RT
    1]
    END
```

```
14. TO MEDIAL.TRIS :NUM :X1 :Y1 :X2
    :Y2 :X3 :Y3
    IF :NUM = 0 STOP
    TRI :X1 :Y1 :X2 :Y2 :X3 :Y3
    MEDIAL.TRIS :NUM - 1 (:X1 +
      :X2)/2 (:Y1 + :Y2)/2 (:X2 +
      :X3)/2 (:Y2 + :Y3)/2 (:X3 +
      :X1)/2 (:Y3 + :Y1)/2
    END

    TO TRI :X1 :Y1 :X2 :Y2 :X3 :Y3
    PU
    SETXY :X1 :Y1
    PD
    SETXY :X2 :Y2
    SETXY :X3 :Y3
    SETXY :X1 :Y1
    END
```

Chapter Test

1. 16

2. (i) The slopes of the three segments determined are each $\frac{3}{4}$. **(ii)** Labeling $(4, 2)$, $(0, {}^-1)$ and $({}^-4, {}^-4)$ as A, B, and C, respectively, we find that $AB = 5$, $AC = 10$, and $BC = 5$, so that $AB + BC = AC$. Hence, A, B, and C are collinear.

3. (a)

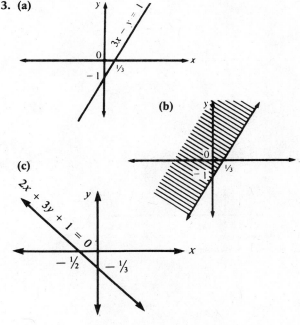

237

4. (a) $x = \dfrac{-4}{3}x - \dfrac{1}{3}$ **(b)** $x = {}^{-}3$ **(c)** $y = 3$

5. (a) $y = \dfrac{4}{3}x + \dfrac{7}{3}$ **(b)** $y = 5$ **(c)** $\left(\dfrac{3}{4}, 5\right)$

6. $y = \dfrac{3}{2}x - \dfrac{1}{3}$

7. (a) $\left(\dfrac{21}{5}, \dfrac{-3}{5}\right)$ is the unique solution. **(b)** $\left(\dfrac{10}{9}, \dfrac{4}{3}\right)$ is the unique solution. **(c)** No solution

8. 80 regular and 30 deluxe.

9. (a) $\left(1, \dfrac{-1}{2}\right)$ **(b)** $({}^{-}7, 3)$

10. (a)

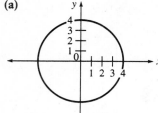

(b)

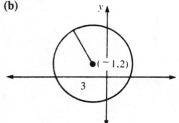

(c)

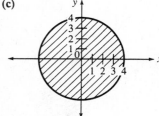

11. $(x + 3)^2 + (y - 4)^2 = 25$

12. (a)

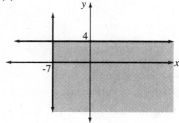

(b)

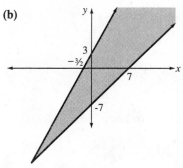

13. 9 red and 3 black

14. 275 freshmen and 500 sophomores

15. Hoover, 15,957,537; Roosevelt, 22,521,525

CHAPTER 15

Problem Set 15-1

1. 9 bounces

2. $\dfrac{x}{2} + \dfrac{x}{4} + \dfrac{x}{5} + 9 = x$

$20\left(\dfrac{x}{2} + \dfrac{x}{4} + \dfrac{x}{5} + \dfrac{9}{1}\right) = 20x$

$\qquad 19x + 180 = 20x$

$\qquad\qquad\; 180 = x$

Thus Jim has saved $180

3. Because $\dfrac{H}{381} \doteq 0.291$, then $H \doteq 110.871$. If x is the number of hits he must get by the end of the year, then we must solve the following.

$\dfrac{110.871 + x}{441} > .300$

$\qquad x > 21.43$ Thus, he must get 22 hits.

4. The horse that runs 10 feet from the rail runs 800 feet on the straight areas. The distance covered on the curved area is equal to the circumference of a circle of radius feet. Thus, the total distance covered is (800 + 120π) feet. Similarly, the distance covered by the horse 20 feet from the rail is (800 + 140π) feet. Thus the difference in the distance traveled is 20π feet, or approximately 62.8 feet.

5. If the distance between the center of the coin and a grid line is less than or equal to $\dfrac{1}{4}$ inch, the coin will touch a grid line. If the coin lands within the boundaries of a square that measures $2\dfrac{1}{2}$ inches on a side, which is located inside each 3-inch square, the coin will not touch. Thus, the probability of the coin not touching a grid line is given by the ratio of the areas of the squares that measure $2\dfrac{1}{2}$ inches and 3 inches, respectively.

Hence, the probability is $\dfrac{6.25}{9}$, or $69.\overline{4}\%$.

6. Distance is given by multiplying speed times time, or $d = s \cdot t$. Because the distance is the same going up and back, we can equate speed times time in both cases. Thus, if C represents the rate of the current, then we have the following

$$(4 - C) \cdot 2 = (4 + C) \cdot 1$$
$$8 - 2C = 4 + C$$
$$4 = 3C$$
$$\frac{4}{3} = C$$

Hence, the current rate is $1\frac{1}{3}$ miles per hour.

7. The minimum number of weights is 10. The weights are 1, 2, 4, 8, 16, 32, 64, 128, 256, 512. Notice that these are just the powers of 2 contained in 680.

8. The table below shows the number of digits scanned for each of the intervals given.

Interval	Number of Numbers	Number of Digits
1–9	9	9
10–99	90	180
100–999	900	2,700
1,000–9,999	9,000	36,000
10,000–99,999	90,000	450,000
100,000–999,999	900,000	5,400,000
1,000,000–9,999,999	9,000,000	63,000,000

Hence, the number of digits scanned is the sum of the numbers in the last column plus 1, or 68,888,890.

9. We reduce the problem to simpler cases, look for pattern, and generalize. A table for various exponents and remainders is given below.

Exponent	Remainder
1	5
2	4
3	6
4	2
5	3
6	1
7	5
8	4
9	6

Exponents 1–6 form a Repeating block.

To see how many times this block repeats in our problem, we divide 999,999 by 6 to obtain 166,666 with a remainder of 3. Thus, the block repeats 166,666 times and then goes three steps further. Because the third number in the repeating block is 6, this is the desired answer.

10. A tree diagram for this experiment is as follows:

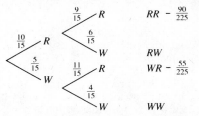

Thus the probability of a red ball on the second draw is $\frac{90}{225} + \frac{55}{225}$, or $\frac{145}{225}$.

11. The distances run by each of the runners when Tom and Dick finish the 2-km race are given below.

	Tom	Dick	Harry
(1)	2000 m	1900 m	x m
(2)		2000 m	1800 m

To find x we solve the following proportion: $\frac{1900}{2000} = \frac{x}{1800}$. Thus, $x = 290$ m.

12. To obtain exactly 7 L, the following steps could be made. 1. Fill the 5-L pail. 2. Empty the 5-L pail into the 3-L pail; 2 L remain in the 5-L pail. 3. Empty the 3-L pail. 4. Pour 2 L from the 5-L pail into the 3-L pail. 5. Fill the 5-L pail and we have the desired 7 L.

13. (a) The short way to do this problem is to realize that if there are 98 players and only 1 winner, there must be 97 losers. To obtain 97 losers, 97 matches must be played. **(b)** By similar reasoning, there must be $(n - 1)$ matches.

14. (a) The outside runner should be given a head start of $2\pi(41 - 40)$, or 2π m. **(b)** The outside runner should again be given a head start of 2π m.

15. $2^{12} \cdot 5^8 = 2^4 \cdot (2^8 \cdot 5^8) = 2^4 \cdot (2 \cdot 5)^8 = 16 \cdot 10^8$. Hence the number of digits is 10.

16. (a) The numerators form a sequence of numbers, each of which (except the first) is 4 greater than the previous term. The denominations form a sequence starting with 5, in which each number is 2 greater than its numerator. **(b)** $\frac{3999}{4001}$ **(c)** It can be shown that every fraction in the sequence has the form $\frac{4n - 1}{4n + 1}$.

Suppose there is a number such that $d|(4n + 1)$ and $d|(4n - 1)$. Then $d|(4n + 1) - (4n - 1)$, or $d|2$. The only numbers that divide 2 are 1 and 2. Since $4n - 1$ and $4n + 1$ are both odd numbers, 2 cannot divide them. Hence the only common divisor is 1, and the fractions are reduced.

17. (a) 1, 5, 4 + 5, 4 + 4 + 5, 4 + 4 + 4 + 5, 4 + 4 + 4 + 4 + 5, ...; i.e., 1, 5, 9, 13, 17, 21, ...
(b) $4(n - 2) + 5$, or $4n - 3$

18. Since $BC = BE$ it can be shown that $\triangle ABC \cong \triangle DEB$. (Hint: Use complementary angles.) Thus, $AB = DE = 9$ m and $BE = AC = 12$ m. Thus, $AD = AB + BD = 21$ m. Now $(CB)^2 = 12^2 + (AB)^2 = 12^2 + 9^2 = 225$. Therefore, $CB = 15$ m.

19. Let x be the number of sheets of paper and y be the number of envelopes. Then for Ann we have $x - 50 = y$, or $x = y + 50$. For Sue we have $3(y - 50) = x$. Thus, $y + 50 = 3(y - 50)$ and $y = 100$, $x = 150$. There were 150 sheets of paper in each box.

20. The sum of the digits of a five-digit number can be at most $5 \cdot 9$, or 45. Because the sum is 43, which is 2 less than 45, we have the following two possibilities: **(a)** One of the digits is 7 and the rest are 9s. The five possibilities are: 79,999; 97,999; 99,799; 99,979; 99,997. **(b)** Two digits could be 8s and the other three could be 9s. The possibilities in this case are; 88,999; 89,899; 89,989; 89,998; 98,899; 98,989; 98,998; 99,889; 99,898; 99,988.

Thus, there are 15 five-digit numbers, the sum of whose digits is 43. Using the divisibility test for 11, we find that among these, only three numbers, 97,999, 99,979, and 98,989, are divisible by 11. Thus the desired probability is $\frac{3}{15}$, or $\frac{1}{5}$.

21. Let x be the length of the bottom and y be the depth of the water when the bottom is level. The volume of the water is $10xy$. When the aquarium is tilted, the water forms a right triangular prism with an altitude of 10 inches. The volume of this triangular prism is $\frac{1}{2} \cdot 10 \cdot 8 \left(\frac{3}{4} \cdot x \right)$, which is $30x$. Setting the volumes equal, we obtain $10xy = 30x$, and therefore $y = 3$. Thus, the water depth is 3 inches.

22. (a) Square: 6.25 square units; rectangle: 6 square units; equilateral triangle: $\frac{100\sqrt{3}}{36} \doteq 4.81$ square units; right isosceles triangle: $\frac{25}{2}(2 - \sqrt{2}) \doteq 4.29$ square units; circle: $\frac{25}{\pi} \doteq 7.96$ square units. **(b)** Circle

23. Let x be the amount Susan made 2 years ago. Because her salary increased 50% each year, her salary after the first year was $1.5x$, and after the second year, $(1.5) \cdot (1.5)x$. Thus $(1.5)^2 \cdot x = \$100,000$ and $x = \$44,444.44$, or $\$44,444$.

24. Let W stand for team A winning and L for team A losing. A tree for team A winning two games before team B wins 3 is:

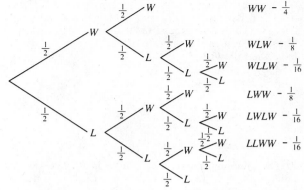

Thus, the probability of A winning the series is $\frac{11}{16}$. The odds in favor of A winning are 11 to 5.

25. Let d be the integer. Since the remainders are the same, then $d | (13,903 - 13,511)$ and $d | (14,589 - 13,903)$. That is, $d | 392$ and $d | 686$. Since $GCD(392, 686) = 98$, then $d = 98$.

26. For a two-digit number, we have $(a \cdot 10 + b) - (b \cdot 10 + a) = 9a - 9b = 9(a - b)$, which is divisible by 9. For a three-digit number, we have $(a \cdot 10^2 + b \cdot 10 + c) - (c \cdot 10^2 + b \cdot 10 + a) = (a - c) \cdot 10^2 + (c - a) = (a - c) \cdot (10^2 - 1) = (a - c)99$, which is divisible by 9. The property can be proved for any n-digit number.

27. In one hour, the hour hand covers $\frac{360°}{12} = 30°$.

Thus, in 15 minutes it covers $\frac{30°}{4} = 7°30'$.

Consequently, the angle between the hands at 2:15 is $30° - 7°30' = 22°30'$.

28. Draw a line connecting the given point P in the plane with the center of the circle circumscribing the hexagon. The line PO, as shown, divides the hexagon into two congruent parts, $GABCH$ and $HDEFG$. To prove this it is sufficient to show $\triangle AGO \cong \triangle DHO$ by AAS.

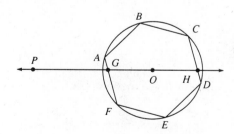

240

29. Pair the numbers as follows:
999,999,998 and 1
999,999,997 and 2
999,999,996 and 3
999,999,995 and 4
999,999,994 and 5
$$\vdots \qquad \vdots$$
500,000,000 and 499,999,999
There are 499,999,999 pairs and the sum of the digits in each pair is $9 \cdot 9$, or 81. The unpaired numbers are 999,999,999 and 1,000,000,000. The sums of the digits in these numbers are 81 and 1, respectively. Hence the total sum of the digits is $499,999,999(81) + 1(81) + 1$ $= 500,000,000(81) + 1 = 40,500,000,001$.

30. Because the point $(2, ^-1)$ does not satisfy either of the given equations, it is the intersection point of the other two sides. The lines containing the other two sides go through $(2, ^-1)$ and are parallel to the given lines.

The slope of the line $3x - 2y = 6$ is $\frac{3}{2}$. The equation of the line through $(2, ^-1)$ and parallel to $3x - 2y = 6$ is given by $y - (^-1) = \frac{3}{2}(x - 2)$. Thus, $y = \frac{3}{2}x - 4$.

Similarly, the equation of the line parallel to $5x + 4y = 21$ and passing through $(2, ^-1)$ is given by $y - (^-1) = \frac{^-5}{4}(x - 2)$. Thus we obtain $y = \frac{^-5}{4}x + \frac{3}{2}$. To find the intersection point of the diagonals, find two endpoints and then find the midpoint. One endpoint is $(2, ^-1)$ and the other is the intersection of the line $3x - 2y = 6$ and $5x + 4y = 21$. Solving these equations, we obtain $x = 3$ and $y = \frac{3}{2}$. From the midpoint formula, we have $x = \frac{2 + 3}{2}$ and $\frac{5}{2}$ and $y = \frac{^-1 + \frac{3}{2}}{2} = \frac{1}{4}$. Thus, the point where the diagonals intersect is $\left(\frac{5}{2}, \frac{1}{4}\right)$.

31. Let (x, y) be the center of the circle; then, using the distance formula, we have $x^2 + y^2 = (x - 4)^2 + y^2$ and $x^2 + y^2 = (x - 1)^2 + (y + 3)^2$. These two equations reduce to $16 - 8x = 0$ and $3y - x + 5 = 0$. Solving these equations, we find $x = 2$ and $y = ^-1$. Hence the center is at $(2, ^-1)$. The radius is the distance from any point—for example, $(0, 0)$ to the center $(2, -1)$. Thus, $r = \sqrt{2^2 + 1^2} = \sqrt{5}$.

32. Let M_1 and M_2 denote the first and second meeting points, respectively. Let C be the circumference of the circle.

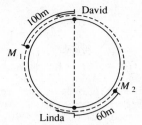

Let r_D and r_L be David's and Linda's speeds, respectively. The formula for distance, d, is $d = r \cdot t$, where t is the time. Since the time it takes for each to travel to a meeting point is the same and since $t = \frac{d}{r}$, then for the first meeting, we have the following:
$$\frac{100}{r_D} = \frac{\frac{C}{2} - 100}{r_L}$$
For the second meeting we have:
$$\frac{\frac{C}{2} + 60}{r_D} = \frac{C - 60}{r_L}$$
From the first equation, we obtain:
$$\frac{r_D}{r_L} = \frac{100}{\frac{C}{2} - 100}$$
From the second equation, we obtain:
$$\frac{r_D}{r_L} = \frac{\frac{C}{2} + 60}{C - 60}$$
Thus, $\dfrac{100}{\frac{C}{2} - 100} = \dfrac{\frac{C}{2} + 60}{C - 60}$.

Solving for C, we obtain $C = 480$ m.

33. Let x be the number that voted against the bill the first time. Then we have the following:

	Against	For
First vote	x	$400 - x$
Second vote	$400 - \frac{12}{11}x$	$\frac{12}{11}x$

In the second vote, the bill passed by twice the margin, so,

$$2[x - (400 - x)] = \frac{12}{11}x - \left(400 - \frac{12}{11}x\right)$$
$$2(2x - 400) = \frac{12}{11}x - 400 + \frac{12}{11}x$$
$$20x = 4400$$
$$x = 220$$

241

The difference between the "for" votes the first and second time is $\frac{12}{11}x - (400 - x) = \frac{12}{11}(220) - (400 - 220) = 60$, or 60 votes.

34. First show that $FG = GH = HE = EF$. It can be shown by SAS that $\triangle DCN \cong \triangle BAP$, and hence $\angle DNC \cong \angle APB$ and $\angle APB \cong \angle PBC$ because they are alternate interior angles for parallel lines BC and AD. Thus $\angle DNC \cong \angle PBC$. Because $\angle DNC$ and $\angle PBC$ are congruent corresponding angles, it follows that $\overleftrightarrow{BP} \parallel \overleftrightarrow{ND}$. Because $BN = NC$, it follows that $HG = GC$. Similar arguments show that $GF = FD$, $EF = EA$, and $EH = BH$. Using congruent triangles BAP, ADO, DCN, and CHB, it can be shown that $\triangle BHM \cong \triangle CGN \cong \triangle DFO \cong \triangle AEP$ by ASA. From this it follows that $BH = AE = DF = GC$, and consequently that $HE = EF = FG = GH$. Because $\angle APB \cong \angle AOD$ and $m(\angle OAD) + m(\angle AOD) = 90°$, it follows that $m(\angle OAD) + m(\angle APB) = 90°$, and hence $m(\angle AEP) = 90°$. Thus $HGFE$ is a square. **(b)** Let $AD = a$; then $OD = \frac{a}{2}$. Let $AE = x$; then from (a) we have $EF = x$ and $OF = \frac{x}{2}$ (because $\triangle DFO \sim \triangle DGC$). Thus $AO = x + x + \frac{x}{2} = \frac{5x}{2}$. Applying the Pythagorean Theorem to $\triangle ADO$, we have

$$\left(\frac{5x}{2}\right)^2 = a^2 + \left(\frac{a}{2}\right)^2$$
$$\frac{25x^2}{4} = a^2 + \frac{a^2}{4} = \frac{5a^2}{4}$$

and therefore $x^2 = \frac{a^2}{5}$. Thus the area of $HGFE$ is $\frac{1}{5}$ of the area of $ABCD$; that is, $\frac{1}{5} \cdot 100$ cm² $= 20$ cm².

35. (a) 1, 8, 28, 56, 70, 56, 28, 8, 1; 1, 9, 36, 84, 126, 126, 84, 36, 9, 1 **(b)** $s_1 = 1$, $s_2 = 2$, $s_3 = 4$, $s_4 = 8$, $s_{10} = 512$, $s_n = 2^{n-1}$ **(c)** The alternate sum in each row after row 1 is zero. **(d)** Answers may vary.

36. That the sum of the numbers in any row is given by 2^{n-1} can be justified by noticing that the sum of the numbers in each row is really twice as much as the sum in the preceding row. For example, consider the fourth and fifth row, as shown below:

4th Row   1   4   6   4   1

5th Row (1 + 4) (4 + 6) (6 + 4) (4 + 1)

Each of the numbers in the fourth row appears twice as many times in the sum of the numbers in the fifth row. Similarly, the sum of the number in any row is twice as great as the sum in the preceding row. Because the sum in row one is $1 = 2^0$, then the next sums are given as shown below.

Row	Sum
1	$1 = 2^0$
2	$2 = 2^1$
3	$4 = 2^2$
4	$8 = 2^3$
5	$16 = 2^4$
⋮	⋮
n	2^{n-1}

37. Each country received one bar more than the next smaller country. Suppose the smallest country received n bars of gold. Then, the next larger country received 1 bar more, and the next larger country 2 bars more, and so on. That is, the countries in order of size received n bars, $(n + 1)$ bars, $(n + 2)$ bars, and so on. The number of countries is unknown, so we designate that number by k.

Ordering countries according to size from smallest to largest and making a table reveals a pattern. The kth country receives $n + (k - 1)$ bars of gold.

Order of Country	Number of Bars Received
1	n
2	$n + 1$
3	$n + 2$
4	$n + 3$
5	$n + 4$
⋮	⋮
k	$n + (k - 1)$

The total number of gold bars is 1000. Because the total number of bars received by all countries is 1000, we have

$$n + (n + 1) + (n + 2) + (n + 3) + \cdots + (n + k - 1) = 1000$$

Thus, the problem involves finding a sum of consecutive natural numbers.

$$1 + 2 + 3 + 4 + \cdots + 100$$
$$100 + 99 + 98 + 97 + \cdots + 1$$
$$\overline{101 + 101 + 101 + 101 + \cdots + 101}$$

There are 100 sums of 101 in twice the desired sum, so we divide by 2 to obtain $\frac{100(101)}{2} = 5050$.

A similar approach can be used to find the sum $n + (n + 1) + (n + 2) + (n + 3) + \cdots + (n + k - 1)$.

$$n + (n+1) + (n+2) + \cdots + (n+k-1)$$
$$(n+k-1) + (n+k-2) + (n+k-3) + \cdots + n$$
$$\overline{(2n+k-1) + (2n+k-1) + (2n+k-1) + \cdots + (2n+k-1)}$$

There are k sums of $2n + k - 1$ shown above and this is twice the desired sum. Hence, we divide by 2 to obtain $\frac{k(2n + k - 1)}{2}$. This result can be used as follows.

$$n + (n + 1) + (n + 2) + \cdots + (n + k - 1) = 1000$$
$$\frac{k}{2}(2n + k - 1) = 1000$$
$$k(2n + k - 1) = 2000$$

The last equation has two unknowns, k and n. To find k and n, we need another equation involving k and n. Unfortunately, no other condition that yields an additional equation is given in the problem.

A useful strategy in solving any problem is to make sure that no important information is neglected. One condition of the problem states that the number of countries k is the least number possible and $k \neq 1$. Also, because no bar can be broken, n and k must be natural numbers. Keeping these conditions in mind, we focus on $k(2n + k - 1) = 2000$. Because k and $2n + k - 1$ are natural numbers, they are factors of 2000. Also, k is the least number possible, so we start with $k = 2$. If $k = 2$, then $2 \cdot (2n + 2 - 1) = 2000$ and $n = 499\frac{1}{2}$, which is not a natural number. Hence, $k \neq 2$. Similarly, if $k = 4$, the next factor of 2000, then $n = 248\frac{1}{2}$, and hence, $k \neq 4$. However, if $k = 5$, then $n = 198$. Thus, the smallest country receives 198 bars of gold, and, consequently, the five countries receive 198, 199, 200, 201, and 202 bars, respectively.

APPENDIX I

Problem Set A1

1. (a), (b) and **(f)**

2. (a) $X \wedge 2 + Y \wedge 2 - 3*Z$ **(b)** $(24*34/2) \wedge 3$
(c) $A + B - C \wedge 2/D$ **(d)** $(A + B)/(C + D)$
(e) $15/(A*(2*B \wedge 2 + 5))$

3. (a) 7 **(b)** 7 **(c)** 6 **(d)** 3 **(e)** 16 **(f)** ⁻44

4. (a) 35,200,000 **(b)** 0.0000193 **(c)** ⁻0.000001233
(d) ⁻7402

5. Answers may vary depending upon the computer used.

6. (a)
```
5 REM WE INPUT THE VALUE OF
  THE VARIABLE X
10 INPUT X
20 LET Y = 13*X ^ 5 - 27/X + 3
30 PRINT "WHEN X = ";X;", Y =
   "; Y
40 END
```
(b) (i)
```
RUN
? 1.873
WHEN X = 1.873, Y = 288.247015
```
(ii)
```
RUN
? 7
WHEN X = 7, Y = 218490.143
```

7. (a)
```
10 REM THIS PROGRAM CONVERTS
   DEGREES FAHRENHEIT
20 REM TO DEGREES CELSIUS
30 PRINT "THE NUMBER OF
   DEGREES FAHRENHEIT IS ";
40 INPUT F
50 LET C = 5/9*(F - 32)
60 PRINT F; " DEGREES
   FAHRENHEIT = ";C;" DEGREES
   CELSIUS"
70 END
```
(b) (i)
```
THE NUMBER OF DEGREES
FAHRENHEIT IS? 212
212 DEGREES FAHRENHEIT =
100 DEGREES CELSIUS
```
(ii)
```
THE NUMBER OF DEGREES
FAHRENHEIT IS? 98.6
98.6 DEGREES FAHRENHEIT =
37 DEGREES CELSIUS
```
(iii)
```
THE NUMBER OF DEGREES
FAHRENHEIT IS? 68
68 DEGREES FAHRENHEIT = 20
DEGREES CELSIUS
```
(iv)
```
THE NUMBER OF DEGREES
FAHRENHEIT IS? 32
32 DEGREES FAHRENHEIT = 0
DEGREES CELSIUS
```
(v)
```
THE NUMBER OF DEGREES
FAHRENHEIT IS? -40
-40 DEGREES FAHRENHEIT =
-40 DEGREES CELSIUS
```
(vi)
```
THE NUMBER OF DEGREES
FAHRENHEIT IS? -273
-273 DEGREES FAHRENHEIT =
-169.444444 DEGREES CELSIUS
```

8.
```
10 REM THIS PROGRAM FINDS THE
   VOLUME OF A RIGHT RECTANGULAR
   PRISM
20 PRINT "TYPE THE LENGTH, WIDTH,
   AND HEIGHT SEPARATED BY
   COMMAS."
30 INPUT L,W,H
35 REM V IS THE VOLUME OF THE
   PRISM
40 LET V = L*W*H
50 PRINT "THE VOLUME OF A BOX
   WITH LENGTH ";L;", WIDTH ";W;
60 PRINT " AND HEIGHT ";H;" IS
   ";V
70 END
TYPE THE LENGTH, WIDTH, AND
HEIGHT SEPARATED BY COMMAS.
? 8,5,3
THE VOLUME OF A BOX WITH LENGTH
8, WIDTH 5 AND HEIGHT 3 IS 120
```

9. (a) ```
PRINT 100*1.18 ^ 25
6266.8628
```
(b) ```
5 REM N IS THE NUMBER OF YEARS
  THE MONEY IS INVESTED
10 INPUT N
15 REM B IS THE BALANCE
20 LET B = 100*1.18 ^ N
30 PRINT "AFTER ";N;" YEARS,
   THE BALANCE IS $";B
40 END
```
(The balance in (b) is the same as in (a).)

10. Answers may vary depending upon the computer used.

11. (a) ```
HEY YOU OUT THERE
```
(b) ```
HEY YOU OUT THERE
HEY YOU OUT THERE
HEY YOU OUT THERE
HEY YOU OUT THERE
HEY YOU OUT THERE
HEY YOU OUT THERE
HEY YOU OUT THERE
```

Outputs are different because of the placement of the PRINT statement being outside the loop in (a) and inside the loop in (b).

12. (a) ```
10 FOR N = 1 TO 20
10 PRINT 2*N
30 NEXT N
40 END
```
(b) ```
10 FOR N = 1 TO 20
20 PRINT 2*N " ";
30 NEXT N
40 END
```

13. ```
5 REM THIS PROGRAM COMPUTES THE
  SUM OF THE SQUARES OF THE
6 REM FIRST 100 POSITIVE
  INTEGERS
7 REM N IS A POSITIVE INTEGER
10 FOR N = 1 TO 100
15 REM Y IS USED TO ACCUMULATE
20 LET Y = Y + N*N
30 NEXT N
40 PRINT Y
50 END
5050
```

14. ```
10 PRINT "THIS PROGRAM IS TO
   PRACTICE MULTIPLYING."
20 PRINT "TYPE THE TWO NUMBERS
   TO BE MULTIPLIED";
21 PRINT "SEPARATED BY A COMMA."
25 REM A AND B REPRESENT THE
   NUMBERS TO BE MULTIPLIED
26 REM X INITIALIZES A COUNTER
27 REM C REPRESENTS THE PRODUCT
   OF A AND B
28 LET X = 0
30 INPUT A,B
35 LET X = X + 1
40 PRINT "AFTER THE QUESTION
   MARK, TYPE THE PRODUCT."
50 PRINT A;"*";B;"=";
60 INPUT C
70 IF A*B > C THEN 100
80 PRINT "SORRY, TRY AGAIN."
90 GOTO 40
100 PRINT "VERY GOOD. DO YOU
    WANT TO MULTIPLY OTHER
    NUMBERS?"
110 INPUT D$
120 IF D$ = "YES" THEN 20
130 PRINT "THE NUMBER OF
    ATTEMPTED EXERCISES WAS ";X
140 END
```

15. ```
5 REM THIS PROGRAM COMPUTES
  SQUARES AND SQUARE ROOTS
8 REM N REPRESENTS A NATURAL
  NUMBER
10 PRINT "NUMBER","SQUARE
   ROOT","SQUARE"
20 FOR N = 1 TO 10
30 PRINT N,SQR(N),N^2
40 NEXT N
50 END
```

16. ```
5 REM THIS PROGRAM WILL
  DETERMINE IF A POSITIVE
  INTEGER IS PRIME
6 REM N REPRESENTS A POSITIVE
  INTEGER
7 REM A REPRESENTS AN INTEGER
  BETWEEN 1 AND N
8 REM Y REPRESENTS THE QUOTIENT
  N/A
10 INPUT N
15 IF N = 1 THEN 60
16 IF N = 2 THEN 80
20 FOR A = 2 TO N - 1
30 LET Y = N/A
40 IF Y = INT(Y) THEN 60
50 NEXT A
55 GOTO 80
60 PRINT N;" IS NOT A PRIME."
70 GOTO 90
80 PRINT N;" IS PRIME."
90 END
```

17. ```
10 REM THIS PROGRAM CONVERTS
   DEGREES FAHRENHEIT
20 REM TO DEGREES CELSIUS
25 REM F REPRESENTS A NUMBER OF
   DEGREES FAHRENHEIT
26 REM C REPRESENTS A NUMBER OF
   DEGREES CELSIUS
30 PRINT "DEGREE FAHRENHEIT",
   "DEGREE CELSIUS"
40 FOR F = -40 TO 220 STEP 10
50 LET C = 5/9*(F - 32)
60 PRINT F,,C
70 NEXT F
80 END
```
```

```
18.  10  REM THIS PROGRAM CALCULATES
         THE AREA
     20  REM AND THE CIRCUMFERENCE OF
         A CIRCLE
     25  REM R IS THE RADIUS; C IS THE
         CIRCUMFERENCE; A IS THE AREA
     30  PRINT "WHAT IS THE RADIUS";
     40  INPUT R
     50  LET A = 3.14159*R^2
     60  LET C = 2*3.14159*R
     70  PRINT "RADIUS",
         "AREA","CIRCUMFERENCE"
     80  PRINT R,A,C
     90  END
19.  10  REM THIS PROGRAM CALCULATES N!
     15  REM N IS A NATURAL NUMBER
     16  REM T IS USED TO ACCUMULATE
         PRODUCTS
     17  REM A IS USED AS A COUNTER
     20  PRINT "WHAT IS THE VALUE OF N";
     30  INPUT N
     40  LET T = 1
     50  FOR A = 1 TO N
     60  LET T = T*A
     70  NEXT A
     80  PRINT "N","N!"
     90  PRINT N,T
    100  END
20.  10  REM LAURA'S LOTTERY
     11  REM P IS THE PRIZE
     12  REM A IS THE AMOUNT
         ACCUMULATED
     13  REM N IS A COUNTER
     14  REM P IS THE DIFFERENCE IN A
         AND $10000
     15  LET N = 0
     20  LET P = 50000
     30  LET A = P*(1 + .15)
     40  LET N = N + 1
     50  LET P = A - 10000
     60  IF P <= 0 THEN 80
     70  GOTO 30
     80  PRINT "YOU'RE OUT OF MONEY."
     90  PRINT "IT LASTED ";N - 1;"
         YEARS."
    100  END

     YOU'RE OUT OF MONEY.
     IT LASTED 9 YEARS.
21.  10  REM SUM OF CUBES EQUALS
         SQUARES OF SUM OF INTEGERS
     15  REM N IS AN INTEGER
     16  REM Y IS THE CUBE OF N
     17  REM K IS TO ACCUMULATE THE
         SUM OF CUBES
     18  REM Z IS TO ACCUMULATE THE
         SUM OF THE NUMBERS
     19  REM S IS TO SQUARE Z
```

```
     20  PRINT "1^3 + 2^3
         +...+N^3","(1 + 2 + 3
         +...+N)^2"
     25  LET K = 0
     26  LET Z = 0
     30  FOR N = 1 TO 10
     40  LET Y = N^3
     50  LET K = K + Y
     60  LET Z = Z + N
     70  LET S = Z^2
     80  PRINT K,,S
     90  NEXT N
    100  END
22.  10  REM THIS PROGRAM COMPUTES THE
         SUM OF THE
     20  REM FIRST 1000 ODD NATURAL
         NUMBERS
     21  REM A IS A NATURAL NUMBER
     22  REM N DETERMINES ODD NATURAL
         NUMBERS
     23  REM Y ACCUMULATES THE SUM OF
         THE ODD NATURAL NUMBERS
     24  LET Y = 0
     30  FOR A = 1 TO 1000
     40  LET N = 2*A - 1
     50  LET Y = Y + N
     60  NEXT A
     70  PRINT "THE SUM OF THE FIRST
         1000 ODD NATURAL ";
     80  PRINT "NUMBERS IS ";Y
     90  END
23.  10  REM HARMONIC SERIES
     11  REM K IS A COUNTER
     12  LET K = 0
     13  REM Y ACCUMULATES THE SUM
     14  LET Y = 0
     20  PRINT "HOW MANY TERMS DO YOU
         WANT";
     30  INPUT N
     40  LET K = K + 1
     50  LET Y = Y + 1/K
     60  IF k >= N THEN 80
     70  GOTO 40
     80  PRINT "THE VALUE OF THE FIRST
         ";N;" TERMS OF THE ";
     90  PRINT "HARMONIC SERIES IS ";Y
    100  END

     HOW MANY TERMS DO YOU WANT? 100
     THE VALUE OF THE FIRST 100 TERMS
     OF THE HARMONIC SERIES IS
     5.187377
24.  10  REM PLASTIC CARD COMPANY
         BILLS
     11  REM O1 IS THE AMOUNT FOR
         FIRST METHOD
     12  REM O2 IS THE AMOUNT FOR
         SECOND METHOD
```

```
13 REM O3 IS THE AMOUNT FOR
   THIRD METHOD
20 PRINT "WHAT IS THE CUSTOMER
   ID NUMBER";
30 INPUT I
40 PRINT "WHAT IS THE BILL";
40 INPUT B
60 LET O1 = B - 5/100*B
70 LET O2 = B
80 LET O3 = B + 2/100*B
90 PRINT "ID#","OPTION
   1","OPTION 2","OPTION 3"
100 PRINT I,O1,O2,O3
110 END
```

25.
```
10 REM TABLE OF CUBES AND CUBE
   ROOTS
11 REM N IS A NATURAL NUMBER
20 PRINT "NUMBER","CUBE","CUBE
   ROOT"
30 FOR N = 1 TO 20
40 PRINT N,N^3,N^(1/3)
60 NEXT N
70 END
```

26.
```
10 REM THIS PROGRAM PRINTS
   INTEREST COMPOUNDED DAILY
15 REM N IS A COUNTER
16 REM B IS THE AMOUNT
   ACCUMULATED
17 LET N = 0
20 LET N = N + 1
30 LET B = 1000*(1 + 5/36500)^N
40 IF B > 5000 THEN 60
50 GOTO 20
60 PRINT "AFTER ";N;" DAYS, THE
   BALANCE EXCEEDS $5000."
70 END
```

```
AFTER 11750 DAYS, THE BALANCE
EXCEEDS $5000.
```

27.
```
5 REM THIS PROGRAM PRINTS
   FIBONACCI NUMBERS
10 REM X IS THE FIRST TERM
11 REM Y IS THE SECOND TERM
12 REM A COUNTS THE TERMS AFTER
   THE THIRD
13 REM Z FINDS SUCCESSIVE TERMS
14 PRINT "HOW MANY TERMS OF THE
   SEQUENCE DO YOU WANT";
15 INPUT N
20 LET X = 1
30 PRINT X; " ";
40 IF N = 1 THEN 140
50 LET Y = 1
60 PRINT Y; " ";
70 IF N = 2 THEN 140
80 FOR A = 3 TO N
90 LET Z = X + Y
100 LET X = Y
110 LET Y = Z
120 PRINT Z; " ";
130 NEXT A
140 END
```

```
HOW MANY TERMS OF THE SEQUENCE
DO YOU WANT? 10
 1  1  2  3  5  8  13  21  34  55
```

28.
```
10 REM THIS PROGRAM OUTPUTS
   BATTING AVERAGES
11 REM K COUNTS THE PLAYERS
12 REM A IS THE BATTING AVERAGE
13 REM R IS THE BATTING AVERAGE
   IN THOUSANDTHS
15 LET K = 0
20 PRINT "HOW MANY PLAYERS ARE
   THERE";
30 INPUT N
40 PRINT "PLAYER #","# OF
   BATS","# OF HITS","BATTING
   AVERAGE"
50 LET K = K + 1
60 PRINT "AFTER THE QUESTION
   MARK, TYPE THE # OF AT BATS,"
70 PRINT "THE # OF HITS OF
   PLAYER ";K;" SEPARATED BY
   COMMAS."
80 INPUT B,H
90 LET A = H/B
100 LET R = INT(1000*A)
105 LET R = R/1000
110 PRINT K,B,H,R
120 IF K < N THEN 50
130 END
```

29.
```
10 REM THIS PROGRAM DOUBLES
   SALARY
11 REM D COUNTS DAYS
12 REM S COMPUTES SALARY FOR DAY
13 REM T ACCUMULATES SALARY
14 LET T = 0
20 FOR D = 1 TO 15
30 LET S = 2^(D - 1)
35 IF D = 15 THEN 60
40 LET T = T + S
50 NEXT D
60 PRINT "THE DIFFERENCE OF THE
   15TH DAY'S SALARY AND"
70 PRINT "THE TOTAL FOR 14 DAYS
   IS ";S - T
80 END
```

```
THE DIFFERENCE OF THE 15TH DAY'S
SALARY AND THE TOTAL FOR 14 DAYS
IS 1.
```

30.
```
10 REM SUM OF TWO SQUARES
11 REM X AND Y REPRESENT
   POSSIBLE NUMBERS
12 REM Z IS THE SUM OF X^2 AND
   Y^2
20 FOR X = 1 TO 6
30 FOR Y = 1 TO 6
40 LET Z = X^2 + Y^2
50 IF X >= Y THEN 70
60 IF Z < 40 THEN 100
70 NEXT Y
80 NEXT X
90 GOTO 120
100 PRINT Z;"=" ;X;"^2 +";Y;"^2"
110 GOTO 70
120 END
```

```
 5 = 1^2 + 2^2
10 = 1^2 + 3^2
17 = 1^2 + 4^2
26 = 1^2 + 5^2
37 = 1^2 + 6^2
13 = 2^2 + 3^2
20 = 2^2 + 4^2
29 = 2^2 + 5^2
25 = 3^2 + 4^2
34 = 3^2 + 5^2
```

APPENDIX II

Problem Set AII-1

1. (a) 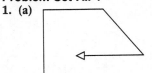   (b)

(c)    (d)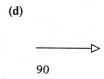

90

(e) 0

2. The answer may vary depending on the type of computer being used.

3. (a) 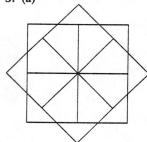   (b)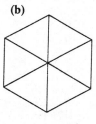

(c) 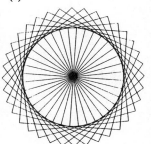   (d) 0

(c)
```
TO HAT
    REPEAT 2 [FORWARD 20 RIGHT 90
     FORWARD 30 RIGHT 90]
    PENUP LEFT 90 FORWARD 30
    PENDOWN
    REPEAT 2[LEFT 90 FORWARD 6
     LEFT 90 FORWARD 90]
END
```
(d)
```
TO T
    FORWARD 60 LEFT 90
    FORWARD 30 BACK 60
END
```
(e)
```
TO RHOMBUS
    RIGHT 20 FORWARD 40
    RIGHT 70 FORWARD 80
    RIGHT 110 FORWARD 40
    RIGHT 70 FORWARD 80
END
```
(f)
```
TO CENTER.SQUARE
    REPEAT 4[FORWARD 60 RIGHT 90]
    RIGHT 20 PENUP
    FORWARD 20 LEFT 90 FORWARD 20
    PENDOWN
    REPEAT 4[FORWARD 20 RIGHT 90]
END
```
5. Answers may vary.
```
TO LOGO
    PENUP LEFT 90 FORWARD 90 RIGHT
     90
  PENDOWN L
  SPACE O
  SPACE G
  SPACE O
END
```
4. Answers may vary.
(a)
```
TO RECT
    REPEAT 2[FORWARD 30 RIGHT 90
     FORWARD 60 RIGHT 90]
END
```
(b)
```
TO FLAG ·
  FORWARD 40
    REPEAT 2 [FORWARD 20 RIGHT 90
     FORWARD 60 RIGHT 90]
END
```

Brain Teaser (p. 875)
```
TO TEASER
  LEFT 45 FORWARD 70.7
  LEFT 135 FORWARD 50
  REPEAT 3[LEFT 90 FORWARD 50]
  REPEAT 2[RIGHT 120 FORWARD 50
  RIGHT 75 FORWARD 70.7
END
```

Problem Set AII-2
1. Type the procedures on the computer.
2. Type procedures on the computer.

```
TO L
  FORWARD 40 BACK 40
  RIGHT 90 FORWARD 20
  BACK 20 LEFT 90
END
TO O
  REPEAT 2[FORWARD 40 RIGHT 90
    FORWARD 25 RIGHT 90]
END
TO G
  FORWARD 40 RIGHT 90 FORWARD 25
  PENUP RIGHT 90 FORWARD 20
    PENDOWN
  RIGHT 90 FORWARD 10 BACK 10
  LEFT 90 FORWARD 20 RIGHT 90
    FORWARD 25 RIGHT 90
END
TO SPACE
  PENUP RIGHT 90
  FORWARD 35 LEFT 90
  PENDOWN
END
```
6. Answers may vary
```
  TO SQUARE1
    REPEAT 4[FORWARD 50 RIGHT 90]
  END
  TO TRIANGLE1
    REPEAT 3[FORWARD 50 RIGHT 120]
  END
```
  (a)
```
  TO SQUARE.PILE
    REPEAT 4[SQUARE1 RIGHT 90]
  END
```
  (b)
```
  TO DIAMOND
    RIGHT 30 TRIANGLE1
    RIGHT 60 FORWARD 50 RIGHT 120
    TRIANGLE1
  END
```
  (c)
```
  TO RECT1
    REPEAT 2[FORWARD 60 RIGHT 90
      FORWARD 30 RIGHT 90]
  END
  TO RECL.SWIRL
    REPEAT 4[RECT1 LEFT 90]
  END
```
  (d)
```
  TO TRI.SWIRL
    RIGHT 30
    REPEAT 3[TRIANGLE1 RIGHT 120]
  END
```
  (e)
```
  TO STAR
    RIGHT 30
    REPEAT 4[TRIANGLE1 RIGHT 60
      FORWARD 50 RIGHT 30]
  END
```
  (f)
```
  TO FLAG1
    FORWARD 10
    REPEAT 2[FORWARD 5 RIGHT 90
      FORWARD 8 RIGHT 90]
  END
```

```
TO FLAG.TOP
  SQUARE1
  FORWARD 50 RIGHT 30
  TRIANGLE1
  FORWARD 50 LEFT 30
  FLAG1
END
```
7. Answers may vary.
  (a)
```
  TO SQUARE.FACE
    SQUARE 60
    FORWARD 5 PENUP RIGHT 90
    FORWARD 25
    LEFT 90 PENDOWN
    SQUARE 10 PENUP FORWARD 18
    PENDOWN RIGHT 30
    TRIANGLE 10
    PENUP LEFT 30 FORWARD 15 LEFT
      90 FORWARD 10
    RIGHT 90 PENDOWN
    SQUARE 10 PENUP RIGHT 90
    FORWARD 20 LEFT 90 PENDOWN
    SQUARE 10
  END
  TO SQUARE :S
    REPEAT 4[FORWARD :S RIGHT 90]
  END
  TO TRIANGLE :S
    REPEAT 3[FORWARD :S RIGHT
      120]
  END
```
  (b)
```
  TO BUILD.SQR :S
    SQUARE :S
    SQUARE :S+10
    SQUARE :S+20
    SQUARE :S+30
    SQUARE :S+40
  END
```
  (c)
```
  TO TAIL :S
    SQUARE :S
    FORWARD :S RIGHT 90 FORWARD
      :S LEFT 90
    SQUARE :S/2
    FORWARD :S/2 RIGHT 90 FORWARD
      :S/2 LEFT 90
    SQUARE :S/4
  END
```
  (d)
```
  TO TOWER :S
    SQUARE :S
    FORWARD :S RIGHT 90 FORWARD
      :S/4 LEFT 90
    SQUARE :S/2
    FORWARD :S/2 RIGHT 90 FORWARD
      :S/8 LEFT 90 SQUARE :S/4
  END
```

```
8. TO DOG
     FULLSCREEN
     PENUP BACK 50 LEFT 90 FORWARD 50
      RIGHT 90 PENDOWN
     BODY BACK 50
     LEG PENUP RIGHT 90 FORWARD 90
      LEFT 90 PENDOWN
     LEG RIGHT 90 FORWARD 10 LEFT 90
      FORWARD 100
     TAIL LEFT 90 FORWARD 100 RIGHT
      90 BACK 20
     HEAD FORWARD 20 EAR
     PENUP LEFT 90 FORWARD 25 RIGHT
      90 FORWARD 15 PENDOWN
     EYE PENUP BACK 30 LEFT 90
      FORWARD 15 RIGHT 90 PENDOWN
     NOSE
   END
     TO BODY
      REPEAT 2[FORWARD 50 RIGHT 90
       FORWARD 100 RIGHT 90]
     END
     TO LEG
      REPEAT 2[FORWARD 50 RIGHT 90
       FORWARD 10 RIGHT 90]
     END
     TO TAIL
      REPEAT 2[FORWARD 30 RIGHT 90
       FORWARD 10 RIGHT 90]
     END
     TO HEAD
      REPEAT 2[FORWARD 50 LEFT 90
       FORWARD 40 LEFT 90]
     END
     TO EAR
      REPEAT 2[FORWARD 30 LEFT 90
       FORWARD 15 LEFT 90]
     END
     TO EYE
      REPEAT 4[FORWARD 5 RIGHT 90]
     END
     TO NOSE
      REPEAT 2[FORWARD 15 LEFT 90
       FORWARD 5 LEFT 90]
     END
9. TO KITE
     LEFT 45
     REPEAT 4[FORWARD 40 RIGHT 90]
     RIGHT 45
     REPEAT 3[BACK 20 K.TAIL RIGHT
      120]
     BACK 20 FORWARD 80 RIGHT 45
      FORWARD 30
     RIGHT 90 FORWARD 80
   END
```

```
   TO K.TAIL
     RIGHT 60
     REPEAT 3[FORWARD 10 RIGHT 120]
     LEFT 180
     REPEAT 3[FORWARD 10 LEFT 120]
   END
10. (a) TO RECT :L :W
         REPEAT 2[FORWARD :L RIGHT 90
          FORWARD :W RIGHT 90]
       END
    (b) Use the RECT procedure from part (a).
       TO FLAG :S
         FORWARD :S
         RECT :S/3 :S/2
       END
    (c) TO HAT :S
         RECT :S :S/2
         PENUP LEFT 90 FORWARD :S/2
          PENDOWN
         REPEAT 2[LEFT 90 FORWARD
          :S/10 LEFT 90 FORWARD
          :S+:S/2]
       END
    (d) TO T :S
         FORWARD :S LEFT 90
         FORWARD :S/2 BACK :S
       END
    (e) TO RHOMBUS :S :A
         REPEAT 2[FORWARD :S RIGHT
          (180-:A) FORWARD :S RIGHT
          :A]
       END
    (f) TO CENTER.SQUARE :S
         SQUARE :S
         RIGHT 90
         PENUP FORWARD :S/3 LEFT 90
          PENDOWN
         SQUARE :S/3
       END
       TO SQUARE :S
         REPEAT 4[FORWARD :S RIGHT 90]
       END
11. TO BLADES :S
     REPEAT 12[FORWARD :S
      PARALLELOGRAM :S*3/2 :S 30
      RIGHT 30]
   END
   TO PARALLELOGRAM :S1 :S2 :A
     REPEAT 2[FORWARD :S1 RIGHT :A
      FORWARD :S2 RIGHT (180-:A)]
   END
12. TO RECTANGLES :S
     LEFT 90
     REPEAT 4[RECTANGLE :S/3 :S
      RIGHT 90 FORWARD :S/3]
   END
   TO RECTANGLE :S1 :S2
     REPEAT 2[FORWARD :S1 RIGHT 90
      FORWARD :S2 RIGHT 90]
   END
```

3. Answers may vary.
   (a)
```
TO STRETCH :S
  IF :S<5 STOP
  SQUARE :S
  FORWARD :S RIGHT 90
  FORWARD :S LEFT 90
  STRETCH :S-10
END
```
   (In Apple Logo II, replace IF :S<5 STOP with IF :S<5 [STOP].)

   (b)
```
TO TOWER :S
  IF :S<5 STOP
  SQUARE :S
  FORWARD :S RIGHT 90 FORWARD
   :S/4
  LEFT 90 TOWER :S/2
END
```
   (In Apple Logo II, replace IF :S<5 STOP with IF :S<5 [STOP].)

   (c)
```
TO PISA :S :A
  IF :S<5 STOP
  SQUARE :S
  FORWARD :S LEFT :A
  PISA :S*0.75 :A
END
```
   (In Apple Logo II, replace IF :S<5 STOP with IF :S<5 [STOP].)

   (d)
```
TO CONSQRS :S
  IF :S<5 STOP
  SQUARE :S
  PENUP FORWARD :S/3 RIGHT 90
   FORWARD :S/3
  LEFT 90 PENDOWN
  CONSQRS :S/3
END
```
   (In Apple Logo II, replace IF :S<5 STOP with IF :S<5 [STOP].)

   (e)
```
TO ROW.HOUSE :S
  IF :S<5 STOP
  HOUSE :S
  SETUP :S
  ROW.HOUSE :S/2
END
```
   (In Apple Logo II, replace IF :S<5 STOP with IF :S<5 [STOP].)
```
TO HOUSE :S
  SQUARE :S
  FORWARD :S
  RIGHT 30 TRIANGLE :S
  LEFT 30
END
TO SETUP :S
  BACK :S RIGHT 90
  FORWARD :S LEFT 90
END
```

   (f)
```
TO TRI.TOWER :S
  IF :S<5 STOP
  RIGHT 30 TRIANGLE :S
  SETUP :S
  TRI.TOWER :S/2
END
```
   (In Apple Logo II, replace IF :S<5 STOP with IF :S<5 [STOP].)

```
TO TRIANGLE :S
  REPEAT 3[FORWARD :S RIGHT
   120]
END
TO SETUP :S
  FORWARD :S LEFT 120
  FORWARD :S/4 RIGHT 90
END
```

4.
```
TO NEST.TRI :S
  IF :S<10 STOP
  RIGHT 30 TRIANGLE :S
  FD :S/2 RIGHT 30
  NEST.TRI :S/2
END
```
   (In Apple Logo II, replace IF :S<10 STOP with IF :S<10 [STOP].)
```
TO TRIANGLE :S
  REPEAT 3[FORWARD :S RIGHT 120]
END
```

5. Answers may vary.
6. Type the procedure on computer.
7. Answers may vary.
```
TO SPIN.SQ :S
  IF :S<5 STOP
  SQUARE :S
  RIGHT 20
  SPIN.SQ :S-5
END
```
   (In Apple Logo II, replace IF :S<5 STOP with IF :S<5 [STOP].)
```
TO SQUARE :S
  REPEAT 4[FORWARD :S RIGHT 90]
END
```

8. Answers may vary.
```
TO STAR :N :S
  IF :N=6 STOP
  FORWARD :S*(SQRT 2)/3 LEFT 45
PENDOWN
  SQUARE :S PENUP RIGHT 45 BACK
   :S*(SQRT 2)/3
  RIGHT 60 PENDOWN
  STAR :N+1 :S
END
```
   (In Apple Logo II, replace IF :N=6 STOP with IF :N=6 [STOP].)
```
TO SQUARE :S
  REPEAT 4[FORWARD :S RIGHT 90]
END
```

9. Answers may vary.
```
TO SQ.TOWER :S
  IF :S<5 STOP
  SQUARE :S FORWARD :S
  SQ.TOWER :S/2
  SQUARE :S FORWARD :S
END
```
   (In Apple Logo II, replace IF :S<5 STOP with IF :S<5 [STOP].)
```
TO SQUARE :S
  REPEAT 4[FORWARD :S RIGHT 90]
END
```

CHAPTER ONE
Selected Bibliography

An excellent bibliography is available in *Problem Solving in School Mathematics*, 1980, yearbook published by the National Council of Teachers of Mathematics, S. Krulick and R. Reys, eds.

Bartalo, B. "Calculators and Problem-Solving Instruction: They Were Made for Each Other." *Arithmetic Teacher* 30 (January 1983): 18-21.

Bernard, J. "Creating Problem-Solving experiences with Ordinary Arithmetic Processes." *Arithmetic Teacher* 30 (September 1982): 52-53.

Billstein, R. "Checkerboard Mathematics." *Mathematics Teacher* 86 (December 1975): 640-646.

Bransford, J. , and B. Stein. *The Ideal Problem Solver*. New York: W. H. Freeman, 1984.

Brown, S., and M. Walter. *The Art of Problem Posing*. Philadelphia: Franklin Institute Press, 1983.

Bruni, J. "Problem Solving for the Primary Grades." *Arithmetic Teacher* 29 (February 1982): 10-15.

Burns, M. "How to Teach Problem Solving." *Arithmetic Teacher* 29 (February 1982): 46-49. *The I Hate Mathematics Book*, Boston: Little, and Brown, 1975.

Bush, W. , and A. Fiala. "Problem Stories: A New Twist on Problem Posing." *Arithmetic Teacher* 34 (December 1986): 6-9.

Butts, T. "In Praise of Trial and Error." *Mathematics Teacher* 78 (March 1985): 167-173.

Campbell, P. "Using a Problem-Solving Approach in the Primary Grades." *Arithmetic Teacher* 32 (December 1984): 11-14.

Charles, R. "The Role of Problem Solving." *Arithmetic Teacher* 32 (February 1985): 48-50.

Charles, R., and F. Lester. *Teaching Problem Solving: What, Why, and How*. Palo Alto, Calif.: Dale Seymour, 1982

Curcio, F., ed. *Teaching and Learning: A Problem-Solving Focus*. Reston, Va.: National Council of Teachers of Mathematics, 1987.

Day, R. "A Problem-Solving Component for Junior High School Mathematics." *Arithmetic Teacher* 34 (October 1986): 14-17.

Dick, T. "The Continuing Calculator Controversy." *Arithmetic Teacher* 35 (April 1988): 37-41.

Dimana, F., and A. Osborne. "Chasing a Calculator: Four Function Foul-ups." *Arithmetic Teacher* 35 (March 1988): 2-3.

Dolan, D., and J. Williamson. *Teaching Problem-Solving Strategies*. Menlo Park, Calif.: Addison-Wesley, 1983.

Easterday, K., and C. Clothiaux. "Problem-Solving Opportunities." *Arithmetic Teacher* 32 (January 1985): 18-20.

Frank, M. "Problem Solving and Mathematical Beliefs." *Arithmetic Teacher* 35 (January 1988): 32-34.

Gadanidis, B. "Problem-Solving: The Third Dimension in Mathematics Teaching." *Mathematics Teacher* 81 (January 1988): 16-21.

Greenes, C., R. Spungin, and J. Dombrowski. *Problem-mathics*. Palo Alto, Calif.: Creative Publications, 1977.

Halmos, P. "The Heart of Mathematics." *American Mathematical Monthly* 87 (July 1980): 519-524.

Hembree, R. "Research Gives Calculators a Green Light." *Arithmetic Teacher* 34 (September 1986): 18-21.

Hembree, R., and D. Dessant. "Effects of Hand-held Calculators in Precollege Mathematics Education: A Meta-Analysis." *Journal for Research in Mathematics Education* 17 (March 1986): 83-89.

Hirsch, C., ed. *Activities for Implementing Curricula Themes: From the Agenda for Action*. Reston, Va.: National Council of Teachers of Mathematics, 1986.

Johnson, J. "Do You Think You Might Be Wrong? Confirmation Bias in Problem Solving." *Arithmetic Teacher* 34 (May 1987): 13-16.

Johnson, M., and T. Offerman. "How Do You Evaluate Problem Solving." *Arithmetic Teacher* 35 (April 1988): 49-51.

Jones, B. "Put Your Students in the Picture for Better Problem Solving." *Arithmetic Teacher* 30 (April 1983): 30-33.

Kantowski, M. "The Microcomputer and Problem Solving." *Arithmetic Teacher* 30 (February 1983): 20-21, 58-59.

Kenney, M., and S. Bezuszka. "A Square Share: Problem Solving with Squares." *Mathematics Teacher* 77 (September 1984): 414-420.

Krulik, S, and R. Reys, eds. *Problem Solving in School Mathematics: 1980 Yearbook of the National Council of Teachers of Mathematics*. Reston, Va.: National Council of Teachers of Mathematics, 1980.

Krulik, S., and J. Rudnick. "Developing Problem-Solving Skills." *Mathematics Teacher* 78 (December 1985): 685-692, 697-698.

Krulik, S., and J. Rudnick. "Strategy Gaming and Problem Solving-An Instructional Pair Whose Time Has Come." *Arithmetic Teacher* 31 (December 1983): 26-29.

Krulik, S., and J. Rudnick. "Suggestions for Teaching Problem Solving-A Baker's Dozen." *School Science and Mathematics* 81 (January 1981): 37-42.

Laing, R. "Extending Problem-Solving Skills." *Mathematics Teacher* 78 (January 1985): 36-44.

Lappan, B., et al. "Powers and Patterns: Problem Solving with Calculators." *Arithmetic Teacher* 30 (October 1982): 42-44.

Lee, K. "Guiding Young Children in Successful Problem Solving." *Arithmetic Teacher* 29 (January 1982): 15-17.

Mason, J., L. Burton, and K. Stacey. *Thinking Mathematically*. Reading, Mass.: Addison-Wesley, 1985.

Meyer, C., and T. Sallee. *Make it Simpler: A Practical Guide to Problem Solving in Mathematics*. Menlo Park, Calif.: Addison-Wesley, 1983.

Morris, J. *How to Develop Problem Solving Using a Calculator*. Reston, Va.: National Council of Teachers of Mathematics, 1981

O'Daffer, P. "Problem Solving: Tips for Teachers." *Arithmetic Teacher* 32 (September 1984 through May 1985).

Polya, B. *How to Solve It*. Princeton, N.J.: Princeton University Press, 1957.

Schaaf, O. "Teaching Problem-Solving Skills." *Mathematics Teacher* 77 (December 1984): 694-699.

Seymour, D., and E. Beardslee. *Critical Thinking Activities*. Palo Alto, Calif.: Dale Seymour, 1988.

Slesnick, T. "Problem Solving: Some Thoughts and Activities." *Arithmetic Teacher* 31 (March 1984): 41-43.

Souviney, R. *Solving Problems Kids Care About*. Glenview, Ill.: Scott, Foresman, 1981.

Spencer, J., and F. Lester. "Second Graders Can Be Problem Solvers." *Arithmetic Teacher* 29 (September 1981): 15-17.

Szetela, W. "The Checkerboard Problem Extended, Extended, Extended..." *School Science and Mathematics* 86 (March 1986): 205-222.

Szetela, W. "The Problem of Evaluation in Problem Solving: Can We Find Solutions?" *Arithmetic Teacher* 35 (November 1987): 36-41.

Talton, C. "Let's Solve the Problem Before We Find the Answer." *Arithmetic Teacher* 36 (September 1988): 40-45.

Thompson, A. "On Patterns, Conjectures, and Proof: Developing Students." *Arithmetic Teacher* 33 (September 1985): 20-23.

Van de Walle, J., and C. Thompson. "Let's Do It: Promoting Mathematical Thinking." *Arithmetic Teacher* 34 (February 1985): 7-13.

Wheatley, C., and G. Wheatley. "Problem Solving in Primary Grades." *Arithmetic Teacher* 31 (April 1984): 22-25.

Williams, D. "Calculator-integrated Curriculum: The Time Is Now." *Arithmetic Teacher* 34 (February 1987): 8-9.

Wilmot, B. "Creative Problem Solving and Red Yarn." *Arithmetic Teacher* 33 (December 1985): 3-5.

Worth, J. "Problem Solving in the Intermediate Grades: Helping Your Students Learn to Solve Problems." *Arithmetic Teacher* 29 (February 1982): 16-19.

CHAPTER TWO
Selected Bibliography

Brieske, T. "Functions, Mappings, and Mapping Diagrams." *Mathematics Teacher* 66 (May 1973): 463-468.

Bruni, J., and H. Silverman. "Using Classification to Interpret Consumer Information." *Arithmetic Teacher* 24 (January 1977): 4-12.

Cetorelli, N. "Teaching Function Notation." *Mathematics Teacher* 72 (November 1979): 590-591.

Coltharp, F. "Mathematical Aspects of the Attribute Games." *Arithmetic Teacher* 21 (March 1974): 246-251.

Geddes, D., and S. Lipsey, "The Hazards of Sets." *Mathematics Teacher* 62 (October 1969): 454.

Horak, V., and W. Horak. "Let's Do It: 'Button Bag' Mathematics." *Arithmetic Teacher* 30 (March 1983): 10-16.

Johnston, A. "Introducing Function and Its Notation." *Mathematics Teacher* 80 (October 1987): 558-560.

Liedtke, W. "Experiences with Blocks in Kindergarten." *Arithmetic Teacher* 22 (May 1975): 406-412.

McGinty, R., and J. Van Beynen. "Deductive and Analytical Thinking." *Mathematics Teacher* 78 (March 1985): 188-194.

National Council of Teachers of Mathematics. *Topics in Mathematics for Elementary School Teachers*. Booklet Number 1. Sets. 1964.

O'Regan, P. "Intuition and Logic." *Mathematics Teacher* 81 (November 1988): 664-668.

Papy, F. *Graphs and The Child*. New Rochelle, N.Y.: Cuisenaire Company of America, Inc., 1970.

Papy, F. *Mathematics and The Child*. New Rochelle, N.Y.: Cuisenaire Company of America, Inc., 1971.

Pereira-Mendoza, L. "Graphing and Prediction in the Elementary School." *Arithmetic Teacher* 24 (February 1977): 112-113.

Sanders, W., and R. Antes. "Teaching Logic with Logic Boxes." *Mathematics Teacher* 81 (November 1988): 643-647.

Schoen, H. "Some Difficulty in the Language of Sets." *Arithmetic Teacher* 21 (March 1974): 236-237.

Spence, L. "How Many Elements Are in a Union of Sets?" *Mathematics Teacher* 80 (November 1987): 666-670, 681.

Vance, I. "The Large Blue Triangle: A Matter of Logic." *Arithmetic Teacher* 22 (March 1975): 237-240.

Vilenkin, N. *Stories about Sets*. New York and London: Academic Press, 1969.

Warman, M. "Fun with Logical Reasoning." *Arithmetic Teacher* 29 (May 1982): 26-30.

Woodward, E., and L. Schroeder. "Detective Stories." *Arithmetic Teacher* 29 (December 1982): 26-27.

CHAPTER THREE
Selected Bibliography

Arcavi, A. "Using Historical Materials in the Mathematics Classroom." *Arithmetic Teacher* 35 (December 1987): 13-16.

Baroidy, A. "Children's Difficulties in Subtraction: Some Causes and Cures." *Arithmetic Teacher* 32 (November 1984): 14-19.

Bates, T., and L. Rousseau. "Will the Real Division Algorithm Please Stand Up?" *Arithmetic Teacher* 33 (March 1986): 42-46.

Beard, E., and R. Polis. "Subtraction Facts with Pattern Explorations." *Arithmetic Teacher* 29 (December 1981): 6-9.

Beattie, I. "Modeling Operations and Algorithms." *Arithmetic Teacher* 33 (February 1986): 23-28.

Beattie, I. "The Number Namer: An Aid to Understanding Place Value." *Arithmetic Teacher* 33 (January 1986): 24-28.

Bernard, J. "Creating Problem-Solving Experiences with Ordinary Arithmetic Process." *Arithmetic Teacher* 30 (September 1982): 52-53.

Boykin, W. "The Russian-Peasant Algorithm: Rediscovery and Extension." *Arithmetic Teacher* 20 (January 1973): 29-32.

Bradbent, F. "Lattice Multiplication and Division." *Arithmetic Teacher* 34 (January 1987): 28-31.

Brown, R. "A 'No Borrow' Subtraction Algorithm." *Mathematics Teacher* 75 (September 1982): 467-468.

Brulle, A., and C. Brulle. "Basic Computational Facts: A Problem and a Procedure." *Arithmetic Teacher* 29 (March 1982): 34-36.

Colton, B. "Subtraction Without Borrowing." *Mathematics Teacher* 73 (March 1980): 196.

Duncan, D., and B. Litwiller. "Calculators, Quotients, and Number Patterns." *Mathematics Teacher* 79 (February 1986): 108-112.

Dunkels, A. "More Popsicle-Stick Multiplication." *Arithmetic Teacher* 29 (March 1982): 20-21.

Engelhardt, J. "Using Computational Errors in Diagnostic Teaching." *Arithmetic Teacher* 29 (April 1982): 16-19.

Ewbank, W. "Subtraction Drill with a Difference." *Arithmetic Teacher* 31 (January 1984): 49-51.

Ferguson, A. "The Stored-Ten Method of Subtraction." *Arithmetic Teacher* 29 (December 1981): 15-18.

Folsom, M. "Operations on Whole Numbers." *Mathematics Learning in Early Childhood, 1975 Yearbook*. Reston, Va.: National Council of Teachers of Mathematics, 1975.

Hall, W. "Using Arrays for Teaching Multiplication." *Arithmetic Teacher* 29 (November 1981): 20-21.

Harrison, M., and B. Harrison. "Developing Numeration Concepts and Skills." *Arithmetic Teacher* 33 (February 1986): 18-22.

Hendrickson, A. "Verbal Multiplication and Division Problems: Some Difficulties and Some Solutions." *Arithmetic Teacher* 33 (April 1986): 26-33.

Hope, J. "Estimation and Mental Computation." *Arithmetic Teacher* 34 (November 1986): 16-17.

Hope, J., B. Reys, and R. Reys. *Mental Math in the Middle Grades*. Palo Alto: Dale Seymour Publishing, 1987.

Kami, C., and L. Joseph. "Teaching Place Value and Double-Column Addition." *Arithmetic Teacher* 35 (February 1988): 48-52.

Katterns, B., and K. Carr. "Talking With Young Children About Multiplication." *Arithmetic Teacher* 33 (April 1986): 18-21.

Kolb, J. "When Does a Subtraction Algorithm Involve Borrowing?" *Mathematics Teacher* 75 (December 1982): 771-775.

Kulm, G. "Multiplication and Division Algorithms in German Schools." *Arithmetic Teacher* 27 (May 1980): 26-27.

Laing, R., and R. Meyer. "Transitional Division Algorithms." *Arithmetic Teacher* 29 (May 1982): 10-12.

Lazerick, B. "Mastering Basic Facts of Addition: An Alternate Strategy." *Arithmetic Teacher* 28 (March 1981): 20-24.

Lessen, E., and C. Cumblad. "Alternatives for Teaching Multiplication Facts." *Arithmetic Teacher* 31 (January 1984): 46-48.

McKillip, W. "Computational Skill in Division: Results and Implications from National Assessment." *Arithmetic Teacher* 28 (March 1981): 34-35.

Moore, T. "More on Mental Computation." *Mathematics Teacher* 79 (March 1986): 168-169.

Musser, G. "Let's Teach Mental Algorithms for Addition and Subtraction." *Arithmetic Teacher* 29 (April 1982): 40-42.

O'Neil, D., and R. Jenson. "Strategies for Learning the Basic Facts." *Arithmetic Teacher* 29 (December 1981): 6-9.

Patrick, S. "Expanded Division." *Arithmetic Teacher* 30 (November 1982): 44-45.

Payne, J. "Ideas." *Arithmetic Teacher* 34 (September 1986): 26-32.

Payne, J. "Place Value For Tens and Ones." *Arithmetic Teacher* 35 (February 1988): 64-66.

Quintero, A. "Conceptual Understanding of Multiplication: Problems Involving Combination." *Arithmetic Teacher* 33 (November 1985): 36-39.

Reardin, C., Jr. "Understanding the Russian Peasant." *Arithmetic Teacher* 20 (January 1973): 33-35.

Reys, B. "Estimation and Mental Computation: It's About Time." *Arithmetic Teacher* 34 (September 1986): 22-23.

Reys, B. "Mental Computation." *Arithmetic Teacher* 32 (February 1985): 43-46.

Reys, R. *Computational Estimation (Grades 6, 7, and 8)*. Palo Alto: Dale Seymour Publishing, 1987.

Rightsel, P., and C. Thornton "72 Addition Facts Can Be Mastered by Mid-grade 1." *Arithmetic Teacher* 33 (November 1985): 25-26.

Robitaille, D. "An Investigation of Some Numerical Properties." *Arithmetic Teacher* 29 (May 1982): 13-15.

Robold, A. "Grid Arrays for Multiplication." *Arithmetic Teacher* 30 (January 1983): 14-17.

Sawada, D. "Mathematical Symbols: Insight through Invention." *Arithmetic Teacher* 32 (February 1985): 20-22.

Shaw, J., and M. Cliatt. "Number Walks." *Arithmetic Teacher* 28 (May 1981): 9-12.

Shaw, R., and P. Pelosi. "In Search of Computational Errors." *Arithmetic Teacher* 30 (March 1983): 50-51.

Singer, R. "Estimation and Counting in the Block Corner." *Arithmetic Teacher* 34 (January 1987): 28-31.

Spitler, G. "Painless Division with Doc. Spitler's Magic Division Estimator." *Arithmetic Teacher* 28 (March 1981): 34-35.

Stuart, M., and B. Bestgen. "Productive Pieces: Exploring Multiplication on the Overhead." *Arithmetic Teacher* 29 (January 1982): 22-23.

Suydam, M. "Improving Multiplication Skills." *Arithmetic Teacher* 32 (March 1985): 52.

Thompson, C., and D. Hendrickson "Verbal Addition and Subtraction Problems: Some Difficulties and Some Solutions." *Arithmetic Teacher* 33 (March 1986): 21-25.

Thompson, C., and J. Van de Walle. "Modeling Subtraction Situations." *Arithmetic Teacher* 32 (October 1984): 8-12.

Thompson, C., and J. Van de Walle. "The Power of 10." *Arithmetic Teacher* 32 (November 1984): 6-11.

Thompson, C., and J. Van de Walle. "Transition Boards: Moving from Materials to Symbols in Subtraction." *Arithmetic Teacher* 28 (January 1981): 4-7.

Tierney, C. "Patterns in the Multiplication Table." *Arithmetic Teacher* 32 (March 1985): 36.

Trafton, P. "Computation - It's Time For Change." *Arithmetic Teacher* 34 (November 1986): 2.

Tucker, B. "Give and Take: Getting Ready to Regroup." *Arithmetic Teacher* 28 (April 1981): 24-26.

Vance, I. "More on Subtraction Without Borrowing." *Mathematics Teacher* 75 (February 1982): 128-129.

Van de Walle, J. "The Early Development of Number Relations." *Arithmetic Teacher* 35 (February 1988): 15-21.

Van de Walle, J., and C. Thompson. "Estimate How Much." *Arithmetic Teacher* 32 (May 1985): 4-8.

Whitin, D. "More Magic With Palindromes." *Arithmetic Teacher* 33 (November 1985): 25-26.

Woodward, E. "Calculators with a Constant Arithmetic Feature." *Arithmetic Teacher* 29 (October 1981): 40-41.

Young, J. "Uncovering the Algorithms." *Arithmetic Teacher* 32. (November 1984): 20.

CHAPTER FOUR
Selected Bibliography

Ballowe, J. "Teaching Difficult Problems Involving Absolute-value Signs." *Mathematics Teacher* 81 (May 1988): 373-374.

Battista, M. "A Complete Model for Operations on Integers." *Arithmetic Teacher* 30 (May 1983): 26-31.

Billstein, R. "Teach a Turtle to Add and Subtract." *The Computing Teacher* 14 (May 1987): 47-50.

Brumfiel, C. "Teaching the Absolute Value Function." *Mathematics Teacher* 73 (January 1980): 24-30.

Charles, R. "Get the Most Out of Word Problems." *Arithmetic Teacher* 29 (November 1981): 39-40.

Crowley, M., and K. Dunn. "On Multiplying Negative Numbers." *Mathematics Teacher* 78 (April 1985): 252-256.

DiDomenico, A. "Discovery of a Property of Consecutive Integers." *Mathematics Teacher* 72 (April 1979): 285-286.

Grady, M. "A Manipulative Aid for Adding and Subtracting Integers." *Arithmetic Teacher* 26 (November 1978): 40.

Jencks, S., and D. Peck. "Hot and Cold Cubes." *Arithmetic Teacher* 24 (January 1977): 70-71.

Johnson J. "Working With Integers." *Mathematics Teacher* 71 (January 1978): 31.

Kilhefner, D. "Equation Hangman." *Arithmetic Teacher* 27 (January 1979): 46-47.

Kindle, G. "Droopy, The Number Line, and Multiplication of Integers." *Arithmetic Teacher* 23 (December 1976): 647-650.

Kohn, J. "A Physical Model for Operations with Integers." *Mathematics Teacher* 71 (December 1978): 734-736.

Morrow, L. "Flow Charts for Equation Solving and Maintenance of Skills." *Mathematics Teacher* 66 (October 1973): 499-506.

Peterson, J. "Fourteen Different Strategies for Multiplication of Integers, or Why $(^-1)(^-1) = (^+1)$." *Arithmetic Teacher* 19 (May 1972): 396-403.

Richardson, L. "The Role of Strategies for Teaching Pupils to Solve Verbal Problems." *Arithmetic Teacher* 22 (May 1975): 414-421.

Schoenfeld, A., and A. Arcavi. "On the Meaning of Variable." *Mathematics Teacher* 81 (September 1988): 420-427.

Sconyers, J. "Something New on Number Lines." *Mathematics Teacher* 67 (March 1974): 253-254.

Shoemaker, R. "Please, My Dear Aunt Sally." *Arithmetic Teacher* 27 (May 1980): 34-35.

Usiskin, Z. "Why Elementary Algebra Can, Should, and Must Be an Eighth-Grade Course for Average Students." *Mathematics Teacher* 80 (September 1987): 428-438.

Zlot, W., and R. Roberts. "The Multiplication of Signed Numbers." *Mathematics Teacher* 75 (April 1982): 302-304.

Zweng, M. "One Point of View: The Problem of Solving Story Problems." *Arithmetic Teacher* 27 (September 1979): 2.

CHAPTER FIVE
Selected Bibliography

Adams, V. "A Variation on the Algorithm for GCD and LCM." *Arithmetic Teacher* 30 (November 1982): 46.

Avital, S. "The Plight and Might of Number Seven." *Arithmetic Teacher* 25 (February 1978): 22-24.

Bezuszka, S. "Even Perfect Numbers-An Update." *Mathematics Teacher* 74 (September 1981): 460-461.

Bezuszka, S. "A Test for Divisibility by Primes." *Arithmetic Teacher* 33 (October 1985): 36-38.

Bezuszka, S., and M. Kenney. "Challenges For Enriching the Curriculum: Arithmetic and Number Theory." *Mathematics Teacher* 76 (April 1983): 250-252.

Brown, S. *Some Prime Comparisons*. Reston, Va.: National Council of Teachers of Mathematics, 1978.

Burton, B., and J. Knifong. "Definitions for Prime Numbers." *Arithmetic Teacher* 27 (February 1980): 44-47.

Cassidy C., and B. Hodgson. "Because A Door Has to Be Open or Closed..." *Mathematics Teacher* 75 (February 1982): 155-158.

Bearing, S., and B. Holtan. "Factors and Primes with a T Square." *Arithmetic Teacher* 34 (April 1987): 34.

Bunham, W. "Euclid and the Infinitude of Primes." *Mathematics Teacher* 80 (January 1987): 16-17.

Edwards, F. "Geometric Figures Make the LCM Obvious." *Arithmetic Teacher* 34 (March 1987): 17-18.

Engle, J. "A Rediscovered Test for Divisibility by Eleven." *Mathematics Teacher* 69 (December 1976): 669.

Fischer, F. "Exploring Number Theory with a Microcomputer." *Mathematics Teacher* 79 (February 1986): 120-122.

Freitag, H. "Exploring Number Theory." *Mathematics Teacher* 79 (September 1986): 433.

Hadar, N. "Odd and Even Numbers-Magician's Approach." *Mathematics Teacher* 75 (May 1982): 408-412.

Henry, L. "Another Look at Least Common Multiple and Greatest Common Factor." *Arithmetic Teacher* 25 (March 1978): 52-53.

Hoffer, A. "What You Always Wanted to Know about Six But Have Been Afraid to Ask." *Arithmetic Teacher* 20 (March 1973): 173-180.

Hohfold, J. "An Inductive Approach to Prime Factors." *Arithmetic Teacher* 29 (December 1981): 28-29.

Hopkins, M. "Number Facts or Fantasy." *Arithmetic Teacher* 34 (March 1987): 38-42.

Klein, P. "Resurrecting an Odd Idea." *Mathematics Teacher* 81 (November 1988): 648-650.

Lamb, C., and L. Hutcherson. "Greatest Common Factor and Common Multiple." *Arithmetic Teacher* 31 (April 1984): 43-44.

Lappan, G., and M. Winter. "Prime Factorizations." *Arithmetic Teacher* 27 (March 1980): 24-27.

Litwiller, B., and D. Duncan. "Pentagonal Patterns in the Addition Table." *Arithmetic Teacher* 32 (April 1985): 36-38.

Long, C. "A Simpler '7' Divisibility Rule." *Mathematics Teacher* 64 (May 1971): 473-475.

Meyer, R., and J. Riley. "Cross-Out." *Arithmetic Teacher* 33 (September 1985): 43.

Robold, A. "Patterns in Multiples." *Arithmetic Teacher* 29 (April 1982): 21-23.

Schatzman, B. "252/7: A Divisibility Pattern." *Mathematics Teacher* 79 (October 1986): 542-546.

Sconyers, J. "Prime Numbers-A Locust's View." *Mathematics Teacher* 74 (February 1981): 105-108.

Shaw, J. "A-Plus for Counters." *Arithmetic Teacher* 31 (September 1983): 10-14.

Sherzer, L. "A Simplified Presentation For Finding the LCM and the GCF." *Arithmetic Teacher* 21 (May 1974): 415-416.

Singer, R. "Modular Arithmetic and Divisibility Criteria." *Mathematics Teacher* 63 (December 1970): 653-656.

Smith, L. "A General Test of Divisibility." *Mathematics Teacher* 71 (November 1978): 668-669.

Steffen, M. "Evenness." *Mathematics Teaching* 113 (December 1985): 2-3.

Stern, P. "GCF and LCM, Korean Style!" *Arithmetic Teacher* 32 (December 1984): 3.

Stock, M. "On What Day Were You Born?" *Mathematics Teacher* 65 (January 1972): 73-75.

Szetela, W. " A General Divisibility Test for Whole Numbers." *Mathematics Teacher* 73 (March 1980): 223-225.

Tirman, A. "Pythagorean Triples." *Mathematics Teacher* 79 (November 1986): 652-655.

Tucker, B. "The Division Algorithm." *Arithmetic Teacher* 20 (December 1973): 639-646.

White, P. "An Application of Clock Arithmetic." *Mathematics Teacher* 66 (November 1973): 645-647.

Wyatt, C. "Clock Beaters." *Arithmetic Teacher* 34 (September 1986): 20.

Yazbak, N. "Some Unusual Test of Divisibility." *Mathematics Teacher* 69 (December 1976): 669.

CHAPTER SIX
Selected Bibliography

Beede, R. "Dot Method for Renaming Fractions." *Arithmetic Teacher* 33 (October 1985): 44-45.

Bennett, A., Jr., and P. Davidson. *Fraction Bars*. Palo Alto, Calif.: Creative Publications.

Carlisle, E. "Fractions and Popsicle Sticks." *Arithmetic Teacher* 27 (February 1980): 50-51.

Chiosi, L. "Fractions Revisited." *Arithmetic Teacher* 31 (April 1984): 46-47.

Collyer, S. "Adding Fractions." *Mathematics Teaching* 116 (September 1986): 9.

Coxford, A., and L. Ellerbruch. "Fractional Numbers." *In Mathematics Learning in Early Childhood, 37th Yearbook of the National Council of Teachers of Mathematics*. Reston, Va.: National Council of Teachers of Mathematics, 1975.

Edge, D. "Fractions and Panes." *Arithmetic Teacher* 34 (April 1987): 13-17.

Ellerbruch, L., and J. Payne. "A Teaching Sequence from Initial Concepts Through the Addition of Unlike Fractions." *In Developing Computational Skills, 1978 Yearbook of the National Council of Teacher of Mathematics*. Reston, Va.: National Council of Teachers of Mathematics, 1978.

Ettline, J. "A Uniform Approach to Fractions." *Arithmetic Teacher* 32 (March 1985): 42-43.

Feinberg, M. "Is It Necessary to Invert?" *Arithmetic Teacher* 27 (January 1980): 50-52.

From the File. "Fractions." *Arithmetic Teacher* 32 (January 1985): 43.

From the File. "Fractions Made Easy." *Arithmetic Teacher* 32 (September 1985): 39.

Hollis, L. "Teaching Rational Numbers-Primary Grades." *Arithmetic Teacher* 31 (February 1984): 36-39.

Jacobson, M. "Teaching Rational Numbers-Intermediate Grades." *Arithmetic Teacher* 31 (February 1984): 40-42.

Jencks, S., D. Peck, and L. Chatterley. "Why Blame the Kids? We Teach Mistakes." *Arithmetic Teacher* 28 (October 1980): 38-42.

Kalman, D. "Up Fractions! Up n/m!" *Arithmetic Teacher* 32 (April 1985): 42-43.

Kennard, R. "Interpreting Fraction Form." *Mathematics Teaching* 112 (September 1985): 46-47.

Kiernen, T. "One Point of View: Helping Children Understand Rational Numbers." *Arithmetic Teacher* 31 (February 1984): 3.

Lester, F. "Teacher Education: Preparing Teachers to Teach Rational Numbers." *Arithmetic Teacher* 31 (February 1984): 54-56.

Liebeck, P. "Are Fractions Numbers?" *Mathematics Teaching* 111 (June 1985): 32-34.

Malcom, P. S. "Understanding Rational Numbers." *Mathematics Teacher* 80 (October 1987): 518-521.

Payne, J. "Curricular Issues: Teaching Rational Numbers." *Arithmetic Teacher* 31 (February 1984): 14-17.

Prevost, F. "Teaching Rational Numbers-Junior High School." *Arithmetic Teacher* 31 (February 1984): 43-46.

Quintero, A. "Helping Children Understand Ratios." *Arithmetic Teacher* 34 (April 1987): 17-21.

Scott, W. "Fractions Taught by Folding Paper Strips." *Arithmetic Teacher* 28 (January 1981): 18-21.

Shookoohi, G-H. "Readiness of Eight-Year-Old Children to Understand the Division of Fractions." *Arithmetic Teacher* 27 (March 1980): 40-43.

Skypek, D. "Special Characteristics of Rational Numbers." *Arithmetic Teacher* 31 (February 1984): 10-12.

Sweetland, R. "Understanding Multiplication of Fractions." *Arithmetic Teacher* 32 (September 1984): 48-52.

Trafton, P., and J. S. Zawojewski. "Teaching Rational Number Division: A Special Problem." *Arithmetic Teacher* 31 (February 1984): 20-22.

Trayton, P., J. Zawojewki, R. Reys, and B. Reys. "Estimation with 'Nice' Fractions." *Mathematics Teacher* 79 (November 1986): 629-630.

Van de Walle, J., and C. Thompson. "Fractions with Fraction Strips." *Arithmetic Teacher* 32 (December 1984): 48-52.

Wiebe, J. "Discovering Fractions on a "Fraction Table.'" *Arithmetic Teacher* 33 (December 1985): 49-51.

CHAPTER SEVEN
Selected Bibliography

Binder, C. "Periodic Decimal Fractions with Computers." *Mathematics Teacher* 77 (December 1984): 688-690.

Boling, B. "A Different Method for Solving Percentage Problems." *Mathematics Teacher* 78 (October 1985): 523-524.

Carpenter, T., et al. "Decimals: Results and Implications from National Assessment." *Arithmetic Teacher* 28 (April 1981): 34-37.

Chow, P., and T. Lin. "Extracting Square Root Made Easy." *Arithmetic Teacher* 29 (November 1981): 48-50.

Coburn, T. "Percentage and the Hand Calculator." *Mathematics Teacher* 79 (May 1986): 361-367.

Cole, B., and H. Weissenfluh. "An Analysis of Teaching Percentages." *Arithmetic Teacher* 21 (March 1974): 226-228.

Dana, M., and M. Lindquist. "Let's Do It: From Halves to Hundredths." *Arithmetic Teacher* 26 (November 1978): 4-8.

Dewar, J. "Another Look at the Teaching of Percent." *Arithmetic Teacher* 31 (March 1984): 48-49.

Firl, D. "Fractions, Decimals and Their Futures." *Arithmetic Teacher* 24 (March 1977): 238-240.

Glatzer, D. "Teaching Percentage: Ideas and Suggestions." *Arithmetic Teacher* 31 (February 1984): 24-26.

Grossman, A. "Decimal Notation: An Important Research Finding." *Arithmetic Teacher* 30 (May 1983): 32-33.

Hilferty, M. "Some Convenient Fractions for Work with Repeating Decimals." *Mathematics Teacher* 65 (March 1972): 240-241.

Hutchinson, M. "Investigation the Nature of Periodic Decimals." *Mathematics Teacher* 65 (April 1972): 325-327.

Jacobs, J., and E. Herbert. "Making $\sqrt{2}$ Seem 'Real'." *Arithmetic Teacher* 21 (February 1974): 133-136.

Kidder, F. "Ditton's Dilemma, or What to Do About Decimals." *Arithmetic Teacher* 28 (October 1980): 44-46.

Manchester, M. "Decimal Expansions of Rational Numbers." *Mathematics Teacher* 65 (December 1972): 698-702.

McGinty, R., and W. Mutch. "Repeating Decimals, Geometric Patterns, and Open-Ended Questions." *Mathematics Teacher* 75 (October 1982): 600-602.

Pauli, S. "Balancing a Checkbook: Children Using Mathematics Skills." *Arithmetic Teacher* 33 (May 1986): 32-33.

Prielipp, R. "Decimals." *Arithmetic Teacher* 23 (April 1976): 285-288.

Robidoux, D., and N. Montefusco. "An Easy Way to Change Repeating Decimals to Fractions-Nick's Method." *Arithmetic Teacher* 24 (January 1977): 81-82.

Rossini, B. "Using Percent Problems to Promote Critical Thinking." *Mathematics Teacher* 81 (January 1988): 31-34.

Schmalz, R. "A Visual Approach to Decimals." *Arithmetic Teacher* 25 (May 1978): 22-25.

Sherzer, L. "Expanding the Limits of the Calculator Display." *Mathematics Teacher* 79 (January 1986): 20-21.

Skypek, D. "Special Characteristics of Rational Numbers." *Arithmetic Teacher* 31 (February 1984): 10-12.

Soler, F., and R. Schuster. "Compound Growth and Related Situations: A Problem-Solving Approach." *Mathematics Teacher* 75 (November 1982): 640-643.

Sullivan, K. "Money--A Key to Mathematical Success." *Arithmetic Teacher* 29 (November 1981): 34-35.

Teahan, T. "How I Learned to Do Percents." *Arithmetic Teacher* 27 (January 1979): 16-17.

Wagner, S. "Fun with Repeating Decimals. " *Mathematics Teacher* 26 (March 1979): 209-212.

Wiebe, J. "Manipulating Percentages." *Mathematics Teacher* 79 (January 1986): 23-26, 21.

Zawojewski, J. "Initial Decimal Concepts: Are They Really So Easy?" *Arithmetic Teacher* 30 (March 1983): 52-56.

CHAPTER EIGHT
Selected Bibliography

Armstrong, R., and P. Pederson, eds. *Probability and Statistics*. St. Louis, Mo.: Comprehensive School Mathematics Project, 1982.

Bernklau, B. "A Look at Frequency Distributions for Sport Scores." *Mathematics Teacher* 81 (March 1988): 212-218.

Billstein, R. "A Fun Way to Introduce Probability." *Arithmetic Teacher* 24 (January 1977): 39-42.

Boas, R. "Snowfalls and Elephants, Pop Bottles and π." *Mathematics Teacher* 74 (January 1981): 49-55.

Bruni, J., and H. Silverman. "Developing Concepts in Probability and Statistics—and Much More." *Arithmetic Teacher* 33 (February 1986): 34-37.

Burns, M. "Put Some Probability in Your Classroom." *Arithmetic Teacher* 30 (March 1983): 21-22.

Carpenter, T., M. Corbitt, H. Kepner, Jr., M. Lindquist, and R. Reys. "What Are the Chances of Your Students Knowing Probability?" *Mathematics Teacher* 74 (May 1981): 342-344.

Choate, S. "Activities in Applying Probability Ideas." *Arithmetic Teacher* 26 (February 1979): 40-42.

Curlette, W. "The Randomized Response Technique: Using Probability to Ask Sensitive Questions." *Mathematics Teacher* 73 (November 1980): 618-621,627.

Engel, A. *A Short Course in Probability*. St. Louis, Mo.: Comprehensive School Mathematics Project, 1970.

Enman, V. "Probability in the Intermediate Grades." *Arithmetic Teacher* 26 (February 1979): 38-39.

Falk, R, R. Falk, and I. Levin. "A Potential for Learning Probability in Young Children." *Educational Studies in Mathematics* 11 (1980): 181-204.

Fennell, F. "Ya Gotta Play to Win: A Probability and Statistics Unit for Middle Grades." *Arithmetic Teacher* 31 (March 1984): 26-30.

Geometric Probability. Reston, Va.: National Council of Teacher of Mathematics, 1988.

Halpern, N. "Teaching Probability—Some Legal Applications." *Mathematics Teacher* 80 (February 1987): 151-153.

Heiny, R. "Gambling, Casinos and Game Simulation." *Mathematics Teacher* 74 (February 1981): 139-143.

Hinders, D. "Monte Carlo, Probability, Algebra, and Pi." *Mathematics Teacher* 74 (May 1981): 335-339.

Horak, V., and W. Horak. "Take a Chance." *Arithmetic Teacher* 30 (May 1983): 8-15.

Houser, L. "Baseball Monte Carlo Style." *Mathematics Teacher* 74 (May 1981): 340-341.

Jones, B. "A Case For Probability." *Arithmetic Teacher* 26 (February 1979): 37, 57.

Kerrich, J. F. *An Experimental Introduction to the Theory of Probability*. Copenhagen: J. Jorgensen and Co., 1964, p.14.

Lappan, G., et al. "Area Models and Expected Value." *Mathematics Teacher* 80 (November 1987): 650-654.

Lappan, G., et al. "Area Models for Probability." *Mathematics Teacher* 80 (March 1987): 217-23.

Lappan, G., and M. Winter. "Probability Simulation in Middle School." *Mathematics Teacher* 73 (September 1980): 446-449.

Milton, S., and J. Corbet. "Strategies in Yahtzee: An Exercise in Elementary Probability." *Mathematics Teacher* 75 (December 1982): 746-750.

Mullet, G. "Watch the Red, Not the Black." *Mathematics Teacher* 73 (May 1980): 349-353.

Noone, E. "Chuck-a-luck: Learning Probability Concepts with Games of Chance." *Mathematics Teacher* 81 (February 1988): 121-123.

Phillips, E., et al. *Probability*, Middle School Mathematics Project, Menlo Park, Calif.: Addison-Wesley, 1986.

Ptak, D. "Probability and the Seating Chart." *Mathematics Teacher* 81 (May 1988): 393-397.

Scheinok, P. "A Summer Program in Probability and Statistics for Inner-City Seventh Grades." *Mathematics Teacher* 81 (April 1988): 310-314.

Shaw, J. "Roll 'n' Spin." *Arithmetic Teacher* 31 (February 1984): 6-9.

Shulte, A. "Learning Probability Concepts in Elementary School Mathematics." *Arithmetic Teacher* 34 (January 1987): 32-33.

Shulte, A., ed. *The Teaching of Statistics and Probability, 1981 Yearbook of the National Council of Teachers of Mathematics*. Reston, Va.: National Council of Teachers of Mathematics, 1981.

Sterba, D. "Probability and Basketball." *Mathematics Teacher* 74 (November 1981): 624-627, 656.

Stone, J. "Place Value and Probability (with Promptings from Pascal)." *Arithmetic Teacher* 27 (March 1980): 47-49.

Travers, K., and K. Gray. "The Monte Carlo Method: A Fresh Approach to Teaching Probabilistic Concepts." *Mathematics Teacher* 74 (May 1981): 327-334.

Vissa, J. "Sampling Treats from a School of Fish." *Arithmetic Teacher* 34 (March 1987): 36-37.

Woodward, E. "An Interesting Probability Problem." *Mathematics Teacher* 75 (December 1982): 765-768.

Woodward, E. "A Second-Grade Probability and Graphing Lesson." *Arithmetic Teacher* 30 (March 1983): 23-24.

CHAPTER NINE
Selected Bibliography

Barbella, P. "Realistic Examples in Elementary Statistics." *Mathematics Teacher* 80 (December 1987): 740-743.

Bestgen, B. "Making and Interpreting Graphs and Tables: Results and Implications from National Assessment." *Arithmetic Teacher* 28 (December 1980): 26-29.

Bruni, J., and H. Silverman. "Graphing as a Communication Skill." *Arithmetic Teacher* 22 (May 1975): 354-366.

Bryan, E. "Exploring Data With Box Plots." *Mathematics Teacher* 81 (November 1988): 658-663.

Burrill, G. "Statistical Decision Making." *NCTM Student Math Notes* (1988).

Christopher, L. "Graphs Can Jazz Up the Mathematics Curriculum." *Arithmetic Teacher* 30 (September 1982): 28-30.

Collis, B. "Teaching Descriptive and Inferential Statistics Using a Classroom Microcomputer." *Mathematics Teacher* 76 (May 1983): 318-322.

Dickinson, J. "Gather, Organize, Display: Mathematics for the Information Society." *Arithmetic Teacher* 34 (December 1986): 12-15.

Ewbank, W. "The Summer Olympic Games: A Mathematical Opportunity." *Mathematics Teacher* 77 (May 1984): 344-348.

Fennell, F. "Ya Gotta Play to Win: A Probability and Statistics Unit for the Middle Grades." *Arithmetic Teacher* 31 (March 1983): 26-30.

Haylock, D. "A Simplified Approach to Correlation." *Mathematics Teacher* 76 (May 1983): 332-336.

Henningsen, J. "An Activity for Predicting Performances in the 1984 Summer Olympics." *Mathematics Teacher* 77 (May 1984): 338-341.

Horak, V., and W. Horak. "Collecting and Displaying the Data Around Us." *Arithmetic Teacher* 30 (September 1982): 16-20.

Huff, D. *How to Lie with Statistics.* New York: Norton, 1954.

Hyatt, D. "M and M's Candy: A Statistical Approach." *Arithmetic Teacher* 24 (January 1977): 34.

Jacobson, M. "Graphing in the Primary Grades: Our Pets." *Arithmetic Teacher* 26 (February 1979): 25-26.

Jamski, W. "Introducing Standard Deviation." *Mathematics Teacher* 74 (March 1981): 197-198.

Johnson, E. "Bar Graphs for First Graders." *Arithmetic Teacher* 29 (December 1981): 30-31.

Joiner, B., and C. Campbell. "Some Interesting Examples for Teaching Statistics." *Mathematics Teacher* 68 (May 1975): 364-369.

Kelly, I., and J. Beamer. "Central Tendency and Dispersion: The Essential Union." *Mathematics Teacher* 79 (January 1986): 59-65.

Kimberling, C. "Mean, Standard Deviation, and Stopping the Stars." *Mathematics Teacher* 77 (November 1984): 633-636.

Klitz, R., and J. Hofmeister. "Statistics in the Middle School." *Arithmetic Teacher* 26 (February 1979): 35-36.

Landwehr, J., and A. Watkins *Exploring Data*, Palo Alto, Calif.: Dale Seymour Publishing, 1987.

Landwehr, J., and A. Watkins. "Stem-and-Leaf Plots." *Mathematics Teacher* 78 (October 1985): 528-532, 537-538.

MacDonald, A. "A Stem-Leaf Plot: An Approach to Statistics." *Mathematics Teacher* 75 (January 1982): 25, 27, 28.

Newman, C., and S. Turkel. "The Class Survey: A Problem-Solving Activity." *Arithmetic Teacher* 32 (May 1985): 10-12.

Noether, G. "The Nonparametric Approach in Elementary Statistics." *Mathematics Teacher* 67 (February 1974): 123-126.

Olson, A. "Exploring Baseball Data." *Mathematics Teacher* 80 (October 1987): 565-569, 584.

Scheinok, P. "A Summer Program in Probability and Statistics for Inner-City Seventh Graders." *Mathematics Teacher* 81 (April 1988): 310-314.

Shulte, A. "A Case for Statistics." *Arithmetic Teacher* 26 (February 1979): 24.

Shulte, A., ed. *Teaching Statistics and Probability*. Reston, Va.: National Council of Teachers of Mathematics, 1981.

Smith, R. "Bar Graphs for Five Year Olds." *Arithmetic Teacher* 27 (October 1979): 38-41.

Sullivan, D., and M. O'Neil. "THIS IS US! Great Graphs for Kids." *Arithmetic Teacher* 28 (September 1980): 14-18.

Tukey, J. *Exploring Data Analysis*. Menlo Park, Calif.: Addison-Wesley, 1977.

Zawojewski, J. "Research into Practice: Teaching Statistics: Mean, Median, and Mode." *Arithmetic Teacher* 35 (March 1988): 25.

CHAPTER TEN
Selected Bibliography

Alexick, H., and F. Kidder. "Why Is a Rectangle Not a Square?" *Arithmetic Teacher* 27 (December 1979): 26-27.

Billstein, R., and J. Lott. "The Turtle Deserves a Star." *Arithmetic Teacher* 33 (March 1986): 14-16.

Bledsoe, G. "Guessing Geometric Shapes." *Mathematics Teacher* 80 (March 1987): 178-180.

Borneson, H. "Teaching the Process of Mathematical Investigation." *Arithmetic Teacher* 33 (April 1986): 36-38.

Bright, G. "Using Tables to Solve Some Geometry Problems." *Arithmetic Teacher* 25 (May 1978): 39-43.

Bright, G., and J. Harvey. "Games, Geometry, and Teaching." *Mathematics Teacher* 81 (April 1988): 250-259.

Bright, G., and J. Harvey. "Learning and Fun with Geometry Games." *Arithmetic Teacher* 35 (April 1988): 22-26.

Burke, M. "Star Rec." *Student Math Notes* (January 1989).

Campbell, P. "Cardboard, Rubber Bands, and Polyhedron Models." *Arithmetic Teacher* 31 (October 1983): 48-52.

Carroll, W. "Cross Sections of Clay Solids." *Arithmetic Teacher* 35 (March 1988): 6-11.

Charles, R. "Some Guidelines for Teaching Geometry Concepts." *Arithmetic Teacher* 27 (April 1980): 18-21.

Clements, D., and M. Battista. "Geometry and Geometric Measurement." *Arithmetic Teacher* 33 (February 1986): 29-32.

Coxford, A., et al. *Geometry*. Chicago: The University of Chicago Press, 1987.

Craig, B. "Polygons, Stars, Circles, and Logo." *Arithmetic Teacher* 33 (May 1986): 6-11.

Damarin, S. "What Makes a Triangle." *Arithmetic Teacher* 29 (September 1981): 39-41.

Fuys, D., D. Geddes, and R. Tischler. *The van Hiele Model of Thinking in Geometry Among Adolescents*. Reston, Va.: National Council of Teachers of Mathematics, 1988.

Henderson, G., and C. Collier. "Geometric Activities for Later Childhood Education." *Arithmetic Teacher* 20 (October 1973): 444-453.

Hilton,P., and J. Pederson. *Build Your Own Polyhedra*. Menlo Park, Calif.: Addison-Wesley, 1988.

Hoffer, A. "Geometry Is More Than Proof." *Mathematics Teacher* 74 (January 1981): 11-18.

Hoffer, A. "Making A Better Beer Glass." *Mathematics Teacher* 75 (May 1982): 378-379.

Hoffer, A. *Van Hiele-based Research*. In R. Lesh and M. Landau, *Acquisition of Mathematics Concepts and Processes*. New York: Academic Press, 1983.

Jacobs, H. *Geometry*, 2d ed. New York: W. H. Freeman and Company, 1987.

Lichtenberg, D. "Pyramids, Prisms, Antiprisms, and Deltahedra." *Mathematics Teacher* 81 (April 1988): 261-265.

Lindquist, M., and A Shulte, eds. *Learning and Teaching Geometry, K-12*, 1987 Yearbook. Reston, Va.: National Council of Teachers of Mathematics, 1987.

Maletsky, E. "Generating Solids." *Mathematics Teacher* 76 (October 1983): 499, 500, 504-507.

Miller, W. "Puzzles that Section Regular Solids." *Mathematics Teacher* 81 (September 1988): 463-468.

Morrell, L. "GE-O-ME-TR-Y." *Arithmetic Teacher* 27 (March 1980): 52.

O'Daffer, P., and S. Clemens. *Geometry: An Investigative Approach*. Reading, Mass.: Addison-Wesley, 1976.

Olson, A. "Logo and the Closed-Path Theorem." *Mathematics Teacher* 79 (April 1986): 250-255.

Poggi, J. "An Invitation to Topology." *Arithmetic Teacher* 33 (December 1985): 8-11.

Pohl, V. "Producing Curved Surfaces in the Octahedron: Enrichment for Junior High School." *Arithmetic Teacher* 34 (November 1986): 30-33.

Prevost, F. "Geometry in the Junior High School." *Mathematics Teacher* 78 (September 1985): 411-418.

Reynolds, J. "Build a City." *Arithmetic Teacher* 33 (September 1985): 12-15.

Shaughnessy, J., and W. Burger. "Spadework Prior to Deduction in Geometry." *Mathematics Teacher* 78 (September 1985): 419-428.

Steinhaus, H. *Mathematical Snapshots*. 3d ed. Oxford: Oxford University Press, 1983.

Suydam, M. "The Shape of Instruction in Geometry: Some Highlights from Research." *Mathematics Teacher* 78 (September 1985): 481-486.

Walle, J., and C. Thompson. "Promoting Mathematical Thinking." *Arithmetic Teacher* 32 (February 1985): 7-13.

Walter, M. "Frame Geometry: An Example in Posing and Solving Problems." *Arithmetic Teacher* 28 (October 1980): 16-18.

Wenninger, M. *Polyhedron Models for the Classroom*. Reston, Va.: National Council of Teachers of Mathematics, 1975.

Winter, M., et al. *Middle Grades Mathematics Project Spatial Visualization*. Menlo Park, Calif.: Addison-Wesley, 1986.

Young, J. "Improving Spatial Abilities with Geometric Activities." *Arithmetic Teacher* 30 (September 1982): 38-43.

Zaslavsky, C. "Networks—New York Subways, A Piece of String, and African Traditions." *Arithmetic Teacher* 29 (October 1981): 42-47.

CHAPTER ELEVEN
Selected Bibliography

Battista, M. "MATHSTUFF Logo Procedures: Bridging the Gap between Logo and School Geometry." *Arithmetic Teacher* 35 (September 1987): 7-11.

Billstein, R., S. Libeskind, and J. Lott, *Apple Logo, Programming, and Problem Solving*. Menlo Park, Calif.: Benjamin/Cummings, 1986.

Billstein, R., S. Libeskind, and J. Lott. *Logo, MIT Logo for the Apple*. Menlo Park, Calif.: Benjamin/Cummings, 1985.

Brown, R. "Making Geometry a Personal and Inventive Experience." *Mathematics Teacher* 75 (September 1982): 442-446.

Burger, W. "Geometry." *Arithmetic Teacher* 32 (February 1985): 52-56.

Edwards, R. "Discoveries in Geometry by Folding and Cutting." *Arithmetic Teacher* 24 (March 1977): 196-198.

Friedlander, A., and G. Lappan. "Similarity: Investigations at the Middle Grade Level." *In Learning and Teaching Geometry, K-12*. Reston, Va.: National Council of Teachers of Mathematics, 1987.

Hiatt, A. "Problem Solving in Geometry." *Mathematics Teacher* 65 (November 1972): 595-600.

Hurd, S. "An Application of the Criteria ASASA for Quadrilaterals." *Mathematics Teacher* 81 (February 1988): 124-126.

Lappan, G., and R. Even. "Similarity in the Middle Grades." *Arithmetic Teacher* 35 (May 1988): 32-35.

Lappan, G., and E. Phillips. "Spatial Visualization." *Mathematics Teacher* 79 (November 1984): 618-623.

Lennie, J. "A Lab Approach for Teaching Basic Geometry." *Mathematics Teacher* 79 (October 1986): 523-524.

Lott, J., and I. Dayoub. "What Can Be Done with a Mira?" *Mathematics Teacher* 70 (May 1977): 394-399.

Mathematics Resource Project. *Geometry and Visualization*. Palo Alto, Calif.: Creative Publications, 1985.

Moulton, J. "Some Geometry Experiences for Elementary School Children." *Arithmetic Teacher* 21 (February 1974): 114-116.

Newton, J. "From Pattern-Block Play to Logo Programming." *Arithmetic Teacher* 35 (May 1988): 6-9.

Pawley, R. "5-Con Triangles." *Mathematics Teacher* 60 (May 1967): 438-443.

Reid, J. "Cutting Across a Circle." *Arithmetic Teacher* 26 (April 1979): 27.

Robertson, J. "Geometric Constructions Using Hinged Mirrors." *Mathematics Teacher* 79 (May 1986): 380-386.

Tartre, L. "Dropping Perpendiculars the Easy Way." *Mathematics Teacher* 80 (January 1987): 30-31.

Thomas, D. "Geometry in the Middle School: Problem Solving with Trapezoids." *Arithmetic Teacher* 26 (February 1979): 20-21.

Troccolo, J. "The Rhombus Construction Company." *Mathematics Teacher* 76 (January 1983): 37-42.

Van de Walle, J., and C. Thompson. "A Triangle Treasury." *Arithmetic Teacher* 28 (February 1981): 6-11.

Van de Walle, J., and C. Thompson. "Promoting Mathematical Thinking." *Arithmetic Teacher* 32 (February 1985): 7-13.

Walter, M. Boxes, *Squares and Other Things*. Reston, Va.: National Council of Teachers of Mathematics, 1970.

CHAPTER TWELVE
Selected Bibliography

Bidwell, J. "Using Reflections to Find Symmetric and Asymmetric Patterns." *Arithmetic Teacher* 34 (March 1987): 10-15.

Billstein, R., S. Libeskind, and J. Lott. *Logo: MIT Logo for the Apple*. Menlo Park, Calif.: Benjamin/Cummings, 1985.

Brieske, T. "Visual Thinking with Translations, Half-turns, and Dilations." *Mathematics Teacher* 77 (September 1984): 466-469.

Brown, R. *Transformational Geometry*. Palo Alto, Calif.: Dale Seymour Corporation, 1989.

Byrne, D. "The Bank Shot." *Mathematics Teacher* 79 (September 1986): 429-430,487.

DeTemple, D. "Reflection Borders for Patchwork Quilts." *Mathematics Teacher* 80 (February 1986): 138-143.

Lott, J. "Escher-like Logo-type Tessellations." *Logo Exchange*. 6 (November 1987): 7-11.

Lovell, R. "Flip, Twist, Shuffle, Snap, and Compose." *Mathematics Teacher* 79 (November 1986): 636-638.

Mansfield, H. "Projective Geometry in the Elementary School." *Arithmetic Teacher* 32 (March 1985): 15-19.

May, B. "Reflections on Miniature Golf." *Mathematics Teacher* 78 (May 1985): 351-353.

Ranucci, E., and J. Teeters. *Creating Escher-type Drawings*. Palo Alto, Calif.: Creative Publications, 1977.

Reesink, C. "Crystals: Through the Looking Glass with Planes, Points, and Rotational Symmetry." *Mathematics Teacher* 80 (May 1987): 377-388.

Renshaw, B. "Symmetry the Trademark Way." *Arithmetic Teacher* 34 (September 1986): 6-12.

Sawada, D. "Symmetry and Tessellations from Rotational Transformations on Transparencies." *Arithmetic Teacher* 33 (December 1985): 12-13.

Shyers, J. "Reflective Paths to Minimum-Distance Solutions." *Mathematics Teacher* 79 (March 1986): 174-177, 203.

Thompson, P. "A Piagetian Approach to Transformation Geometry via Microworlds." *Mathematics Teacher* 78 (September 1985): 465-471.

Van de Walle, J., and C. Thompson. "Cut and Paste for Geometric Thinking." *Arithmetic Teacher* 32 (September 1984): 8-13.

Willcutt, B. "Triangular Tiles for Your Patio." *Arithmetic Teacher* 34 (May 1987): 43-45.

Woods, J. "Let the Computer Draw the Tessellations That You Design." *Mathematics Teacher* 81 (February 1988): 138-141.

Zurstadt, B. "Tessellations and the Art of M. C. Escher." *Arithmetic Teacher* 31 (January 1984): 54-55.

CHAPTER THIRTEEN
Selected Bibliography

Barnett, D. "A 'Metric Review Show.'" *Mathematics Teacher* 77 (February 1984): 106-107.

Binswanger, R. "Discovering Perimeter and Area with Logo." *Arithmetic Teacher* 36 (September 1988): 18-24.

Bright, G., and J. Harvey. "Games, Geometry, and Teaching." *Mathematics Teacher* 81 (April 1988): 250-259.

Changming, L. "A Geometric Solution to a Problem of Minimization." *Mathematics Teacher* 81 (January 1988): 61-64.

Clements, D. C., and M. Battista. "Geometry and Geometric Measurement." *Arithmetic Teacher* 33 (February 1986): 29-32.

Courant, R., and H. Robbins. *What Is Mathematics*. New York: Oxford University Press, 1986.

Harrison, W. "How to Make a Million." *Arithmetic Teacher* 33 (September 1985): 46-47.

Hart, K. "Which Comes First—Length, Area, or Volume?" *Arithmetic Teacher* 31 (May 1984): 16-18.

Hawkins, V. "The Pythagorean Theorem Revisited: Weighing the Results." *Arithmetic Teacher* 32 (December 1984): 36-37.

Hiebert, J. "Why Do Some Children Have Trouble Learning Measurements?" *Arithmetic Teacher* 31 (March 1984): 19-24.

Hildreth, D. "The Use of Strategies in Estimating Measurements." *Arithmetic Teacher* 30 (January 1983): 50-54.

Hirstein, J., C. Lamb, and A. Osborne. "Student Misconceptions About Area Measure." *Arithmetic Teacher* 25 (March 1978): 10-16.

Hunt, J. "How High Is a Flagpole?" *Arithmetic Teacher* 25 (February 1978): 42-43.

Jamski, W. "So Your Students Know About Area?" *Arithmetic Teacher* 26 (December 1978): 37.

Jensen, R. "Concept Formation in Geometry: A Computer-aided, Student-centered Activity." *Arithmetic Teacher* 35 (March 1988): 34-36.

Jensen, R., and D. O'Neil. "Informal Geometry Through Geometric Blocks." *Arithmetic Teacher* 29 (May 1982): 4-8.

Jensen, R., and D. Spector. "Geometry Links the Two Spheres." *Arithmetic Teacher* 33 (April 1986): 13-16.

Kilmer, J. "Triangles of Equal Area and Perimeter and Inscribed Circles." *Mathematics Teacher* 81 (January 1988): 65-69.

Lindquist, M., and M. Dana. "The Neglected Decimeter." *Arithmetic Teacher* 24 (October 1977): 10-17.

Litwiller, B., and D. Duncan. "Areas of Polygons on Isometric Dot Paper: Pick's Formula Revises." *Arithmetic Teacher* 30 (April 1983): 38-40.

Loomis, E. *The Pythagorean Proposition*. Washington, D. C.: National Council of Teacher of Mathematics, 1972.

National Council of Teacher of Mathematics. *1976 Yearbook: Measurement in School Mathematics*. Reston, Va.: NCTM, 1976.

Nelson, R., and D. Whitaker. "Another Use for Geoboards." *Arithmetic Teacher* 30 (April 1983): 34-37.

Ott, J., D. Sommers, and K. Creamer. "But Why Does C = πd?" *Arithmetic Teacher* 31 (November 1983): 38-40.

Shaw, J. "Exploring Perimeter and Area Using Centimeter Squared Paper." *Arithmetic Teacher* 31 (December 1983): 4-11.

Thomas, D. "Geometry in the Middle School: Problem Solving with Trapezoids." *Arithmetic Teacher* 26 (February 1979): 20-21.

Thompson, C., and J. Van de Walle. "Learning About Rulers and Measuring." *Arithmetic Teacher* 32 (April 1985): 8-12.

Tolman, M. "The 'Steps' of Metric Conversion." *Arithmetic Teacher* 30 (November 1982): 32-33.

Walter, M. "A Common Misconception About Area." *Arithmetic Teacher* 17 (April 1970): 286-289.

Walter, M. "Frame Geometry: An Example in Posing and Solving Problems." *Arithmetic Teacher* 28 (October 1980): 16-18.

CHAPTER FOURTEEN
Selected Bibliography

Burrill, J., and H. Kepner. "Relating Graphs to Their Equations with a Microcomputer." *Mathematics Teacher* 79 (March 1986): 185-197.

Dossey, J. "Do all Graphs Have Points with Integral Coordinates?" *Mathematics Teacher* 74 (September 1981): 455-457.

Dugdale, S. "Green Globs: A Micro-computer Application for Graphing of Equations." *Mathematics Teacher* 75 (March 1982): 208-214.

Freidland, H. "Chalkboard Coordinates." *Arithmetic Teacher* 31 (November 1983): 10.

Hopkinson, R. "Interpreting and Applying the Distance Formula." *Mathematics Teacher* 80 (October 1987): 572-579.

Kalman, D. "Up n/m!" *Arithmetic Teacher* 32 (April 1985): 42-43.

Kline, M. *Mathematics in Western Culture*. New York: Oxford, 1953.

Lappan, G., and M. Winter. "A Unit on Slope Functions—Using a Computer in Mathematics Class." *Mathematic Teacher* 75 (February 1982): 118-122.

Ruppel, E. "Business Formulas as Cartesian Curves." *Mathematics Teacher* 75 (May 1982): 398-403.

Smith, R. "Coordinate Geometry for Third Graders." *Arithmetic Teacher* (April 1986): 10.

Tall, D. "The Gradient of a Graph." *Mathematics Teaching* 3 (June 1985): 48-52.

Terc, M. "Coordinate Geometry—Art and Mathematics." *Arithmetic Teacher* 33 (October 1985): 22-24.

Wallace, E. "A New Look at Some Old Formulas." *Mathematics Teacher* 78 (January 1985): 56-58.